DRAMA FOR DEVELOPMENT

DRAMA FOR DEVELOPMENT

CULTURAL TRANSLATION
AND SOCIAL CHANGE

Edited by

Andrew Skuse
Marie Gillespie
Gerry Power

⑤SAGE www.sagepublications.com
Los Angeles • London • New Delhi • Singapore • Washington DC

First published in 2011 by

 SAGE Publications India Pvt Ltd **The Open University**
B1/I-1 Mohan Cooperative Industrial Area
Mathura Road, New Delhi 110 044, India **BBC World Service Trust**
www.sagepub.in

SAGE Publications Inc
2455 Teller Road
Thousand Oaks, California 91320, USA

SAGE Publications Ltd
1 Oliver's Yard, 55 City Road
London EC1Y 1SP, United Kingdom

SAGE Publications Asia-Pacific Pte Ltd
33 Pekin Street
#02-01 Far East Square
Singapore 048763

Published by Vivek Mehra for SAGE Publications India Pvt Ltd, typeset in 10/12 pt Times New Roman by Star Compugraphics Private Limited, Delhi and printed at Chaman Enterprises, New Delhi.

Library of Congress Cataloging-in-Publication Data
Drama for development : cultural translation and social change / edited by
  Andrew Skuse, Marie Gillespie, and Gerry Power.
      p. cm.
  Includes bibliographical references and index.
1. Intercultural communication.   2. Mass media in community development.
3. Cultural pluralism.   4. Social change. I. Skuse, Andrew, 1964– II. Gillespie,
Marie, 1953– III. Power, Gerry, 1960– IV. BBC World Service Trust.

HM1211.D73   303.48'209172'4—dc22   2011   2011010074

ISBN: 978-81-321-0591-6 (HB)

The SAGE Team: Elina Majumdar, Anupam Choudhury, and Deepti Saxena

For Jo, Alex and Evie.

*Without their support and love
this book could not have been realised.*

—Andrew Skuse

For my mother, Margaret Gillespie, with love.

—Marie Gillespie

For Sandra Ball-Rokeach.

—Gerry Power

Thank you for choosing a SAGE product! If you have any comment, observation or feedback, I would like to personally hear from you. Please write to me at contactceo@sagepub.in

—Vivek Mehra, Managing Director and CEO,
SAGE Publications India Pvt Ltd, New Delhi

Bulk Sales

SAGE India offers special discounts for purchase of books in bulk. We also make available special imprints and excerpts from our books on demand.

For orders and enquiries, write to us at

Marketing Department
SAGE Publications India Pvt Ltd
B1/I-1, Mohan Cooperative Industrial Area
Mathura Road, Post Bag 7
New Delhi 110044, India
E-mail us at marketing@sagepub.in

Get to know more about SAGE, be invited to SAGE events, get on our mailing list. Write today to marketing@sagepub.in

❧☙

CONTENTS

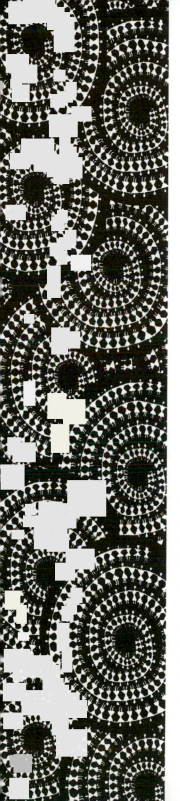

ACKNOWLEDGEMENTS

This book is based on collaborative research between The Open University, the University of Adelaide and the BBC World Service Trust and was funded by the United Kingdom's Arts and Humanities Research Council's Migration Diaspora and Identities Programme (www. diasporas.ac.uk). Details of the research project entitled 'Tuning In: Diasporic Contact Zones at the BBC World Service' (award reference AH/ES58693/1) can be found at www8.open. ac.uk/researchprojects/diasporas/. This collaboration has also been generously supported by the Centre for Research on Socio-Cultural Change (www.cresc.ac.uk). We would also like to acknowledge and thank the various funders that enabled the BBC World Service Trust dramas examined in this book to be developed (see Appendix 1 for a full list).

Several colleagues played crucial roles at different stages of the research. Lizz Frost Yocum offered many important and vital insights in the earliest phases of the research. Carol Morgan and Emily Richter at the BBC World Service Trust provided sterling research administration support. We are grateful to Chiv Linna and Kate Ribet for their efforts in translation and transcription. Also, Sophie West and Stephanie Lowe are to be thanked for their invaluable research support. Tom Cheesman provided excellent editorial advice and guidance. Finally, we would also like to express our gratitude to the following colleagues who gave generously of their time over the last three years: Gordon Adam, Rukhsana Ahmad, Chhaya Amara, Devika Bahl, Helen Bassey-Osijo, Mike Battcock, Ashley Burgess, Jonathan Curling, Jessica Dromgoole, Warren Feek, Anji Loman Field, Lucy Hannah, Mary Hare, Nicola Harford, Sok Kunthy, Fiona Ledger, Nabila Malick, Chheang Marida, Karen Merkel, Akim Mogaji, Kate Lloyd Morgan, Mary Myers, Farjad Nabi, Eze Eze Ogali, Fiona Power, Matthew Robinson, Colin Rogers, Rishi Sankar, Shirazuddin Siddiqi, Ath Sotheavy, Arif Waqar, David Wood and Nicola Woods.

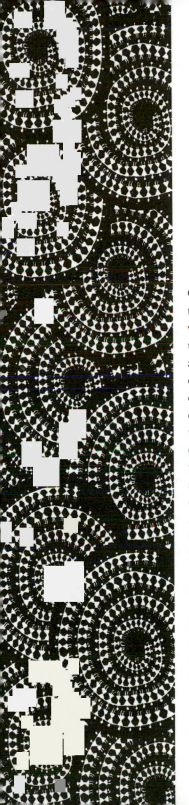

INTRODUCTION

DRAMA FOR DEVELOPMENT—CULTURAL TRANSLATION AND SOCIAL CHANGE

ANDREW SKUSE, MARIE GILLESPIE AND GERRY POWER

Can serial radio and television dramas, designed to promote development, change the social worlds or behaviour of their audiences? How are their narratives understood and shaped by their audiences? What are the challenges facing producers and dramatists who have to create strategic development narratives, as well as entertaining dramas, that can travel and translate across multiple linguistic and cultural boundaries? These questions and many others lie at the heart of a transformation in broadcasting that has accelerated over recent decades, namely, the blending of entertainment with education (commonly abbreviated to E-E) in pursuit of specific development outcomes such as improved nutrition, conflict reduction or greater gender equity.

The BBC World Service Trust (BBC WST), the international charity of the BBC, has been at the forefront of these developments over the last decade.[1] However, their work in the field of drama for development has received little sustained academic scrutiny or critical appraisal from scholars or practitioners. This edited volume is the first attempt to provide an analytical framework that brings into dialogue practitioners and academics in order to assess the opportunities

and constraints within which serial dramas must operate, and to identify the factors driving success and failure. Crucial to the aspirations
of social change embedded in dramas for development are cultural
translation practices that ensure key global development themes travel
and translate across diverse national, linguistic and cultural boundaries. This book hopes to shed light on these processes that are typically
hidden from view.

From rural Afghanistan to urban Nigeria, audiences have been
tuning in to BBC WST drama containing 'instructive' messages for
nearly two decades, in the same way that BBC Radio 4's the *Archers*
was, and still remains, instructive of rural ways for its British audience
(see Appendix 1 for a detailed summary of the dramas produced by the
BBC WST). A former *Archers* producer notes:

> When the Archers first started in Britain after the war it was intended to
> help farmers increase their productivity. The young hero kept pigs. If he
> made enough profit, he would have the money to marry the beautiful
> heroine. The wedding was on/off/on/off according to how successful his
> various attempts to increase pig productivity were. The whole of Britain
> was hooked on the romantic side of this storyline. It just so happened that
> at the same time, the whole of Britain became expert in pig rearing.
>
> (Rigbey, 1993: 6)

Shift contexts to the BBC WST's Afghan Education Projects (BBC AEP)
broadcasting in Afghanistan, and the similar storyline takes on a harder
edge. The young hero keeps sheep. His daily journey to tend them is
fraught with risks of unexploded mines. He wants to marry the heroine
but her father wants too big a bride price (a payment paid to the bride's
family for the loss of a daughter). Having lost five sheep to landmines
in only three months, he does not see how his family will ever raise the
necessary money. Despondent, he seeks solace in opium. Meanwhile,
Afghans become no less expert in rearing sheep![2]

Behind such storylines lies a complex interweaving of development
goals, donor objectives, processes of cross-cultural translation, creative dialogue and debate between local and expatriate dramatists and,
not least, the responses and interpretations of dramatic development
narratives by audiences. From such a perspective, organisations such as
the BBC WST can be seen to be actively engaged in crafting complex

development concepts and issues into local frames by applying specific cultural, social and political filters to render these concepts and narratives intelligible. At the BBC WST, these filters are informed by formative and ongoing audience research and evaluation that feeds into production in ways that enable audiences to play an active role in the evolving serial narratives. These cultural filters are also shaped by partnerships with local development agencies. Such processes and relationships raise important questions. How do transcultural creative processes work in practice? Which development concepts travel and translate with ease and which are difficult to translate or are deemed untranslatable? Do production teams manage to avoid the pitfalls of ethnocentrism or eurocentrism? How do local dramatists and audiences resist or subvert attempts to integrate development narratives in popular dramas? What constitutes success for different stakeholders involved in producing and consuming these productions?

At the heart of this book lies an examination of what cultural and linguistic translation means in a critical and academic sense, what practices and accommodations it entails, and what imaginative investments it requires. In applying a critical and analytical lens to the drama for development work of the BBC WST and their partners, *Drama for Development: Cultural Translation and Social Change* offers unique insights into a wide range of highly popular radio and television productions broadcast in contexts as diverse as Afghanistan, Burma, Cambodia, Nepal, Pakistan, India, Nigeria and Rwanda. In doing so, this book draws together contributions and experiences from academics and researchers working in both the university sector and within the BBC WST (Research and Learning Group). The book emerges from a unique research collaboration between the UK's The Open University, the University of Adelaide and the BBC WST. It is based on a three-year research project funded by the UK Arts and Humanities Council Project.[3]

This larger research project—of which the focus on drama for development at the BBC WST constitutes one strand—examines how the BBC World Service functions as a cross-cultural 'contact zone' and an agent of cultural and public diplomacy. It seeks to analyse the kinds of transnational and transcultural knowledge and translation practices that give the BBC World Service its global reputation. But the project, like our book, also takes a critical distance from the BBC World Service in order to assess the extent to which, as an international broadcaster, it complies with or challenges political objectives and neo-colonial cultural encounters, and truly serves the needs of its audiences. The project thus situates the BBC World Service in the wider context of contemporary international broadcasting. The collaboration brings together numerous media and development institutions and academics working in the anthropology of development and of media into a critical dialogue with producers, audience evaluators, actors, commentators and editors working at the BBC World Service. The larger research project is without parallel in terms of the access afforded to the BBC World Service and the level of collaboration that has resulted.

The present volume uses BBC WST dramas—and the creative work involved from their conception to consumption—as a prism through which to critically assess practices of cultural translation and situate their work in a wider international and academic context. Our collaborative research is itself an example of the varied transcultural and translation processes that we are exploring. As a transnational team of researchers, we have engaged in a creative intellectual collaboration with dramatists and development workers sharing ideas and data, collaboratively analysing material and co-authoring key chapters across sectors (BBC WST and academic) and continents. Inevitably, intellectual tensions arise from the collision of different perspectives and priorities in such a project, but rather than concealing these we explore them, creatively. The resulting dialogue is much more critical, engaged and informed as a consequence, and is able to challenge some of the central assumptions of Entertainment-Education (E-E) theory and practice, whilst garnering insights from the anthropology of development, the anthropology of media, post-colonial studies, cultural studies and media research. The volume is truly 'global' in the sense that it speaks to the diffusion of drama for development and to the significance of the BBC WST, and seeks to project the plurality of 'voices' and insights of media producers and consumers working in transcultural contexts and in countries and places that are rarely heard of in western academic and media contexts—from Cambodia to Nigeria and Nepal.

Drama for Development: Cultural Translation and Social Change offers a unique window into the social and media worlds that typically remain closed to academic inquiry. But it goes beyond the conventional concerns of drama for development to explore 'the social life of methods'[4] or the myriad ways in which the methods that we use to study the social and media worlds of audiences are not culturally neutral tools, but are active agents in themselves that can become a force for social change. This book seeks to break new ground in how we think about, create and research serial drama to effect progressive social change. Its implications extend well beyond the contexts studied in Africa and Asia to highlight the dynamics of the universal and the particular as well as the global and the local in contemporary television and radio serial drama (see Appendix 2 for a summary of the structure of different forms of dramatic and serial narrative).

Chapters 1–3 set the context for the case studies to follow. In the opening chapter, 'Re-framing Drama for Development', Andrew Skuse, drawing on nearly two decades experience of field research, assesses the development and range of analytical frameworks applied to researching drama for development and E-E projects. He argues for the need to bring qualitative inquiry into closer dialogue with the kind of quantitative surveys that appear to offer number crunching certainties, but which can often lack in-depth understanding of cultural dynamics and change. He proposes that mixing ethnographic, community-based and participatory approaches enables more socially sensitive research on transnational circuits of production and consumption as dynamic cultural processes, and stresses the importance of cultural translation—not just translation from one language to another, but wider processes that involve the negotiation of cultural values, practices and traditions that may be mobilised for or against development goals. While stressing this approach, Skuse also recognises that a willingness to engage the 'other' in a cosmopolitan sense constitutes a core attribute of drama for development writers and producers. Making one's way 'through' another culture is an endeavour of some magnitude that requires skills associated not only with exactness or mastery, but also with cultural approximation and playfulness. Thus, how the creative rendering of a representation of society through drama allows maximum audience engagement, one that cuts across different ethnicities and language groups, also constitutes a main animating topic of not only Chapter 1, but also the broader volume.

The history of drama for development work at the BBC WST is the subject of Chapter 2, 'Great Expectations and Creative Evolution: The History of Drama for Development at the BBC World Service Trust' by Caroline Sugg and Gerry Power. Drawing upon 10 years' experience working to support over 15 drama serials, the authors map 'overlapping' processes or stages in the evolution of drama production at the BBC WST, including: an early phase where the export of drama to developing and transitional countries was underpinned by a rather traditional BBC drama centric approach to development; a 'development sensitisation' phase during which the priorities of its funders were reflected in the dramas; a phase of 'great expectations' where theories of behaviour change and development communication were prominent and a more recent phase that they refer to as a 'creative coalescence' when the expectations about what drama can achieve in development terms have matured, been refined and redefined. This chapter is particularly useful in offering an overview of the dramas produced over the last 10 years by the BBC WST—a body of work that is extremely varied, but which can also be distinguished by a set of key characteristics (see Appendix 1).

Gerry Power, in Chapter 3, examines the history and cultural politics of the BBC WST's 'Audience Research in Drama for Development', emphasising its role as a cross-cultural 'contact zone' where daily practices of translation and transnational knowledge production meet and inform creative decisions about drama formats, characters, narrative themes and plotlines. He examines four sets of dynamics that have to be taken into account in understanding, researching and delivering dramas to audiences: (*a*) *London and Local* or the relations between London and local researchers and how this translocal cultural field operates; (*b*) *Practitioner and Academic* or the tensions between the pursuit of audience research that has all the hallmarks of good, applied social science and the practical, cultural and time constraints with which researchers and dramatists have to deal; (*c*) *Researcher and the researched* and the ideological influence of a northern social sciences paradigm; (*d*) Western and non-Western dynamics remind us that contact zones are also zones of tension, marked by asymmetries of power and the history of colonial and post-colonial relations.

In Chapter 4, 'Creative Tensions: Audience Research and the Representational Challenge of Dramatising Opium Substitution in Afghanistan', Andrew Skuse explores the challenges faced by national and international broadcasters in establishing meaningful community-level dialogue and partnerships due to the inevitable social distance that separates the usually liberal, urban, highly educated, professional media producers and dramatists from their often rural and highly conservative audiences. Audience research seeks to reduce this 'social distance' and promote the inclusion of community voices in broadcasting, but it is also a mechanism whereby dominant western development 'messaging' and neo-liberal discourses may be imposed on information-poor and entertainment-hungry developing world audiences. In assessing the specific functions of qualitative audience research within the field of drama for development, this chapter focuses on the BBC AEP's long-running radio drama *New Home, New Life* (see Chapters 7 and 13). A critical theme of the drama, opium, crop substitution strategies and the allied effects of widespread drug addiction and conflict constitute key concerns for donors, the Afghan national government and non-government agencies. He shows how qualitative audience research, paradoxically, both enhances and restrains the 'utopianism' of development discourse.

Issues of gender are addressed in Chapter 5, 'Considering Men, Masculinity and Drama' by Charlotte Lapsansky and Joyce S. Chatterjee. Not only is women's equity an important goal in its own right, but it has also been shown to have significant effects on public health outcomes. In recent years, a number of dramas for development have tackled the issue of women's rights and gender equity. However, understanding audiences' engagement and commitment to gender equity is a nuanced and culturally complex task, the mapping of which presents a significant methodological challenge. This chapter explores the use of the Gender Equitable Men (GEM) scale as an analytical tool to help identify audience gender-related attitudes and key areas of intervention for storyline development. The GEM tool is the only existing gender attitudes scale that has been created specifically for evaluation of international development and public health interventions. While originally developed for evaluation, this chapter discusses the potential of the GEM scale as a formative research tool for understanding drama for development audiences. The authors present their work with the

BBC WST and the use of the GEM scale as a formative research tool audience assessment for the Trust's radio drama interventions in India, *Jasoos Vijay* and *Life Gul Mohar Style*.

Chapter 6, 'Telling Other People's Stories: Cultural Translation in Drama for Development' by Emily LeRoux-Rutledge, Gerry Power and Carol Morgan tackles the question raised earlier by Gerry Power (see Chapter 3) of how translocal dynamics operate: how dramatists, working on drama for development projects, negotiate the challenges of drama production across cultural and linguistic boundaries. Translating development themes into good dramas requires a basic 'cross-cultural literacy' if dramatists are to play the role of successful 'cultural brokers' (see Chapter 1). How is a foundational 'cultural literacy' achieved? What roles do local translators and cultural intermediaries play in informing and enculturating the dramatists? How do these cross-cultural translation processes shape creative decision-making? This chapter examines the competing and often-conflicting tensions placed on dramatists by various stakeholders (audiences, media partners, donors, government and so on), and proposes a conceptual framework onto which the creative decisions made by dramatists may be mapped.

Andrew Skuse and Marie Gillespie, in Chapter 7, 'Broadcasting "The State"', examine the enduring significance of tribal power and local hierarchies that may militate against any westernised notions of citizenship in Afghanistan. They examine the mutually constituting relationships that are forged between radio drama producers, editors, scriptwriters and audiences through the related practices of audience evaluation and media engagement. The chapter takes a longitudinal approach examining documents and reanalysing research data conducted over the period of the BBC AEP's *New Home, New Life* production (1993/4–present). The chapter presents a conjunctural analysis of the politics represented in three distinctly different political moments in recent Afghan political history: *Mujahideen* rule (1989–1996), the Taliban era (1997–2001) and the post-Taliban democratic period of US/NATO influence (2002–present). Each of these 'moments' in Afghan history forced the producers and writers to make specific choices over how aspects of politics and citizenship should be represented. The chapter shows how modern neo-liberal state practices and institutions in traditional tribal and non-tribal rural communities in Afghanistan have been resisted, with state attempts to effect radical social change generating hostility, distrust and resentment. It shows how social realist dramas are constructed in the interplay between the social realities of the audience, as identified through audience research (see Chapter 4), the neo-liberal development themes of donors and the liberal politics of media producers.

In Chapter 8, 'Dramatising "New Nepal"', Andrew Skuse and Michael Wilmore examine an innovative Nepali language production *Katha Mitho Sarangiko (Sweet Tales from the Sarangi)*. The chapter shows how this drama overturns established drama for development conventions by using a series of social realistic techniques: improvisation based on loose synopses; recording on location; using local people in non-key roles (as fathers, mothers-in-law, bus drivers, butchers, postal workers). The chapter also highlights the challenges of linking diverse Nepalese geographical and cultural contexts, rural and urban, as well as upper and lower castes. This is achieved through the imaginative deployment of a stock character in traditional oral culture—the wandering *Sarangi* (a small bowed lute) player and itinerant storyteller. In analysing some of the dramatic devices used and production choices made in this drama, the chapter poses some searching questions about the translation of genres, dramatic techniques and formats: How did audiences respond to the use of social realist techniques? Did the use of improvisation and real people present the drama in a more vivid or convincing way in the view of audiences? What are the opportunities and constraints on creative innovation in contexts where genre conventions are often rigidly adhered to? To what extent are the development goals of the production met and enhanced by such a method?

In Chapter 9, 'A Dynamic Encoding Process: Making the Cambodian "Taste of Life" Drama', Lizz Frost Yocum examines the shifting priorities of and power relations between key players involved in making a drama for development. The chapter traces how various logics of practice influence how and when key actors (dramatists, audiences, producers, managers, editors) exercise power (cultural, creative, editorial and financial) at varying stages of the drama-making process. It highlights the tensions between their competing and, at times, conflicting logics of practice in making an entertaining and educational drama that engages audiences while simultaneously seeking to achieve development-oriented outcomes focused on social change that can be measured and assessed. It argues that the roles of key actors in the transnational cultural circuits that constitute drama for development have to be understood and analysed as a dynamic, active and creative process of cultural translation where neither the encoding of 'messages' nor the responses or outcomes of audiences can be predicted in advance.

In Chapter 10, we return (see Chapter 5) to HIV and AIDS-focused television drama in India. In *'Jasoos Vijay*: Self-Efficacy, Collective Action and Social Norms in the Context of an HIV and AIDS Television Drama', Lauren B. Frank, Sonal Tickoo Chaudhuri, Anurudra Bhanot and Sheila T. Murphy, a typical BBC WST transnational team, examine how sensitivities to cultural values and social norms were handled in the popular Indian television detective drama, *Jasoos Vijay* (*Detective Vijay*). In this drama, viewers are exposed to different perspectives of people living with HIV and AIDS. The chapter explores audience responses as re-presented in qualitative (letters, e-mails, texts) and quantitative (survey) data. The chapter examines the profile of viewers that research identifies as 'most likely' to be responsive to messages that characterise shifts in attitudes and norms regarding HIV and AIDS. They go on to identify the key elements of drama for development (characters, messages, discussion of the programme with others, etc.) that resonate with normative understandings of HIV and AIDS, and how such attitudes might be changed. The chapter concludes with recommendations for optimising viewer engagement in drama for development.

Cultural translation in a drama about transnational families as well as among key players involved in its production is the subject of Chapter 11, '"Passport to Love": Dramatising Forced Marriage between Pakistan and the Pakistani Diaspora' by Sadaf Rizvi. The BBC WST Urdu language radio drama *Piyar ka Passport* (Passport to Love) was broad-cast in Pakistan and the United Kingdom for a trial period in 2006. It was produced to raise awareness and stimulate dialogue on human rights and social and gender issues in Pakistan and in the diaspora. The chapter analyses processes by which British, global and Pakistani perspectives are negotiated by donors, dramatists, development and policy actors and audience researchers. It examines the processes of cross-cultural exchange and translation, and highlights the differences between donors and dramatists on the issue of forced marriage. While unpacking the idea of forced marriage, the chapter addresses issues of autonomy, the balancing of loyalties and implications of decisions about marriage in Pakistani culture. The drama provides a focused cross-cultural 'contact zone' to understand the connections and the differences between media practitioners, human rights and development constituencies, donors and audiences. The negotiations between donors and dramatists present an interesting evolution and development narrative.

Chapter 12, '*Urunana* Audiences at Home and Away: Together "Hand in Hand"?' by Helen M. Hintjens and Fortunee Bayisenge, examines this award winning drama serial and women's responses to it 'at home' and within the Rwandan diaspora (where they can listen to the drama online). Drawing on qualitative data, including interviewing and focus group discussions, this chapter considers how Kinyarwanda speaking women (in Rwanda and The Netherlands), in diverse local settings are connected by the soap, how they talk about the storylines from the *Urunana* ('Hand in Hand') radio drama broadcast by the BBC World Service and produced by the NGO Health Unlimited. The chapter asks: How do different Kinyarwandan speaking women 'translate' and appropriate the themes of *Urunana*? How do women audiences interpret the same storylines in different settings? Whatever the themes of the episodes discussed (which ranged from marriage, hygiene and HIV, women in leadership, barriers to contraceptives, adultery, teenage pregnancy, etc.), the key starting point is: How do listeners themselves frame the topics and interpret the themes whether in relation to their own life experiences or to external events in the wider society—or simply as entertainment? The authors examine the impact of context, life-stage, class and wider patterns of media consumption on responses to the drama. It is argued that by combining perspectives from media and development studies literature, feminist and social constructionist approaches to framing development issues, this chapter advances our understanding of how audiences listen to and make use of radio drama to make sense of their own lived experiences and of wider processes of social change in both national and diasporic communities.

Gossip is a central feature of both serial and real-life dramas and a powerful tool for debating, affirming and/or transforming social norms.

In Chapter 13, 'Gossiping for Change: Dramatising "Blood Debt" in Afghanistan', Andrew Skuse and Marie Gillespie examine the kind of gossip about social transgressions that the Afghan serial drama *New Home, New Life* inspires about the moral propriety of characters. The authors argue that the complexities of real life and soap gossip as a potent form of communication in close-knit and intimate social networks remains a source of influence that drama for development practitioners and theorists could use to convey key themes and issues. Gossip and rumour have their own rules and norms, but because of the way the audience is knitted into the serial drama over time, generating debate via soap gossip is an effective tool of social communication (see Appendix 2). We examine the distinctive qualities of serial drama and the ways in which it produces temporal structures conducive to gossip and, by implication, the negotiation of cultural translation and social change.

Across the chapters, we develop a distinctive approach to drama for development. We argue that a focus on transnational circuits of cultural production, translation and consumption is necessary to avoid the sometimes limiting assumptions of many early drama projects aimed at changing audiences' behaviours without a deep and full understanding of the social and cultural contexts of their lives. We advocate the use of ethnographic methods and 'thick descriptions' of cultural dynamics and processes to complement other forms of research and to underpin the important work that drama for development can do to improve the lives of poor people, through the provision of relevant information that enables audiences and publics themselves to make up their minds rather than be the subjects of media didacticisms.

Analysing drama for development as a cross-cultural contact zone, with cosmopolitan potential (see Chapter 1), is only one, albeit important step and, we hope, an intervention in this field. But drama for development studies needs to be further contextualised in the wider milieu of interstate relations and geopolitical priorities, western (and therefore culturally specific) neo-liberal doctrines of democracy and freedom, the financial and power play of donor constituencies and challenges of participatory development practice.

We hope that we have shown how our integrated and relational approach to examining how key actors in the circuits of drama production and consumption cooperate, collide, collude and conflict will shed light on the enormous creative and financial challenges that the BBC WST, the lynchpin holding together the dramas analysed in this book, faces and deals with on a daily basis with a great deal of goodwill and expertise.

Notes

1. The BBC WST is externally funded through donor contributions and grants, and works in partnership with local broadcasters to address humanitarian challenges and constraints on development through the application of media (see Chapters 1 and 2 in this volume for more detail on the organisation of the BBC WST).
2. This example conflates a number of actual storylines presented by the *New Home, New Life* production during the mid-1990s for the purpose of illustration.
3. 'Tuning in: Diasporic Contact Zones at the BBC World Service' (see http://www8. open.ac.uk/researchprojects/diasporas/).
4. http://www.cresc.ac.uk/our-research/cross-theme-research/social-life-of-methods

1

RE-FRAMING DRAMA FOR DEVELOPMENT

A<small>NDREW</small> S<small>KUSE</small>

Introduction

'Writing about soap opera is a perilous business,' suggests Geraghty, of the difficulties inherent in choosing melodrama as an object of study (1991: 7). Her peril is essentially that of any researcher faced with the task of fixing in time that which is designed always to be in narrative and dramatic motion. By way of example, during the period of her own research in the early 1990s, she recalls that 'Pamela left *Dallas* and Fallon, via a space ship, came back to *Dynasty*; Angie and Den left *Eastenders* and the factory in *Coronation Street* was demolished; *Crossroads* was killed off and *Dynasty* came to an abrupt halt' (ibid.). These popular British and American television drama serials and soap operas stir instant recognition for audiences internationally, yet the dramas that constitute the focus of this book are far less familiar to global audiences, though are equally popular in the Asian and African contexts of their production (Liebes and Katz, 1993). Like their mainstream counterparts, BBC World Service Trust (BBC WST) dramas such as Nigeria's *Wetin Dey* (*What's Up?*), India's *Jasoos Vijay* (*Detective Vijay*) and Afghanistan's *Khana-e-nau, Zindagi-e-nau* (*New Home, New Life*) fire both the imagination and emotions of diverse audiences watching and listening in diverse socio-cultural contexts, therein promoting discussion of where the narrative will go next and how it can possibly be resolved (see Appendix 2).

There is broad agreement that mass-mediated serial narratives (in the form of drama serials or soap operas) are emotionally affective, engage audiences like few other media genres can and constitute an important semantic element of everyday social interaction, discussion and dissension (Abu-Lughod, 1995, 2005; Allen, 1985, 1995; Ang, 1985; Buckingham, 1987; Gillespie, 1995, 2006; Singhal et al., 2004; Tufte, 2003). As an organisation, the BBC has been engaged in media production towards 'pro-social' ends for many decades (albeit generally domestically and without the explicit goal orientation of the BBC World Service Trust's contemporary international drama for development productions). For example, in the post-war era the long-running domestic BBC Radio 4 drama *The Archers* began, addressing some of the key social and economic challenges facing rural Britain during this period, while more recent BBC productions such as BBC One's *Eastenders* television soap opera has addressed issues as diverse as racism, HIV and domestic violence (Buckingham, 1987; Geraghty, 1991; Rigbey, 1993; Walker, 1992). Though very much 'drama-led', 'social concerns' can be seen to permeate much mainstream BBC contemporary drama broadcasting (see Chapter 3). In particular, BBC television drama since the 1960s has espoused social realist values and cultural detail of the type associated with what is popularly termed British 'kitchen sink' drama (Heritage, 1988). This suggests that hard-hitting BBC drama that problematises social issues and contradictions, and which, contains clear social commentary has thrived far beyond the domains of communication for development or so-called Entertainment-Education (E-E) interventions for many years (Singhal et al., 2004).[1] Such mainstream drama broadcasting is typically reactive to social trends and concerns that permeate society. However, in recent years, as interest in media and development has been rekindled by the emergence of new information and communication technologies, many international broadcasters, the BBC World Service, Radio Netherlands and the Australian Broadcasting Corporation included, have strived to more clearly define their roles in relation to the board of communication for development.

Established in 1999, the BBC WST is an independent charity that sits within the Global News Division of the BBC that includes the BBC World Service, BBC World News and BBC Monitoring. Funded from a mix of external grants, voluntary contributions and in-kind support from the BBC, the BBC WST's organisational location allows it to draw: '... on the extensive experience and expertise of the BBC, adhering to the corporation's values, making use of its technical resources and maintaining the highest professional standards of BBC broadcasting and programme-making in all of its outputs' (BBC World Service Trust, 2008: 8).

The manner in which the BBC WST is organised within the broader BBC, allied to its role in utilising media in support of processes of social change, is perhaps unique amongst the organisations active in the field of 'communication for development' (see Chapter 2). The institutional relationships that exist between the BBC WST, its funders (such as the UK Department for International Development) and their local producing/broadcast partners significantly frame the objectives of each drama production and allied audience research activities (see Appendix 1 for a detailed list of BBC WST drama for development productions). Further, such relationships are defined by international poverty reduction targets (such as the United Nations Millennium Development Goals) that in turn generate specific power dynamics (North to South) and create sets of expectations concerning outcomes that shape orientations and assumptions about audiences, research and the effects or impacts of the dramas produced (Abrahamsen, 2004; UNDP, 2001). More simply stated, in numerous contexts the drama production of the BBC WST faces the daunting challenge of translating complex—often external—development themes and priorities into locally intelligible frames by applying specific cultural and political filters informed by research, evaluation and partnership at the local level.

In recognising this challenge, this book conceptualises the various contexts of BBC WST drama for development production and audience consumption in dynamic terms, as cross-cultural 'contact zones' in which various forms of translation, flow and interpretation occur. Where possible, each chapter reflects the creative labour of drama production, the multiple mediations of audiences and specific organisational relationships that facilitate production. Thus, each contribution seeks to promote an understanding of BBC WST drama in 'relational' terms—production to consumption and vice versa. This position helps to advance our understanding of both institutional arrangements and creative processes, while linking these to audience interpretation. In doing so, this pushes the publicly available analysis beyond that of conventional audience-focused 'impact' studies with their narrow focus on knowledge, attitudes and behaviour towards a more holistic, critically engaged and fundamentally qualitative appreciation of the inherently relational complex that is media production and consumption (Dornfeld, 1998; Gillespie, 2005; Hall, 1999; Morley, 1992). Too often, the cultural nature of media consumption is separated from the contexts, specificities and cultures of production, with this failing being attributed to the analytical preference for 'cultural texts' or 'audience effects' over the significant factors of political economy, organisational relations, cultures of creativity and cosmopolitanism evident in production. In recognition of this critical 'lack', Dornfeld (1998) suggests we must urgently address the 'interpretative frameworks' of producers and 'production practices'.

Since Dornfeld (1998) made this appeal, modest inroads into the analysis of 'cultures of media production' have been made (Ginsburg et al., 2002; Skuse, 2002, 2005; Tufte, 2002; Wilk and Askew, 2002).[2] However, the way in which producers situate themselves with regard to wider institutional arrangements, their audiences, how they utilise audience research, specific theoretical and professional concepts or dedicated media genres, and how these are reflected in their media representations is of critical concern to understanding how media contributes to and shapes wider public culture (Dornfeld, 1998: 7). Such concerns are apposite when we consider the drama for development work of the BBC WST, the transnational nature of the wider BBC, the developing world contexts of their production, the diasporic and expatriate staff critical to their realisation and their creative endeavour of translating local and international development concerns into stimulating melodrama.

Locating Drama for Development at the BBC World Service Trust: Alternative Creative Traditions and Theoretical Approaches

Drama production at the BBC WST draws upon a number of communication theories and psycho-social approaches related to behaviour change modelling, as well as upon a 'pro-social/social-realist' dramatic tradition that has grown up independently of communications theorising (see Chapter 2). The institutional arrangements that allow the BBC WST to draw upon domestic BBC 'expatriate' expertise yields creativity and cross-cultural encounters that cannot be proscribed in theory. The Kabul-based BBC Afghan Education Projects' (BBC AEP) long-running (1994–present) radio drama *New Home, New Life* is a case in point. Developed with the assistance of a former *Archers* editor, utilising a group of Afghan dramatists that previously worked for various incarnations of the Afghan Communist Government (1978–1989) influenced by Soviet Socialist Realism, made for a creative encounter that was both unique, but also not informed in significant way by theorising or behavioural modelling. Yet, with the emergence of the discrete field of communication for development and the establishment of the BBC WST (1999) as a charity principally funded by external organisations, the dramatic traditions of the wider BBC have since been incorporated into a body of communications theory that seeks to account for the potential and seemingly innate power of mass media to modify human behaviour, promote modernity and stimulate socio-cultural change.

The conceptual approach and practice of the BBC WST is referenced by contemporary communications and psycho-social theorising, which began to emerge, along with the Cold War, in the 1950s (Lerner, 1958). The following theoretical summary seeks to identify dominant sectoral trends, rather than explicitly 'pin-down' a specific BBC WST approach, which in practice reflects a bricolage of different vertical and horizontal communication strategies. In the post-war period, mass media were increasingly viewed as tools via which visions of modernity (socialist or liberal-democratic) could be pushed, especially in developing country contexts deemed to be 'at risk'. The explosion of pro-modernity and democracy *radio-* and *telenovelas* in Latin America from the 1950s onwards represents a case in point (Hagedorn, 1995;

Martín-Barbero, 1995; Vink, 1988). Many contemporary communication frameworks and psycho-social theories support, often uncritically, notions of social, behavioural or material change. Nonetheless, they constitute a *lingua franca* for organisations that practice in the field of communication for development and have become a critical component of the discourse and rhetoric that circulates around the role of mass media in processes of development.

Typically, communication for development interventions such as those promoted by the BBC WST seek to enhance knowledge, bring about broad shifts in public awareness and alter people's individual and group practices, their norms, attitudes and behaviours (see Chapman et al., 2003; Torero and Von Braun, 2005). In this respect, Inagaki suggests:

> The hallmark of development communication interventions is the explicit and implicit desire to change the way people behave. The role of the communication experts is to design and implement a communication message or system of information flows that would trigger reactions leading to the adoption of the desirable behavioural patterns.
>
> (2007: 24)

In espousing similar principles, the approach of the BBC WST links to a body of communication and psycho-social theory that plays on the notion that: (*a*) certain people are predisposed to change and that these people—following suitable media mobilisation—can act as 'reagents' or 'opinion leaders', pushing their own societies towards social reforms, development and therein, modernity and (*b*) many people lack alternative visions of the future or how to overcome a specific problem and can address such problems by mimicking the behaviour of 'reagents' or positive media role models. Such theorising is heavily dependent on notions of 'self-realisation' or 'self-efficacy' in which information provision, such as health-messaging, combined with positive role modelling can lead to lasting social change (Rogers, 1962).[3]

The work of Rogers (1962) is perhaps the best known of a basket of approaches to communication and change that fall broadly within the 'psycho-social' category. Other models such as the health belief model, theory of reasoned action, social cognitive theory, and so on, all draw upon the notion that individuals are able to rationalise their actions and behaviours and upon reflection change them (Dutta-Bergman, 2005; Waisbord, 2001). However, such models tend to pay little attention to how appealing the advocated changes may appear to the target group/audience or whether there is scope to undergo change within the socio-cultural, economic or political context (UNAIDS, 1999). Early top–down and didactic media interventions generally failed to inspire audiences, with the stubborn persistence and deepening of global poverty and inequality in the decades since the 1960s suggesting that if the poor did seek modernity and change, it wasn't the form of modernity and change that was envisaged by development planners and communicators (Waisbord, 2001). Nonetheless, the notion that society is populated with 'opinion leaders' or 'reagents' and 'role models' who are located at the vanguard of social change has enduring appeal for organisations such as the BBC WST, and much of their drama work focuses on 'modelling positive and negative behaviour' through various role models and transgressors.

Both televised and radio-based drama for development variants tend to rely on the 'dilemma' quality of storylines and the notion that there are social 'heroes', and by association 'villains'. Theoretically and practically, many contemporary drama for development interventions link closely with the work of Bandura (1977) and Sabido (2004) and social learning theory (an evolution of earlier psycho-social models), which proceeds from the premise that individuals learn from actively assessing both positive and negative behaviour. Thus, many drama productions adopt common sense notions that audiences face various dilemmas within their lives that they must rationalise or negotiate and that drama is a particularly well-suited genre for highlighting the positive and negative consequences of a given behaviour or action. Typically, though characters are heard/seen to waiver between the 'good' and the 'bad', more often than not, characters adopt the advocated positive stance (Das, 1995; Miller, 1995). It is through the choice of this positive stance that the dominant meaning of potentially long-run and complex storyline threads is communicated.

Galavotti et al. (2001) suggest that 'alternative narratives' are urgently required within the developing world and that a combination of mass-mediated drama, plus 'interpersonal reinforcement at the community level' is being viewed as a potentially effective mechanism for broaching developmental and behavioural 'alternatives'. With regard to the deepening HIV crisis, Galavotti et al. suggest:

> In the face of ... public health threats, women and men in developing countries have a limited ability to imagine other futures and other choices. They are held hostage by a societal narrative in which the cycle of early marriage, unprotected sexual behaviour, multiple unplanned births, HIV infection, and early death is seen as unavoidable, and where patterns of personal behaviour are thought to be unalterable.
>
> (2001: 1602)

Increasingly, communication for development is perceived in terms of generating meaningful dialogues with the poor and recent approaches—Galavotti et al. (2001) included—now advocate a more holistic and contextual understanding of human behaviour. This move is in response to the failure of earlier theories to locate individuals within communities and environments that actively constrain action and behaviour change (UNAIDS, 1999). Those advocating a 'behaviour change' approach, such as the BBC WST, have sought to reposition their work towards a greater recognition of the need for community 'ownership' (of interventions) and dialogue. In seeking to understand culturally specific domains, socio-economic impediments and specific behaviours, such approaches now recognise that individual behaviour change is not simply a matter of social-psychology and rationalisation on an individual basis, but an outcome of numerous complex and interlocking factors (UNAIDS, 1999).[4] In turn, this has heralded significant investments in audience research capacity within organisations committed to this field, the BBC WST included.

Whilst much communication for development remains 'top–down' and informed by quite dated psycho-social models, rapidly expanding community media and deepening of access to interactive media such as the Internet has heralded the emergence of a considerable 'citizen media' sector in the South that is actively building a more horizontal orientation to communication (CFSC/Rockefeller Foundation, 2002; Inagaki, 2007). Whilst all communication inevitably entails hierarchies, citizen media included, many communication for development practitioners are acutely aware that in addition to raising broad public awareness through traditional 'top–down' broadcasting, there is the parallel need to engage communities via other channels and forms of communication. Rarely are development communication interventions reliant upon standalone mediums, and there is broad consensus that impact is raised exponentially when a '360° messaging' approach is adopted (Yoder et al., 1996). Thus, the more consistently and frequently messages are targeted at, for example, certain health risk groups, the more effective the impact of the communication.[5] Multi-channel communication is forcing the coalescence of multiple communication approaches, this point being reinforced by Inagaki, who notes that: '... applied development communication is thus characterised by the co-presence of multiples frameworks. Constructive cross-pollinations between different frameworks are much desired, but such prospects are not taken for granted' (2007: 8).

What is clear from theorising and model-building in communications for development through the past four decades is that there has been an increasingly significant interest in developing 'evidence based' interventions in terms of interventions that respond to actual needs, actual issues, work in partnership with affected populations and which seek to understand and amend their media content in an iterative way through an ongoing process of evaluation of impacts and outcomes (Batchelor and Scott, 2005).

The push towards building a solid evidence base relating to communications for development interventions is placing an increasing emphasis on building more subtle evaluation mechanisms and particularly on expanding the role of qualitative research (Marker et al., 2002). Formative qualitative evaluation has long played a key role in project design, in communicating the information needs of target groups and audiences to planners and content producers and increasingly, more systematic and ongoing forms of qualitative feedback are being sought by project implementers (Skuse et al., 2007). This is because large-scale communication campaigns, whilst seeking to integrate mass, community, participatory and interpersonal (peer education and counselling) communication in the methodological bricolage, tend to be organised in the national metropolis and feature considerable aspects of social distance, i.e., the physical and sociocultural, economic and political distance between audiences and content producers, such as actors, dramatists and presenters (Allen, 1985, 1995; cf. Fairhead and Leach, 1996; Long and Long, 1992). Much of the effort of BBC WST qualitative evaluation involves attempts to close this distance, to realise an ongoing and representative voice for the 'national audience' within production especially, whilst at the same time providing insights into the impact of the content and the development 'messages' therein (see Chapter 4).

Evidence-based approaches are now seen as a key 'hallmark' of effective communication for development. Here, Inagaki (2007) cites five different forms of 'evidence' typically cited, namely: (*a*) evidence of behaviour change; (*b*) shifts in knowledge and attitudes; (*c*) the empowerment and capacity building (of individuals, groups and organisations); (*d*) evidence of coalition building and partnership around a given problem and (*e*) tangible community resources being developed as a result of the communication intervention about a problem. By far the dominant concern of communication for development interventions is that of changing behaviour, the precursor of which is typically viewed in terms of raised awareness or knowledge, as well as shifts in attitudes about a given issues. Since behaviour change may occur over a very long period, the stock-in-trade of impact evaluation tends to reside with analysis of knowledge attained and attitudes affected (Mytton, 1999). However, this trend, which is driven principally by the project implementers' need to demonstrate accountability against their stated objectives to their donors, obscures much from analytical view. It obscures the depth of qualitative research undertaken by organisations such as the BBC WST; more specifically, it obscures the lengths to which interventions will go to reduce social distance between producers and audiences in the attempt to integrate the voices and perspectives of audiences into the production process.

Increasingly longer term ethnographic approaches to evaluation are being adopted in some communication interventions, as both a project development tool and a route to sustained qualitative evaluation (Skuse et al., 2007). Tufte (2002) in a recent study of 'edutainment' interventions suggests that increasingly there is a concern to understand how audiences 'make meaning' in the sense of the culturally and socially framed discussions that occur over content. Tufte suggests that a focus on 'mediations' within the audience can help reveal the complexity of communication, including: 'The set of influences that structure, organise and reorganise the understanding of the reality of that an audience lives. Mediation is the process in which sense is made in the communication process' (Tufte, 2002: 2).

Understanding the 'mediations' concerning the content of communications for development shifts our attention away from the ostensibly quantitative approaches of surveying knowledge and attitudes towards understanding things like how knowledge is negotiated, how attitudes are altered, why certain media content is accepted, whilst other content is rejected. Tufte's (2003) study of Brazilian *telenovelas* and earlier ethnographic work on the ethnography of drama for development (Mandel, 2002; Skuse, 1999, 2002, 2005) production and consumption alerts us to the fact that: (*a*) audiences are complex and bring many differing mediations to the same content; (*b*) that audiences are embedded in and constrained by socio-cultural, political and economic fields that affect their ability to act on informative content or even interpret it and (*c*) that the 'meanings' derived from content tend to derive from collective dialogues and negotiation within these fields. Tufte (2002) defines several points of entry to the ethnographic study of drama for development that resonate to earlier media theory, that (*a*) '*telenovelas* articulate strong emotional engagement and increase audience involvement' (cf. Ang, 1985); (*b*) 'telenovelas increase dialogue and debate, and can break the silence around controversial or taboo issues' (Gillespie, 1995; Miller, 1995); and (*c*) 'telenovelas socialize viewers [or listeners] to new lifestyles and articulate cultural citizenship' (Martín-Barbero, 1995; Rofel, 1995; Tufte, 2002, 2003; Vink, 1988).

The analytical focus provided by Tufte (2002) links to the rapid growth of media anthropology and audience ethnography (Ginsburg et al., 2002; Mankekar, 1999; Wilk and Askew, 2002), and is conventional in that there is a clear privileging of audiences and audience mediations over processes of media production. There is a significant dearth of qualitative work undertaken in media studies and media anthropology concerning contexts of media production. There are though exceptions (Dornfeld, 1998; Graffman, 2004; Skuse 2002, 2005; Wilmore, 2008), and such work highlights the clear value of understanding processes of mediation in their entirety, namely, in understanding the 'flow' of content through moments of design, production, dissemination and consumption. Tufte (2002), like many others before him, highlights Hall's (1999) seminal 'encoding-decoding' model of media production, circulation and consumption, but fails to fully recognise the value of understanding production fields. Whilst audiences mediate and garner 'preferred' or 'oppositional' readings of content, or even 'remediate' content to generate entirely new and unexpected meanings, we must recognise that media producers are engaged in similar processes as they work to form media content. This is of particular importance when we bear in mind that the producers of pro-social media content such as the BBC WST are actively seeking to integrate 'beneficial' messages concerning a range of issues within content that seeks to resonate with the socio-cultural realities of their target audiences.

From this perspective we can see that there is clear merit in adopting a 'political economy' approach to the study of processes of development communication. Such an approach seeks to locate such processes within context-specific social, cultural, political and economic frames, frames that are critically reflective of patterns of power, social exclusion, inequality and intergenerational poverty (Bracking, 2003; de Haan, 1998; Garnham, 1997; Mattelart, 1996; UNAIDS, 1999). For example, Mansell (2002) has argued that there is clear neglect of political economy in research on new media diffusion to the developing world and this means that 'the overall social and economic dynamics of the production and the consumption of new media [in developing countries] continue to be subjects of speculation'. Echoing the assertions of UNAIDS (1999), Mansell (2002) recognises that having information or knowledge and being able to act on it are two very different things, which returns us to the key contention that in order to understand the complex dynamics of communication at community level a more rigorous, relational (in the sense of production-consumption-production) and longer term qualitative mode of inquiry is preferential. This volume, with its singular focus on the drama for development work of the BBC WST, seeks to interrogate such dynamics. In doing so, it locates the work of the BBC WST firmly within the remit of cosmopolitanism.

Drama for Development Production and Cosmopolitan Competency

The chapters in this book all speak to an essentially cosmopolitan endeavour. The BBC WST approaches the craft of drama and its role in development—as outlined in the section above—from the perspective that it is 'capable' of effecting or contributing to social change on an individual and community basis. Its audience research work seeks to understand perceived 'negative' behavioural practice (such as not wearing condoms when at risk from HIV) and wider development constraints in order that they may be problematised and overcome. Here, drama provides the vehicle for stimulating debate and interpersonal communications, the provision of information, positive role modelling and welcome entertainment. In engaging in 'other' cultural terrains within the developing world the BBC WST brings to bear a set of competencies that, it argues, reflects in the wider values of professionalism, technical and research expertise, creativity and impartiality commonly associated with the BBC. Perceiving drama for development production in terms of a range of creative and cultural competencies thus provides an interesting analytical oeuvre, one that intrinsically links to notions of cosmopolitanism, cross-cultural encounter and translation.

Examination of notions of cultural competency in turn forces a discussion of how culture, as both a term and concept, is employed and understood by the BBC WST. Analysis suggests that culture tends to be understood in reified, reductionist and practical/vernacular ways by drama producers and the wider BBC WST. First, culture is reified because it is often discussed and approached in a generalised way. From this perspective culture is a 'thing' that has certain rules, norms and mores, but importantly, this thing can be changed and manipulated. Second, culture is used in an essentialised 'stripped-down' way, in which complex cultural practices such as caste or sexual behaviour are focused upon and reduced to sets of understandable and challengeable concepts, norms and mores. Finally, culture is understood in practical and vernacular ways, as something that you 'do' or something that is constructed in the process of expatriate and local dramatists, producers and development specialists interacting (cf. Baumann, 1997). A multi-faceted approach to culture moves us beyond the notion that drama for development production is concerned with a mechanistic translation—one culture (or class) to another—of complex development concepts and issues. Rather, drama for development production reflects a complex milieu, in which culture is made, contested, adapted, understood, misunderstood, reified, reduced, essentialised and made practical. In considering culture and the BBC WST it is also reasonable to stress that as an organisation, the fine-grained understandings of culture generated by anthropology and ethnographic method are typically beyond the reach and remit of such organisations, yet cultural competency is very much a contemporary hallmark of communication for development and especially, so-called behaviour change interventions. Behaviour is cultural and changing behaviour necessarily implies the cultural (however it is understood). Further, cultural competency is closely associated with notions of cosmopolitanism and attendant abilities to interpret and intuit 'Other' cultures.

Conventionally, the term cosmopolitanism is used 'loosely, to describe just about anybody who moves about in the world' (Hannerz, 1990: 238). Hannerz rightly warns that 'the cosmopolitan' is often contrasted to the 'local', with the former being seen to engage in social relationships that are freed from 'territorial boundaries' while the latter is regarded as being bound by 'face-to-face' localised interactions. This is a useful way of not only conceiving of individuals, but also institutions such as the BBC WST, which though international, in a practical sense seek to 'work through' and understand 'the local'. Hannerz (1990) notes that we can no longer think of the world in terms of hard-edged cultural boundaries; rather, he envisages deepening cultural 'overlap and mingle' in a rapidly globalising world marked by evolving processes of commercial, material and political interconnection, hybridity and transformation, of which, the wider BBC is intrinsically a part. Clearly, the local can neither be discounted nor divorced from processes of globalisation or from cosmopolitan practices, such as drama for development production. Further, in discounting the universalising dimensions of cosmopolitanism and globalisation, Hall suggests that these processes intrinsically connect to: ' ... disjunctive histories, the very early and the very late, the too late and the too early, the developed, the developing and the underdeveloped, the colonised and the colonisers, the pre- and the post-colonial, etc.' (in conversation with Werbner [2008: 345]).

This view of globalisation helps to open critical spaces for thinking about cosmopolitanism in terms of temporality and the discursive flow of concepts and ideas such as those that relate to development and social change. Further, it presses us to think about the role that mass media production and broadcasting plays in promoting such potentially cosmopolitan concepts as 'development' (Gillespie and Baumann, 2007).

Following Hannerz (1990), we can think about some of the competencies that are implied within the practice of drama for development production. We can think about the 'competencies' of drama writers and their attendant ability to 'read' the world, in a cultural sense, with a degree of 'success'. Thus, cosmopolitan 'competency' can usefully refer to the processes and practices entailed in translating 'worlds of difference', herein understood as the development concepts and cultural landscapes in which these concepts must make sense. For drama writers, editors and producers this means adapting key development themes/goals to the specific cultural frames of context. Thus, we can locate drama for development production in terms of a specific 'orientation' and 'willingness' to engage the 'Other' in pursuit of development and cultural change. Hannerz suggests that this reflects 'an intellectual and aesthetic stance of openness towards divergent cultural experiences, a search for contrasts rather than uniformity' (1990: 239).

In 'engaging the other', the BBC WST typically seeks to transform culture and society by changing behaviour and challenging norms and mores that are deemed 'negative' or which act as a potential 'brake on development' (see Chapter 5). Given this, expatriate and local dramatists and producers must inevitably 'work through' and 'incorporate' aspects of cultural difference within their productions by virtue of the fact that the cultural, caste and class positions that they strive to represent are fundamentally remote from them (Allen, 1985, 1995). As such, dramatists and producers can be perceived as cultural brokers, attempting to catalyse processes of social and political transformation through mass mediated cultural engagement (Gillespie and Baumann, 2007). The cosmopolitan competence of this endeavour can be located in the ways in which they appropriate, adapt and confront cultural dynamics and the skill with which they underpin their 'fictions' with genre specific (i.e., Bollywood- or Nollywood-style production) or socially 'realistic' representations that mediate the imagining of concepts (some more abstract than others) such as the nation, development, human rights, government or equality. Thus, cosmopolitan competence invokes:

> … a state of readiness, a personal ability to make one's way into other cultures, through listening, looking, intuiting and reflecting … Competence … itself entails a sense of mastery, as an aspect of the self. One's understandings have expanded, a little more of the world is somehow under control. Yet there is a curious, apparently paradoxical interplay between mastery and surrender here. It may be one kind of cosmopolitanism where the individual picks from other cultures only those

pieces which suit himself. In the long term, this is likely to be the way a cosmopolitan constructs his own unique personal perspective out of an idiosyncratic collection of experiences.

(Hannerz, 1990: 239–240)

Dramatists and producers claim (with few exceptions) rigorous social realist credentials, which suggests a close reading by drama writers of the material, political and cultural conditions of audience contexts. Indeed, convention dictates that drama for development productions are well researched, planned and organised communicative interventions. However, as Margulies (2002) points out, realist serial narratives rarely capture the full scope of the mundane qualities of 'real life' but instead reflect a strategic and inevitably dramatic approach designed to capture the 'gritty contradictions' of modernity. In turn, Porton contends that much 'realist' drama reflects a desire to 'fuse didactic realism with popular theatrical traditions' (2002: 165). Many of the chapters presented in this volume speak to notions of realism and creative assumptions that social realism enhances the potential for social impact, though this is far from a universal trend.

While drama for development writers, editors and producers aspire to cosmopolitan competency, social realism and professional rigour, the idea of competence as some form of 'mastery' is limiting. Margulies (2002) argues that we can cast the cultural competency of drama writers and editors rather differently, as being geared towards a looser and more entertaining rendering of 'social reality'. Further, what does 'mastery' imply in both practice and context? Such doubts lend weight to a more critical appreciation of cosmopolitanism, understood as a 'socially situated process' or set of practices in which issues of cultural contestation and the inevitable impossibility for 'accurate' cultural translation come to the fore (Gillespie and Baumann, 2007). A critical approach to cosmopolitanism focuses our attention on the fact that drama for development productions may not change behaviour or deep-seated cultural norms at all, may stimulate change in unanticipated ways, may send the wrong 'messages', misread culture and/or be contested by audiences. In turn, this forces us to think about how we can usefully assess the impact of such interventions in contexts marked by rapidly deepening media complexity (see Chapter 3).

Conclusion

If, as Hall (2008) suggests, we try to understand cosmopolitans—such as BBC WST drama writers, editors or producers—in terms of their capacities to 'connect' cultural formations, histories and narratives across time and space, how do we understand the notion of 'competency' as it relates to the essentially cosmopolitan practice of drama for development production? What degree of cultural 'mastery' is enough to produce an effective development-oriented drama? What values, practices and processes are necessary to achieving such a daunting creative enterprise? The chapters in this volume speak to such critical questions, but also to a tension evident between upholding drama for development production as a practice reflective of an almost 'scientific' mastery of culture and a creative enterprise that is much less socio-culturally precise. Accordingly, many of the analyses contained in this volume highlight the cosmopolitan competencies employed by drama writers, editors and producers to be those of cultural playfulness and approximation, rather than any sense of strict cultural mastery, competence or realism. Indeed, knowing the bounds of the culturally permissible, in the sense of the application of cultural propriety, decency and taste, and thereafter engaging in creative 'play' through drama writing can potentially be perceived as the essence of drama production seeking 'social and behavioural change'. Here, a looser rendering of culture and society may be the very thing that ensures wide socio-cultural appeal across diverse national audiences.

Notes

1. Edutainment (E-E) is a term used to refer to any mass or interpersonally mediated genre of entertainment—from puppet shows to street plays to television soap operas—that feature pro-social messages concerning aspects of social development (Singhal et al., 2004). Possibly the best known and most extensively used genre of E-E is that of radio and television drama or soap opera.
2. Numerous analyses of serial drama and soap opera, in providing insights into audience consumption, tend either to ignore production or to generate unsubstantiated inferences concerning production processes or relations. These include Ang's (1985) study of *Dallas*, Liebes and Katz's (1993) work on the same series, Hobson's (1982) study of the British television soap opera *Crossroads*, to a host of others (Buckingham, 1987; Gillespie, 1995). Allen (1985), Cantor and Pingree (1983), plus Vink (1988),

offer limited insights into drama production, but these are vague and predicated on analysis of the popular press, for which soap opera remains an ever-popular subject. Thus, when Allen (1985) talks of 'soap opera's mode of production' or its 'division of labour', it is done so in the broadest of terms.

3. Rogers' (1962) 'diffusion of innovation' model is especially influential and provides a simple and seemingly logical 'five step' approach to change, namely: (*a*) awareness of an issue/problem is raised by mass media; (*b*) individuals are 'empowered' with knowledge about this issue/problem; (*c*) being empowered with knowledge the individual decides he/she should change their behaviour related to this issue/problem; (*d*) the individual decides to trial a different behaviour and (*e*) the individual decides to adopt or reject the behaviour in the longer term.

4. The UNAIDS communication framework (1999) marked a watershed in thinking on the role of communication in development and sought to identify some of these factors, and in doing so highlighted the extent to which issues such as livelihood insecurity, chronic vulnerability and low socio-economic status, lack of rights, poor government policy and gender inequality act as barriers to social and behavioural change. Subsequently, UNICEF/UNAIDS (2002), drawing on the Communication for Social Change (2002) approach have suggested that development professionals need to 'pass ownership [of communications interventions] to community groups' and 'stop *doing* and start *facilitating*'. This shift brings with it a reorientation in approach that places a critical emphasis on: (*a*) community dialogue, rather than didactic messages; (*b*) social norms, policies and culture, rather than the individual; (*c*) community participation and ownership, rather than external experts; (*d*) peer and life skills, rather than formal epidemiological education and (*e*) indigenous models of communications best practice, rather than imported western models.

5. Galavotti et al. (2001) highlight five key features of successful behavioural interventions: (*a*) the use of role models to provide examples of 'how to change'; (*b*) drama elicits strong affective responses in the sense of catharsis or empathy for those characters suffering this or that fate, which in terms aids information retention; (*c*) effective/ affective E-E links to existing social and cultural narratives that are familiar to audiences; (*d*) personalisation in the sense of having the key messages reinforced via interpersonal communication strengthens self-efficacy and the scope for implementing behavioural change and (*e*) link to services and commodities and recognise impediments and potential facilitators.

References

Abrahamsen, R. (2004) 'The Power of Partnerships in Global Governance', *Third World Quarterly*, 25(8): 1453–1467.

Abu-Lughod, L. (1995) 'The Objects of Soap Opera: Egyptian Television and the Cultural Politics of Modernity', in D. Miller (ed.), *Worlds Apart: Modernity Through the Prism of the Local*. London: Routledge.

Abu-Lughod, L. (2005) *Dramas of Nationhood: The Politics of Television in Egypt*. Chicago: University of Chicago Press.

Allen, R. (1985) *Speaking of Soap Operas*. Chapel Hill: The University of North Carolina Press.

———. (1995) 'Introduction', in R. Allen (ed.), *To Be Continued ... Soap Operas around the World*. New York: Routledge.

Ang, I. (1985) *Watching Dallas: Soap Opera and Melodramatic Imagination*. New York: Routledge.

Bandura, A. (1977) *Social Learning Theory*. Englewood Cliffs, NJ: Prentice-Hall.

Batchelor, S. and Scott, N. (2005) *Good Practice Paper on ICTs for Economic Growth and Poverty Reduction*. Paris: OECD.

Baumann, G. (1997) 'Dominant and Demotic Discourses of Culture: their Relevance to Multi-Ethnic Alliances', in P. Werbner and T. Modood (eds), *Debating Cultural Hybridity: Multicultural Identities and the Politics of Anti-racism*. London–New York: Zed Press.

BBC World Service Trust. (2008) *Annual Review*. London: BBC WST.

Bracking, S. (2003) 'The Political Economy of Chronic Poverty', Working Paper 23, IDPM/Chronic Poverty Research Centre, University of Manchester.

Buckingham, D. (1987) *Public Secrets: Eastenders and its Audience*. London: British Film Institute.

Cantor, M. and Pingree, S. (1983) *The Soap Opera*. Beverley Hills: Sage Publications.

CFSC/Rockefeller Foundation. (2002) *Communication for Social Change: An Integrated Model for Measuring the Process and its Outcomes*. New York: Rockefeller Foundation.

Chapman, R., Slaymaker, T., and Young, J. (2003) *Livelihoods Approaches to Information and Communication in Support of Rural Poverty Elimination and Food Security*. Rome and London: FAO and DFID.

Das, V. (1995) 'On Soap Opera: What Kind of Anthropological Object is it'? in D. Miller (ed.), *Worlds Apart: Modernity through the Prism of the Local*. London: Routledge.

De Haan, A. (1998) 'Social Exclusion—an Alternative Concept for the Study of Deprivation'? *IDS Bulletin*, 29(1): 10–19.

Dornfeld, B. (1998) *Producing Public Television, Producing Public Culture*. Princeton: Princeton University Press.

Dutta-Bergman, M. J. (2005) 'Theory and Practice in Health Communication Campaigns: A Critical Interrogation', *Health Communication*, 18(2): 103–122.

Fairhead, J. and Leach, M. (1996) *Misreading the African Landscape*. Cambridge: Cambridge University Press.

Galavotti, C., Pappas-De Luca, K. and Lansky, A. (2001) 'Modelling and Reinforcement to Combat HIV: The MARCH Approach to Behaviour Change', *American Journal of Public Health*, 91(10): 1602–1607.

Garnham, N. (1997) 'Political Economy and the Practice of Cultural Studies', in M. Ferguson and P. Golding (eds), *Cultural Studies in Question*. London: Sage Publications.

Geraghty, C. (1991) *Women and Soap Opera: A Study of Prime Time Soaps*. Cambridge: Polity Press.

Gillespie, M. (1995) *Television, Ethnicity and Cultural Change*. London: Routledge.

———. (2005) 'Television Drama and Audience Ethnography', in M. Gillespie (ed.), *Media Audiences*. Maidenhead: The Open University Press.

———. (2006) 'Narrative Analysis', in M. Gillespie and J. Toynbee (eds), *Analysing Media Texts*. Maidenhead: Open University Press.

Gillespie, M. and Baumann, G. (2007) 'Diaspora, Diplomacy and Cosmopolitan, Impartiality: An Inter-disciplinary Study of the BBC World Service', Online Working Paper available at http://www8.open.ac.uk/researchprojects/diasporas/publications/working-paper/diaspora-diplomacy-and-cosmopolitanism-at-the-bbc-world-service-1942–2000 (accessed on 21.4.2011).

Ginsburg, F., Larkin, B. and Abu-Lughod, L. (2002) *Media Worlds: Anthropology on New Terrain*. Berkeley: University of California Press.

Graffman, K. (2004) 'The Cruel Masses: How Producers at a Swedish Commercial Television Production Company Construct their Viewers', Media Anthropology Network Working Paper, University of Uppsala, Uppsala, Sweden.

Hagedorn, R. (1995) 'Doubtless to be Continued: A Brief History of Serial Narrative', in R. Allen (ed.), *To Be Continued … Soap Operas around The World*. London: Routledge.

Hall, S. (1999) 'Encoding, Decoding', in S. Buring (ed.), *The Cultural Studies Reader*. London: Routledge.

———. (2008) 'Cosmopolitanism, Globalisation and Diaspora', in P. Wernber (ed.), *Anthropology and the New Cosmopolitanism*. Oxford: Berg.

Hannerz, U. (1990) 'Cosmopolitans and Locals in World Culture', in M. Featherstone (ed.), *Global Culture: Nationalism, Globalisation and Modernity*. London: Sage Publications.

Heritage, P. (1988) 'The Promise of Performance: True Love/Real Love', in R. Boon and J. Plastow (eds), *Theatre Matters: Performance and Culture on the World Stage*. Cambridge: Cambridge University Press.

Hobson, D. (1982) *Crossroads: The Drama of a Soap Opera*. London: Methuen.

Inagaki, N. (2007) *Communications for Development: Recent Trends in Empirical Research*. Washington DC: World Bank.

Lerner, D. (1958) *The Passing of Traditional Society*. New York: Free Press.

Liebes, T. and Katz, E. (1993) *The Export of Meaning: Cross-cultural Readings of 'Dallas'*. Cambridge: Polity Press.

Long, N. and Long, A. (1992) *Battlefields of Knowledge: The Interlocking of Theory and Practice in Social Research and Development*. London and New York: Routledge.

Mandel, R. (2002) 'A Marshall Plan of the Mind: The Political Economy of a Kazakh Soap Opera', in F. Ginsburg, L. Abu-Lughod and B. Larkin (eds), *Media Worlds: Anthropology on New Terrain*. California: University of California Press.

Mankekar, P. (1999) *Screening Culture, Viewing Politics: An Ethnography of Television, Womanhood and Nation in Post-colonial India*. Durham: Duke University Press.

Mansell, R. (2002) 'From Digital Divides to Digital Entitlements in Knowledge Societies', *Current Sociology*, 50(3): 407–426.

Margulies, I. (2002) 'Bodies Too Much', in I. Margulies (ed.), *Rites of Realism: Essays on Corporeal Cinema*. Durham: Duke University Press.

Marker, P., McNamara, K. and Wallace, L. (2002) *The Significance of Information and Communication Technologies for Reducing Poverty*. London: DFID.

Martín-Barbero, J. (1995) 'Memory and Form in the Latin American Soap Opera,' in R. Allen (ed.), *To Be Continued … Soap Operas around The World*. London: Routledge.

Mattelart, A. (1996) *The Invention of Communication*. Minnesota: University of Minnesota Press.

Miller, D. (1995) 'The Consumption of Soap Opera: *The Young and the Restless* and Mass Consumption in Trinidad', in R. Allen (ed.), *To Be Continued … Soap Operas around the World*. London: Routledge.

Morley, D. (1992) *Television, Audiences and Cultural Studies*. London: Routledge.

Mytton, G. (1999) *Handbook on Radio and Television Audience Research*. Paris: UNICEF and UNESCO.

Porton, R. (2002) 'Mike Leigh's Modernist Realism', in I. Margulies (ed.), *Rites of Realism: Essays on Corporeal Cinema*. Durham: Duke University Press.

Rigbey, L. (1993) *How to Write a Radio Soap Opera*. Mimeo.

Rofel, L. (1995) 'The Melodrama of National Identity in Post-Tiananmen China', in R. Allen (ed.), *To Be Continued … Soap Operas around the World*. London: Routledge.

Rogers, E. (1962) *Diffusion of Innovation*. New York: Free Press.

Sabido, M. (2004) 'The Origins of Entertainment-Education', in A. Singhal, M. Cody, E. Rogers and M. Sabido (eds), *Entertainment-Education and Social Change: History, Research, and Practice*. Mahwah: Lawrence Erlbaum Associates.

———. (2004) 'The Status of Entertainment-Education Worldwide', in A. Singhal, Michael J. Cody, Everett M. Rogers, Miguel Sabido (eds), *Entertainment-Education and Social Change: History, Research, and Practice*. New York: Lawrence Erlbaum Associates, Inc.

Singhal, A., Cody, M., Rogers, E. and Sabido, M. (2004) *Entertainment-Education and Social Change: History, Research, and Practice*. New York: Lawrence Erlbaum Associates, Inc.

Skuse, A. (1999) *Negotiated Outcomes: An Ethnography of the Production and Consumption of a BBC World Service Radio*, PhD thesis, University College London, London.

———. (2002) 'Vagueness, Familiarity and Social Realism: Making Meaning of Radio Soap Opera in South-east Afghanistan', *Media Culture and Society*, 24(3): 409–427.

———. (2005) 'Voices of Freedom: Afghan Politics in Radio Soap Opera', *Ethnography*, 6(2): 159–181.

Skuse, A., Fildes, J., Tacchi, J., Martin, K. and Baulch, E. (2007) *Poverty and Digital Inclusion*. New Delhi: UNESCO.

Torero, M. and Von Braun, J. (2005) *Information and Communication Technologies for the Poor*. Washington DC: International Food Policy Research Institute.

Tufte, T. (2002) *Soap Operas and Sense-Making: Mediations and Audience Ethnography*. Mimeo.

———. (2003) *Living With the Rubbish Queen: Telenovelas, Culture and Modernity in Brazil*. Indiana: Indiana University Press.

UNAIDS. (1999) *Communications Framework for HIV/AIDS: A New Direction*. Geneva: UNAIDS.

UNDP. (2001) *Human Development Report: Making New Technologies Work for Human Development*. New York: UNDP.

UNICEF/UNAIDS. (2002) 'Communication from a Human Rights Perspective: Responding to the HIV/AIDS Pandemic in Eastern and Southern Africa', Nairobi/Pretoria: UNICEF/UNAIDS.

Vink, N. (1988) *The Telenovela and Emancipation: A Study on TV and Social Change in Brazil*. Amsterdam: Royal Tropical Institute.

Waisbord, S. (2001) *Family Tree of Theories, Methodologies and Strategies in Development Communication*. New York: The Rockefeller Foundation.

Walker, A. (1992) *A Skyful of Freedom: 60 Years of the BBC World Service*. London: Broadside Books.

Wilk, R. and Askew, K. (eds) (2002) *The Anthropology of Media: A Reader*. Oxford: Blackwell.

Wilmore, M. (2008) *Developing Alternative Media Traditions in Nepal*. Lanham: Lexington Books.

Yoder, P., Hornik, R. and Chirwa, B. (1996) 'Evaluating the Program Effects of a Radio Drama about AIDS in Zambia', *Studies in Family Planning*, 27(4): 188–203.

2

GREAT EXPECTATIONS AND CREATIVE EVOLUTION

THE HISTORY OF DRAMA FOR DEVELOPMENT AT THE BBC WORLD SERVICE TRUST

CAROLINE SUGG AND GERRY POWER

Introduction

This chapter reviews the history of drama for development work at the BBC World Service Trust (BBC WST). In doing so, it draws upon the authors' collective involvement with the production of more than 15 drama serials over the past 10 years. The chapter identifies four overlapping processes or stages in the evolution of drama production at the BBC WST: (*a*) 'BBC Drama Exported'—a period in which the BBC's assumptions about the public benefits of drama informed projects in developing and transitional countries; (*b*) 'Development Sensitisation'—a phase during which the BBC WST increasingly focused its dramas to deliver specific international development outcomes, in line with the priorities of its funders; (c) 'Great Expectations'—a stage during which the dramas produced by the BBC WST were particularly influenced by theories of behaviour change communication (BCC); and (d) 'Creative Coalescence'—a period during which the BBC WST's expectations about what drama can achieve in development terms have matured and been refined.

We argue that the evolution in creativity witnessed over the past 10 years has been informed by the interplay between two sets of 'institutional relationships' that have defined the BBC WST's approach to drama, namely, the relationship between the BBC WST and the wider BBC and the relationship between the BBC WST and the development organisations/donors that fund this work. A review of the dramas produced over the last 10 years uncovers a body of work that is extremely varied, but that can also be distinguished by a set of key characteristics each of which we outline below. We conclude with a set of considerations relating to meeting donor expectations and the delivery of drama for development in less-developed parts of the world.

The BBC WST's relationship with the BBC has, without doubt, been critical to its broader success. The level of credibility and trust afforded to the BBC brand has enhanced the BBC WST's standing with donor organisations and audiences alike, while connections with the BBC have provided the BBC WST with privileged access to highly qualified and experienced media professionals willing to engage in its development projects worldwide. The BBC WST emerged from within the BBC in the late 1990s and continues to forge numerous creative connections to the wider organisation. This results in the promotion of core BBC values (including editorial independence, impartiality and honesty), approaches to production (high technical and creative quality) and assumptions about the purpose of programme making (entertaining, educational, informative) among staff (see www.bbc.co.uk/aboutthebbc/purpose/). Meanwhile, the BBC WST's dependence on institutional donors (such as the UK Department for International Development [DFID]) to fund its activities clearly frames its work as a development organisation. The relationships with donor organisations have shaped the BBC WST's approach to its work and created certain expectations about the potential change that drama projects can deliver. The divergence between the professional culture of drama-making at the BBC and the way in which the expectations of institutional donors have been interpreted by project managers at the BBC WST have led to creative tensions within the organisation at particular points within its short history (see Chapter 11). These tensions have shifted, however, as the organisation has matured and developed a more refined and contextually nuanced understanding of the role that drama can play in development.

The Body of Work and its Defining Characteristics

Since 1999, the BBC WST has produced serial dramas for television, radio and online platforms, working in 14 countries and in over 21 different languages, with many local broadcast partners. Appendix 1 details these dramas, including information about the funding donor, the development objectives for each and when and where each was broadcast. A review of these dramas demonstrates significant diversity within the body of work produced. The phrase 'drama for development' is widely used as if it were a single genre, reflecting a uniform approach to production, but, in fact, this blanket term covers a broad range of production activities determined by a number of factors including: (a) donor objectives and expectations; (b) budget, which affects both the scale and longevity of a project; (c) local audience needs; (d) the media landscape and media consumption habits; and (e) production capacity of both the BBC WST and their local partners. Dramas are also differentiated by where and by whom they are produced; the intended broadcast platform for the drama, and whether they are broadcast on a standalone basis or as part of a wider campaign. These defining criteria are discussed in more detail below.

Purpose and Objectives

Serial dramas have been produced in support of all of the major thematic areas addressed by the BBC WST: health, governance and human rights, livelihoods, humanitarian response and climate change. Some of these dramas have been highly focused in terms of the outcomes they seek to deliver, whilst others are far broader in scope. While *Jasoos Vijay, Wetin Dey* and *Taste of Life,* for instance, focused purely on health-related objectives, others such as *Ruga Mi Pisha* in Albania or *Story Story* in Nigeria have far wider pro-social or pro-development agendas.

Many of the dramas produced by the BBC WST have aimed primarily to stimulate debate and discussion of certain social and development issues, whilst others have had an overtly educational purpose or specifically sought to encourage measurable changes in audience knowledge, attitudes and behaviours. Some objectives agreed with project donors are more challenging to achieve than others—for instance, if a highly popular drama is produced and broadcast on a radio or television station with good audience reach, it might be relatively straightforward to increase knowledge that a certain health service is available. On the other hand, objectives that involve achieving shifts in complex and established social norms—for instance, addressing the low value ascribed to women in certain societies—are clearly far harder to achieve.

Where projects receive funding from multiple development donors, it is often a requirement that dramas address multiple themes and pursue multiple objectives within a short timeframe. This can be a challenge for production teams striving to create engaging programmes that will entertain an audience, as well as deliver development outcomes. At the other extreme, production teams also struggle when donors have broad, but unspecific, expectations of what a drama project will deliver.

Diverse Formats

Regardless of how directed a drama is in terms of its objectives, all BBC WST drama producers are encouraged to realise the creative imperative of their work and to create programming that will have mass public appeal. Project managers understand that a drama that is overly didactic or that is perceived as simply being a vehicle for messages rather than, first and foremost, a form of entertainment, is unlikely to generate an audience and risks failure. With the ability to access the services of highly creative dramatists, both internationally and locally, the BBC WST is in a privileged position to produce highly engaging and entertaining drama. Warren Feek, Director of the Communications Initiative (see www.comminit.com), notes the importance of good storytelling:

> Audiences are extremely sophisticated. They know when they're being preached at and they know when they're being entertained, so the trick in effective entertainment is … making the educational parts of the drama, the informative parts of it or the key issue-driven parts of it—essential to the plot that's taking place.
>
> (Warren Feek, Interview with Stephanie Lowe, 2009)

Reflecting the importance that the BBC WST places on the creativity and entertainment value of its dramas, dramatists employed by the BBC WST are encouraged to innovate and support local creative interpretation within their work. Building local capacity and mentoring local talent is central to creating a localised drama. The relationship between the dramatist and the local creative team is multi-layered and defined by cultural, linguistic, professional and hierarchical norms. Navigating the challenging waters of creativity is difficult even when these norms are known, but the territory of transnational creative teams is uncharted territory for many and the canon of professional practice is not yet established.

Funding proposals rarely specify the exact nature of the drama format to be produced, enabling audience tastes, local conventions and the creative ideas of a production team to shape the nature of the final output produced. Moreover, there are no prescribed rules about the creative processes to be employed during the production of dramas at the BBC WST. This has resulted in a range of formats being produced by local teams (within the broad genre of serial drama and as reflected in the chapters presented in this volume) ranging from more traditional village and family-based soap operas such as *Thabyegone Ywa* (*Eugenia Tree Village*) in Myanmar/Burma or *New Home, New Life* in Afghanistan, to a detective drama in India or sets of self-contained improvised radio plays linked together by common characters, such as *Katha Mitho Sarangiko* (*Sweet Tales of the Sarangi*) in Nepal.

Longevity

The serial dramas produced by the BBC WST vary significantly in terms of the length of time for which they are on-air. Longevity is driven both by the complexity and range of the issues being addressed and the level of donor funding available. *Piyar Ka Passport (Passport to Love)* consisted of only 12 episodes (see Chapter 11), while *Story Story* has been broadcast since 2004 and *New Home, New Life* since 1994. In most cases dramas are broadcast for between one and three years, reflecting typical donor project funding cycles. Clearly, long-running dramas to which audiences are exposed year after year, which build a strong identity and become part of the fabric of a society can be expected to have a more far-reaching impact than dramas that are more ephemeral. However, the development of long-running drama often requires the commitment of substantial donor funding upfront and the development of local fundraising capacity, so that financing can be secured to enable long-term production, broadcasting and distribution.

Production Centre

The BBC WST's modus operandi involve, primarily, the development and production of dramas in the country where they will be heard or watched. It is viewed as particularly important to develop storylines and scripts locally and where possible involving scriptwriters and producers from the same 'culture' as the intended audience in order to ensure that dramas produced are locally and culturally appropriate and relevant. Of course, mobility and migration, class educational differences may diminish shared culture-specific understandings within a particular social or societal context. Nevertheless, the work of cultural translation is essential to the success of the dramas produced. For the production of the television soap *Taste of Life,* more than 70 Cambodian staff were employed, including researchers, writers, producers, directors and technical crew (see Chapter 9). Similar teams have been built in Afghanistan, India, Nigeria and Nepal.

In rare cases and when donor funds are extremely limited, the 'in-country' base may be smaller in scale and be established for only a short period of time. For the production of *Piyar Ka Passport,* for instance, the script-writing process was managed remotely from London, while a small team in Pakistan handled recording. In some extreme cases, where it is impossible for the BBC WST to establish a base in-country, production takes place elsewhere. For example, in the case of pro-gramming developed for Myanmar/Burma—where the BBC is unable to operate—dramas were written and produced in Thailand by Burmese scriptwriters, actors and producers. Similarly, the *New Home, New Life* drama for Afghanistan was produced for many years in the city of Peshawar in northern Pakistan due to the ongoing Afghan civil war and lack of stability.

The BBC WST recognises that local scriptwriting does not neces-sarily lead to the production of programming that resonates perfectly with its target audience, since often the writers engaged on a drama project are socially, culturally or politically removed from a drama's intended audience (see Chapter 6). Moreover, in the worst-case scenario, power dynamics within a team—for instance between an experienced expatriate producer and a team of young or inexperienced local writers—might impact upon the extent to which local sensibilities are fully taken in account. In order to overcome these issues, the BBC WST emphasises the importance of formative audience research and 'pre-testing episodes' of a drama (see Chapter 3).

Campaign Context

While many of the BBC WST's dramas are run as standalone inter-ventions, the organisation recognises the value of embedding a drama within a comprehensive media campaign consisting of other outputs for broadcast and print. For instance, drama serials can be complemented by factual programmes that enable the delivery of more specific and detailed information to viewers and listeners, discussion programmes that facilitate in-depth and reality-based exploration of the issues raised in the drama, or creatively executed public service announcements (PSAs) that enable the repeated delivery of key messages to specific target audiences. In many instances, it has been the BBC WST's health-focused dramas that have formed part of wider campaigns. *Taste of Life* was broadcast in conjunction with numerous PSAs for radio and television, four radio call-in programmes designed to appeal to different target audiences, and the dissemination of comic books and leaflets. *Wetin Dey* was part of a similarly designed campaign, as were the early series of *Jasoos Vijay*.

This approach has gone on to influence the BBC WST's work in other thematic areas. Some series of *Story Story* were complemented by a radio discussion show, *Talk Talk*, whilst the radio drama *Katha Mitho Sarangiko* in Nepal is part of a larger project, which also encompassed the production and broadcast of *Sajha Sawal (Common Questions)*, a weekly political debate programme for television. In addition to em-bedding dramas within broader media campaigns, many BBC WST projects complement broadcast programming with the establishment of listener's groups where community members can gather together to listen to or watch programmes, and then discuss them. This process can be supported by the development of tailored supporting materials, as one country director explains:

> … a drama made for broadcast can be repackaged and modified into a multi-media toolkit for use by NGOs. We made a DVD set of *Jasoos Vijay* episodes accompanied by a manual demonstrating how the TV pro-gramme can be used to generate community discussion. The toolkit also includes relevant games to help stimulate learning … it's great value for money if TV content can have a shelf life long after the broadcast run has ended.
>
> (Yvonne MacPherson, Personal Communication, 2010)

Broadcast Platforms

Where relevant audience data is available or can be collected, broadcast platforms for the dramas produced by the BBC WST are selected according to an analysis of which media channels have the greatest reach amongst the intended audience for a given project. These data are analysed alongside considerations of the cost of airtime in a given media market. The broadcast channel selected for a drama transmission might be a local public or commercial broadcaster, or a BBC World Service language service, such as the Persian or Urdu Service.

The Export of Drama Serials

Although organisationally, BBC WST sits alongside the BBC World Service (BBC WS) within the Global News Division of the BBC, it is, in fact, an independent charity with its own board of trustees and a funding model that is distinct from that of other parts of the corporation. A licence fee levied from the general public (of the United Kingdom) funds the BBC and the BBC WS is funded by a Parliamentary Grant-in-Aid that is administered by the UK's Foreign and Commonwealth Office (FCO). The BBC WST, on the other hand, like many charities, is funded by a range of development partners including 'bilateral' donors (country-to-country direct assistance such as that provided by the UK Department for International Development), the so-called 'multi-laterals' (UN agencies, UN-organised thematic funds and the European Union) and a number of private foundations (for instance The Bill and Melinda Gates Foundation and The David and Lucile Packard Foundation). The international development landscape within which the BBC WST operates is fundamental to its overall objectives, the methodologies it employs, the design of projects it delivers and the content of its programmes.[1] The BBC WST is driven by an organisational mission and set of objectives that differ from those of the BBC WS and the wider BBC. The mission of the BBC is to enrich people's lives with programmes and services that inform, educate and entertain, while the BBC WS aims to be the world's best known, most creative and most respected voice in international news. Distinct from this, and informed by the objectives of its donors, the BBC WST works in developing and transitional countries, with a mission to use the power of media and communications to provide accurate and reliable information to enable people to make decisions about their lives. The BBC WST also aims to promote individual and social change in support of political, economic and social development.

Despite these organisational distinctions between the BBC WST, the BBC WS and the wider BBC, the close association with its two 'parent' organisations has undoubtedly been beneficial for the BBC WST both in terms of its fundraising for, and delivery of, drama for development projects. It is an opinion widely held by the BBC WST's staff that the fact that many donor organisations are familiar with, and have positive associations with, the BBC brand assists in the process of raising funds. Further, the familiarity of some donors with BBC dramas provides a common frame-of-reference for exploring new project ideas. In addition, the BBC's long track record in the production of serial dramas with wide reach and mass appeal instils in donors a confidence that the BBC WST will exercise the craft of drama-making according to similar standards. The 'legitimising effect' of the BBC brand is perhaps one reason that, once donors have approved a project proposal and a detailed set of objectives for a drama series, there is little negotiation between the BBC WST and the donor organisation about the precise content or detail of the programmes produced. The association with the BBC also gives the BBC WST privileged access to a pool of skilled drama practitioners, who can be employed as expatriate editors or drama trainers/advisors. Indeed, almost all of the international drama staff employed by the BBC WST have been previously employed and trained by the BBC. Thus, because of these relationships, the BBC's approach to making drama strongly informs the BBC WST's approach to drama, although this has not gone unchallenged.

Dramatic Traditions

The BBC unapologetically values drama as a form of popular enter-tainment in its own right. However, it also perceives a public service role for drama. Public documents from the BBC emphasise the part that broadcasting, including the broadcasting of drama, has to play in providing a 'network of shared values, traditions and experiences that people hold in common [...] sometimes known as social capital', arguing that, in this regard, broadcasting 'helps to build higher levels of trust, tolerance and shared understanding that can make many aspects of a society's operations, from business and politics to people's daily lives, easier and more productive' (BBC, 2004: 36).

Dramas are also perceived by the BBC to have public value in that they can 'tackle important social issues in a responsible and accessible way' (BBC, 2004: 33). In defence of the public value of the BBC, for example, the popular soap opera *Eastenders* is argued to be 'watched by people of all ages, all social classes and [...] all ethnic backgrounds, providing a basis for talking points between groups that may otherwise lack common frames of reference' (BBC, 2004: 37). BBC programming, including drama, is positioned as serving a role in fostering positive inter-group relations in the UK:

> Take, for example, the contribution that the BBC can make to building trust and tolerance between the UK's different cultures through [...] portrayal of a diverse UK in dramas like *Casualty* (a hospital-based drama), and documentaries about racial issues. If the BBC did not exist, other tools of public policy might be needed to achieve the same ends—perhaps through race agencies or the education system—or society would be worse off. (BBC, 2004: 45)

Literature on drama for development makes regular reference to the history of the production of 'educational drama' at the BBC, in particular to the Radio 4 production *The Archers*, which was first developed in the 1950s as a vehicle for providing instructive information to rural audiences in an entertaining fashion (Rigbey, 1993). However, there is little reference to drama as an educational tool in current BBC discourse. While producers at the BBC recognise that audiences may 'learn' or derive educational value from serial dramas and soap operas, they are keen to claim that the dramas produced by the BBC are not intended to be didactic and are not designed even to raise specific issues, let alone to promote particular views or behaviours. Buckingham (1987) notes in his study of the BBC soap opera *Eastenders* that, although it was intended that the soap would tackle controversial social issues, producers claim that it is not an 'issues-based' production (i.e., although storylines are topical and inevitably reactive to what is going on in society, they are not developed to illustrate particular predetermined issues). Moreover, while producers accept that the programme has an educational function, raising issues of concern for audiences, they claim to be more concerned with raising questions than with offering solutions to problems (Buckingham, 1987).

The ways in which the BBC articulates its understanding of the public and social value of drama is echoed in the discourse and methodologies of the BBC WST. This is primarily because many of its early senior managers, drama producers and creative advisers have previously been employed and trained by the wider BBC. The BBC WST project managers and producers describe drama as an effective platform through which to tackle important social issues and argue that drama can encourage discussion of important development themes. There is also an inherent assumption within the work of the BBC WST that, as a popular format that can generate mass audience appeal, drama can make a contribution towards social cohesion.

The early years of the BBC WST could be characterised as a period in which the BBC's assumptions about the public benefits of drama were 'exported' to 'developing and transitional country' contexts. The *Marshall Plan of the Mind* (MPM) was one of the three organisations incorporated within the BBC WST when it was formed in 1999. The initiative was established—in the wake of the collapse of the Soviet Union—with the underlying assumption that 'helping Russia along the road to a free enterprise civil society was … a task for which the BBC was well suited' (BBC WS, 1999). Through the MPM—created in 1992 to make radio and television programmes for Russian audiences—the BBC WS had already been involved with international drama projects with broadly defined 'development' objectives. Funded mainly by the British Government's Know How Fund, the MPM produced a number of programmes including 'a soap opera set in a Moscow apartment building with strong human interest storylines and looking at characters striving to come to terms with very changed circumstances' (BBC WS, 1999). The aims of *Rruga Me Pisha* (*Pine Street*), a radio serial drama developed for Albanian audiences in 1999 were similarly broad, namely, 'to promote tolerance and understanding in Albania' and 'to raise awareness and stimulate debate on issues and dilemmas common to everyday life' (see Appendix 1).[2]

Clearly, the discourse around the dramas produced by the BBC WST in the years immediately following its establishment focused very much on the broad social value of dramas, reflecting the kind of language used by the BBC itself to describe the public purpose of drama. As the BBC WST grew and matured as an organisation this discourse was challenged by a growing familiarity with the objectives and language of the international development community and the new institutional donors funding its work.

Development Sensitisation

In particular, the ways in which the potential outcomes of certain drama-based projects were described began to evolve.[3] At the same time, those in leadership positions within the BBC WST had ambitions to extend the scope and the size of the organisation's operations, building on its past successes. This saw the BBC WST enter a new playing field, driven by the imperative to increase levels of funding to enable the development and delivery of increased numbers of projects and related social impact. This in turn led to the BBC WST deepening its relationships with its existing donors, engaging with new donors and developing a closer understanding of the BBC WST's position alongside other organisations working in the field. In the period between 1999 and 2006, the funding raised by the BBC WST grew from £3m to over £17m and several staff with development and research backgrounds joined the organisation from outside the BBC.

This shift was increasingly reflected in the language with which the objectives of drama projects were defined. *Story Story: Voices from the Market*, a radio drama produced by the BBC WST in Nigeria, aimed 'to tackle the poverty issues that stifle development and which form the eight targets set by United Nations, or the Millennium Development Goals', to 'explore issues such as governance, rights and responsibilities' and 'to draw attention to the empowerment of women, education and environmental sustainability in particular'.[4] These goals explicitly reflected the aims and objectives of DFID Nigeria, the project's funder, at the time the project began. Similarly, the objectives of the DFID-funded radio drama *Thabyegone Ywa (Eugenia Tree Village)* set a specific 'developmental agenda' for the programme. In accordance with DFID's goals, the primary purpose of the drama was to 'open up public debate on HIV/AIDS and poverty related diseases'. It was expected that the project would 'change the attitudes of poor people towards health issues' and 'empower citizens to present their views and state their demands with confidence'.[5] This focus on specific donor-driven development goals signified a new phase in the Trust's evolution—a phase in which the objectives of its dramas started to more clearly be distinguished from those of the dramas produced by the domestic BBC.

Great Expectations: The Behaviour Change Paradigm

At the time that *Story Story* and *Thabyegone Ywa* were being produced by the BBC WST's then Education and Social Action Unit, staff working in the BBC WST's Health Unit were becoming more familiar with BCC theories. These theories argue that the delivery of tailored messages through a variety of communication channels can foster positive behaviour, promote and sustain individual, community and societal behaviour change and help to maintain behaviour deemed to be appropriate and consistent with development objectives (see Chapter 1 for an overview of influential communication theories relevant to social and behavioural change). These theories include the E-E approach, based in part on Sabido's work in television soap opera in Mexico in the 1970s and the work of Bandura (1977). It is argued that through engagement and identification with characters in a television or radio drama audiences can be encouraged to adopt certain 'desired' behaviours (Singhal et al., 2004). Another model that strongly influenced the thinking of the BBC WST at this stage of its history was the MARCH model (Modelling and Reinforcement to Combat HIV) which argues that entertainment formats (and particularly serial drama) can be used as a vehicle for education, to promote behavioural changes that reduce the risk of HIV transmission and create normative environments in which behavioural changes can be sustained (Galavotti et al., 2001).

These theories overtly underpin the work of a large number of organisations working in the field of Communications for Development at this time, particularly in the area of public health. These organisations include the Soul City Institute, FHI (Family Health International) and PSI (Population Services International), the Population Media Center (PMC), the CDC (Centers for Disease Control and Prevention) and The Johns Hopkins Center for Communications Programmes, which the BBC WST now saw itself competing for project funding. PSI, for example, employs dramas as part of larger social marketing campaigns. They note: 'PSI is a leader in behavior change communications (BCC), information exchange tailored to specific groups to encourage health-seeking behaviors.'[6] Soul City, in southern Africa, on the other hand describes its focus as 'social change':

The Soul City Institute for Health and Development Communication is a social change project which aims to impact on society at the individual, community and socio-political levels ... The edutainment [E-E] vehicle is at the core of the model ... Through personal identification with characters, as well as through moving storylines, the dramatic genre is emotive and persuasive. This enables it to shift social norms, impacting on deeply held negative attitudes, and practices.[7]

Although many organisations use the language of E-E as part of their work, the format and approach is central to the work of PMC:

At the heart of PMC's work is a unique form of entertainment-education... A highly successful and proven mass media instrument, the Sabido methodology of entertainment-education has shown a unique capacity for not only raising awareness among large numbers of people ... but for actually motivating audiences to adopt new behaviors. (http://www.populationmedia.org/what/our-method/ accessed on 21 December 2009)

At the BBC WST there was a growing familiarity with these models of change and with the language employed by other organisations working in the field of Communications for Development. This was combined with the increased recognition that, if it was to grow in size and be able to deliver more projects at scale, the organisation would need to develop funding proposals and projects that responded to the concrete and specific objectives of donor organisations, including behaviour change objectives. The language of many development donors—particularly those working in the domain of public health—suggest high levels of expectation for drama as a tool that can deliver specific and measurable changes both at an individual and societal level. These, often 'great expectations' are clearly reflected in the statements of some leading development donors:

A pioneering national radio drama series produced by the Population Media Center dramatically impacted Ethiopians' awareness of reproductive health issues ... Ethiopian families eagerly followed the broadcasts' role models. Women flocked to reproductive health service centers, citing the broadcasts as their inspiration for seeking help.

Requests for contraceptives and HIV tests rose sharply among the programs' audience, compared to non-listeners.

(The David and Lucile Packard Foundation, 2007)

USAID supports a locally produced TV series in Zimbabwe, called *Studio 263*, which presents social issues about HIV and AIDS in sensitive ways that help people question long-accepted behavior patterns. [Research] revealed that these messages influenced 48% of 15–19 year-olds to delay the onset of sexual activity; 33% of 25–29 year-olds to use voluntary counselling and testing services; and 26% of 25–29 year-olds to discuss HIV testing with their spouse/partner.

(USAID, 2010)

It could be an episode of *Eastenders* or *Coronation Street* but instead it's a storyline that has gripped South African audiences in one of the country's most popular soap operas. Soul City is just one of many television and radio dramas that DFID funds across the developing world to promote messages such as safe sex, reporting corruption, or the right to vote.

(DFID, 2010)

As early as 2001, the Health Unit of the BBC WST was beginning to implement a new drama-based project with specific behaviour change objectives. *Jasoos Vijay*, the Indian detective drama, which aimed to increase knowledge of how HIV is transmitted, to encourage people to get tested for HIV, to challenge the culture of discrimination towards people who are HIV positive and to promote support and treatment for those living with HIV. Building on this work, and in response to the trends described above, many BBC WST staff increasingly argued that the organisation should incorporate BCC theories more explicitly into both its approach to the development and production of drama and the way in which it articulated the role of drama in its work. As many staff tried to more rigorously articulate the concrete and measurable contribution that they believed drama could make to development goals and to optimise the resonance that the language used by the BBC WST had with its funders, arguably the organisation's own expectations of what drama could deliver also grew.

Promoting Change in Health Behaviours:
BBC Meets E-E Discourse

In 2001 and 2002, a large-scale multi-media project was being developed by the BBC WST to combat HIV/AIDS in Cambodia and specifically to promote sexual behaviour change, as well as to increase knowledge levels and change attitudes about HIV and AIDS. *Taste of Life* was one of the media outputs produced as part of this project—perhaps the most ambitious television drama that the BBC WST has ever produced in terms of the 'scientific' way in which it attempted to integrate a large number of specific health messages, tailored to specific sub-audiences, into a long-running series of programmes (see Chapter 9).

The methodologies used to produce *Taste of Life* were indicative of an evolution in the thinking of many BBC WST staff—an evolution that led to internal tensions in the way that drama was defined and developed within the organisation as two often conflicting discourses, the 'BBC discourse' about the public value of drama, and the discourse of E-E and BCC—came together. Some managers insisted that the primary function of drama for development was to create shared social experiences and frames of reference, arguing that drama should offer a discussion of topics of concern, but remain more concerned with raising questions than with offering answers. Others focused far more on the language of behaviour change, developing projects that specifically intended to deliver measurable shifts in the actual behaviour of audiences, in addition to attitudinal shifts and changes in levels of knowledge about given subjects. Managers in this second camp were supported by the growth and development of the BBC WST's internal Research and Learning teams which built up local research capacity to enable the delivery of large-scale quantitative audience surveys intended to measure the 'impact' of projects on audience knowledge, attitudes and behaviours (see Chapter 3). Previous research had focused almost entirely on either informing programme content or measuring the audience reach of a given programme. In this regard, distinct differences began to emerge between the approaches of the BBC WST's Education and Social Action Units—mostly influenced by BBC philosophies and assumptions about drama—and those of its Health Unit, which were increasing influenced by BCC theories and approaches.

Many of the dramas developed by the BBC WST's Education and Social Action Unit—including early series of *Story Story* in Nigeria, *Our Town Our Future* in Bosnia and *Thabyegone Ywa* in Myanmar/Burma were guided by narrative briefs setting out issues to be discussed and explored, enabling a relatively 'free-flowing' script development process. In some cases the storylines developed by the BBC WST writers were then refined through a process of ongoing interaction with project donors. On the other hand, the increasing focus of the Health Unit's drama projects (for instance *Taste of Life* in Cambodia and *Wetin Dey* in Nigeria) on specific behaviour change objectives led to the development of new techniques used by project managers for briefing (in terms of preferred content and change objectives) and then managing the drama professionals that they employed. At project inception, the objectives outlined in a project proposal were further developed in line with the findings of formative audience research, and communicated in detail to drama producers through a message brief—a document detailing specific project objectives in terms of changes to knowledge, attitudes and behaviours, and key messages to be conveyed to members of a drama's target audience.

The 'great expectations' of many project managers about what drama could achieve in development terms and implementation of these new methodologies led, on occasion, to disagreement both among members of the management team at the BBC WST, and between project managers and the drama producers and advisers that they employed. Many of these drama professionals had worked for the BBC in the past and whilst they tended to overtly accept that the BBC WST had development goals, many felt unfamiliar with the notion of drama being used to convey messages or deliver development outcomes. Imbued with the BBC's own discourse, which makes far fewer assumptions about what drama can achieve in terms of social effects, producers often felt uncomfortable when presented with a message brief by a project manager and conversations often ensued about the benefits of creative freedom and the nature of drama as an art rather than a science. Tensions were often exacerbated when producers perceived that there were too many precise messages to be conveyed within a given programme or series, or that the focus of a serial was too narrow. As one drama producer at the BBC WST protested 'there are only so many programmes we can make about diarrhoea' (Mathew Robinson, Personal Communication, 2005)! Fundamental to the success of the BBC WST in resolving these issues as they emerged within projects was the key role of the project manager in managing these tensions, as well as expectations. The project managers typically negotiate with both drama producers and donors to ensure that the donor's objectives for a drama are realistic, and that producers understand and accept the donor's ambitions for the output being produced.

Creative Coalescence

While differences of opinion between drama practitioners and project management staff at the BBC WST may still emerge from time to time, the tensions caused by attempts within the BBC WST to accommodate BBC approaches to drama with theories of BCC have lessened in recent years. The reasons for this relate to organisational changes, and subtle shifts in the way in which the BBC WST articulates the precise role of drama in its development projects. In 2007, the BBC WST was restructured along regional lines and its Education, Health Units and Media Development units were disbanded. This led to the departure of some staff from the BBC WST and the remaining staff from these units working more closely together in their new teams rather than competing with each other on philosophical grounds. Perhaps also, aware of some of the potential tensions involved with drama for development productions, project managers at the BBC WST became more adept at briefing new drama practitioners prior to project inception. Provided with orientation about the specific development goals of the BBC WST and the particular objectives of a drama production at the outset, dramatists are in a better position to understand the expectations of its donors and the ways in which the BBC WST implements its work.

Moreover, the BBC WST's own discourse about drama and the role it can play in development is now more nuanced. Those working at the BBC WST share an appreciation that drama alone cannot, of course, change the world—poverty reduction, peace building and public health depend on large-scale efforts and investments by governments and stakeholders working at multiple levels. As a drama producer currently working for the BBC WST notes:

> But both the potential for messaging and the limits should … be better understood. Beyond the control of the donors, the production team and the managers behind them, there can be some brutal systemic realities latent in any country in which the project is undertaken: a society where subservience is the price you pay for finding a husband and children, a health service where nurses are demoralised and bad tempered and unhygienic in their habits, an education system where a female student feels she must sleep with her teacher to get good marks.
>
> (Fiona Ledger, Personal Communication, 2009)

The BBC WST now explicitly acknowledges the limits of what drama can achieve and the fact that the impact of its media interventions will be heightened if delivered in conjunction with comprehensive development programmes, or linked to related grassroots activities. Again, the benefit of this interplay is recognised by donors and experts in the field of drama for development:

> The radio drama should be in support of something else, proper health care or well-digging or good governance or paying policemen instead of allowing them to be wildly corrupt. You can't make policemen less corrupt by having a nice policeman in your drama … dramas have to work completely hand in hand with practical initiatives.
>
> (Mary Myers, Personal Communication, 2010)

Where feasible, the BBC WST links its dramas, and other media outputs, to related development activities. For instance, *Wetin Dey* in Nigeria was embedded within a larger DFID-funded HIV prevention programme that included the rollout of health services such as voluntary counselling and testing (VCT), which could be promoted within the BBC WST's media outputs. Similarly, the *Katho Mitho Sarangiko* drama was funded by the UNDP as part of a much wider initiative on peace-building and conflict resolution (see Chapter 8). Likewise, the television drama *Bishaash (Believe)* is part of a much larger initiative designed to teach English in Bangladesh. The overall programme has multiple implementing partners and includes the development of materials and curricula for use in schools across the country.

Without doubt, many project managers have developed a more subtle and sophisticated understanding of what drama can achieve in development terms. As the BBC WST has become more established as an organisation, project managers have become more confident about articulating this approach to donors. Despite widespread support for BCC approaches both within the BBC WST and the wider field of Communication for Development, there is growing recognition that the concept of messaging through drama can be interpreted in an over-simplistic way and that serial drama is not a 'silver bullet' through which individual behaviour change or social change can automatically be re-alised. Where they are still employed, message briefs are used in a more fluid way within the scriptwriting process—as a point of reference, a way to set the agenda for the drama in broad terms, rather than being overly prescriptive. This more 'measured' sense of what drama can achieve is reflected in the following comments from current BBC WST staff:

> Donors want a message—'value women', 'participate in the political process', 'stay healthy'—embedded in the drama, but they don't always accept the painful and complicated route the message must take before it is acted on by the audience. And of course, there are no guarantees that the audience receiving the message will react exactly in the way the funders want. Development drama is not a science.
>
> (Fiona Ledger, Personal Communication, 2010)

> Drama should entertain and inspire and never message or judge. Drama should provide the tools to allow people to think for themselves.
>
> (Rishi Sankar, Personal Communication, 2009)

However, in spite of these caveats, comments from staff currently working at the BBC WST reveal that the belief that drama can play a strong role in development is still firmly held and the expectations of those responsible for production are equally great. Some focus on the potential of the format to include diverse perspectives and to sug-gest alternative ways of thinking (as Galavotti et al.'s [2001] MARCH model advocates). Shirazuddin Siddiqi, BBC WST Country Director, Afghanistan suggests that: 'Drama cuts through social, religious, pol-itical and ethnic obstacles and appeals to almost everyone in the society. [It] helps people to think differently and do things differently by role modelling and storytelling, using a very simple form of spoken language.' Similarly, Rishi Sankar, the BBC WST Series Producer in Bangladesh, believes that:

> Stories can change the way people think and the way people see the world without being didactic; stories can show a vast multitude of points of view without passing judgment; stories can confront taboos without making people turn away; these are perhaps the key ways that drama can play a decisive role in development.
>
> (Rishi Sankar, Personal Communication, 2010)

Others focus more on the outcomes of the drama within the audience. Fiona Ledger, the radio dramatist in Nepal, notes the way in which drama can provoke constructive discussion among listeners: 'Successful development drama acknowledges the painful realities experienced by the individual and society. By doing this and suggesting choices and strategies to dealing with these realities, it can trigger a debate about positive change in individuals, in communities and society' (Fiona Ledger, Personal Communication, 2010). Yvonne MacPherson, the BBC WST country director in India goes even further, noting the power of the format to affect social norms: 'Drama as a format is ideal not only for communicating life-saving information and creating demand for services, but also for depicting positive attitudes and defining and establishing social norms' (Yvonne MacPherson, Personal Communication, 2010).

Conclusion

The creative evolution described in this chapter occurred during a period of dramatic growth for the BBC WST and reflected the ongoing influence of two primary institutional forces: the BBC and the donor community. The analysis herein firstly explored some of the implications of the BBC WST's origins within the BBC and identified how the tradition of BBC drama-making and BBC values were exported within the early dramas for development that it produced.

Secondly, the chapter has described a period of development sensitisation during which BBC WST staff, and particularly project managers, became more precise in terms of how they described the potential for dramas on radio and television to contribute to the achievement of specific development objectives. Over time, the BBC WST has increasingly embraced theories of BCC employed by other development organisations—partly in response to donors' great expectations about what dramas could and should deliver in development terms. These shifts—both in the language used to describe drama-making at the BBC WST, and in expectations about what dramas could 'achieve' in development terms—at times led to tensions between project management staff and creative teams.

More recently, drama-making at the BBC WST has witnessed a period of 'creative coalescence' through which earlier tensions have been resolved as staff work consciously and carefully to balance the imperatives of the craft of drama production and the need to focus on specific objectives directed to particular audiences. Dramas continue to be developed that strive to meet the 'great expectations' of donors, while simultaneously addressing the needs and tastes of their audiences across a range of complex development issues. A review of the diversity of work produced by the BBC WST has identified a set of criteria that define the entire body of work—the purpose and objectives, the diversity of formats, the longevity of the broadcast, the establishment of a production centre, the campaign context and the selection of a broadcast platform.

As the BBC WST proceeds with its work in drama for development, it continues to work to build in-depth agreement and shared understanding between donors and dramatists about what dramas can deliver in development contexts. Expectations should remain 'great' but also realistic, supported by a more precise and shared articulation of what constitutes success and failure in drama for development initiatives.

Notes

1. The BBC WST retains final editorial control over all of its programme outputs.
2. See http://www.bbc.co.uk/worldservice/trust/news/story/2005/08/010509_soapopera.shtml.
3. The work of the BBC WST can be divided into two, often overlapping, categories— Media Development and Development Communications. Media Development activities aim to strengthen the media sector in developing and transitional countries

through training and change management programmes, while Development Communications work focuses on the production of creative programming that both engages and informs audiences around key development issues, including governance and human rights, health, livelihoods, disaster preparedness and humanitarian response, and climate change. Across the world, the BBC WST's staff and partners produce content for radio, television, online, mobile and print platforms. Programme formats produced include serial dramas, films, debate programmes and magazine programmes, PSAs and documentaries—each designed to achieve specific development objectives (usually in combination with each other).

4. See http://www.bbc.co.uk/worldservice/trust/mediacoverageresources/story/2005/12/051207_dev-gateway-storystory.shtml.
5. Ibid.
6. See http://www.psi.org/our-work/changing-behaviors.
7. See http://www.soulcity.org.za/about-us/institute-for-health-development.

References

Bandura, A. (1977) *Social Learning Theory*. Englewood Cliffs, NJ: Prentice-Hall.

BBC World Service. (1999) *Memorandum Submitted by the Select Committee on Foreign Affairs*. London: BBC World Service.

British Broadcasting Corporation (BBC). (2004) *Building Public Value: Renewing the BBC for a Digital World*. London: BBC.

Buckingham, David. (1987) *Public Secrets: Eastenders and its Audience*. London: BFI.

Department for International Development (DFID). (2010) 'DFID Sponsored TV and Radio'. Available online at http://www.dfid.gov.uk/getting-involved/dfid-sponsored-tv—radio/ (accessed on 15 December 2009).

Galavotti, C., Pappas-De Luca, K. and Lansky, A. (2001) 'Modelling and Reinforcement to Combat HIV: The MARCH Approach to Behaviour Change', *American Journal of Public Health*, 91(10): 1602–1607.

Rigbey, L. (1993) Unpublished Manuscript. 'How to Write a Radio Soap Opera'.

Singhal, A., Cody, M., Rogers, E. and Sabido, M. (2004) *Entertainment-Education and Social Change: History, Research, and Practice*. New York: Lawrence Erlbaum Associates, Inc.

The David and Lucile Packard Foundation. (2007) 'Population Report—Ethiopia'. Available online at http://www.packard.org/assets/files/population/program%20review/2007_pop_report_ethiopia_041707.pdf (accessed on 21 December 2009).

United States Agency for International Development (USAID). (2010) 'Studio 263 TV – HIV/AIDS Programming A Hit'. Available online at http://www.usaid.gov/stories/zimbabwe/cs_zimbabwe_aidstv.html (accessed on 15 December 2009).

3

AUDIENCE RESEARCH IN DRAMA FOR DEVELOPMENT

A CONTACT ZONE OF TRANSLATION AND TRANSNATIONAL KNOWLEDGE PRODUCTION*

GERRY POWER

Introduction

The BBC World Service has a long history of conducting audience research throughout the developing world, primarily focused on establishing the reach of broadcasting services (Mytton, 1993a, 1993b).[1] This chapter examines how audience research, as it has developed at the BBC World Service Trust (BBC WST) constitutes a site of transnational knowledge production. García Canclini and Roncagliolo propose that 'transnationalisation is not the simple abolition of differences: it is also the creation of hybrid

*The author acknowledges the comments on an early draft of this chapter from Connie Della-Piana, Darrin Hodgetts, Caroline Howie, Emily LeRoux-Rutledge, Linje Manyozo, Bella Mody, Liz Nelson and Emily Richter.

spaces in which, to the rhythm of conflicts, both the hegemonic and the subaltern sectors refunctionalise objects and dominant practices' (1988: 151). Further, the chapter provides a critical reflection on the research methods employed and the impact of the audience research on the dramas produced by the BBC WST. I employ Pratt's (1991) notion of a contact zone, defined as 'social spaces where cultures meet, clash, and grapple with each other, often in contexts of highly asymmetrical relations of power'. Gillespie and Baumann describe the diasporic 'contact zones' at the BBC World Service as 'sites of transnational and diasporic creativity and representation, and forums for cross-cultural dialogue and, potentially, of cosmopolitan translations' (2007: 5). Audience research activities can also be regarded as 'contact zones' of cross-cultural negotiation and interpretation where knowledge is produced and is used to inform creative and representational decisions about drama formats, characters, plotlines and stories.

The role of research in the construction of identity in developing countries is well documented in anthropology (L'Estoile, 1997; Ribeiro, 2006) and social psychology (Hodgetts et al., 2010). The contact zones of audience research at the BBC WST—where the emic and the etic interface—comprise the discussions, debates and decisions between local and London-based researchers and the production teams. These interactions focus on refining research questions, agreeing the profile of research participants, the locations of data gathering and the meaning-making of the final results. Of particular import is the involvement of local researchers in the design, analysis and interpretation of the research in the countries where dramas are made. The answers, reactions and impressions of local populations to the dramas produced become the grist for the intellectual labour of a cross-cultural research team to interpret the information gathered (Pe-Pua, 2006). There is a sense in which the role of the research in drama-making approximates what Foucault (1980) in *The Order of Things* refers to as an episteme. The episteme 'is the "apparatus" which makes possible the separation, not of the true from the false, but of what may from what may not be characterised as scientific' (Foucault 1980: 197).

There are, at least, four sets of realities and priorities in the 'translation challenge' evident in both BBC WST research practice and drama production. First, the research is achieved through the face-to-face and mediated interactions of London-based and local researchers. Second, the research is designed to inform a body of practice—programme production, rather than address a purely academic inquiry. Third, the methods employed, as part of the research practice, define a set of social relations that privilege one participant, the researcher over the other, the one researched. Fourth, the social science paradigm underlying the research and the methods used are western and inherently limited in understanding the cultural norms of local cultures in the South (see Chapters 5 and 10). These four sets of contrasting realities and priorities combined pose a significant challenge to the validity and reliability of the knowledge produced from the research and its influence on the drama production process (Van de Vijver and Leung, 1997).

London and Local

From 1999, the BBC WST engaged a range of research consultants to support drama and other projects. I joined the BBC WST in 2003, as a full-time research manager, working within the then Health Unit. My remit was to support health projects, primarily in India and Cambodia, with audience research. There was an explicit expectation to design research that would capture the impact of our dramas in a robust manner. The approach adopted was a hybrid model, informed by academic principles and methods commonly employed in health promotion practice. Such methods are heavily reliant on knowledge, attitude and practice (KAP) indicators and draw partly on the methods employed by commercial market researchers, with their focus on meeting the needs and expectations of consumers of media content. Both of these influences are still manifest in the research approach at the BBC WST today. While many organisations in the development sector deliver their research activities, often referred to as Monitoring and Evaluation (M&E), by employing expatriate experts and consultants, the BBC WST made a strategic decision to invest in building local research capacity (see Chapter 4). This decision has proven to be invaluable in enhancing the design and implementation of the research for our dramas, most importantly in interpreting the findings of our studies.

In early 2005, the BBC WST established a standalone Research and Learning Group (R&L) to provide research support to all BBC WST's projects in health, governance, humanitarian response, livelihoods and climate change. The discrete practice of research within the organisation affords an important critical distance between the project teams and the researchers. The research team has grown to more than 50 people with a core team based in London and local researchers based in BBC WST offices in 14 countries. Researchers come from a variety of backgrounds, including the academic, commercial, government and not-for-profit sectors. This diversity facilitates a breadth of research perspectives and expertise. There is a strong commitment to building the research skills of the team in the spirit of action research, from reflective processes to social action. This is achieved through distance mentoring, an online network and 'master-classes' and workshops.

There are multiple challenges to conducting research in developing countries and it is imperative to build in strict quality control mechanisms. In the case of the BBC WST, these quality control procedures are largely implemented by the local research teams on the ground. When conducting research, face-to-face methods are most commonly employed where appropriate and necessary, but telephone and online methodologies are also used. Local researchers conduct interviews, moderate focus group discussions, convene listening groups and manage large-scale survey efforts and receive technical support from the team in London. Further, where appropriate, unobtrusive methods such as media content analysis and discourse analysis are also used. The sampling methodology employed for each study is very specific and will usually be defined in terms of demographic and psychographic (typically, values, characteristics, attitudes and so on) characteristics as well as media use patterns and preferences. The research group specialises in gathering data from rural, remote and hard-to-reach populations. Data are analysed using a variety of software packages, qualitative tools and statistical techniques.

The dominant assumption in the interactions between London-based and local researchers is that the research activities will inform the drama-making in a manner that makes the drama more appealing to audiences and so makes key development messages more efficacious. Sillitoe (2002a) discusses the problematic nature of labelling different types of knowledge in development research and the implied hierarchies in the interface between science and indigenous knowledge. At the BBC WST, the perspective of the London research team is framed largely as 'technical', whereas the perspective of the in-country researchers is framed largely in terms of their 'local' identity. This dynamic pretends to neutralise the value of the non-local perspective as 'technical' and frames the local perspective as aware, sensitised and in-tune. This is not to suggest that local knowledge is everything that is left when the technical aspects of the research are removed, but rather that the site of knowledge production is formed by a contact zone of primarily technical London and primarily local in-country staff. It is also not the case that the technical is assumed to be superior to the local. On the contrary, the prevailing paradigm within the group—in line with contemporary development practice—is that local knowledge makes the technical possible. While decisions about research design, sampling and analysis are primarily driven from London, the intelligence about appropriate language, translation, question formats and access to hard-to-reach populations typically comes from the local team. For example, in the interests of avoiding undue interpersonal influence, the 'technical requirement' that focus group participants not know each other is often challenged by local researchers who, quite sensibly, argue that it is anathema in many cultures— particularly in more remote areas—for strangers to gather in public places. Inevitably, the local knowledge prevails over technical expertise, and the requirements of the cultural context for knowledge production will take precedence over the formal requirements of 'scientific method'. Oftentimes, this is unspoken and there is an implicit trust in the judgment of the local knowledge, in deference to the practical focus of the research. This approach is consistent with Sillitoe (2002a, 2002b), who defines knowledge as a continuum comprising the constant interrogation of knowledges.

The research team shares the mantra and one of the core values of the larger BBC that 'audiences are at the heart of everything we do'. The underlying assumptions about the audience in the BBC WST's approach to research can be summarised as follows: (*a*) asking questions of audience members in research can uncover how issues are understood, defined and communicated; (*b*) audiences are regarded as heterogeneous in terms of demographic, psychographic and media/technographic characteristics. The most common demographic attributes are age, social class and location (urban/rural). However, demographic categories in less-developed countries are not equivalent to those in the west, where, for example, life expectancy is relatively short, men and women marry at a relatively younger age, social class is defined according to very precise set of context-specific criteria and urban/rural distinctions vary and shift; (c) audiences understand the expectation that they will draw on their experience, knowledge and sense of preference in order to respond to questions and (d) audiences will ultimately benefit from the application of the research findings to development interventions. This final assumption is not always explicit in research practice or articulated in such terms to research participants.

These assumptions about the character and identity of the audience are typically negotiated in the 'contact zone' between the technical and local research forces and are reflected in the study design and methodology employed in the final research studies that are conducted. For example, because of low literacy levels, particularly in rural areas, all research is conducted face-to-face, with few exceptions; because of the variety of languages and dialects spoken, research instruments are customised to resonate with specific sub-groups; permission to speak to research participants is often granted not by the individual themselves but by others, in the case of some females by their husbands or fathers and among some rural communities by tribal or village elders; the social hierarchy will often dictate who can speak and who cannot; matching the identity of the interviewer with all of the salient characteristics of the interviewee will minimise experimenter effect (in which a researcher can influence the outcome of research) and social desirability (in which interview respondents provide answers that a perceived as 'favourable' or 'politically correct').

The research approach adopted at the BBC WST is akin to the action research tradition of Kurt Lewin (1946, 1948), which 'involves a cyclical process of theorizing, planning, conducting, gaining feedback on, implementing, evaluating and revising a research project in dialogue with a range of stakeholders from the beginning to the end of a project' (Hodgetts et al., 2010: 7). Further, the critical reflections are framed in a manner consistent with the tradition of Martín-Baró (1994) and the importance he placed on understanding human behaviour in the local context and conditions in which it exists and the rejection of a universal, impartial psychology. The tensions between the requirements of a scientific research practice and the influence of an understanding of local knowledge and conditions are also manifest in the 'contact zone' of audience research with drama for development projects.

Practitioner and Academic

Dramas can be (and are) made without ever consulting the audience, yet audience research at the BBC WST plays a significant role in their development, their storylines and characters. Such dramas are placed in dialogue with their audiences and are not simply imposed on or transmitted to them. Audience research 'with' rather than 'on' people achieves this dialogue. Sillitoe calls for:

> ... the formulation of research strategies that meet the demands of development—to be cost effective, to be time effective, to generate appropriate insights, to be readily intelligible to non experts etc. while not compromising anthropological expectations, so downplaying the difficulties attending the excogitation of others' knowledge as to render the work effectively valueless.
>
> (2002b: 14)

Since 1993, the Afghan drama *New Home, New Life*—part of the BBC Afghan Education Projects (BBC AEP) and which preceded the establishment of the BBC WST—had embedded within it a robust 'locally grounded' content and impact research programme. The local Afghan team, trained by international development experts, travelled throughout the country, gathering stories and insights from audiences. The team employed a variety of research methods heavily influenced by Participatory Rural Appraisal (PRA) techniques (see Chapter 4). The research in Afghanistan, however, was not designed to establish the extent or nature of the listenership to the drama, but rather to collect anecdotes and scenarios to weave into the drama storyline.

More recent research has sought to establish the extent and nature of listenership and listener attitudes. Much current non-academic research on drama audiences takes a largely mechanistic approach to aggregating responses and reactions to elements of the drama. One strand of audience research is focused on testing a range of creative decisions and is characterised by understanding likes and dislikes, comprehension and engagement with characters, likelihood of viewing, relevance and appropriateness. A second body of audience research explores the profile of the audience for the drama in demographic, lifestyle/life-stage and psychographic terms. When this is quantitative research, the emphasis is on estimating the size of the audience or sub-audiences. A qualitative approach typically differentiates audience members based on their attitudes and beliefs about some development issue. In both cases, the result is usually to classify and label the audience members into discrete categories in order to support the creation of content in the dramas that will speak to the diversity of viewpoints represented. The classification, although based on local meaning structures often result in disembodied sanitised references that 'speak to' the extent of media consumption (high, medium and low exposure), their relative importance to the objectives of the drama (primary, secondary, tertiary audience) or the availability of different media (media rich or media dark).

The practices described above resonate with Appadurai's (1990) notions of 'ethnoscapes', 'technoscapes', 'mediascapes' and 'ideoscapes' that offer irregular configurations of cultural mixing and disjunction on a global scale. For example, in response to the request from a donor to produce episodes of *New Home New Life* that would explore the issue of poppy cultivation, a qualitative study was commissioned in 2008 to examine opinions about poppy cultivation among Afghan radio listeners (see Chapter 4). The analysis produced by the research segmented the audience into three discrete groups based on their attitudes toward growing poppy and then further refined the three groups by their urban/rural location, education and religious beliefs (see Table 3.1 below). This type of non-academic or practitioner-based audience research is designed not to question the political and economic motivations of the donors' interest in the public's opinion about poppy cultivation, but rather to aid the dramatists in understanding the range of potential dominant and oppositional readings of the 'text' of the drama (Hall, 1980). These readings, as the results show, are inherently politically and economically motivated. Herein lies the practical benefit of the research—knowing the

Table 3.1

**Three Categories of Listeners Identified Based on Opinions
about Poppy Cultivation in Afghanistan**

Profile	Rejectionists—never alright	Justifiers—sometimes alright	Supporters—always alright
Position	- More urban than rural residents - More educated - More religious - People with economic options - Reject poppy on moral or religious grounds - Reject poppy out of respect for civic order	- More rural than urban residents - Less educated - More flexible with religious beliefs - Less access to economic opportunities - Justify based on economic need - Justify based on belief it does not negatively impact what is important to them	- Minority of population - Both urban and rural - Economically and politically motivated - No moral, religious or civic concerns about poppy cultivation - View as legitimate business

Source: Author.

audience increases the likelihood that the drama episodes will resonate with the breadth of listeners' lived experience and therein generate a 'pro-social' impact.

In 2002, the BBC WST commissioned an external academic consultant to conduct research to evaluate the impact of the Indian television drama, *Jasoos Vijay* ('Detective Vijay', see chapter 10 of this volume). The consultant employed a panel or cohort approach to the survey research—where the same individuals would be surveyed over a period of time and their levels of knowledge, attitudes and self-reported behaviour tracked over time, relative to their consumption of the drama and other outputs. In order to maintain the integrity of the research, when individuals indicated by their answers that they had misconceptions about modes of transmission and prevention of HIV, they could not be provided with the correct information as this would interfere with the potential attribution of increases in knowledge to the drama.

What ensued was a protracted tense debate between the BBC WST research team and the academic organisation about the 'pros' and 'cons' of cross-sectional and longitudinal survey research designs and the types of errors introduced depending on the choices made. There was clearly a clash of two life-worlds—the development and the academic.

The development perspective advocated debriefing those participants identified as having 'incorrect knowledge' and avoiding the risk of reinforcing misconceptions that would not otherwise be held. For example, some research questions testing people's knowledge suggested that it was possible to transmit HIV by a handshake or eating food prepared by an HIV positive person. The academic perspective advocated retaining the integrity of the research design and abdicated all responsibility for such educational efforts to local social workers. These were two worlds deriving their professional lives from the same effort—asking poor people in developing countries about a television drama. The common language was the audience research methods, but the academic and development objectives collided.

The 'contact zone' of audience research and knowledge production activity punctuated the meeting point of two worlds—the habitus of academic inquiry and the habitus of practical development research (Bourdieu, 1972). This event, early on in the history of research at the BBC WST, brought to the fore the clash of worldviews between professional academics interested in the media and development phenomenon for publication purposes and professional audience researchers interested in understanding populations in developing countries, which in turn informs the practice of drama production. The academic research can often be concerned with questioning the motivations of all the stakeholders—the donors, the BBC WST, the dramatists, the local governments and even the audiences. On the other hand, the focus of the practical research is typically on mining the data to inform decision-making about the drama to make it more engaging, to increase audience size and to establish the strength of the relationship between exposure to the drama and shifts in development indicators. The convergence of these two fields is a hybrid space that few occupy comfortably, as the priorities of practical and academic research rarely coincide.

Researcher and Researched

Research methods, like research, are sites of contestation. They define who is spoken to, who is not spoken to, what questions are asked and what questions are not asked. They pose ethical dilemmas and often become the focus of moral debates about inclusion and exclusion, over and above the social class differences of those asking questions and those providing answers. The protocols for gathering data, therefore, establish the terms of engagement both on physical and inter-personal terms, akin to what Foucault (1979) describes in the *History of Sexuality* as 'the examination'. The research method, like the examination, can be regarded as an instrument of discipline that combines the techniques of both hierarchical observation and normalising judgment, to effect a 'normalising gaze' through which individuals may be classified and judged. In 'the examination' are manifested 'the subjection of those who are perceived as objects and the objectification of those who are subjected [...]. In this slender technique are to be found a whole domain of knowledge, a whole type of power' (Foucault 1979: 185).

Throughout the production process of making a drama at the BBC WST, there are typically four stages of research that use different methods. At the formative stage, ideas and concepts are explored in order to establish more definite parameters for project design (see Chapter 9, this volume). The second stage is the 'pre-testing' phase when audiences are asked to provide feedback on the format and content of outputs in order to check that they are comprehensible, relevant, culturally appropriate and targeted to the right audience. Third, when programmes are on air, monitoring is a valuable tool to understand how they are resonating with the people for whom they were designed. Finally, when projects have finished, the most important evidence to capture is whether outputs have had the desired result. Impact may be defined in terms of numbers of people reached, knowledge or skills acquired, attitude or social change or the adoption of new practices.

Acutely aware of the imbalance of power relations in the social science research canon, as a development organisation, we have attempted to draw on research methods that seek to redress the differences in power between 'the researcher' and 'the researched'. Part of this effort has included using participatory methods. The concept of participation dominates many facets of development work. It underpins 'meaningful' practice. It is assumed that change will be greater and more sustainable when people themselves participate in defining and assessing the 'change process' (Schönhuth, 2002). Chambers' (2007) work on participatory methodology is noteworthy, especially where he critiques both the reductionist approach, which he characterises as standardised, non-contextual, quantitative, employing questionnaire surveys, and the particularistic approach, which is idiosyncratic, contextual, qualitative and uses participant observation. As an alternative, Chambers (2007) advocates a participatory approach to research, that he claims is pluralist, interactive, multidimensional and facilitates poor people's own analysis. Within the media for development world, the participatory approach to research that has dominated the field is the Communication for Social Change model (CFSC), which 'focuses on the process by which dialogue—as a participatory form of communication—is related to collective action' (Figueroa et al., 2002: iii).

The time and resource commitment at the community level and the capacity building of citizens required to support the CFSC approach is prohibitive for the BBC WST to use in developing its dramas. However, we borrow many of its principles of community engagement, in which people identify and define their own information needs. It is also imperative to recognise that the reification of the data and of the research practice gives authority and legitimacy to the results and can shift attention away from the voices of the original speakers. While audiences are consulted continuously throughout the drama-making process, the research effectively becomes 'the voice' of the citizen/consumer and mediates between the viewers and listeners and the production teams.

When the primary purpose of the research falls within a different domain, the politicised nature of the research relationship is punctuated. Purcell and Akinyi Onjoro suggest that 'the notion of development almost always involves inequality between those receiving development and those from whom ideas about the process and goal emanate' (2002: 164). The choice of research method is typically underscored by multiple motivations—the desire to confirm strongly held beliefs, to test out new ideas and alternative hypotheses, to demonstrate selective impacts and to fulfil donor requirements. All of these motivations, although some of them conflicting, sit comfortably within the parameters of the overall development mission of audience research and they do not cause great unease. In contrast, the choice of research method becomes a battleground when the research is used for non-development purposes.

It is not the case that the dramatists or production teams always adhere to the implicit recommendations in the research findings. The findings, however, provide an important point of reference. For example, when research participants in Cambodia repeatedly described an attractive female actress as ugly and unappealing, further investigation uncovered that it was her indigenous appearance that was off-putting to these particular viewers, nonetheless the decision was made to include her in the drama. In Myanmar (Burma), a country where little population data exists for NGOs and others to inform their work, the BBC WST carried out extensive qualitative and quantitative audience research on its radio drama, *Thabyegone Ywa* (*Eugenia Tree Village*). In this case, the audience research proved to be invaluable in confirming the priorities, over and above the perspective of the production team. The director responsible for the Myanmar project at the time contrasts the approach to drama production that relies solely on the opinions of producers with an approach that is informed by embedding audience research within the production process:

> I would never dispute the original production team's idea to go out and say we need to do such and such, because then you've got something to test. But they completely failed in their duty to find out from the audience whether that idea would work and whether that was what was needed … and had they done that, I think it would have been different. And I think it's my very very best example of how the two [research and drama] worked hand in hand, because we were able to mine and mine and mine the audience research material and know—because it had been done so carefully—and know that we would be sure footed, which is unusual.
>
> (Interview with Karen Merkel, BBC WST, 2009)

The audience research on drama for development at the BBC WST is driven by a desire to inform a host of practical and production decisions about broadcast platforms, when people view and listen, who they view and listen with, what characters they like and dislike, what language resonates with them and so on. The interaction between London and local researchers in defining these questions and interpreting the answers often blurs the lines between the emic and etic, resulting in a body of knowledge that reflects both perspectives.

The West and the Rest

There is a significant body of literature from the developing world that challenges the hegemony of Western social science, particularly as it has framed and intellectualised the south. These works on the western construction of southern identity include the writings on the 'subaltern' by Guha and Spivak (1988); the contributions to the sociology of knowledge of Akiwowo (1986); as well as Said's (1978) classic work, *Orientalism*. Reflecting on the seductive appeal of Enlightenment meta-narratives, Hall notes that:

> These days I find myself recruited to many of the Enlightenment aspirations, but I have to remind myself that it never understood difference, never understood that it was underpinned by a particularly Western conception of reason, never came to terms with the supporting ideological underpinning of its 'liberalism', of this particular notion of cosmopolitanism, and of the ways the claims to universalism were embedded in a certain form of historical particularity. (2008: 349)

In her historical analysis of the intimate relationship between sociology, the new science of 'society', and the expansion of North Atlantic power, Connell argues that:

> Sociology was formed within the culture of imperialism, and embodied an intellectual response to the colonized world. This fact is crucial in understanding the objects and subjects of analysis and the methodological approaches that have developed in sociology, as well as the discipline's wider cultural significance. (2007: 9)

Connell advocates a body of literature (some of which is cited above) from thinkers in the South as a valuable contribution to social theory in a global context.

The challenge to respond to the epistemological opportunity afforded by the transnational space of audience research is achieved largely by adopting the principles of the 'problem posing method' as defined by Freire (1990). Rather than imposing a particular approach or definition of an issue in a drama, the knowledge and insights of audiences gathered in the research process are privileged in the creative process. However, we are conscious that the ways of 'coming to know' and gaining insight are derived from a Western worldview and practice, rather than from what Hodgetts et al. (2010) refer to as 'indigenous cosmologies'. The practice within the social sciences of asking questions of people according to an established set of protocols that are based on a set of theoretical principles is grounded in a particular socio-cultural tradition. This approach may not be the most appropriate to capture the essence of non-Western peoples. As an alternative, Hodgetts et al. (2010) suggest that indigenous cosmologies routinely pose such questions as Who am I? Where do I fit in? Where am I going? What are important things to do? They note that for 'many Europeans of the old world, [*sic*] these questions were answered through Judeo-Christian beliefs in one God, who created heaven and earth and all that is between including mankind' (Hodgetts et al., 2010). These are not the guiding principles of the faith and belief systems that dominate in most of the cultural contexts where BBC WST dramas air, where Buddhism, Hinduism, Islam and animist traditions tend to prevail (see, for example, the work of Shariati [1979] on the Sociology of Islam). Hodgetts et al. (2010) propose an indigenous approach to research as part of a 'decolonisation project', where research and action strategies privilege the lived experiences of individuals and their communities. They emphasise the importance of valuing different forms of knowledge, ways of knowing and practice: that is, praxis as part of working against oppression and exclusion. Finally, Hodgetts et al. (2010) argue that it is imperative to promote everyday practices that recognise our embeddedness in socio-political realities, as the process of working for change at individual, interpersonal and institutional levels. These principles of the 'decolonisation project' constitute a benchmark against which we calibrate the value of the knowledge gathered in our research projects, while recognising the practical challenges of gathering information that will guide the decision-making of the drama production teams. There is a strong and explicit imperative, therefore, to create drama that is grounded in the everyday lives of the audiences. However, this challenge is often not a balance between local and international identities, but rather between various local ethnic, religious, socio-economic and urban/rural realities.

In 2004, the BBC WST launched *Story Story—Voices from the Market*, a radio drama that uses what are intended to be dynamic storylines and true-to-life characters to encourage debate amongst its listeners about local and global issues within the Nigerian context of production. The drama was part of the wider *Voices* project, a national public education broadcasting intervention. The BBC has a long history in Nigeria—the BBC trained and assisted the Nigerian Broadcasting Service, which began in 1950. The BBC broadcasts in Hausa and English and has a weekly audience (for all programmes) of 26 million (BBC GND/IPSOS, May 2009). Audience research conducted by the global news division (GND) of the BBC suggests that the BBC has a 'strong brand heritage' in Nigeria and is regarded as a highly trustworthy news source.

Story Story explores topics such as poverty, governance, rights and HIV and AIDS; it also focuses on specific development issues that inform the Millennium Development Goals (MDGs), such as the empowerment of women, education and environmental sustainability. Broadcast on more than 50 radio stations around Nigeria, as well as on the BBC World Service, the drama is currently being produced in the Hausa, Yoruba and Igbo languages. Set in a busy fictional market in the heart of West Africa, the series features characters—traders, farmers and people with money and power who inhabit the market—that aim to give a voice to real people. Stories of debt, romance, rubbish, holes in the road, self-help and community spirit entwine these characters as they try to earn a living in the bustling market.

In an effort to make the drama as relevant as possible, the series is written, performed and directed by a Nigerian creative team. Rather than recording in a studio environment, the series is recorded 'on-location'—a strategy designed to create a unique broadcasting sound through scenes recorded in an open courtyard, corridors and open fields with the winds blowing. *Story Story* is supplemented by a discussion and debate programme called *Talk Talk*. A radio programme that has been expanded to television, *Talk Talk* takes topics from *Story Story* and looks at the impact they have in 'real life'. Each programme uses an excerpt from the drama and also features a 'location report' from around the country. One of the key strategies is to put ordinary Nigerians in touch with people in power, asking what everyone can do to make their world a better place. The idea is that 'real stories' are the most effective way of exploring a subject and making the programme interesting, while still raising important development issues.

Audience research conducted on *Story Story* confirmed that 7 million people listened to the English language version and that 11 million people listened to the Hausa version of the drama. In addition, 80 per cent of *Story Story* listeners spoke to friends and family about issues raised in the drama and 51 per cent of listeners said the drama had made them think differently about some of the issues featured. One of the key themes of the production that emerges repeatedly in audience research is how the drama format captures the ethnic, regional and religious diversity of Nigeria—an aspect that is highly valued by listeners. This acknowledgement is particularly significant in a country as diverse as Nigeria, with 370 different ethnic groups and a multitude of languages. The research also uncovered that while most listeners expressed a preference for characters 'like them' certain characters were more broadly appealing and transcended the formal boundaries of religion, ethnicity and language. This learning about the potential and limitations of characters and the imperative to create a 'real' drama informed the development of a new HIV and AIDS-related television drama in Nigeria called *Wetin Dey* (Pidgin for *What's Up?*) that was launched by the BBC WST in 2007. *Wetin Dey* was a drama series exploring the social realities facing young people in Nigeria; it was designed to raise HIV and AIDS awareness. It attracted immediate attention from young Nigerians both offline and online. Here an online comment from a viewer calling themselves '6footplus' enthuses:

> Have you guys seen the 'Wetin Dey' TV Show? That's by far 1 of d best *naija* shows [dramas] i've seen in a long time, d production na 4 shizzles o! even the story telling is awesome, how dey take it from each characters' POV and then begin his/her story. i would [encourage] anyone who hasnt seen it 2 find out more on wetindey.tv its funny, smart, well-produced, i cud go on all night!
>
> (Comment posted on 23 July 2007 on www.nairaland.com)

The *Wetin Dey* drama was broadcast on Nigerian television and was part of a wider project funded between 2005 and early 2008 by the UK Department for International Development (DFID) to address sexual and reproductive health (e.g., HIV and AIDS) among Nigerian youth aged 15–24 years. The project, delivered in partnership with the Society for Family Health (SFH) in Nigeria, was a mass media intervention designed to engage the audience around six key HIV and AIDS issues that were developed with input from SFH, DFID and other leading HIV and AIDS organisations in Nigeria. The project included a broad array of mutually reinforcing outputs on radio, television and film, designed specifically to appeal to youth. *Wetin Dey* was produced alongside two interactive youth radio programmes in both Nigerian English and Hausa, called *Flava* (Pidgin for *Flavour*) and *Ya Take Ne?* (Hausa for *What's Up?*). In addition, a series of television and radio spots in four languages featuring testimonials from people living with HIV and AIDS was also produced. Further, the project worked in partnership with the Nigerian film industry to incorporate HIV and AIDS messages into the storylines of certain 'Nollywood' films.[2]

Wetin Dey was a multi-strand, multi-character 30-minute weekly television drama running for 52 episodes. It was broadcast by Nigerian National Television (NTA) at 8.00 p.m. on Sunday and later changed by NTA to 10.30 p.m. The characters spoke to the diversity of the target audience, which varied by age, gender, ethnic affiliation, religion, first language, education and sexual activity. The drama was designed to focus on lower socio-economic groups, with an emphasis on the daily lives of ordinary Nigerians. In the beginning, a group of senior African drama experts were brought in to inform the thinking on the *Wetin Dey* production. Among them, Gabriel Gbadamosi, who explains how audience research informed his approach to the drama:

> As dramaturg for this 52-part drama series aimed at addressing an emerging crisis of HIV/AIDS in Nigeria, I devised the scenario and worked with a team of 20 writers and producers to set up a framework of stories and characters, establishing the dramaturgical principles for the drama's continuing development. Embedded in each of the half-hour episodes, *separation* and *sacrifice* were the key principles I derived from primary research conducted by the BBC World Service BBC WST into Nigerian responses to the epidemic and from the context of a multi-faith and profoundly religious society. *Separation* was used to identify and contrast characters in a range of crisis situations—including but not

limited to HIV/AIDS—while *sacrifice* was used to focus potential responses and carry through a principle of change or *'courage'* in the development of character.

(Interview, June 2007)

In this case, the creative process incorporated the knowledge produced from the audience research as a guide on general themes likely to resonate across a diverse body of television viewers. However, this guide was contextualised by a culturally informed interpretation of the dual task of delivering on development objectives and simultaneously anticipating the varying reactions of the population. Again, Gbadamosi explains:

> The aim was to stimulate critical awareness of the choices available to Nigerians in creating television drama and in responding to the health crisis. Knowledge of and sensitivity to a range of Nigerian conceptions of moral character and psychological development allowed me to negotiate existing preoccupations with *judgment* among both writers and audiences. Judgment was juxtaposed with alternative responses to sickness and disability—such as the *healing* and *compassion* encoded in the traditional Yoruba narrative of Obatala's children: the outcast is the child of God.

(Interview, June 2007)

The awareness of the common purpose, on one hand, and the plethora of likely oppositional readings based on competing moral and emotional responses, on the other, also guided the story-writing and the drama-making process. Here Gbadamosi notes that: 'Contrasting stories, each with a different ethos brought by individual writers, were combined to increasingly contest the space for possible viewer responses to the evolving characters, situations and dilemmas in a diverse community confronting a still silent HIV/AIDS crisis' (Interview, July 2007). Audience research for serial drama-making in developing contexts affords the opportunity to converge competing bodies of knowledge—diasporic drama experts, audience research findings, indigenous writers—to produce a product that 'promises' or 'pretends' to deliver on a construction of identity that is grounded and real (see Chapter 8). Gbadamosi explains further:

> Contributing to the development of new Nigerian writing for performance, *Wetin Dey* provided a rich platform for practice-led research into

the process of critical dialogue, skills exchange and capacity building between its African-British and Nigerian participants. It allowed me to cross-reference skills and knowledge as both a British and Nigerian practitioner across both industries and cultural contexts, and to disseminate that learning, together with the possibilities for innovation, clearly and effectively.

(Interview, June 2007)

The recognition of the value of different types of knowledge from different sources resists an essentialist view of a Nigerian or African identity that is only knowable if one is Nigerian or African. As Ahluwalia (2002) notes: 'In a dichotomous discourse that equates "African" with indigenous ethnic identity, there is no place for significant groups of intellectuals whose African identity has other grounds' (cited in Connell, 2007: 108). To produce a great drama for development requires a unique set of conditions: a national policy that does not prevent the growth of the creative industries, a donor agency that is not averse to the belief that cultural production is an integral part of how societies develop, a knowledge of the audience, a knowledge of the culture, a knowledge of the craft of drama-making and the creativity to 'make magic' (personal correspondence with Karen Merkel, BBC WST, 2010). Only the audience(s) can judge how effectively the knowledge production processes have been in constructing identities that are meaningful to their lives and that stimulate critical awareness about the choices available to them.

Conclusion

Four dimensions define the audience research conducted on drama at the BBC WST that further constitutes it as a 'contact zone' of transnational knowledge production. They include the relations between London and local researchers, the practical rather than academic focus, the dynamic between the researcher and the researched and ideological influence of a western social sciences paradigm. Reflecting over the last seven years on the work of the BBC WST's R&L, several observations associated with conceptual, methodological and operational challenges are worthy of mention.

First, building local researcher capacity has grounded the approach to drama production in local realities and challenged the assumptions of London-based and international staff. The insights of the local research teams have refined the language use, character development and plotlines of the dramas. Local knowledge has adapted the technical requirements of London-based research designs, methods and sampling strategies to achieve more meaningful data gathering activities to produce more nuanced interpretations of local realities. The interactions between 'London' and 'local' research staff constitute a hybrid space where the 'us' and the 'them' is blurred and a focus emerges on generating a body of knowledge that is internally and externally valid and reliable.

Second, 'practical' research is the essence of the audience research practice at the BBC WST. While theoretical and critical arguments abound in the academic literature, there is a dearth of empirical research on many of the practice-based issues that the audience research programme at the BBC WST is actively exploring. Because of the quick turnaround demands of a production cycle and the often-limited budget, there is a tendency to focus on manageable issues and questions, rather than more macro-level sociological concerns. While these may overlap, the emphasis is inevitably on the former to guide practical decisions. Consequently, research results are delivered in a parsimonious and easily accessible manner to the dramatist and production teams. Audiences are classified and labelled and counted in a manner that often simplifies what they say they know, what they say they believe and what they say they do. These simplified (and in academic terms what might be deemed as essentialised or reified) cultural and social insights enable the creative teams to feel more 'sure-footed' as they engage in production.

Third, the politics of research on drama and other formats at the BBC WST are often manifest in the methods chosen to gather the data. While participatory research methods, such as those advocated by Chambers (2007), Manyozo (2007) and others are grounded in well-established theory and practice regarding empowerment and the sustainability of change, their adoption at a mass or population level, rather than a community context, has not been demonstrated. Further, the use of data for purposes beyond their original intention to inform creative decisions about the dramas has, at times, been a source of tension. The academic and development research endeavours have not always been motivated by a common purpose.

Finally, the theories and methods of audience research commonly used to study the BBC WST dramas have their origins in a western social science paradigm and tradition, yet are repeatedly applied in southern contexts. This raises the question about the extent to which prevailing paradigms in the west limit the understanding of southern contexts and thinking. As a 'contact zone' of knowledge production, audience research at the BBC WST constitutes only one source within a constellation of other cultural 'references' and 'readings'. As a source of influence within a given society, the formats created by the BBC WST, including drama are not assumed to exist in a vacuum, but rather constitute part of a complex environment of conflicting and contradictory sources of competing information and belief systems. It is imperative to incorporate these sources of influence into any approach attempting to understand the role of drama in advancing human development.

Notes

1. Hilda Matheson played a key role in the development of MI5 during the First World War. She was recruited to the BBC in 1926 by John Reith 'to develop and enhance the BBC's "Talks" coverage of British culture'. She is described as 'founding BBC radio journalism and responsible for laying down the foundations of qualitative cultural programming'. She resigned from the BBC in 1931 and went on to oversee The African Survey and to run the Joint Broadcasting Committee during WWII (see www.bbc.co.uk and www.ma-radio.gold.ac.uk).
2. Nollywood is Nigeria's video drama production industry. It is the third-largest film industry in the world after the United States and India.

References

Ahluwalia, P. (2002) 'The Struggle for African Identity: Thabo Mbeki's African Renaissance', *African and Asian Studies*, 1(4): 265–277.
Akiwowo, A. (1986) 'Contributions to the Sociology of Knowledge from an African Oral Poetry', *International Sociology*, 1(4): 343–358.
Appadurai, A. (1990) 'Disjuncture and Difference in the Global Cultural Economy', *Public Culture*, 2(2): 1–23.
Bourdieu, P. (1972) *Outline of a Theory of Practice*. Cambridge: Cambridge University Press.

Chambers, R. (2007) 'Poverty Research: Methodologies, Mindsets and Multi-dimensionality', Working Paper 293, Institute of Development Studies, Brighton, United Kingdom.

Connell, R. (2007) *Southern Theory*. Cambridge: Polity.

de L'Estoile, B. (1997) 'The "Natural Preserve of Anthropologists": Social Anthropology, Scientific Planning and Development', *Social Science Information*, 36(2): 343–376.

Figueroa, M., Kincaid, D., Bani, M. and Lewis, G. (2002) *Communication for Social Change Working Paper Series—Communication for Social Change: An Integrated Model for Measuring the Process and its Outcomes*. New York: The Rockefeller Foundation.

Foucault, M. (1979) *The History of Sexuality*. London: Penguin.

———. (1980) *Power/Knowledge: Selected Interviews and Other Writings, 1972–1977*. New York: Pantheon.

Freire, P. (1990) *Pedagogy of the Oppressed*. New York: Continuum.

García Canclini, N. and Roncagliolo, R. (1988) *Cultura Transnacional y Cultural Populares*. Lima: Inistituto para América Latina.

Gbadamosi, G. (2007) 'Dramaturg, Wetin Dey'. Available online at http://www.gold.ac.uk/drama/staff/g-gbadimosi/fellowship-projects/wetin-dey/ (accessed on 7 July 2007).

Gillespie, M. and Baumann, G. (2007) 'Diasporic Citizenships, Cosmopolitanisms, and the Paradox of Mediated Objectivity: An Interdisciplinary Study of the BBC World Service', Working Paper. Available online at http://www8.open.ac.uk/researchprojects/diasporas/publications/working-paper/diasporic-citizenships-cosmopolitanismsand-the-paradox-of-mediated-object (accessed on 21 April 2011).

Guha, R. and Spivak, G. (1988) *Selected Subaltern Studies*. New York: Oxford University Press.

Hall, S. (1980) 'Cultural Studies: Two Paradigms', *Media, Culture and Society*, 2: 57–72.

———. (2008) 'Cosmopolitanism, Globalisation and Diaspora', in P. Wernber (ed.), *Anthropology and the New Cosmopolitanism*. Oxford: Berg.

Hodgetts, D., Drew, N., Sonn, C., Stolte, O., Nikora, N. and Curtis, C. (2010) *Social Psychology and Everyday Life*. Basingstoke: Palgrave/MacMillan.

Lewin, K. (1946) 'Action Research and Minority Problems', *Journal of Social Issues*, 2(4): 34–46.

———. (1948) *Resolving Social Conflicts*. New York: Harper and Brothers.

Manyozo, L. (2007) 'Method and Practice in Participatory Radio: Rural Radio Forums in Malawi', *Ecquid Novi: African Journalism Studies*, 28(1–2): 11–29.

Martín-Baró, I. (1994) 'Towards a Liberation Psychology', trans. A. Aron, in A. Aron and S. Corne (eds), *Writings for a Liberation Psychology: Ignacio Martín-Baró*. Cambribge: Harvard University Press.

Mytton, G. (1993a) *Handbook on Radio and Television Audience Research*. Paris: UNICEF and UNESCO.

———. (1993b) *Global Audiences: Research for Worldwide Broadcasting*. London: John Libbey & Company Limited.

Pe-Pua, R. (2006) 'From Decolonizing Psychology to the Development of a Cross-Indigenous Perspective in Methodology: The Philippine Experience', in U. Kim., K. Yang and K. Hwang (eds), *Indigenous and Cultural Psychology: Understanding People in Context*. New York: Springer.

Pratt, M.L. (1991) 'Arts of the Contact Zone', pp. 33–40, *Profession 91*.

Purcell, T. and Akinyi Onjoro, E. (2002) 'Indigenous Knowledge, Power and Parity: Modes of Knowledge Integration', in P. Sillitoe, A. Bicker and J. Pottier (eds), *Participating in Development: Approaches to Indigenous Knowledge*. London: Routledge.

Ribeiro, G. (2006) 'World Anthropologies: Cosmopolitics for a New Global Scenario in Anthropology', *Critique of Anthropology*, 26: 363–386.

Said, E. (1978) *Orientalism*. London: Routledge and Kegan Paul.

Schönhuth, M. (2002) 'Negotiating with Knowledge at Development Interfaces: Anthropology and the Quest for Participation', in P. Sillitoe, A. Bicker and J. Pottier (eds), *Participating in Development: Approaches to Indigenous Knowledge*. London: Routledge.

Shariati, A. (1979) *An Approach to Understanding of Islam*, trans. Venus Kaivantash. Tehran: The Shariati Foundation and Hamdami Publishers.

Sillitoe, P. (2002a) 'Globalizing Indigenous Knowledge', in P. Sillitoe, A. Bicker and J. Pottier (eds), *Participating in Development: Approaches to Indigenous Knowledge*. London: Routledge.

———. (2002b) 'Participant Observation to Participatory Development: Making Anthropology Work', in P. Sillitoe, A. Bicker and J. Pottier (eds), *Participating in Development: Approaches to Indigenous Knowledge*. London: Routledge.

Van de Vijver, F. and Leung, K. (1997) *Methods and Data Analysis for Cross-Cultural Research*. Thousand Oaks: Sage Publications.

4

CREATIVE TENSIONS

AUDIENCE RESEARCH AND THE REPRESENTATIONAL CHALLENGE OF DRAMATISING OPIUM SUBSTITUTION IN AFGHANISTAN

ANDREW SKUSE

Introduction

National and international radio broadcasting is often perceived as a 'one way media' reflective of 'active' producers and 'passive', yet receptive, audiences (Crisell, 1986; Hilmes, 1997). Though such broadcasting is not 'interactive' in the sense of newer information and communication technologies, this simplistic conception fails to recognise the significant efforts that radio producers put into forming meaningful and ongoing relationships with their audiences, typically through complex audience research processes (Skuse et al., 2007). Inevitably, national and international radio broadcasters cannot interact with 'all' of their audience; nonetheless, audience research processes do afford them the opportunity for 'some' of their audience's voices and perspectives to be realised within their programming (cf. Allen, 1985). This is of particular importance when considering the humanitarian goals of communications for development interventions, such as 'pro-social drama for development', with its obligation of addressing the information needs of the poor, the excluded or the displaced.

Increasingly, the drive to connect the abstract domain of communication for development theorising with that of practice (such as drama production) is being expressed through commitments to qualitative audience research in particular (Inagaki, 2007; Waisbord, 2001). Overtly didactic modernist psycho-social theoretical approaches (see Chapter 1) developed from the 1950s onwards have given way to more nuanced qualitative and participatory approaches and models within recent years, in pursuit of 'communication partnerships' and 'critical dialogue' at the community level (cf. Lerner, 1958; Rogers, 1962; CFSC, 2002; Gumucio Dagron, 2001; UNAIDS, 1999). That given, establishing meaningful community-level dialogue and partnership remains problematic for national and international broadcasters due to the inevitable social distance that separates liberal and urbane media producers and writers from their often rural and highly conservative audiences. From a production perspective, audience research represents a key 'interface' critical to closing this 'social distance' and promoting the inclusion of community voices in broadcasting (cf. Long and Villareal, 1994). More cynically, it also constitutes one of the key mechanisms whereby communication for development interventions more skilfully impose dominant development perspectives and neo-liberal discourses upon information-poor and entertainment-hungry developing world audiences. This is particularly evident when we consider the core development 'themes' of democratisation, accountability and good governance, which Abrahamsen (2004) suggests are 'hegemonic' within contemporary global development frameworks, initiatives and discourse.

This hegemony is reflected in commentary on the potential of audience research and its centrality to communication for development interventions. Mytton suggests that it:

> ... can be used as a means of maximising the effectiveness of public advocacy campaigns, and of improving and enhancing education and information for effective democracy and good government. Audience research is a means of providing essential information to aid the creative

process of programme making. It can be used as a means of maximising the efficient and cost-effective use of limited resources. And it can be used to test if the objectives of any educational or information campaign have been successful.

(1999: 17)

The role of audience research as both technique and tool of governmentality is unequivocal, yet little by way of grounded examination of audience research processes exists within the literature on drama for development or E-E. In part, this is because project implementers tend to fixate on bringing quantitative evidence of impact to the public domain—with the immediacy of its knowledge, attitudes and practice statistics—therein leaving the scope of the ongoing dialogical qualitative research relationships that exist between audiences and producers relatively under-investigated in comparison (Batchelor and Scott, 2005; Inagaki, 2007). This is despite the mainstream literature on E-E recognising the merits of establishing qualitative audience 'feedback loops' that have the 'potential' to add to the rigour, reflexivity and efficacy of 'pro-social' media interventions (Singhal and Rogers, 2004; Tacchi et al., 2008). In assessing the specific functions of qualitative audience research within the field of drama for development, this chapter focuses upon the BBC Afghan Education Projects (BBC AEP) long-running radio drama *New Home, New Life* (see Chapters 7 and 13). Produced first in Pakistan and then Afghanistan, it remains one of the most enduringly popular Afghan radio productions, having been broadcast three times per week in the languages of Pashtu and Dari (Afghan Persian) for over 15 years.

Qualitative audience research provides much of the dramatic raw material that *New Home, New Life's* creative team thrives upon. The establishment of such qualitative feedback loops are understood by producers and drama writers in terms of helping them to ground their self-purported 'social realist' dramatic narratives in what they perceive to be the 'actual problems' or development 'realities' routinely experienced by their audiences (Skuse, 2002). In examining this dynamic, this chapter draws out the connections evident between neo-liberal donor-driven agendas and the craft of synopsis development, the various inputs that qualitative audience research affords the scripting process, as well as the audience 'critique' that qualitative research can help to level back at productions such as *New Home, New Life* (cf. Dornfeld, 1998; Tufte, 2002). In recognising the dialogical relationship that can exist between drama producers and the 'partial' audience, this chapter grounds its discussion in the theme of 'opium', which has broad currency within Afghanistan and beyond. A critical theme of the *New Home, New Life* drama, opium, crop substitution strategies and the allied effects of widespread drug addiction and conflict constitute key concerns for donors, the Afghan national government and non-government agencies (Ward et al., 2008).

In addressing this theme, analysis draws upon a range of qualitative data collected over the period 1996–2008. Ethnographic field research was conducted by the author within both Afghanistan and Pakistan (then the location of the BBC AEP production unit) between 1996–1998, with a further field visit to Afghanistan being conducted in 2002 in the wake of the US-led invasion and collapse of the Taliban regime in the preceding year. This research resulted in large quantities of ethnographic data and project-related documentation being collected across disparate locations that include the cities of Kabul and Jalalabad, as well as in rural areas of Paktia and Wardak Provinces. This research is further complimented by more recent data (2002–2008) derived from the BBC AEP. These data include full scripts, consultative notes, extensive focus group material and individual interviews conducted in the Afghan provinces of Helmand, Herat, Paktia and Nangarhar (2006–2008).

Opium: Donor Themes, Production and the Role of Qualitative Research

Established in 1993 (and first broadcast in early 1994) at the height of the Afghan civil war, the BBC AEP's radio drama *New Home, New Life* has been at the forefront of the humanitarian information response of the international development community for nearly twenty years. During this period, the political, economic and socio-cultural fortunes of Afghanistan have waxed and waned, with conflict of varying intensity being ever-present. From the early days of the *jihad* (holy war) against the Soviet occupiers (1979–1989) opium production has been critical to both the funding of numerous politico-religious groups prosecuting conflict, as well as to the livelihoods of poor farmers within poppy growing regions such as Helmand, Farah and Nimroz Provinces (Roy, 1990). A recent report commissioned by the UK Department for International Development (DFID) and World Bank on Afghan opium production identifies its significant scale:

> In the last two decades, Afghanistan has become the world's predominant supplier of illicit opiates, accounting for over 90% of world production and trade. Total gross revenues from the illegal drug trade in Afghanistan are equivalent to over one-third of licit GDP. Millions of Afghans benefit directly or indirectly from the opium economy.
>
> (Ward et al., 2008: iii–iv)

Further, the connection between conflict and raw opium production is well understood by donors and efforts to reduce its influence centre on what are termed 'crop-substitution' strategies, in which high-value crops such as opium are replaced with alternative crops of high value such as vegetables, along with related technical and material assistance schemes. Ultimately, while opium 'eradication' is sought, donors such as DFID, as well as the Government of Afghanistan are alive to the political implications of an outright assault on production. Both fear a backlash from poor farmers whose support can easily waiver. They recognise that an outright ban may fuel more conflict than current opium production levels sustain and may also do significant damage to the fragile livelihoods of the poor:

> The government's [of Afghanistan] strategy, with global backing, is to fight drug trafficking and to progressively reduce opium production over time. Where farmers are better off and clearly have viable alternatives, law enforcement measures can be taken. Where farmers are poor, or where landless labourers are involved, government policy is to develop viable alternatives for the rural poor, and only then use sterner measures to enforce a ban on opium poppy cultivation.
>
> (Ward et al., 2008: iii–iv)

Policy aside, *New Home, New Life*, which has been funded by DFID (amongst many other bilateral and multilateral agencies) for many years, is charged (in line with the preferred DFID and Government of Afghanistan joint opium substitution and eradication strategy) with representing a positive shift in Afghan agricultural practice towards crop substitution, while challenging the negative aspects of opium use and opium-related conflict.

Though significantly donor 'directed' in terms of thematic content, *New Home, New Life's* writers and producers feel little sense of overt external 'pressures' being applied to the drama's creative process. A sense of artistic freedom is perceived to characterise the drama, though this freedom inevitably occurs within the limiting bounds of strict production schedules and the said donor-directed themes. Artistic freedom aside, the BBC AEP was quick to recognise the need to invest in qualitative audience research capacity, which it developed from the outset (1993) of production. This capacity was essential to informing many of the themes picked up in the drama and reflected the dearth of quality data available relating to contemporary Afghanistan resulting from the constraints to field research generated by the Afghan–Soviet war (1979–1989). This critical investment served the purposes of providing qualitative research to support storyline development, impact assessment data and audience feedback.

BBC AEP audience research is conducted by an 'in-house' team of evaluators that variously comprises three to five staff members.[1] Field-based research occurs on a quarterly basis and combines two discrete processes. First, a conventional quantitative knowledge, attitudes and practices (KAP) survey of the type most often associated with measures or indicators of behavioural change, i.e., understanding of the dangers of landmines or identification of common diseases. Here, BBC AEP researchers are typically looking for increases—quarter on quarter—in audience knowledge relating to the core development themes of the production. Alongside this process sits an ongoing qualitative 'needs assessment' exercise that draws upon the methodologies of extended individual interviewing and focus group discussions relating to themes to be dramatised in future episodes of *New Home, New Life*. The production uses this assessment to identify storylines that are of relevance to the constraints faced by the wider audience. In turn, this allows some semblance of community 'participation' and audience engagement to be associated with the production, which in turn allows it to connect to key communication for development models and theories (see Chapter 1). The needs assessment process provides BBC AEP writers with a written resource (in the form of audience research evaluations) relating to ongoing 'donor' themes garnered directly from audience members.

Undertaking audience research of any form within Afghanistan has always represented a significant challenge for the production, though it will go to considerable lengths to secure qualitative audience inputs for future storylines. Unsurprisingly, the drama has faced continual conflict-related constraints on its audience research activities, as noted by the Country Director, Shirazuddin Siddiqi:

> ... the current insecurity has made it very difficult for the evaluation team to visit most of the southern provinces like Helmand, Qandahar, Zabul, and Oruzgan where the drama enjoys the most unique listener' loyalty. However, it is still possible to work in most or some parts of other provinces like Logar, Paktia, Khost, Nangarhar, Laghman and Kunar. The last round of needs assessment in February [2008] was conducted [in] the last three provinces. Generally, the team avoids insecure areas but tries to compensate for them by going to other similar [in terms of ethnicity] provinces.
>
> (Interview, London, 2008)

Inevitably challenging in terms of its collection, qualitative audience data plays a key role within *New Home, New Life* and is closely integrated into the production process. This is reflected in the dynamic relationship that exists between the productions' drama writers and producers, its audience researchers, external donors and technical experts. This relationship plays out in illuminating ways:

> ... our funders just come up with the topics. They say for instance, nutrition. UNICEF says nutrition is one of our issues, coughs and colds is another, diarrhoea is another, 'education for all', hygiene and sanitation, water is another, these are the topics, these are not ideas. What we do is create stories around these topics and they [donors] are just providing technical expertise. If there's a good way to treat diarrhoea and we are wrong a doctor comes from UNICEF and says 'you are wrong'. And he says 'this is not exactly the way you treat diarrhoea, this is the way'. We take that information from the specialist and then we *really* do

the wrong thing [typically informed by examples from qualitative field research] in the drama so that we can highlight the need for the right thing.

(Shirazuddin Siddiqi, Interview, Peshawar, 1998)

Whilst referring to a conventional 'E-E' dramatic device, the input of donors and technical experts, despite writers feeling they have complete freedom, is not as simple as a broad development theme being supplied. Indeed, the various donors that support the *New Home, New Life* drama have a significant input to the drama through ongoing engagement with the production process. Each episode of *New Home, New Life* is produced over a three-month period—from initial script development meeting to ultimate broadcast—and this process reveals a number of critical entry points for qualitative audience research. The production process has 12 discrete steps, including: (*a*) the initial script development meeting during which story ideas for 12 episodes of the drama are assessed; (*b*) a consultative committee meeting that assesses these storylines for informational and technical content; (*c*) synopsis writing establishes a content brief for 12 future episodes; (*d*) synopses are sent to funders and technical advisers for information; (*e*) scriptwriting, during which the synopses are fleshed out into full-length scripts by the writing teams; (*f*) the scripts are typed up; (*g*) the scripts are assessed during an editorial meeting; (*h*) script changes emerging from this meeting are undertaken leading to the finalisation of the script that will be used in production; (*i*) the drama is recorded; (*j*) playback of the recording occurs to assess quality; (*k*) following recording 'lead-time' of approximately six weeks occurs which represents the gap between finishing an episode of the production and its actual broadcast and (*l*) broadcast.

With regard to audience research the critical steps within the drama production process outlined above are the script development, consultative committee, synopses writing and editorial meetings. The script development meeting, which occurs on a monthly basis, enables writers, producers and audience researchers to build the broad themes that will be dramatised over the course of a month's worth of episodes. For example, with regard to an early 'opium substitution' storyline the script development process for episodes 223–234, broadcast in 1995, highlights a story idea for future elaboration:

Nek Mohammad [a well-respected elder] has planted some onions in his field, which last year was with Jabbar Khan [a landlord], he was planting opium on it. It turns out that his onions have been more lucrative than last year's opium. Jabbar Khan will later be astonished to see how much he has made out of onions, and later mentions the matter to [his overseer] Nazir.

(BBC AEP Script Development Notes, Episodes 223–234, 1995)

The script development process provides the BBC AEP's audience researchers with an opportunity to engage writers, editors and project managers in discussion of themes and issues emerging from the 'field'. Given that the funders of the drama are concerned with broad and ongoing themes, for example, DFID with opium substitution, UNICEF with child health or WHO with tuberculosis, funding agreements allow the audience research team a degree of certainty that over the course of a year or more such themes will be addressed within the drama and can therefore be picked up in the quarterly qualitative 'needs assessment' research process. The output from this meeting takes the form of a set of notes that are sent to both funders and technical advisors, along with an invitation to the specific consultative committee meeting in which technical feedback, as well as feedback on the cultural propriety of storylines, is provided to the scriptwriters. During such meetings, technical advisers may give very specific information concerning the various drama themes and audience researchers convey what audience members understand about them or what they might actually practice with regard to them. For example, issues such as the temporal fit between storylines and things such as seasonal diseases like coughs and colds or the agricultural cycle may be noted. Like the script development process, the consultative process results in extensive notes (in English) that again are circulated to attendees for any further comments. Following this critical input, the synopses of individual episodes are produced and again circulated amongst funders and advisers for feedback. The following extract from an early set of consultative committee meeting notes reveals how discussion of opium-related conflict between the two villages that feature in *New Home, New Life* (Upper and Lower Village) would develop:

[Summary of discussion] It was agreed that since land disputes are rarely settled amicably in Afghanistan, it would be better to return the storyline to the initial reason behind the conflict between Upper and Lower Villagers, i.e. cultivation of poppy crops [by Lower Village].

[Changes to storyline] The death of Khair Mohammad [a central character] will provide an impetus to settlement. The land dispute will be settled once there is recourse to the document [title deeds], which it will be found no longer exists. The matter will then come down to witness and it will be agreed that the uncultivated land in fact belongs to Upper Village. Following quick settlement of this issue, the matter will come down to opium substitution, i.e. Upper Village will take the lead in finding alternatives to the opium crop of Lower Village which they had taken the lead in [earlier] destroying.

(Consultative Committee Meeting Notes, 10 April 1996)

Though not explicit, the agenda of opium eradication and crop substitution reflected in the meeting notes above is significantly informed by research and is entwined in other themes such as title deeds to land, government corruption, access to water and opium-related conflict. This is in keeping with the multiple storyline threads one typically expects to find in good serial drama. Clearly, audience research can help to add qualitative detail to some of these issues, but it also reveals the problem of opium to be a stubbornly difficult issue to address. In this respect, much audience feedback is openly critical of the proposed 'solutions' that the drama offers and the utopian notions of 'abundance' that it is criticised for portraying. Such critique does not go ignored and consequently it is towards an analysis of critical audience feedback and the role of qualitative research that this chapter now turns.

Promoting 'Development Discourse': The Audience 'Speaks Back'

Inevitably, the *New Home, New Life* drama must tread a careful path in dramatising the issue of opium. The production recognises the presence of the opium situation in Afghanistan—the drug addiction, the issues connected to dry-land farming and crop substitution, the conflict that it can generate—and seeks to develop a moral landscape in which opium can be problematised. In pursuit of a 'realist' agenda, *New Home, New Life* uses audience research to add community-level voices, understandings and experiences to the creative mix. Qualitative research routinely adds colour to dramatic content and this is particularly evident when considering the role of lay medical practice within Afghanistan. In-depth analysis into the traditions of what Afghans describe as Greek (humoral) medicine, which equates health and gender to properties of heat and cold, have generated data that have been routinely fed back to writers for inclusion in the dramatisation process. For example, opium poppy husks (a by-product of opium production) are widely available in bazaars and are used extensively as a cough suppressant to 'cool' the body. Typically, husks are boiled with water and taken by adults and children alike to 'calm them', as reflected in both BBC AEP and ethnographic research data: '[Opium] has a bad effect ... it creates some serious problems in human blood [addiction]. Some mothers in our area give their children poppy in order to make them sleep but they're not informed and their children are becoming thin and weak' (BBC AEP, Interview, 2006).

> My young son developed a cough [most probably as a result of whooping cough] that made it hard for him to breath ... it just wouldn't stop. We live far from a doctor and so was giving him poppy to help him sleep at night. I wanted to just ease his problem, but he became very pale and was crying all the time. I suspected he may have a Hindu *jinn* (malicious spirit or ghost) sitting on him and the mullah gave me *tawiz* [an amulet to ward off evil] for him, but after some time he died.
>
> (Paktia Province, Interview, 1997)

Full of dramatic possibilities, such potential story-threads are routinely collected during periods of audience research.

Equally, audience research plays a critical role in determining if the audience understands storylines in the sense of 'reading' the drama for its dominant meanings, that is, those preferred and promoted by donors. This can be illustrated with regard to one of the production's early opium-related storylines (1996–1998) that was significantly misinterpreted by sections of the *New Home, New Life* audience (this being notably reflected in numerous male listeners' letters and endorsed through qualitative research follow-up): '... we hear from the drama that Upper Village has burnt the opium of Lower Village and destroyed their livelihood. Destroying crops leaves enemies without money or food and this seems like a clever way to make them weak' (Wardak Province, Interview, 1997).

So, along with intended consequences come unintended outcomes, and via audience research drama writers can quickly be alerted to misinterpreted messages and storylines so that corrective measures can be taken. This particular example was difficult to correct in the sense of it being impossible to 'withdraw the deed', but audience feedback did serve to inform writers that this strategy should not be repeated in other conflict-related story-threads. Misinterpretation of storylines is not uncommon amongst audiences who are unfamiliar with the delayed storyline resolution of serial narrative (see Appendix 2).

On a more mundane level, the biggest tension that audience research reflects with regard to opium relates to the availability of and access to physical resources. Here, the socio-economic dilemmas that farmers face in terms of whether or not to engage in opium production are reflected in the comments of a housewife from Helmand Province (a main centre of production):

> Poppy cultivation has lots of benefits, it grows quickly, some drugs [as described above] are made from poppy and a family can have a good life with the money that is earned through poppy cultivation. The negative points are that it has bad effects and creates health problems especially for young people and the person who has used it once like powder [heroin], he will not be able to leave it until death.
>
> (BBC AEP, Interview, 2006)

Similarly, qualitative audience research undertaken in the poppy growing province of Helmand finds listeners broadly supportive of poppy cultivation and aware of the difficulties of crop substitution:

> ... we can better prolong our life with money which is earned through poppy cultivation and also as we know that famine is in our country and we can't afford the expenses of other plants like wheat [which requires significant quantities of water to grow].
>
> (BBC AEP, Interview, 2006)

Simply stated, opium is easy to grow and here such storylines inevitably connect to the issues of access to and control of water resources.

Afghanistan is a considerable distance from any large bodies of water and contains large desert areas. It has a naturally dry climate and exceptionally low average annual rainfall. Accordingly, dry farming is practised, with wheat, barley and increasingly opium representing the most important 'cash' crops. In arid conditions, proper water management is crucial. Water is derived from snowfalls or else is channelled from rivers or underground sources into complex canal systems or *qanats* (Persian wells). Traditionally, villages share water rights in direct relation to the area that is under cultivation with the flow being controlled by the *mir-i-aab* or water caretaker, who maintains canals and water flows. The *mir-i-aab* is not paid, but instead receives a cut of each farmer's harvest in return for his labours. Decades of war have left such institutions significantly weakened and numerous watercourses destroyed. *Qanats* were purposefully destroyed during the Afghan–Soviet conflict (1979–1989) in an attempt to starve people off the land. Thus, water can be regarded as key to both agriculture and political stability. Indeed, control of water can result in local political and economic dominance and this is reflected in *New Home, New Life* through constant squabbles between the two villages over control of water. Here, a male listener from Khost Province notes that:

> In the drama, a bridge was blown up because of mines placed in the waterbed. The villagers came forward and decided that Fateh Khan [one of the chief protagonists in the opium conflict] has to pay for the cost of the bridge. Hats off to the village *jirga* [traditional council]. But the *woleswal* [district government officer] is sitting as a bottle and has nothing to do with anything. If everything is destroyed he does not bother about it, so the *woleswal* should quit his job and the place he has occupied in this drama should be given to someone else.
>
> (Khost Province, Interview, 1998)

Planting landmines in watercourses was a common strategy of the Soviet occupiers (1979–1989) and local warlords seeking to control access to water. Nonetheless, the passage above also highlights a positive response to one of *New Home, New Life*'s critical themes, namely, the strengthening of traditional conflict resolution mechanisms such as local *jirgas*. The respondent questions the lack of administrative action on the part of the *woleswal* and effectively pleads for 'better governance' on the part of this particular local official. With a perennially weak state, the indifference displayed by the administrator character is perhaps unsurprising. Nonetheless, such concerns are routinely fed back by audience researchers and ultimately addressed through formal meetings with *New Home, New Life's* creative staff, as outlined above, and through more ad hoc day-to-day contact with writers in the context of the *New Home, New Life* offices.

The discourses of opium substitution and good governance promoted by donors and taken up in radio drama are to varying degrees utopian and whilst audience research strives to make *New Home, New Life's* dramatic narratives more effective in terms of uptake and impact, the gap between development rhetoric and socio-economic realities remains wide. Here, listeners highlight the fact that the Afghan Government does little to practically support opium crop substitution and that poverty and other political forces leave little choice. Here a female listener notes that: 'The key factor is political affairs in Afghanistan, terrorism and Al-Qaeda's existence. Also people are compelled to grow poppy, because they do not have enough money to feed their family and for the needs of life' (BBC AEP, Interview, 2006).

Whilst advocating opium crop substitution over the past 15 years and highlighting the dangers of drug addiction, trafficking and inter-village conflict, *New Home, New Life* alone has been unable to effect a meaningful reduction in opium production, especially in areas such as Helmand Province where the extension of the state is weak and the influence of the Taliban is significant. Currently, opium production is at decade-long highs and shows little sign of abating. Nonetheless, charged with reflecting the social realities of Afghanistan, attempts to bolster opium substitution remain an enduring feature of its melodrama. Here, needs assessment lists a raft of potential storylines identified through qualitative audience research relating to opium substitution for writers to take up in the scripting process:

How can we store vegetables?
How can we cultivate saffron?
How can we protect our lands from rats and diseases?

Using the cropping methods of cultivating two crops simultaneously, what other things can we cultivate together?
What are the most beneficial vegetable crops?
Advantages/disadvantages of using insecticide?
Any advice regarding insecticides?

(39th Needs Assessment Report Episodes 2053–2088, December 2006)

Routinely, such ideas are channelled to writers who strive to transform these grounded audience concerns into informative, yet entertaining, radio drama. The connection between radio producers and consumers that is forged through audience research can highlight numerous inaccuracies, problems and misinterpretations. Yet, if we think back to Mytton's (1999) assertions regarding its central role to 'pro-social' or 'development-oriented' broadcasting we can see that such feedback provides *New Home, New Life* with an ongoing semantic and critical resource that enables it to constantly revise the tenor of its melodrama in pursuit of more effective behaviour change.

Nonetheless, it would be inaccurate to suggest that listeners only critique the drama's approach. Needs assessment work undertaken in 2006 in Heart, Ningrahar and Paktia Provinces identifies positive responses to opium substitution initiatives, with the provision of detail concerning useful crops and marketing strategies being fed back to writers:

In most [focus] groups the people revealed that they have stopped cultivating poppy and are cultivating wheat, garlic, onion, eggplant, carrot, tomato, radish, turnip, rice, ladyfinger, cauliflower, leek, spinach, sugar cane, and cucumber instead. They thought growing vegetables is better because besides selling them they can use them and give them to friends. They added that they don't have a problem transporting the crops to market but sometimes some of the produce gets damaged or decayed along the way because of the bad conditions of the roads. In this case, the farmers face losses. They said that they first take their share of the crop and then send the rest to market. The crops that grow quickly, leaving the land for the next cultivation, are cauliflower, string bean, cotton, sugar cane, rice, potato and leek. Cultivating onion has two benefits: fresh onions can be sold easily and dried onions bring in more income. The people said they have specified land for cultivating vegetables, and that they cultivate vegetables every year. Some complained of water shortage and that they only have water for one season's cultivation. Some groups said since their district is far from the city they sell all the produce in their own district because transporting it would be too difficult. One group said they usually take their potatoes and onions to Kabul but if they know they are not going to get much benefit there, they sell the vegetables in the farm to merchants.

(39th Needs Assessment Report Episodes 2053–2088, December 2006)

Inevitably, the drama is caught between portraying the benefits of opium substitution, the negative effects of drug addiction and lay medicines, and the reality of the situation in which poor Afghan farmers find themselves. In keeping with the directives of donors and the need to highlight better governance and more morally inclined livelihoods, *New Home, New Life* can be seen to offer listeners a range of alternative options and choices. Galavotti et al. (2001) suggest that in development terms, drama can provide much needed 'alternative narratives' that help viewers or listeners to imagine pathways out of 'perceived' negative traditional practices and cultural constraints. The extent to which these pathways align with neo-liberal development discourse remains a moot point. That given, both ethnographic and audience evaluation data suggest that the listeners of *New Home, New Life* still struggle to imagine alternative livelihoods. Though striving to be a catch-all, yet socially realist, representation of Afghan village life, astute listeners point out that unlike their own villages, the villages in *New Home, New Life* are blessed with a constant water supply (even though it is fought over), fertile land, a nearby forest, a health centre and also work opportunities. Many listeners complain that characters 'have it all' in terms of available resources and services. Nonetheless, such a bountiful representation allows for a very broad range of dramatic and thematic possibilities to be constructed, opium substitution included: '... when you think about it Upper Village is just like a European village because they've got everything, a school, a clinic, facilities and money whenever they need it!' (John Butt, Former BBC AEP Manager, Peshawar, 1997).

Similarly, a female listener rails against *New Home, New Life's* lack of socio-economic realism:

... the people [characters] who work in *New Home, New Life* are nice people and they have good professions. For instance, Mamoor Nek Mohammad has land and he works on it. Rahim is a teacher and Karim is a vet. Shakoor is a commandant and he's got arms and ammunition in his store. Sher Mohammad works for an NGO and would get a good salary. Sarwar is the son of the Khan [local landlord] who has a lot of land. Jandad and Zalmay are also well off. The drama's got lots of ways of life, but it never mentions the daily prices of food items, which are very high, or whether these people [characters] can afford them or not. There are people who don't have land and two or three of their family members have been killed in the war. Their children and wives are left behind and how would they find a living for their family? These are real problems!

(Ghazni Province, Interview, 1997)

Such criticism highlights the production's inability (despite its own discourse of social realism) to accurately reflect certain pressing economic or social realities. Being charged with identifying pathways from poverty New Home, New Life must dramatise a range of economic possibilities, which must be shown to be at least partially successful if they are to inspire the audience to follow suit. The many successes that the production's fictive characters enjoy in this or that economic pursuit stands in stark contradistinction to socio-economic realities, where real life routinely overwhelms, frustrates and confounds economic initiatives. Inevitably, the soap opera must also highlight failures and the potential harm that certain economic activities, such as opium production and use, help to create. By necessity, the context of such productions—as Rigbey suggests—tends towards abundance:

[Drama production] should probably be a few degrees more pleasant than real life. For all the misery you depict there should be laughter and warmth and a feeling of belonging in the soap opera which sadly may be missing from the lives of people.

(Rigbey,1993: 3)

In line with this assessment, utopianism can be identified as a core component of key development discourses such as opium substitution and the drama for development interventions that donors support. Nonetheless, if New Home, New Life is utopian it is also periodically shot through with heart-wrenching commentaries derived from listeners, a responsiveness to critique that is genuinely accepted and acted upon and an inquisitiveness that strives for social and cultural relevance. For the moment, achievement of some of the grander development objectives promoted by donors such as 'good governance' and licit agricultural production remain some way off.

Conclusion

The role that qualitative audience research seeks to play in closing the gap between radio producers and consumers can be understood in terms of improving content, making messages more efficient and storylines culturally appropriate. This to a very large extent 'does' happen and is considerably evidenced by the data presented in this chapter. Yet, the theme of opium proves a particularly stubborn issue to address and this in turn suggests that to a degree audiences still reject notions of state intervention in their affairs (Tapper, 1983). Afghanistan has always been a relatively weak state and local autonomy is fiercely pursued, to the point that in rural areas the state has almost no meaningful presence (see Chapter 7). In such a context, the partnerships forged between development donors and the BBC AEP, which manifests itself in radio drama, creates tensions that are both positive and negative. There is no dominant reading of the opium theme, but also no outright rejection, rather a simple recognition that as a livelihood strategy opium remains a preferred option.

Abrahamsen suggests that: '... specific technologies of global liberal governance [such as audience research] ... help produce modern, self-disciplined citizens and states that can be trusted to govern themselves according to liberal democratic norms' (2004: 1454). However, in a context such as Afghanistan, where much of the rural population has never really trusted or necessarily accepted the right of successive governments to intervene in their local affairs, the state remains largely unable to produce 'self-disciplined' citizens. Therein, opium production remains very much a path of self-determination that radio in and of itself could not realistically hope to address. Nonetheless, it can make contributions. Thus, qualitative audience research plays a complex role. In seeking to further the development goals of donors, but also in acting as a brake on the 'utopianism' of development discourse, in closing the social distance evident between producers and consumers and in challenging productions such as *New Home, New Life* to more accurately reflect the lived experience of listeners.

Note

1. During the period of research (1996–1998 and 2002) the team was comprised of male evaluators, but was lead by a woman, a Pashtun Pakistani woman called Shireen Sultan who has been critical to the production accessing the voices of Afghan women over the past 15 years. The conservatism that pervades Afghan society means that male researchers can generally only interview male informants and vice versa. Whilst, this may introduce a 'male bias' within the research process, the constraints of *purdah* (sexual segregation and control of women) make it very difficult to recruit female researchers capable of undertaking travel within Afghanistan.

References

Abrahamsen, R. (2004) 'The Power of Partnerships in Global Governance', *Third World Quarterly*, 25(8): 1453–1467.

Allen, R. (1985) *Speaking of Soap Operas*. Chapel Hill: The University of North Carolina Press.

Batchelor, S. and Scott, N. (2005) *Good Practice Paper on ICTs for Economic Growth and Poverty Reduction*. Paris: OECD.

CFSC/Rockefeller Foundation. (2002) *Communication for Social Change: An Integrated Model for Measuring the Process and its Outcomes*. New York: Rockefeller Foundation.

Crisell, A. (1986) *Understanding Radio*. London: Methuen.

Dornfeld, B. (1998) *Producing Public Television, Producing Public Culture*. Princeton: Princeton University Press.

Galavotti, C., Pappas-DeLuca, K. and Lansky, A. (2001) 'Modelling and Reinforcement to Combat HIV: The MARCH Approach to Behavior Change', *American Journal of Public Health*, 91(10): 1602–1607.

Gumucio Dagron, A. (2001) *Making Waves: Participatory Communication for Social Change*. New York: Rockefeller Foundation.

Hilmes, M. (1997) *Radio Voices: American Broadcasting 1922–1952*. Minneapolis: University of Minnesota Press.

Inagaki, N. (2007) *Communications for Development: Recent Trends in Empirical Research*. Washington DC: World Bank.

Lerner, D. (1958) *The Passing of Traditional Society*. New York: Free Press.

Long, N. and Villareal, M. (1994) 'The Interweaving of Knowledge and Power in Development Interfaces', in I. Schoones, J. Thompson and R. Chambers (eds), *Beyond Farmer First: Rural People's Knowledge, Agricultural Research and Extension Practice*. London: Intermediate Technology Publications.

Mytton, G. (1999) *Handbook on Radio and Television Audience Research*. London: BBC World Service Training Trust/UNESCO/UNICEF.

Rigbey, L. (1993) '*How to Write a Radio Soap Opera*.' Unpublished Mimeo.

Rogers, E. (1962) *Diffusion of Innovation*. New York: Free Press.

Roy, O. (1990) *Islam and Resistance in Afghanistan*. Cambridge: Cambridge University Press.

Singhal, A. and Rogers, E. (2004) 'The Status of Entertainment-Education Worldwide', in A. Singhal, M.J. Cody, E.M. Rogers, M. Sabido (eds), *Entertainment-Education and Social Change: History, Research, and Practice*. New York: Lawrence Erlbaum Associates, Inc.

Skuse, A. (2002) 'Vagueness, Familiarity and Social Realism: Making Meaning of Radio Soap Opera in South-east Afghanistan', *Media Culture and Society*, 24(3): 409–427.

Skuse, A., Fildes, J., Tacchi, J., Martin, K. and Baulch, E. (2007) *Poverty and Digital Inclusion*. New Delhi: UNESCO.

Tacchi, J., Fildes, J., Martin, K., Baulch, E. and Skuse, A. (2008) *Ethnographic Action Research Handbook*. New Delhi: UNESCO.

Tapper, R. (1983) 'Introduction', in R. Tapper (ed.), *The Conflict of Tribe and State in Iran and Afghanistan*. London: Croom Helm.

Tufte, T. (2002) *Soap Operas and Sense-Making: Mediations and Audience Ethnography*. Mimeo.

UNAIDS. (1999) *Communications Framework for HIV/AIDS: A New Direction*. Geneva: UNAIDS.

Waisbord, S. (2001) *Family Tree of Theories, Methodologies and Strategies in Development Communication*. New York: The Rockefeller Foundation.

Ward, C., Mansfield, D., Oldham P. and Byrd, W. (2008) *Afghanistan: Economic Incentives and Development Initiatives to Reduce Opium Production*. London: DFID/World Bank.

5

CONSIDERING MEN, MASCULINITY AND DRAMA

CHARLOTTE LAPSANSKY AND
JOYEE S. CHATTERJEE

Introduction*

The drama for development field is marked by a long and successful tradition of using entertainment media formats to promote women's empowerment. Innovative drama for development

*The authors wish to acknowledge the support of the members of BBC World Service Trust team in India who took time out to share their experiences and expertise with the authors. In particular, Jaspreet Kaur, Andy Bhanot, Sushree Panigrahi, Sonal Tickoo Chaudhuri and Yvonne Macpherson were key in providing support and insights on the two dramas. Thanks also to our colleagues at USC Annenberg who provided valuable feedback through various stages of this paper, especially, Sheila T. Murphy, Lauren B. Frank, Doe Mayer and Michael Cody. Thanks to the editors, Andrew Skuse, Gerry Power and Marie Gillespie whose comments and insights helped enhance the paper. Joyee S. Chatterjee would like to acknowledge the support of the USC Annenberg Graduate Fellowship grant, which facilitated the preparation of this article.

storylines have been used to encourage women to exercise rights to education, employment and health care and to speak out against domestic violence. However, despite the important role that some men play in ensuring gender justice, drama for development interventions have typically not placed as much emphasis on engaging male audiences in women's rights and gender-related health issues. In this chapter, we discuss the ways that drama for development interventions can contribute to the important work of involving men in promoting women's rights and decreasing gender-based health inequalities—especially in regards to reproductive health and HIV prevention—while challenging rigid gender norms. We start from the premise that mass media, and in particular entertainment media, is an important site for the construction and maintenance of these gender ideologies. Research on gender and media has shown that the mass media communicate powerful messages about cultural norms and values, including those related to gender (Bussey and Bandura, 1999; Morgan, 1982; Smith and Granados, 2009). Media, then, is often implicated in both shaping and reflecting dominant notions of gender and masculinity (Consalvo, 2003; Darling-Wolf, 2004; Hanke, 1990, 1998; Palmer-Mehta, 2006; Soulliere, 2006; Trujillo, 1991). However, it has also been used as a site for modelling alternative ideologies and behaviours, especially in fields of practice concerned with directed social change, such as entertainment-education (E-E), social marketing or drama for development.

In this chapter, we demonstrate the potentially powerful role of mass media—particularly drama for development—in asking male audiences to question, challenge and redefine traditional masculine norms. We start with the prevailing theoretical discussions on masculinity and men in relation to health and the development discourse, before we look specifically at the potential of drama to address these issues. We then point to promising frameworks and strategies from the field for conceptualising such programmes. Finally, we look closely at the production of *Jasoos Vijay* and *Life Gulmohar Style*, two recent BBC World Service Trust (BBC WST) drama interventions in India, drawing from interviews with the production and research team, to illustrate some of the key decisions and concerns that must be addressed when targeting a male audience. We situate this discussion about the role of drama for development in engaging male audiences within a larger trend in social development, which has turned increasing attention towards men and masculinity in the past decades. In doing so, we point to lessons from this larger discourse that can inform future drama for development programming.[1] Further, we advocate frameworks that recognise that both males and females must be involved in changing gender norms and relations, and this involves working with men and engaging the issue of masculinities in more intentional ways. We aim to emphasise gendered approaches to drama for development design—that involve men and boys, as well as women and girls—so as to enable drama for development programmes to go beyond treating the symptoms of gender inequality and address the underlying ideologies that lie at the root of gender-based health vulnerabilities.[2]

Drama for Development and Masculinity

Media effects theorists have argued that images and behaviours we see modelled in popular culture become part of a symbolic system that influences the creation of our gender identities (Bussey and Bandura, 1999; Morgan, 1982; Smith and Granados, 2009). In other words, media personalities and characters vastly expand the range of role models and potential masculine or feminine ideologies available to individuals in their immediate environment (Bussey and Bandura, 1999). Thus, entertainment media and popular culture are heavily implicated as a powerful institution that shapes and upholds gender relations.

Despite the fact that popular culture is often understood as rein-forcing traditional gender norms, many studies in the field of E-E have demonstrated the ways in which drama and other behaviour change media interventions can successfully model new attitudes and behaviours including those related to gender (Morgan et al., 2009; Papa et al., 2000; Rogers et al., 1999; Valente et al., 2007; Valente et al., 1994; Wilkin et al., 2007). Historically the social status and equity of women have been recurring themes in drama for development programming across the globe, especially given the overarching emphasis on HIV/AIDS, reproductive health and maternal health care in these programmes. From early experiments such as *Hum Log* in India, *Soul City* in South Africa and now *Afghan's Women's Hour* in Afghanistan, various communication interventions have addressed women's rights in the context of domestic violence, reproductive health and HIV prevention.

However, given the powerful role that entertainment programmes and media characters play in shaping gendered identities, attention needs to be paid to the ways we construct gendered male and female characters in the name of promoting health goals and women's rights. Given that these characters both communicate and construct gender norms, particular attention must be paid to the way masculinity is constructed if interventions are to shift male gender norms. Whether or not a drama for development programme specifically aims to address gender inequalities, gendered depictions and cultural gender norms communicated in the programme may in turn impact or even hinder the long-term programmatic agenda. As Wilkins and Mody note: 'relying on stereotypical images of gender roles ... may hasten short-term effects of campaign objectives in children's health or population projects but may curtail more progressive long-term goals towards shifting gender roles' (2001: 392).

Evaluations of several past projects illustrate this potential unintended negative consequence. For instance, *Naseberry Street,* an early drama for development intervention in Jamaica, featured a character that had multiple sex partners and numerous illegitimate children, who reflected the prevalent masculine norms. While the writers intended this char-acter to serve as a negative role model, a notable proportion of the male listeners reported not only liking the character, but indicated that they saw him as a 'positive' role model to emulate (Singhal and Rogers, 1999). Similarly, an E-E campaign to promote family planning among men in Zimbabwe found that while men's involvement in family planning increased, this was accompanied by an increase in the proportion of men whose reported decision making behaviour showed that they 'alone' had made the decision to practise family planning, excluding women from the con- versation (Piotrow et al., 1992). The evaluation report concluded: 'the campaign's reliance on traditional masculine images may have reinforced stereotypes about male decision-making and blurred campaign messages about the value of joint decision-making' (Kim et al., 1996: xi).

These studies indicate that, in attempting to propose 'solutions', programme content can unintentionally reinforce gendered norms of behaviour and power structures, which in the long run may create additional barriers to the public health outcomes sought. The ultimate result may in fact curtail or short-circuit the more progressive long-term agenda of promoting equitable gender roles and gender-equitable definitions of manhood. Thus, it is important to not only engage men, but to do so with a clear strategy and an understanding of the different ways that such interventions can both reproduce and challenge masculine norms.

Gendered Strategies: Engaging Men, Transforming Norms

Male involvement in gender equity and reproductive health programming can take many forms. At one end of the spectrum lie service delivery programmes that may give special attention to male clients, but do not address the root cause of inequality. At the other end of the spectrum are programmes that seek to affect transformative cultural changes in gender norms and expectations. We find the World Health Organization's (WHO) distinction between gender-sensitive programmes and gender-transformative programmes to be particularly useful for categorising different approaches to engaging male audiences (WHO, 2007). We briefly describe these two approaches below and then argue that drama for development interventions stand to benefit by taking a gender-transformative approach to involving male audiences.

Gender-sensitive programmes recognise the needs and realities of men within the context of gender norms and gender roles. These programmes often seek to correct the previous emphasis on delivery of reproductive health services to women by targeting men with information and services. They may also address men as partners, aiming to help men recognise their role as gatekeepers to women's access to reproductive health information and services and encourage them to take active roles in reproductive decisions, thus improving programme outcomes. For example, family planning interventions that involve both wives and husbands have been shown to be more effective than those that work solely with women (Terefe and Larson, 1993). These programmes can result in valuable benefits for men and women alike by helping to ensure that men and women receive gender-appropriate services. They do not, however, alter the fundamental inequalities and cultural gender expectations of manhood that contribute to health vulnerabilities, and thus do not affect the problem at the root. This can lead to results that may not pay off in the long run, as illustrated by the case of the E-E programme in Zimbabwe (discussed above) that increased male involvement in family planning *at the expense* of women's involvement.

Gender-transformative programmes, on the other hand, seek to transform gender roles to promote more gender-equitable relationships between men and women (WHO, 2007). Gender-transformative programmes enlist men as agents of social change, encouraging them to question and redefine gender norms and to re-invent social constructions of masculinity, resulting in positive behaviour and attitudinal changes. For example, *Program H*, implemented by Instituto Promundo and its partners in Brazil, aimed to tap into the 'alternative' voices of men who were already challenging traditional views of masculinity in low-income communities. Evaluation of the intervention (which included group education and a community-based poster and billboard campaign) showed positive changes in gender-equitable attitudes, as well as increased safe sexual practices among participants.[3] Other gender-transformative programmes that have shown promising results include *Men as Partners, Stepping Stones, The Strength Campaign* in the United States, and the *Respect Campaign* in Western Europe. Gender-transformative programmes such as these are likely to be more challenging to design, implement and evaluate because they call for a fundamental transformation of cultural norms, which are difficult to change and tricky to measure. However, such programmes, when well designed, have been shown to be more effective in achieving behaviour change among boys and men than programmes that may merely acknowledge or mention gender norms, such as programmes that take a gender-sensitive approach (WHO, 2007).

Gender-transformative programmes have the potential to address not only specific behaviours, but also the gender norms and inequalities that are at the root of women's and men's vulnerabilities. However, while there have been an increasing number of programmes in this area, mass media has not been an important element in much of this work. Yet mass media and popular culture have a clear role to play in achieving both gender-sensitive programme goals as well as gender-transformative ones. As we have argued here, drama for development is particularly well suited to affecting gender norms and questioning masculine ideologies and thus, is a potentially powerful tool for gender-transformative programmes. In addition, we argue that E-E interventions that do not intentionally model transformative gender relations or new masculine norms of behaviour, may in fact further entrench traditional gender ideologies and be counter-productive to the health goals at stake. Thus, it is important that drama for development programmes take a gender-transformative approach to messaging that engages male audiences and challenges rigid norms of masculinity, based on an understanding of the theoretical grounding that influences gender-transformative approaches.

Theorising Gender and Masculinity in Development Programmes

Many of the interventions with men and boys that take a gender-transformative approach are theoretically grounded in a social constructionist gender perspective, inspired by Connell's (1987, 1994) theory of gender and power. A social constructionist approach holds that gender norms—including the social expectations associated with manhood—are not biologically determined, but are cultural and social constructs perpetuated by social institutions like the family, schools, and—most importantly for the purposes of our discussion—the media. At any given time, there may be multiple constructions of gender roles and norms operating in the same culture. Connell (1987, 1994) suggests the use of the plural term 'masculinities' (as opposed to the singular masculinity) to denote the plurality of ways of 'being a man' that may exist in any given society, and this usage has become common in gender and development and public health literature (see Amaro, 1995; Campbell, 1995; Cohen and Burger, 2000; Quina et al., 1997; Rivers and Aggleton, 1998; Worth, 1989).

However, while a plurality of masculinities may exist, not all are valued equally in society. For example, a version of manhood associated with a dominant social class may have more power and legitimacy than others. Similarly, heterosexual masculinity is often granted more legitimacy and power than homosexual or bisexual masculine identities. Connell argues that there is a cultural ideal of masculinity—or a 'hegemonic masculinity'—that achieves dominance through cultural institutions and practices such as mass media, religious doctrine, political debate and educational policy. Hegemonic masculinity is thus the dominant model of masculinity that comes to define 'what it means to be a man' in a particular culture (Hanke, 1990). The power of this hegemonic masculinity is, according to Connell, assured through 'practices that institutionalise men's dominance over women', as well as over other men (including gay men, men of colour, unemployed men and so on) who do not embody this idealised version of manhood (1987: 187). Thus, hegemonic masculinity serves to maintain systems of social power in society that marginalise women as well as many men who do not ascribe to dominant norms. While boys and girls often internalise these hegemonic gender ideologies early in life, individuals can also react to, reject or redefine these norms, enacting alternative models of what it means to be a man or to be a woman. Such alternative models of masculinity may exist alongside the hegemonic norm, yet are not granted the same salience or power (Connell, 1987, 1994).

Again, the media is implicated in the construction and maintenance of this gendered social hierarchy. There is a substantial body of media research that has investigated the ways in which mass media recreate and reinforce notions of dominant hegemonic notions of masculinity (Consalvo, 2003; Darling-Wolf, 2004; Hanke, 1990; Hanke, 1998; Palmer-Mehta, 2006; Soulliere, 2006; Trujillo, 1991). While much of this research focuses on the negative impact of mass media and popular culture, a social constructionist perspective that recognises the existence of multiple masculinities, including hegemonic ones, also implies the possibility of change through intervention, thus suggesting a natural fit between gender-transformative programme goals and media genres such as drama.

Specifically, a gender-transformative approach grounded in social constructionist theorising is helpful in designing media interventions for two reasons. First, the notion of hegemonic masculinity (and the corollary notion that non-dominant alternatives exist alongside the norm) acknowledges the diversity in the lives of men and boys and the various positions of power and powerlessness that influence their enactment of masculinities, as well as their health behaviours and vulnerabilities. This allows for an acknowledgement of the ways in which men and boys are equally put at risk by the pressures to 'be a man' and that many men, especially those who either choose not to or cannot subscribe to dominant masculine ideologies, also face oppression or marginalisation as a result of prevailing gender norms. This recognition of the ways in which hegemonic manhood constrains the choices of men, and creates very real social consequences for them, can help us better understand how to work with men as potential allies and potential advocates for alternative masculine ideologies that place more emphasis on equality and non-violence.

Secondly, a gender-transformative approach suggests that dominant hegemonic masculinities can change and that alternative versions of masculinity exist and can be constructed. An acknowledgement that masculinities are dynamic, and not a singular monolithic construct defined entirely by the hegemonic masculine ideology, allows us to recognise that many men already play positive roles in the lives of their families and communities and already support women's rights in a number of ways. The plurality of masculinities also allows for the possibility of redefining and re-imagining masculinity not only through ongoing processes of social change, but also by intentional intervention to promote alternative masculine ideologies that value equality. For example, some programmes with gender-transformative goals have aimed to model a different masculine ideology by promoting a specific set of norms and behaviours that constitute what Barker terms 'gender-equitable' manhood. According to Barker (2000), 'gender-equitable men' are respectful to women and seek relationships based on equality and intimacy, rather than on sexual conquest; believe that men and women have equal rights; share responsibility with their partners for reproductive health and disease prevention issues; seek to be involved domestic partners and fathers who are responsible for at least some of the household chores and their children's care giving; are opposed to violence against women and homophobia (Barker, 2000; Pulerwitz et al., 2006).

An understanding of the plurality of masculinities and their relationships to power can aid in the creation of gender-transformative programmes that start from the premise that men and boys are allies (both current and potential) in promoting women's rights. In essence, then, gender-transformative media programmes should demonstrate a commitment to enhancing quality of life for men as much as for women. Our argument here is that drama for development programme goals need to go beyond gender-sensitive approaches that merely acknowledge the needs and realities of men or that simply target them with information and services. While a gender-sensitive approach may enable immediate gains by capitalising on exiting gender realities, they fail to truly engage, challenge and transform the gendered norms that are at the root of women's and men's vulnerabilities. Gender-transformative programmes no doubt entail a more concerted effort to question gender norms and re-invent social constructions of masculinity, but they may in turn prove more effective in achieving and sustaining long-term behaviour change among boys and men, with positive health outcomes for both males and females.

Although drama for development interventions that take a gender-transformative approach to masculinity are only just emerging, some recent mass media campaigns addressing male audiences point to the ways in which mass media, entertainment and popular culture can be used as sites for modelling gender-equitable alternative masculine ideologies or norms of behaviour. For example, Breakthrough's *What Kind of Man Are You?*, launched in India in 2005, used a series of public service announcements and a popular music video to encourage men to interrogate the dominant masculine norms that perpetuate domestic violence. Breakthrough's more recent campaign, *Bell Bajao* (Ring the Bell), encourages social intervention by male community members by ringing the doorbell when they hear domestic violence in their community in order to bring domestic violence to a halt. The campaign also includes extensive peer education and ground-level mobilisation to engage men in ending domestic violence and preventing the spread of HIV and AIDS in India. Groups like Soul City (South Africa) and Puntos (Nicaragua) have experimented with media-based drama formats to engage men with gender-transformative messages. For example, *Sexto Sentido*, produced by Puntos, is a weekly telenovela (soap opera) that airs in Nicaragua and other countries in Latin America. It challenges young men and women to question traditional gender norms, with particular emphasis on presenting alternative models of masculinity. The intervention, which also includes a phone-in radio show and community-based activities with youth, has been shown to be effective in promoting gender-equitable attitudes and HIV prevention behaviours (Solorzano et al., 2008). The success of serialised television series such as *Sexto Sentido* suggests that drama is a potentially effective format for grappling with some of these key issues regarding gender and masculinity and that similar interventions stand to make positive impact towards promoting gender-equitable masculinities.

Decades of quantitative and qualitative research in the field of E-E have indicated the power that the drama genre has to change attitudes, spark discussions, influence social norms and provide new behavioural models (Papa et al., 2000; Papa and Singhal, 2008; Rogers et al., 1999; Sharan and Valente, 2002; Sood et al., 2006; Storey et al., 1999; Valente et al., 2007; Yoder et al., 1996). This research and programme experience has contributed to a more complex understanding of how best to reach and engage audiences. The time is right to question the ways that storytelling and character development can be used in increasingly sophisticated ways to move beyond the promotion short-term behaviour adoption to challenging and modelling long-term transformative change in the norms, attitudes and behaviours of male audiences. In the next section, we look closely at the development of two BBC WST drama interventions in India to highlight some of the practicalities and key decisions involved in intentionally engaging a male audience.

Reaching Out to Men: Strategies from Indian Dramas

In recent years, the BBC WST in India has produced a number of large-scale campaigns that have specifically targeted men with messages concerning HIV and AIDS, as well as other health-related issues. In this section, we draw examples from two recent drama interventions produced by BBC WST to highlight some of the practical considerations of engaging male audiences. First, we describe how key decisions regarding format, storytelling and central character development were made during the production of *Jasoos Vijay* (2002–2006), a national television drama to better reach and engage male audiences. Making these decisions requires detailed knowledge of your intended audience, best gained through formative research. We also describe *Life Gulmohar Style* (a radio programme launched in 2009 to promote women's equality and reduce sex-selective abortion) as another example of the promising practices in formative research used by the BBC WST to better understand the male audience.

Jasoos Vijay

Jasoos Vijay (*Detective Vijay*), premiered on *Doordarshan*, India's national broadcasting station, in 2002, as part of a media initiative created in a partnership between the Indian government's National AIDS Control Organization (NACO), the Indian national broadcaster *Prasar Bharati*, the British government's Department for International Development (DFID) and BBC WST. The drama sought to combat stigma and raise awareness of HIV and AIDS in the Hindi Belt (north and central regions), an area of India considered highly vulnerable to increased HIV infection. The show was a fast-paced detective thriller focused on the adventures of Detective Vijay, an HIV-positive detective. At the time when the show went off the air in 2006, *Jasoos Vijay* was among the top 10 most watched programmes on television in India. Nielsen television monitoring data estimated that, during its final year, *Jasoos Vijay* reached a weekly audience of up to 15 million, and over the course of the year, it reached 70 million viewers.

Jasoos Vijay formed the backbone of a campaign with an explicit agenda to engage young, sexually active males in the urban and semi-urban regions of central and northern India. Formative research and careful analysis of the viewing habits of the intended audience—young sexually active men—helped shape creative and programming decisions about the storytelling format. As with any campaign, one of the first practical concerns was determining the media and format that would best reach and attract the intended audience. Television was a strategic choice to enable the campaign to simultaneously gain viewership and create awareness across a large population. National data on viewership trends and 'most watched' programming of the time indicated that crime drama and action-based shows enjoyed the highest viewership among young men in urban and semi-urban centres. Thus the programme—*Jasoos Vijay*—an action-oriented, fast-paced, high production value detective show took shape.

Detective Vijay's character was designed to appeal to an Indian male audience, and accordingly, he was portrayed as a handsome, intelligent, athletic man with a 'real taste for heroic action' who was 'always victorious'. However, as we have argued above, portraying alternative models of masculinity and specifically tailoring underlying messages so as to challenge traditional notions of what it means to be a man can have important positive outcomes in furthering health and gender equity–based goals. Therefore, even while Vijay portrayed the bravery and good looks of the classical male Indian hero, he was also depicted as sensitive, community-oriented and empathetic, and a champion of the rights of the marginalised. This characterisation allowed the programmers to place a positive male role model at the centre of narratives on gender equity–related issues such as domestic violence, rape and dowry. A corresponding strong female lead, Gauri, (Vijay's wife in subsequent seasons) who was equally intelligent, courageous and insightful helped model an equitable relationship.

Studies have suggested that—as in other cultures with highly developed media industries and storytelling traditions—the media environment in India (including movies, television, print and street dramas) provide models of masculinity and sexuality and is an important factor in the construction of Indian masculinity (Pelto et al., 2000). Specifically, studies of Indian mass media have indicated that typical media representations of masculinity tend to eroticise male dominance and female submission, thus communicating that masculinity and male sexuality are linked to male violence and the control of women (Derne, 2000). Although multiple versions of masculinity do exist in Indian culture (see Anandhi et al., 2002; George, 2006; Osella and Osella, 2000), hegemonic constructions of masculinity tend to dominate air time. Thus, Vijay and other positive male characters on the show served to evolve storylines that demonstrated the existence, and social validity, of non-hegemonic models of masculinity in the Indian context. As a positive role model, Detective Vijay's character posed a challenge to traditional media representations, creating a more negotiated depiction of masculinity and providing alternative models to male audience members who are navigating broader media environments as they construct their identities as men. Thus, the gender portrayal of *Jasoos Vijay* as a man who values equity was intended to spark conversations on gender norms and masculine behaviour.

Masculinity, as we described above, is not a monolithic construct and is influenced by socio-economic, cultural and geographical vectors. As such, gender transformative masculine models in a drama for development intervention must be culturally rooted in order to resonate with the audience. Vijay's character was based on extensive formative research and pre-testing with urban and rural audience members. Drawing on this audience feedback, the character was then informed by cultural realties. Vijay's cases were deliberately set in dispersed parts of northern India. Thus, through story arcs that played out over four episodes, producers were able to explore in depth how characters—both male and female—respond to HIV and AIDS, as well as related issues in a range of geographic contexts that featured diverse socio-cultural actors, local issues and indigenous responses. To add to the authenticity, filming of the episodes was done on location, encouraging audience members to identify with familiar locales and local issues.

Gender transformative programmes, as outlined above, need to address men not only as individuals, but also as actors who are implicated in social relations and embedded within communities. Here, *Jasoos Vijay* used an innovative participative audience feedback format to situate the content of the show within larger community discussions. Apart from encouraging audience members to try and solve the cases and send in their solutions to producers, each episode also included an audience interaction segment that directly raised questions and discussion on the issues addressed in each episode. These segments, which featured footage of audience members reacting to and discussing the issues addressed, was anchored by the famous actor Om Puri, who also provided commentaries on the key issues in epilogues for each episode. For instance, an episode tackled the issue of marital violence. The interactive section of that episode featured a group discussion between men and women in a village about whether or not it was right for a man to beat his wife and whther or not violence against women is a desirable masculine trait that should be emulated. These interactive elements, epilogues and commentaries were central to the design format and played an important function in contextualising the issues highlighted in the show as community concerns (whether related to HIV or AIDS-related stigma, health, gender or other social issues) and actively encouraged people to talk to others in their family and community about these issues.

One of the strongest impacts of *Jasoos Vijay* was that it sparked inter-personal discussion amongst its male viewers and this in turn was related to changes in HIV and AIDS-related knowledge, attitude, self-efficacy and behaviour (Chatterjee et al., 2009). Further, the results indicate that discussion with family members as opposed to friends played differential roles in promoting the relevance of the campaign. For example, sexually active males between the ages of 18 and 34 years were more likely to talk either to their family or to their friends about HIV prevention (Chatterjee et al., 2009). Qualitative assessment also repeatedly stressed the impact that the programme had on promoting spousal conversations, as well as conversations among men. These findings regarding interpersonal conversations are relevant as they highlight the potential of dramas like *Jasoos Vijay* in opening up spaces for peer reflection and influence.

Additionally, while the overall campaign received more than 23,000 audience letters, the bulk of these were in response to the *Jasoos Vijay* drama and were overwhelmingly from male viewers (87 per cent). In addition to soliciting information on HIV and AIDS, these letters indicated changes in HIV prevention–related attitudes and behaviour, as well as engagement with the characters of Vijay and Gauri and their relationship and an increased awareness of related issues such as gender discrimination. Focus group discussions and in-depth interviews also indicated young men's engagement with Vijay as a masculine role model and their reflection on the social pressures and norms faced by young men in India (see Chapter 10 for a related analysis of *Jasoos Vijay*).

However, issues such as reproductive health, HIV and AIDS are gendered, and therein are inseparable from the norms and behaviours dictated by prevailing gender attitudes. A failure to recognise this can result in counter-productive outcomes. Thus, it is important to take a purposeful approach to gendered representations and the portrayals of masculine ideologies, even if this is not the primary goal of the inter-vention. In the case of *Jasoos Vijay*, the drama's intentional use of alter-native masculine models and purposeful audience engagement around gender roles was one way in which the programme aimed to make an impact towards its broader goals of addressing HIV and AIDS. In turn, this points to the way in which rethinking and re-imagining masculinity through the media can become a key strategy in promoting health and gender equity–development goals.

Despite the clear ways in which *Jasoos Vijay* both engaged and intentionally rejected the conventions of masculine representation in Indian media, challenging and changing gender norms was not one of the intervention's stated goals and was thus not a focus in the evaluation of the programme. However, as we have discussed, one of the key elements of the drama was to model transformative male models and thus formal evaluation of impact on gendered norms could have yielded additional insights on the gendered dimension of HIV prevention and the role of drama in challenging hegemonic masculinity in the Indian context.

Life Gulmohar Style

Research and learning from *Jasoos Vijay* and subsequent media interventions has created a base of knowledge and thematic foundation for the subsequent development of the BBC WST's most recent drama intervention in India. *Life Gulmohar Style,* a radio drama launched in October 2009, aims to increase the value ascribed to women and girls in Indian society and reduce practices of discrimination and violence against women. The drama depicts the lives of a group of five friends (three women—Chanchal, Manavi and Sarah—and two men, Revant and Chirantan) and their family members and focuses on unravelling and challenging social and cultural attitudes that fuel gender inequalities (including health inequalities). Set in an urban Indian milieu, the drama follows the professional, romantic and familial lives of these five characters, all of whom come from distinct socio-economic and religious backgrounds, and who model a range of urban gendered realities. The primary target groups for this radio show are young female listeners of All India Radio's (AIR) popular FM channel, the BBC WST's broadcast partner. Given that behaviour change among women is not possible without also influencing other social actors that can constrain or enable women's choices, male relatives, as well as family members from older generations, are key secondary target groups for the drama.

A unique aspect of the show has been its strategic focus on men and their role in gender empowerment and reproductive health right from the start. This has required the development of formative and baseline research strategies that tap into cultural norms and male constructions of masculinity. The drama's baseline survey included an Indian adaptation of the Gender-Equitable Men (GEM) scale (as developed by Verma et al., 2008) to help measure men's attitudes and perceptions on gender equity, as well as to provide inputs that could inform storyline development. The GEM scale is a 24-item scale that measures the extent to which respondents ascribe to traditional masculine norms (Pulerwitz and Barker, 2008). The robust nature of this scale, its cross-cultural applicability (Verma et al., 2008) and the correlation between GEM-scale scores and sexual behaviours among young men suggested that it would be a useful tool for both measuring changes in attitude before and after a media intervention, but also as a formative diagnostic of the gendered attitudes of intended audiences.

The GEM scale was developed in Brazil specifically to evaluate the effects of *Program H* (as earlier discussed), an intervention that used workshops, trainings and community-based outreach campaigns to promote alternative voices of young men to challenge traditional gender norms. The GEM scale is unique in that it was created specifically for the evaluation of international development and public health interventions addressing gender and masculinity. The GEM scale is multifaceted and measures multiple domains of male attitudes towards gender norms, including attitudes towards domestic work and childcare, intimate relationships, sexual and reproductive health, disease and violence prevention and attitude towards homosexuality (Pulerwitz and Barker, 2008; Verma et al., 2008). In addition to Brazil, the scale has also been validated in India and Ethiopia and successfully used to evaluate and measure the impact of community-based interventions in these countries, as well as in Kenya and Nicaragua (see http://www.popcouncil.org/horizons/OR-Toolkit/toolkit/gem1.htm). These studies have found that respondents whose GEM-scale score indicates high levels of support for inequitable gender norms are significantly more likely than those whose scores indicate less support for inequitable norms to report physical and sexual violence against partners and symptoms of sexually transmitted infection, suggesting that the GEM scale does indeed tap in to attitudes that influence behavioural outcomes (Pulerwitz and Barker, 2008).

Although the scale has been tested and validated in the context of peer-based and community interventions, the baseline research for *Life*

Gulmohar Style is innovative in its use of the scale for formative and evalu-ative research in the context of a drama for development intervention. The application of this scale for development media campaigns is both innovative and promising for two important reasons. First, the scale has been shown to be an effective tool for pre-post evaluation of community-based programmes and in assessing the transformation of gender roles in target communities towards more gender-equitable norms. It thus provides a robust validated measure of gender-equitable attitudes among men that can help to assess specific changes in gender-equitable attitudes among male audiences following the intervention. Second, given the consistent findings from the field regarding the correlation of these mea-sures to behavioural indicators, it can also serve as a useful formative re-search assessment tool. The GEM measure can help programme planners understand the pervasiveness of dominant male attitudes among a particular intended audience. Knowledge of the extent to which male audiences are likely to be amenable to gender equity messaging can accordingly help programme planners craft appropriate messaging. Specifically, the GEM scale dimensions can be used to strategise in-tervention messages to specifically address those domains on which male audience members may show the most room for positive change. For example, if GEM-scale survey results indicate that the intended audience scores high for gender-inequitable attitudes in the domain of intimate relationships, but shows propensity for equitable attitudes in the domain of domestic work and childcare, a programmatic decision may be made to place more emphasis on modelling gender-equitable forms of intimacy in relationships.

In the case of *Life Gulmohar Style,* formative research indicated that among young men, while there was relatively greater support for women working outside the home, it is in the domain of women's space in the marital home that male attitudes are lower on the equitable scale (e.g., expectations that women will not be involved in issues involving their natal home/parents once they are married; that women should eat only after their husbands have had their meal). Thus, one of the core aims of *Life Gulmohar Style* is to strategically highlight women's issues within the marital home through the characters and storylines. The male characters in the show have been envisioned as complex individuals embedded in a web of social relations, and depending on the contexts, may display both enabling and/or constraining behaviour on gender-equity issues. This not only helps create realistic masculine role models embedded in everyday behaviour and relationships, moving away from binaries of oppressors and victims, but also actively recognises and encourages gender-equitable behaviour that already exists, while challenging those norms and behaviour that constrain women's lives.

Although, at the time of writing, *Life Gulmohar Style* is only at the beginning of its programme cycle, it has pioneered a number of promising formative research strategies. Functional tools like the GEM scale can provide key support to the creative and programme planning teams in conceptualising and evolving strong, culturally rooted messages that speak to the male audiences' particular gendered attitudes. The use of innovative measures like the GEM scale, in conjunction with other conventional attitudinal and behavioural measures, provides a more nuanced gauge of audience perceptions, beliefs and norms and is therefore crucial when designing gender-transformative media programmes.

Conclusion

Shifting development agendas and lessons from programme experiences over the past decades have brought to the forefront the need to promote health and social justice priorities in a holistic manner, by tackling entrenched social inequities and normative social practices. Research has shown that drama offers a rich context for helping varied audiences bring elements of gender norms into engaged conversation. Paradoxically, research has also demonstrated some of the possible pitfalls when the audience interprets the imagery in the drama in the wrong ways. Our analysis highlights the importance of developing more sophisticated and nuanced approaches to gender in development communication interventions that open spaces for audiences to embrace new cultural meanings relating to the role of men and masculinity.

In other words, there is a critical need to understand and engage men as social agents, deeply implicated in affecting in gender relations, and capable of catalysing individual and social change. As a development communication genre, the drama format is especially well suited to build and model alternative definitions of manhood. There is a need to design communication campaigns that ask male and female audiences to question, challenge and ultimately reshape traditional norms of masculinity in ways that not only benefit individual men and women, but also serve broader goals relating to social equity and justice.

An overview of international E-E intervention programmes undertaken by Sood et al. (2004) makes it clear that drama, as a genre, has found its biggest supporters among scholars and practitioners in the arena of health. Such interventions often rely on E-E strategies that call for the scripting of prototypical positive and negative characters who provide models of idealised behaviours in response to particular 'problems', such as HIV or domestic violence. It is, therefore, worth considering the degree to which these idealised characters may (intentionally or unintentionally) reinforce dominant visions of 'being a man'. Careful monitoring and research is needed to systematically assess the degree to which drama interventions and their gendered character portrayals affect cultural norms surrounding gender.

Our argument here is, specifically, for the need to take a gender-transformative programmatic approach to drama for development, whether in design and creative development, the design of formative research tools or impact evaluation. As a report by the International Center for Research on Women and Instituto Promundo notes: 'programs that fail to address social norms [gender included] limit themselves to treating the symptoms without addressing some of the underlying causes of poor health' (2007: 2). Concurrently, there is a very real need to be more gender aware in formative and evaluative research practices and develop research methodologies (including the use of innovative qualitative and participatory approaches that go beyond surveys and focus groups) that are capable of capturing and analysing subtle changes in cultural gender norms. Then, hopefully, we will be better equipped to not only promote behaviour change, but also address the gender inequalities that are the root cause of many risk behaviours.

Notes

1. Here, we are not advocating a focus on men and masculinity at the expense of addressing the needs of women. In recent years, great strides have been made towards ensuring

that development programmes do not overlook the gendered realities of women. We applaud these efforts and recognise the importance of their continuation. We do, however, point to a need to ensure men continue to be part of the conversation.

2. It is now widely accepted that health is a gendered issue. Gender roles and gender norms—defined here as the differential social expectations for appropriate behaviours of men and women—affect behaviours that have sexual and reproductive health-related consequences for both women and men (see Amaro, 1995; Campbell, 1995; Cohen and Burger, 2000; Quina et al., 1997; Rivers and Aggleton, 1998; Worth, 1989). Women's subordinate position in society and their unequal power in intimate relationships contribute to women's vulnerability to a number of health risks, including maternal mortality, sexually transmitted infections, HIV and AIDS, as well as domestic violence (Beadnell et al., 2000; Go et al., 2003; Maman et al., 2002: Pulerwitz et al., 2002). While women are placed at risk by the social expectations men and boys are expected to live up to every day, equally important gender norms also directly influence behaviours that affect men's own health (Barker, 2000; Kimmel, 2000; Morokoff, 2000; Noar and Morokoff, 2001; Pleck et al., 1993; Rivers and Aggleton, 1998). Young men often face normative pressures that encourage sexual risk-taking as a validation of manhood. For example, holding rigid beliefs about masculinity (e.g., that men need more sex than women do, that men should dominate women, etc.) is one of the strongest predictors of risk-taking behaviours, including substance abuse, violence (against women, as well as other men) and unprotected sex (Courtenay, 1998; Pulerwitz and Barker, 2008).

3. An evaluation of the programme results in two communities found that self reported symptoms of sexually transmitted infections declined from 23 per cent to 4 per cent in one community and from 30 per cent to 6 per cent in the other. Condom use increased from 58 per cent to 87 per cent. At six months there was significant positive change in gender-equitable attitudes among male participants, and these changes were maintained at one year follow-up (Pulerwitz et al., 2006).

References

Amaro, H. (1995) 'Love, Sex, and Power: Considering Women's Realities in HIV Prevention', *American Psychologist*, 50(6): 437–447.

Anandhi, S., Jeyaranjan, J. and Krishnan, R. (2002) 'Work, Caste and Competing Masculinities: Notes from a Tamil Village', *Economic and Political Weekly*, 26: 1–16.

Barker, G. (2000) 'Gender Equitable Boys in a Gender Inequitable World: Reflections from Qualitative Research and Program Development with Young Men in Rio de Janeiro', *Sexual and Relationship Therapy*, 15(3): 263–282.

Beadnell, B., Baker, S., Morrison, D. and Knox, K. (2000) 'HIV/STD Risk Factors for Women with Violent Male Partners', *Sex Roles*, 42(7/8): 661–689.

Bussey, K. and Bandura, A. (1999) 'Social Cognitive Theory of Gender Development and Differentiation', *Psychological Review*, 106(4): 676–713.

Campbell, C. (1995) 'Male Gender Roles and Sexuality: Implications for Women's AIDS Risk and Prevention', *Social Science and Medicine*, 41(2): 197–210.

Chatterjee, J., Bhanot, A., Frank, L., Murphy, S. and Power, G. (2009) 'The Importance of Interpersonal Discussion and Self-efficacy in Knowledge, Attitude, and Practice Models', *International Journal of Communication*, 3: 607–634.

Cohen, S. and Burger, M. (2000) *Partnering: A New Approach to Sexual and Reproductive Health*. New York: United Nations Population Fund.

Connell, R. (1987) *Gender and Power*. Stanford: Stanford University Press.

———. (1994) *Masculinities*. Berkeley: University of California Press.

Consalvo, M. (2003) 'The Monsters Next Door: Media Constructions of Boys and Masculinity', *Feminist Media Studies*, 3(1): 27–44.

Courtenay, W. (1998) 'Better to Die Than Cry? A Longitudinal and Constructionist Study of Masculinity and the Health Risk Behavior of Young American Men', *Dissertation Abstracts International*, 59(08A): Publication Number 9902042.

Darling-Wolf, F. (2004) 'Women and New Men: Negotiating Masculinity in the Japanese Media', *The Communication Review*, 7: 285–303.

Derne, S. (2000) *Movies, Masculinity and Modernity. An Ethnography of Men's Film Going in India*. Westport: Greenwood.

George, A. (2006) 'Reinventing Honorable Masculinity; Discourses from a Working-class Indian Community', *Men and Masculinities*, 9: 35–51.

Go, V., Sethulakshmi, C., Bentley, M., Sivaram, S., Srikrishnan, A., Soloman, S. and Celentano, D. (2003) 'When HIV-Prevention Messages and Gender Norms Clash: The Impact of Domestic Violence on Women's HIV Risk in Slums of Chennai, India', *AIDS and Behavior*, 7(3): 263–272.

Hanke, R. (1990) 'Hegemonic Masculinity in Thirty-Something', *Critical Studies in Mass Communication*, 7(3): 231–248.

———. (1998) 'The "Mock-Macho" in Situation Comedy: Hegemonic Masculinity and its Reiteration', *Western Journal of Communication*, 62(1): 74–93.

International Center for Research on Women and Instituto Promundo. (2007) 'Engaging Men and Boys to Achieve Gender Equality: How can we Build on What we have Learned'?, paper presented at International Center for Research on Women, Washington, DC.

Kim, Y., Marangwanda, C. and Kols, A. (1996) *Involving Men in Family Planning. The Zimbabwe Male Motivation and Family Planning Method Expansion Project, 1993–1994*. Report submitted to Baltimore, Johns Hopkins School of Public Health, Center for Communication Programs.

Kimmel, M. (2000) *The Gendered Society*. Oxford: Oxford University Press.

Maman, S., Mbwambo, J., Hogan, N., Kilonzo, G., Campbell, J., Weiss, E. and Sweat, M. (2002) 'HIV-positive Women Report More Lifetime Partner Violence: Findings from a Voluntary Counseling and Testing Clinic in Dar es Salaam, Tanzania', *American Journal of Public Health*, 92: 1331–1337.

Morgan, M. (1982) 'Television and Adolescents' Sex Role Stereotypes: A Longitudinal Study', *Journal of Personality and Social Psychology*, 43(5): 947–955.

Morgan, S., Movius, L. and Cody, M. (2009) 'The Power of Narratives: The Effect of Entertainment Television Organ Donation Storylines on the Attitudes, Knowledge, and Behaviors of Donors and Non-donors', *Journal of Communication*, 59: 135–151.

Morokoff, P. (2000) 'A Cultural Context for Sexual Assertiveness in Women', in C. Travis and J. White (eds), *Sexuality, Society, and Feminism*. Washington, DC: American Psychological Association.

Noar, S. and Morokoff, P. (2001) 'The Relationship between Masculinity Ideology, Condom Attitudes, and Condom Use Stage of Change: A Structural Equation Modeling Approach', *International Journal of Men's Health*, 1(1): 43–58.

Osella, F. and Osella, C. (2000) 'Migration, Money and Masculinity in Kerala', *Journal of the Royal Anthropological Institute*, 6: 117–133.

Palmer-Mehta, V. (2006) 'The Wisdom of Folly: Disrupting Masculinity in *King of the Hill*', *Text and Performance Quarterly*, 26(2): 181–198.

Papa, M. and Singhal, A. (2008) 'How Entertainment-Education Programs Promote Dialogue in Support of Social Change', paper presented at 58th Annual International Communication Association Conference, Montréal, Canada.

Papa, M., Singhal, A., Law, S., Pant, S., Sood, S. and Rogers, E. (2000) 'Entertainment-Education and Social Change: An Analysis of Parasocial Interaction, Social Learning, Collective Efficacy, and Paradoxical Communication', *Journal of Communication*, 50: 31–55.

Pelto, P., Joshi, A. and Verma, R. (2000) *Development of Sexuality and Sexual Behavior among Indian Males: Implications for the Reproductive Health Programme*. New Delhi: Population Council.

Piotrow, P., Kincaid, D., Hindin, M., Lettenmaier, C., Kuseka, I., Silberman, T., Zinanga, A., Chikara, F., Adamchak, D. and Mbizvo, M. (1992) 'Changing Men's Attitudes and Behavior: The Zimbabwe Male Motivation Project', *Studies in Family Planning*, 23(6): 365–375.

Pleck, J., Sonenstein, F. and Ku, L. (1993) 'Masculinity Ideology: Its Impact on Adolescent Males' Heterosexual Relationships', *Journal of Social Issues*, 49(3): 11–29.

Pulerwitz, J. and Barker, G. (2008) 'Measuring Attitudes Towards Gender Norms among Young Men in Brazil: Development and Psychometric Evaluation of the GEM Scale', *Men and Masculinities*, 10: 322–338.

Pulerwitz, J., Amaro, H., De Jong, W., Gortmaker, S. and Rudd, R. (2002) 'Relationship Power, Condom Use, and HIV Risk among Women in the US', *AIDS Care*, 14(6): 789–800.

Pulerwitz, J., Barker, G., Segundo, M. and Nascimento, M. (2006) *Promoting More Gender-Equitable Norms and Behaviors among Young Men as an HIV/AIDS Prevention Strategy*. Washington, DC: Population Council.

Quina, K., Harlow, L., Morokoff, P. and Saxon, S. (1997) 'Interpersonal Power and Women's HIV Risk', in N. Goldstein and J. Manlowe (eds), *The Gender Politics of HIV/AIDS: Perspectives on the Pandemic in the United States*. New York: New York University Press.

Rivers, K. and Aggleton, P. (1998) *Men and the HIV Epidemic, Gender and the HIV Epidemic*. New York: United Nations Development Programme.

Rogers, E., Vaughan, P., Swalehe, R., Rao, N., Svenkerud, P. and Sood, S. (1999) 'Effects of an Entertainment-Education Radio Soap Opera on Family Planning Behavior in Tanzania', *Studies in Family Planning*, 30(3): 193–211.

Sharan, M. and Valente, T. (2002) 'Spousal Communication and Family Planning Adoption: Effects of a Radio Drama Serial in Nepal', *International Family Planning Perspectives*, 28: 16–25.

Singhal, A. and Rogers, E. (1999) *Entertainment-Education: A Communication Strategy for Social Change*. Mahwah, NJ: Lawrence Erlbaum Associates.

Smith, S. and Granados, A. (2009) 'Content Patterns and Effects Surrounding Sex-Role Stereotyping on Television and Films', in J. Bryant and D. Zillmann (eds), *Media Effects: Advances in Theory and Research*. Mahwah, NJ: Lawrence Erlbaum Associates.

Solorzano, I., Bank, A., Pena, R., Espinoza, H., Ellsber, M. and Pulerwitz, J. (2008) *Catalyzing Personal and Social Change around Gender, Sexuality, and HIV: Impact Evaluation of Puntos de Encuentro's Communication Strategy in Nicaragua*. Washington, DC: Population Council.

Sood, S., Menard, T. and Witte, K. (2004) 'The Theory behind Entertainment-Education', in A. Singhal, M. Cody, E. Rogers and M. Sabido (eds), *Entertainment-Education and Social Change: History, Research, and Practice*. Mahwah, NJ: Lawrence Erlbaum Associates.

Sood, S., Shefner-Rogers, C. and Sengupta, M. (2006) 'The Impact of a Mass Media Campaign on HIV/AIDS Knowledge and Behavior Change in North India: Results from a Longitudinal Study', *Asian Journal of Communication*, 16(3): 231–250.

Soulliere, D. (2006) 'Wrestling with Masculinity: Messages about Manhood in the WWE', *Sex Roles*, 55(1–2): 1–11.

Storey, D., Boulay, M., Karki, Y., Heckert, K. and Karmacharya, D. (1999) 'Impact of the Integrated Radio Communication Project in Nepal, 1994–1997', *Journal of Health Communication*, 4(4): 271–294.

Terefe A. and Larson C. (1993) 'Modern Contraception Use in Ethiopia: Does Involving Husbands make a Difference'?, *American Journal of Public Health*, 83: 1567–1571.

Trujillo, N. (1991) 'Hegemonic Masculinity on the Mound: Media Representations of Nolan Ryan and American Sports Culture', *Critical Studies in Mass Communication*, 8(3): 290–308.

Valente, T., Kim, Y., Lettenmaier, C., Glass, W. and Dibba, Y. (1994) 'Radio Promotion of Family Planning in the Gambia', *International Family Planning Perspectives*, 20(3): 96–100.

Valente, T., Murphy, S., Huang, G., Gusek, J., Greene, J. and Beck, V. (2007) 'Evaluating a Minor Storyline on ER about Teen Obesity, Hypertension, and 5 A Day', *Journal of Health Communication*, 12(6): 551–566.

Verma, R., Pulerwitz, J., Mahendra, V., Khandekar, S., Singh, A., Das, S., Mehra, S., Nura, A. and Barker, G. (2008) *Promoting Gender Equity as a Strategy to Reduce HIV Risk and Gender Based Violence among Young Men in India*. Washington, DC: Population Council.

Wilkins, K. and Mody, B. (2001) 'Reshaping Development Communication: Developing Communication and Communicating Development', *Communication Theory*, 11(4): 385–396.

Wilkin, H., Valente, T., Murphy, S., Cody, M., Huang, G. and Beck, V. (2007) 'Does Entertainment-Education Work with Latinos in the United States? Identification and the Effects of a Telenovela Breast Cancer Storyline', *Journal of Health Communication*, 12(5): 455–469.

World Health Organization. (2007) *Engaging Men and Boys in Changing Gender-Based Inequity in Health: Evidence from Programme Interventions*. Geneva: WHO.

Worth, D. (1989) 'Sexual Decision-making and AIDS: Why Condom Promotion among Vulnerable Women is Likely to Fail', *Studies in Family Planning*, 20: 297–307.

Yoder, P., Hornik, R. and Chirwa, B. (1996) 'Evaluating the Program Effects of a Radio Drama about AIDS in Zambia', *Studies in Family Planning*, 27(4): 188–203.

6

TELLING OTHER PEOPLE'S STORIES

CULTURAL TRANSLATION IN DRAMA FOR DEVELOPMENT

**Emily LeRoux-Rutledge,
Gerry Power and Carol Morgan**

Introduction

This chapter explores the question of how 'non-local' dramatists, working on drama for development projects, negotiate the challenges of drama production in cultures which are not their own. Specifically, it seeks to understand how dramatists working on BBC World Service Trust (BBC WST) productions go about 'translating' their ideas into other cultures. The chapter posits that dramatists attempt to develop a degree of 'cultural literacy' in order to assist them in their role as 'cultural translators' or 'brokers'. It then explores how cultural literacy impacts on their creative decision-making during the drama production process. Because of the various tensions placed on dramatists by diverse stakeholders, including audiences, media partners, donors and governments, the chapter proposes a conceptual framework onto which the creative decisions made by dramatists may be mapped. The framework highlights why dramatists sometimes choose to reinforce and sometimes choose to challenge locally grounded cultural norms.

Various organisations, such as The Soul City Institute (www. soulcity.org.za), Sesame Workshop (www.sesameworkshop.org) and the BBC WST (www.bbcworldservicetrust.org), have been involved in the production of drama for development for a number of years. Although different organisations take different approaches to drama production, many face common challenges. One challenge has to do with 'cultural translation'. When creating drama for development, it is often the case that dramatists' lived realities do not closely resemble those of their audience. For example, in *Dramas of Nationhood*, Abu-Lughod notes that, in Egypt, 'those who produce and criticize television [...] are part of the intelligentsia', unlike most viewers (2005: 10). Experienced dramatists may even come from different countries, as is the case with many BBC WST productions. For example, when the BBC WST began HIV and AIDS work in Cambodia in 2005, Cambodia had no locally produced Khmer television drama serials, although successful 'pro-social' radio drama serials had been developed by organisations such as Health Unlimited and Population Services International (PSI). This meant it was necessary to bring in a dramatist with television experience from outside Cambodia—in this case, a former executive producer of the popular British television drama *Eastenders*. Such examples highlight the value of understanding how dramatists go about translating development 'ideas' and 'ideals'—as well as media genres—into different cultures. They also highlight the value of exploring how dramatists come to understand the cultures in which they are working, and how they engage in dramatic decision-making during the production process. Questions of power and negotiation within production teams also warrant close exploration.

In addressing notions of 'translation', negotiation and brokerage in the dramatisation process, this chapter examines a number of popular BBC WST dramas produced in Cambodia, Burma, Pakistan, India, Bangladesh and Nigeria. Specifically, it draws upon data from a series of in-depth interviews conducted with seven dramatists who have worked, or are currently working, on these productions. Four of the dramatists were born in Britain, one in the Caribbean and one in Australia. The final dramatist was born in India, and worked on the popular Indian television drama *Jasoos Vijay* (see Chapter 5 and 10). She provided a basis of comparison for the other dramatists, who were not born in the countries in which their dramas were aired. The interviews formed part of an ongoing dialogue in which many of the dramatists were interviewed multiple times. The dramatists all had extensive drama production experience, and worked with local production and writing teams to produce their respective outputs (see Appendix 1).

The dramas in question included the television series *Taste of Life,* which followed the lives and loves of Cambodian nursing college students. It was designed to address issues around HIV and AIDS, and maternal and child health. *Thabyegone Ywa (Eugenia Tree Village)* was a radio drama for listeners in rural Burma. It included storylines about HIV prevention and stigma, malaria, tuberculosis, acute respiratory infection and alcohol abuse. It also addressed citizenship and livelihood issues pertinent to the lives of people in Burma, such as debt management, drug use, trafficking, petty corruption and the environment. *Piyar ka Passport (Passport to Love)*, set in Pakistan, was a radio drama that looked at the issue of forced marriage on a transnational basis (see Chapter 11). It followed the story of a diasporic family moving from Britain back to Pakistan, and the marriages of the family's daughters. The goal of the drama was to stimulate debate around forced marriage. *Jasoos Vijay* followed the life of an HIV-positive detective in rural India, as he solved mysteries and tackled issues relating to HIV and AIDS. The drama set in Bangladesh, which is titled *Bishaash* and still in production, is designed to engage people with English language learning. Finally, *Wetin Dey (What's Up?)*, set in peri-urban Nigeria, was a television drama with a varied cast of characters that focused on HIV and AIDS issues, and the broader impact of the HIV and AIDS epidemic on Nigerian society. These dramas reflect a range of different cultures, and were produced for both television and radio, yet they display common challenges around issues of production, dramatisation and cultural translation. These challenges are further explored in the following pages.

'Production Development': Critiques and Challenges

Various media scholars have recommended examining institutional cultures of production and consumption (Hall, 1980; Gillespie, 2005). Consumption has been much studied by those, such as Livingstone, who recognise the importance of audience interpretation (1990). Production, however, has received less attention. Dornfeld, in *Producing Public Television*, stresses the importance of production, noting, 'production is a process of negotiation through which ... meanings emerge into public cultural form' (1998: 15). Production has been focused on by scholars such as Cantor (1988), who looked at institutional cultures of film production within the United States. Few scholars have looked at the dynamics of production in a drama for development context, however, and fewer still (this volume excluded) have looked specifically at the BBC WST, despite its considerable history in drama for development over the last 10 years. There are a number of exceptions, including Sood and Nambiar (2006) and Cody et al. (2004). Most notably, Skuse (2007) has examined cultures of production in the context of the BBC Afghan radio drama *New Home, New Life* and Mandel (2002) has studied the creation of the first Kazakh soap opera, produced by the Trust's predecessor, BBC Marshall Plan of the Mind (MPM).

Cultures of production are particularly important to consider in the context of drama for development because of the complexity of stakeholder involvement. It is not unusual for drama for development productions to have managers or producers from one country and writers from another. In addition, donor organisations, such as the UK Department for International Development (DFID), are usually the primary sources of funding, becoming, effectively, 'the clients' for such productions. This creates a unique set of production circumstances and demands not necessarily present in mainstream television drama (see Chapters 9 and 11). This chapter focuses on dramatists specifically, because they are at the heart of drama production practices, which in turn drive the creation of cultural representations (Dornfeld, 1998).

Dramatists at the BBC WST are often 'non-local', and this idea can be problematic for some.[1] However, the notion of some form of cultural distance between media consumers and producers is far from new. Those involved in television production tend to be from the ranks of the educated elite, and it has been hypothesised that they often share the 'dominant codes' of those in power (Hall, 1980). Abu-Lughod sees the TV audience–producer relationship as a relationship between 'a certain elite who, among other things, produces national television for imagined audiences [...] who not only appreciate and enjoy, but critically interpret, select, and evaluate what the elites produce, always in the context of their everyday lives' (2005: 12). Thus, even in a national context, there can be considerable distance evident between producers and consumers. Moreover, most drama for development productions (including those produced by the BBC WST) are produced with the assistance of local production teams, and many such productions that engage 'non-local' expertise prove to be hugely successful with audiences.

It is unlikely, however, that these dramas would have had such appeal had the dramatists not first, in some way, become familiar with the countries and cultures in which they were working. This is, in part, because of audience demand for drama that is authentic and credible. Authenticity does not necessarily equal 'social realism', but in some contexts the two are related. Livingstone (1990) notes that realism is often an important feature for audience engagement and has identified it as one of the key reasons why people watch or listen to soap opera. She remarks that: 'Viewers describe being able to relate to the events, situations and problems portrayed in the soap opera, valuing the realistic true-to-life characters, realistic true-to-life events, situations and problems, and the soap's concern with topical or relevant social problems' (Livingstone, 1990: 56).

Yet, Livingstone also acknowledges that viewers may like to engage in escapism, finding pleasure in the 'realistic illusion' (1990). Moreover, not all countries have the same traditions of mass mediated social realism. Perhaps what viewers and listeners seek is a sense of credibility and authenticity that forges a meaningful connection through universal themes of love, life and death. In any case, for a dramatist working in an unfamiliar culture, ensuring that a new drama has a realistic, credible or authentic feel can be challenging. Accordingly, part of the challenge for these dramatists is to develop a degree of 'cultural familiarity' or 'cultural literacy' within the culture they are charged with representing and, in some cases, challenging.

Culture is a complex and ever-shifting phenomenon. It becomes even more complex when one is charged with examining the creation of cultural products—such as drama—in different cultural contexts. Porter and Samovar suggest that culture is the collective equivalent of personality, and can be defined as: 'The deposit of knowledge, experience, beliefs, values, attitudes, meanings, hierarchies, religion, timing, roles, special relations, concepts of the universe, and material objects and possessions acquired by a large group of people in the course of a generation' (1998: 19; cited in Servaes, 1999).

Relating this to processes of communication, Hirsch conceives of 'cultural literacy' as the 'background knowledge' required for meaningful communication in any given culture (1988: 2). Likewise, Schirato and Yell define it as 'a knowledge of meaning systems and an ability to negotiate those systems within different cultural contexts' (2000: 1). They maintain: 'It is virtually impossible to describe and analyse what is happening in any communication context or practice without using the concept of cultural literacy' (Schirato and Yell, 2000: 1). Dramatists working on development-oriented productions must often acquire a degree of 'cultural literacy' quickly. There is rarely an opportunity to spend a significant amount of time 'learning the culture' (in the way an anthropologist would) and yet the paradox is that they must create 'cultural products' for a local audience using local cultural frames. One important source of insight for dramatists is audience research, which has been widely acknowledged as critical in the Entertainment-Education field (Singhal and Rogers, 1999). The degree of cultural familiarity, or literacy, that dramatists are able to acquire, and the way in which they acquire it, is central to understanding how dramatists respond to the key 'cultural translation' challenges that they face in pursuit of development and social change objectives.

In this context, 'cultural translation' refers not only to the translation of language, but to the translation of ideas, meanings and concepts (Rubel and Rosman, 2003). The concept has been employed by anthropologists to refer to the process by which ethnographic observations made in a foreign culture are described and transmitted to those in the anthropologist's own culture (Rubel and Rosman, 2003). Cultural translation can be usefully adapted to the present context; in creating drama for development, the BBC WST and its local production partners can be seen to be actively 'translating' development concepts and themes into local cultural frames.

Such cultural translation requires a degree of cultural literacy. Here, Rubel and Rosman argue that, 'in its broadest sense, translation means cross-cultural understanding' (2003: 1), with the key criteria to effective translation being that of 'understanding'. Without a degree of cultural literacy, cultural dominance or ethnocentrism is likely to emerge in the translation process. Rubel and Rosman also stress that, 'the values of the culture of the source [...] may be different from those of the target' (2003: 6). To some extent, this is inevitable in the present example, as six of the seven BBC WST dramatists interviewed for this research were non-local to the countries in which they were working; however, there are also scholars who see translation as an act that 'emphasizes the commonality and universality of human experience', something to which dramatists commonly allude (Rubel and Rosman, 2003: 6). However, the BBC WST dramatists' 'translation' task is further complicated by the fact that they have significant decision-making influence and power over and above local writers. Thus, fundamental to the act of 'cultural translation' in such contexts are the processes of creative decision-making and negotiation. It is through creative decision-making that dramatists choose to reinforce or challenge local culture, its norms and mores. An examination of how dramatists negotiate their way through local culture and therein make creative decisions is central to understanding their role as 'cultural translators'.

Creative Decision-making and Negotiation

We have identified a number of key editorial challenges inherent in the production of drama for development. In mainstream drama, if the audience is satisfied, the broadcaster is satisfied. However, in drama for development, demands are placed upon the dramatist to satisfy a wider range of stakeholders, including donors, local writers and local broadcasters, as well as audiences. Later in this chapter, we propose a conceptual framework that maps dramatists' decisions onto a creative spectrum. This analytical tool can be used to explore how and why dramatists make the creative decisions they make—decisions that are often influenced by various power dynamics that play out in the context of production, and which are vital to understanding how dramatists engage in cultural translation.

In framing the central question of this chapter around notions of 'cultural translation' we have assumed that 'non-local' dramatists working on development-oriented productions in other countries are inevitably engaged in some form of 'cultural translation'. Interestingly, when the question was put to them, the dramatists tended to resist the idea. An analysis of their creative decisions, however, shows that in spite of some conceptual resistance, they routinely performed 'cultural translation'—particularly when it was necessary to fulfil the development mandate of the particular dramas on which they were working. Most significantly, all of the dramatists interviewed were keenly aware of the need to learn about the cultures in which they worked. For example, a dramatist on the Pakistani *Piyar ka Passport* production noted: 'You can't make any lazy short cuts about character or about politics [...] or any of those things—there are no lazy shortcuts if you don't belong to the culture' (Interview, 2008).

Another dramatist working on the Cambodian *Taste of Life* stressed the value of having an 'inception period', during which cultural immersion and the development of some form of 'cultural literacy' was possible:

> The 3-year project included a 3-month 'inception period'. The main purpose of this, as I understood it, was to allow the output executive producers, including me as drama producer, to immerse ourselves in local culture and integrate ourselves into local society as far as possible. This period was invaluable. (Interview, 2008)

All of the dramatists interviewed described drawing on a range of sources to acquire a sense of 'cultural literacy'. They watched local films and television, made friends with local people, attended cultural events, read local newspapers and magazines (where possible), took photos, read local literature (sometimes in translated form) and travelled around the country in which they were working. However, the most common reported way of acquiring cultural literacy was through engaging with the locally recruited scriptwriting and production teams. The dramatist on the *Piyar ka Passport* production described getting information on

Pakistani culture 'largely from the writers and [...] from the cast as well', while the *Taste of Life* dramatist noted that: 'If you've got good advisors with you, like your local writers or your local script editors [...] they can tell you if you're going wrong'. The *Wetin Dey* dramatist echoed these sentiments: the 'writers are Nigerian; the script edit team is Nigerian; the director is Nigerian; everyone on the crew is Nigerian [...] It teaches you a lot'. We can see that local writers often help steer dramatists in the right direction, and may even act as a 'brake' on both their creative ambitions and upon cultural misinterpretation.

Interestingly, and in keeping with the literature on media production, the dramatists acknowledged that their writing teams were not typical of the audiences they were trying to reach (Allen, 1995; Dornfeld, 1998). The *Piyar ka Passport* dramatist described her 'crew' as being drawn from the 'educated classes', while the *Taste of Life* dramatist pointed out that his writing team 'had to be relatively proficient in English for this [the drama] to work in the time we had available'. Thus, the 'non-local' dramatists recognised that there were inherent limitations in taking the local writing and production groups to be representative of the audience and that doing so meant the under representation of less-educated voices. The dramatist from the Burmese *Thabyegone Ywa* production was particularly conscious of this, as many of his writers had not lived in Burma for some time. He remarked that you have 'got to be very wary of what people deem to be their own culture. People assume that everyone is like them and people assume they know their culture, and often, they just don't'. However, the time pressures associated with drama, allied to the financial limitations placed on production, mean that writers are often relied upon. As the *Piyar ka Passport* dramatist remarked, the local drama writers were 'obviously not perfectly reflective of society as a whole, [but they were] as close as I could get'.

Another interesting insight that emerged from this research was the relatively limited emphasis that many of the dramatists placed on audience research. Audience research is conducted at various stages of the production process, including the formative stage (to provide insights about the audience) and during output development (in order to 'pre-test' outputs before they are broadcast). Of all the audience research activities, dramatists seemed most keenly aware of the role played by pre-testing. This is not to suggest that the dramatists did not value and apply the insights generated by formative audience research as well, but rather that such research did not come to the forefront of their minds when recalling how they had initially gone about familiarising themselves with the cultures in which they worked. This supports the notion that dramatists are, first and foremost, concerned with creative processes, a positive reception for their outputs and also that they appear to have an innate sense of what their audience wants (Allen, 1995; Dornfeld 1998). However, we should not rule out the potential influence of formative audience research, as clearly evidenced by other chapters in this volume (see Chapters 3 and 4).

While 'cultural immersion' and the acquisition of 'cultural literacy' are constructed as naturalised processes—something dramatists suggest they 'just do'—it is interesting to note that the dramatist currently immersed in the development of *Bishaash* was keenly aware of the importance of formative research. In this respect, he notes:

> We've been travelling around the country, meeting a huge amount of people, talking to as many people as we can, seeing as many elements of the country's culture [...] and alongside that, doing lots of research as to what types of stories people like: What is their favourite story? Who do they like to see in stories? What defines a hero for them? What defines a villain for them? Who are their favourite actors? Who are their favourite actresses? Who is their favourite writer? What's their favourite TV drama?
>
> (Interview, 2008)

While audience research is an important, if at times understated, component of drama production, more important to dramatists were the personal cross-cultural relationships that they developed with local drama writers. In turn, this raises the critical question of how these personal relationships help to facilitate a process of cross-cultural immersion and translation when such writers are only obliquely representative of the wider audience. Further, 'non-local' dramatists tend to underemphasise the inherent power imbalances in their relationships with local writers, preferring instead to identify creative processes that are highly collaborative. The dramatist working on the *Piyar ka Passport* production reflected: 'There wasn't an explicit message that I needed to translate. So really what I was doing was using my facilitating and interpreting skills to try to grow an idea there with writers who were based there'.

Similarly, the *Wetin Dey* dramatist noted that: 'It's scripted, written by Nigerians. The only thing that was coming from us was the technical expertise and how to actually make good episodes—the craft of writing'. Despite assertions that defer all creativity to the Nigerian writing team, the notion of 'craft' highlights a key area in which the power of 'non-local' dramatists resides. Here, local writers often defer to 'experienced others' when it comes to the structuring of dramatic narratives and a key element of cultural translation emerges in terms of the manipulation of 'local' cultural frames into a 'non-local' genre, namely, that of development-oriented drama.

Interestingly, it was the dramatist involved in the *Bishaash* drama production who felt that that drama (which had yet to be written) was being constructed explicitly around audience needs and perceptions based on formative research:

> It's not really us parachuting down our ideas [...] all of our concepts, everything that we are developing, is based on us engaging with this audience first and working out what they want [...] It's not as if we're coming in and saying, 'This is what the drama needs to be about, and this is what we've decided'. We're coming in saying, 'Tell us everything you know; tell us what you like; tell us what you enjoy, and we'll work with practitioners to help us develop an idea'. So that the process of making sure that the idea works for the Bangladeshi context starts before we even put anything down on paper [...] We would have a problem, I think, if we'd just sat and written the whole thing in an office in London, and then come out here and said, 'Alright, this is the show'. Even if we had British Bangladeshi writers, I still think we would have had a problem. That's the opposite of what we've done. (Interview, 2008)

Like many other dramatists, the non-local dramatist working on the Cambodian drama *Taste of Life* rejected the notion that he was engaged in a form of 'cultural translation'. Rather, an appeal to the universalism of human experience was offered: 'I've had this moral argument that people ask [...] How can you come to a completely foreign country [...] and do drama there? Because I don't think it's any different anywhere! Because it's human beings ... it's the same the world over.'

Kloos observes that 'there are two kinds of knowledge [...] the culture-specific and the generally valid' (1984; cited in Servaes, 1999: 8).

It seems that some dramatists view dramatic expertise as more generally valid than culturally specific. The same *Taste of Life* dramatist notes that in drama: '… there's a universal recognition of human weaknesses. Yes, there are cultural traditions and ways of life, but you don't need to know those to make basic good drama.'

Such commentary highlights a tension between notions of 'cultural immersion', as expressed by non-local dramatists and a more universal notion of the human experience. Despite this, dramatists are typically keen not to have their dramas perceived as 'coming from outside', as noted by a 'non-local' dramatist working on *Piyar ka Passport*:

> What the Trust [BBC WST] commissioned me to do was to raise the debate about the kind of moving line between arranged marriage and forced marriage and by raising that debate with the group of writers that we were working with in Pakistan, between them; they did end up with a position on it. But it wasn't something that culturally I was bringing from the UK—it was something that I was trying to define in the storylining … what the message would be from within Pakistan—the sort of peer message from women to women within Pakistan. (Interview, 2008)

These comments helpfully explain their rejection of notions of 'cultural translation' when it was put to the dramatists. Nevertheless, most were able to identify specific moments when they came into conflict with other parties concerning the content of the drama. This conflict tended to occur with the local writers. In examining the circumstances around conflict within the creative decision-making process, we can see that, although the dramatists were fundamentally reluctant to see themselves as 'imposing' external 'ideals' or 'translating' external concepts into other cultures, they often did so to a greater degree than they imagined or perhaps felt comfortable in expressing. The following account of one particular creative decision made by the producer of *Piyar ka Passport* supports this assertion:

> In the course of developing the story there were moments when, as producer, I was making choices in the stories that were being presented to me for development […]. There's a natural beating heart of sexism to *Piyar ka Passport* because it's about fathers making decisions on their daughters' behalf. But I didn't want jokes at the expense of women, or casual cruelty to women that wasn't in some way intelligently connected to

the … message of the piece. So there, I think, I was imposing some of my own sensitivities—but I was very aware of it, and I was trying to justify all those judgments […]. There was an encounter between the father of the Pakistan based family [in the drama] and the maid—and the maid 'cheeked' the father. And when she walked out the writer had decided that [the father] would say 'bitch' to the microphone […] just a shared joke between the father and the audience and it felt like, if I'd allowed it in, it would have felt like a producer-condoned character decision […]. So I fought not to have that […]. And in a way it was defensible just in terms of the complexity of the drama we were making. But I'd have defended it somehow. (Interview, 2008)

This account highlights how the *Piyar ka Passport* dramatist/producer—who was committed to the idea of a drama firmly based in Pakistani culture—struggled with her feelings about sexism, and how this ultimately influenced her creative decision.

An examination of further creative decisions made by dramatists sheds light on the conditions under which dramatists chose either to challenge or reinforce local cultural contradictions and constraints. In considering such decisions we have developed a creative decision-making framework, which visually represents how creative decisions 'fall out' when dramatists are confronted with local cultural norms. However, the issue of what can be legitimately considered as 'culturally authentic' or normative is highly contested; therefore, rather than attempt to define what 'authentic local cultural norms' are, we will explore dramatists' decision-making processes when presented with what we call 'cultural objects'. We use the term, 'cultural object' to refer to anything presented to a dramatist as, 'authentic' or 'accurate' with respect to a given culture. As such, 'cultural objects' are unavoidably tied to the person or institution that presents them. They can be presented by anyone; however, as 'non-local' dramatists in drama for development contexts tend to depend on local writers, it is most often the local writers who present or portray these cultural objects. In the previous example, the 'cultural object' presented to the dramatist was a scene in which a male head of household spoke disrespectfully about a maid.

When a 'cultural object' is presented to a dramatist, the challenge is to assess the extent to which it feels 'authentic' or 'inauthentic'. In order to make this assessment, the dramatist must draw upon whatever 'cultural literacy' he/she has developed. The 'non-local' dramatist must then decide to what degree the drama, through its characters and plotlines, will either reinforce or challenge that 'cultural object'. For analytical purposes, these two related decisions or assessments can be mapped against each other to capture the range of creative decision-making processes that dramatists face.

What is particularly interesting about this mapping is the way in which it enables us to look at the types of decision that land in different quadrants, and the dramatists' rationale for those decisions (Figure 6.1).

Figure 6.1
Creative Decision-Making Framework

———— Dramatist's assessment of the 'cultural object' presented to them

═══ Dramatist's course of action

Does not feel authentic

There is no police corruption in Cambodia (TOL) Medical professionals do not have extra-marital sex (TOL)	Fake antiretroviral drugs are not sold in Nigeria (WD) Students in Cambodia do not talk back to their teachers (TOL)	There is no sex outside of marriage in Cambodia (TOL) Young people in Nigeria are very religious, and therefore do not have sex outside marriage (WD)

Reinforce / Challenge

4 | 1

3 | 2

Rape and marital violence cannot be overtly depicted on Pakistani radio (PKP) A Cambodian matrimonial ceremony involves certain customs and practices (TOL)	Arranged marriages can be successful (PKP) A couple who eloped would face economic hardship (PKP)	A daughter obeys her father's wishes and would accept his choice of husband against her will (PKP) A male head of household would speak disrespectfully of a maid (PKP)

Feels authentic

Key: PKP—*Piyar ka Passport*
TOL—*Taste of Life*
WD—*Wetin Dey*

Source: Author.

In the lower left quadrant, dramatists judge 'cultural objects' to have an 'authentic' feel, and choose to reinforce them. Many of the examples that fall into this quadrant have to do with cultural detail, for example, how to accurately depict a Cambodian wedding. Such cultural specificities help to create a realistic feel to the drama, which, as we have already discussed, may serve to increase audience engagement. Even when the 'cultural objects' that end up in this category are more complex, often the decision to reinforce them stems from a desire not to depart too far from social reality. Here, the *Piyar ka Passport* dramatist notes that:

> The whole issue of arranged marriage and forced marriage is very [...] tied to economics and there's an elopement between two penniless characters in it and they suffer because of their elopement because they were both protected within their own houses. But because it's so tied to economics, it would be madness to suggest they wouldn't suffer. You would like it to be a happy ending for them, but it really couldn't be, and it was only in keeping with the naturalism of the piece. (Interview, 2008)

On the other hand, sometimes when the 'cultural objects' presented to a dramatist do not 'feel' authentic they may choose not to challenge them, as in the upper left quadrant. The decision not to challenge often centres on whether the issue is relevant to the drama's development mandate, and what the consequences of the challenge might be. The *Taste of Life* dramatist, for example, chose not to depict a scene involving police corruption for reasons of political expediency, even though it would have been realistic in the Cambodian context, because he did not want to offend the authorities: 'There was absolutely no point in getting taken off the air after four episodes for a small point'. Likewise, he eliminated a plotline involving a relationship between two senior medical professionals, after a number of real-life medical professionals protested the storyline. Interestingly, the *Jasoos Vijay* dramatist (who was born in India), also found herself changing storylines to avoid alienating sections of the audience:

> It was such a good thing that we were pre-testing [...]. What we found was that one of the story ideas where we were talking about a nice old man going to a sex worker, and how he manages to educate her in the use of a condom—we thought it was a great story line [...]. We went into the field, and [...] you know, [the audience] rejected the story, because they

said, 'Well, if he's such a nice old man, then why the hell is he going to a sex worker?' [...]. And so then of course the storyline had to be changed because it was completely infected. They were not willing to listen to any good sound advice following that. (Interview, 2008)

What is particularly interesting about this example is that the Indian born dramatist struggled to make an appropriate decision and was taken aback by the reaction of the rural audience. Equally interesting is that, rather than going with her creative intuition, she relied on audience research to make the final choice, recognising that the social distance between herself and the audience could be closed through research.

The two quadrants examined thus far help to ground drama for development productions firmly within their local cultural contexts. It is in the remaining two quadrants where issues of cultural translation become more apparent. Here, dramatists actively decide to challenge 'cultural objects', often because the challenge is vital to the drama's development mandate. For example, many of the dramatists interviewed were forced to challenge the sexual norms that were presented to them by local writers in order to address factors driving their local HIV epidemic. With regard to such challenges the *Wetin Dey* dramatist notes that: 'If you're going to write about HIV, you've got to write about sex. And does anyone in Nigeria want to write about sex? No. It's very private. Sex is what you do behind closed doors'. Similarly, the *Taste of Life* dramatist noted:

[There is a] built-in paradox of the drama's key HIV messages clashing with the notion of Cambodian 'values and traditions'. Traditionalists here, indeed many young people too, go along with the nonsense that there's no sex outside Cambodian marriages [...]. I even saw a quote in the papers from the Minister of Health denying that brothels existed in Phnom Penh [...] [but] we depicted several youthful sexual liaisons out of wedlock. Why? We had no choice if we were to illustrate the dangers of HIV and AIDS—50% of our message brief. (Interview, 2008)

These examples illustrate that challenging cultural norms is sometimes vital to the entire drama for development exercise and is fundamentally necessary to satisfying the development requirements of the project.

Finally, and perhaps most interestingly, there are occasions where even though a 'cultural object' feels authentic, a dramatist will choose to challenge it. This is exemplified in *Piyar ka Passport*, when the dramatist decided to remove the scene in which the father insults the maid. Here, even though the 'non-local' dramatist judged the culture to be a certain way, she chose to represent it in a different light, for fear that the portrayal contradicted other key messages. Similarly, the dramatist working on the Burmese drama depicted the 'coming out' of a homosexual character, which was received by the character's friend with tolerance and acceptance. This is, in essence, cultural translation at its most explicit. A dramatist attempts to depict a concept such as 'gender equality' or acceptance of homosexuality, in the hope that it will present viewers with an alternative to what is culturally normative.

The creative decision-making framework proposed in this chapter argues that there are two key criteria that guide such decisions: perception of authenticity and compliance with cultural norms. Thus, it can be a useful heuristic in the analysis of creative decisions in drama-making and also for dramatists themselves, to understand their own practice and the issues of cultural translation inherent in the drama for development process.

Conclusion

This chapter explored how 'non-local' dramatists, working on drama for development projects, negotiate the challenges of drama production in cultures that are not their own. Specifically, the chapter has explored how such dramatists go about 'translating' ideas and ideals into 'other' cultures? Our analysis reveals that they first attempt to cultivate degrees of 'cultural literacy', primarily through developing interpersonal relationships with their local writing and production teams. Subsequently, they engage in processes of creative decision-making during which they sometimes challenge and sometimes reinforce the 'cultural objects' presented to them by different stakeholders as being representative of a particular culture.

Though the dramatists interviewed for this research tended to reject the idea that they were engaged in overt processes of 'cultural translation', examination of the creative decisions they make—when mapped against the creative decision-making framework above—suggests otherwise. 'Non-local' dramatists do engage in 'cultural translation' processes, though they appear to naturalise this as routine drama practice. This is particularly evident when they are faced with challenging specific 'cultural objects'. Our analysis also highlights the various tensions dramatists face in striving for authenticity and cultural sensitivity, while also fulfilling specific development objectives. These challenges reflect the demands of the various stakeholder groups involved in drama for development and the constraints some of the groups are able to exert over the creative process. Future research could attempt to further populate the creative decision-making framework proposed herein with examples from other dramas, to explore if the trends and patterns identified hold true for other 'non-local' dramatists involved in development-oriented drama production.

Note

1. Unsurprisingly, there is a tradition of criticism around communication for development that highlights cultural hegemonic and ethnocentric concerns (Boyd-Barrett, 1977). Such criticism stems from a critique of modernisation and dependency theories, which have dominated development thinking for considerable periods of time in the post-war period (Manyozo, 2007). Drama for development, as a specific genre, can be seen to have emerged from modernisation theorising in particular, with its focus on rationalism, individualism and agency (Manyozo, 2007; Servaes, 1999).

References

Abu-Lughod, L. (2005) *Dramas of Nationhood: The Politics of Television in Egypt*. Chicago: University of Chicago Press.

Allen, R. (1995) 'Introduction', in R. Allen (ed.), *To Be Continued … Soap Operas from around the World*. New York: Routledge.

Boyd-Barrett, O. (1977) 'Media Imperialism: Towards an International Framework for the Analysis of Media Systems', in J. Curran and M. Gurevitch (eds), *Mass Communication and Society*. London: Arnold.

Cantor, M. (1988) *The Hollywood TV Producer: His Work and His Audience*. New Jersey: Transaction Publishers.

Cody, M., Fernandes, S. and Holley, W. (2004) 'Entertainment-Education Programs of the BBC and BBC World Service Trust', in A. Singhal, M. Cody, E. Rogers and M. Sabido (eds), *Entertainment-Education and Social Change: History, Research, and Practice*. New York: Lawrence Erlbaum Associates, Inc.

Dornfeld, B. (1998) *Producing Public Television, Producing Public Culture*. New Jersey: Princeton University Press.

Gillespie, M. (2005) 'Television Drama and Audience Ethnography', in M. Gillespie (ed.), *Media Audiences*. Maidenhead: The Open University Press.

Hall, S. (1980) 'Cultural Studies: Two Paradigms', *Media, Culture and Society*, 2(1): 57–72.

Hirsch, E. (1988) *Cultural Literacy: What Every American Needs to Know*. New York: Random House.

Kloos, P. (1984) *Antropologie als wetenschap*. Muiderberg: D. Coutinho.

Livingstone, S. (1990) *Making Sense of Television: The Psychology of Audience Interpretation*. London: Routledge.

Mandel, R. (2002) 'A Marshall Plan of the Mind: The Political Economy of a Kazakh Soap Opera', in F. Ginsburg, L. Abu-Lughod and B. Larkin (eds), *Media Worlds: Anthropology on New Terrain*. California: University of California Press.

Manyozo, L. (2007) *Communication for Development: An Historical Overview*. Paris: UNESCO.

Porter, R. and Samovar, L. (1998) 'Cultural Influences on Emotional Expression: Implications for Intercultural Communication', in P. Andersen and L. Guerrero (eds), *Handbook of Communication and Emotion*. San Diego: Academic Press.

Rubel, P. and Rosman, A. (eds) (2003) *Translating Cultures: Perspectives on Translation and Anthropology*. Oxford: Berg Publishers.

Schirato, T. and Yell, S. (2000) *Communication and Cultural Literacy: An Introduction*. Sydney: Allen and Unwin.

Servaes, J. (1999) *Communication for Development: One World, Multiple Cultures*. New Jersey: Hampton Press.

Singhal, A. and Rogers, E. (1999) *Entertainment-Education: A Communication Strategy for Social Change*. New Jersey: Lawrence Erlbaum Associates.

Skuse, A. (2007) 'Misreading Romance: The BBC World Service, Afghan Radio Soap Operas and the Politics of Production and Consumption', *Southern Review*, 39(3): 52–70.

Sood, S. and Nambiar, D. (2006) 'Comparative Cost-Effectiveness of the Components of a Behavior Change Communication Campaign on HIV/AIDS in North India', *Journal of Health Communication*, 11(1): 143–162.

7

BROADCASTING 'THE STATE'

TRIBE, CITIZENSHIP AND THE POLITICS OF RADIO DRAMA PRODUCTION IN AFGHANISTAN

Andrew Skuse and Marie Gillespie

Introduction

This chapter examines shifts in how the Afghan state is represented in the popular radio drama serial *New Home, New Life* which, since 1994, has been produced by BBC Afghan Education Projects (BBC AEP). Based on *The Archers*, BBC Radio 4's longest running serial drama, *New Home, New Life* dramatises the everyday life of a fictional rural village community, weaving educational and development messages into its multiple narrative strands (see Appendix 2). The chapter examines how the producers of *New Home, New Life* embed and promote liberal conceptions of the state and citizenship in the drama.

The Afghan state is imagined, enacted and performed through a dialogical and often a critical exchange with media discourses (Herzfeld, 1992; Gupta, 1995). For nearly 20 years, and in a context of limited Afghan media, *New Home, New Life* has played a significant role in representing the state and civil society to Afghan audiences. Routine BBC AEP surveys (1996–1998) indicated that up to 83 per cent of respondents tune in to *New Home, New Life*. During and after episodes they debate a host of humanitarian and social issues, but fostering debate about the duties and responsibilities of state and citizens have posed formidable challenges to the producers. State formation in Afghanistan has been a slow and troublesome process with myriad tribal affiliations, especially in ethnically Pashtun areas, competing for loyalties. The chapter highlights how local and translocal dynamics are played out in the production and reception of *New Home, New Life*, and how varying forms of patronage, dependency and allegiance are negotiated (Edwards, 1996; Tapper, 1983). We highlight how the BBC's concerns with impartiality shaped the representational strategy of the drama at key political moments, and how the 'absent presence' of the Taliban in the drama poses a range of difficult questions for dramatists, development professionals and the BBC.

The state is often regarded as an impersonal, remote, abstract entity, unlike the nation which is given form and expression through cultural representations. Yet the state is 'implicated in the minute texture of everyday life, a texture made tangible and imaginable through a range of discrete and discursive practices'—not least in the intersections of national and local media discourses (Gupta, 1995: 375). According to Gupta, this enables: '... a certain construction of the state that meshes the imagined translocal institution with its localized embodiments. The government, in other words, is being constructed here in the imagination and in the everyday practices of ordinary people' (1995: 389–390).

Gupta's ethnography of local bureaucracy and corruption in Northern India shows that, far from being abstract and 'unknowable' entity, the 'state' is constructed through clearly observable everyday processes, practices and 'traceable' discourses. In this chapter we examine how notions of state, governance and citizenship are rendered visible, legible and audible in *New Home, New Life* during three key moments: the *Mujahideen* era (1989–1996), Taliban rule (1997–2001) and the post-Taliban democratic period of US/NATO influence (2002–present).

Each of these three political 'moments' in recent Afghan history forced the producers and writers of *New Home, New Life* to make strategic decisions about how aspects of the state, government and citizenship should be represented. In Afghanistan, the development of centralised state institutions and modern practices of governance in tribal and non-tribal rural communities has generally been weak. Attempts to effect radical social change invariably are met with hostility, distrust and resentment (Roy, 1990; Tapper, 1984). However, a notion of the 'state' as the centre of political authority is not necessarily rejected out of hand by Afghans. Traditional rural leaders, for example, recognise that it is a potential resource, a source of funds to be secured and redistributed among local solidarity groups. They appreciate that the advent of a modern state may actually serve to strengthen local hegemonies. Yet attempts to modernise rural areas have often floundered because of the desire of local tribal groups to maintain their autonomy in political, economic and religious affairs (J. Anderson, 1983; Roy, 1990; Tapper, 1983).

Modernity in Afghanistan is a predominantly urban phenomenon where education and relative affluence tends to foster a liberal conception of the state and a positive attitude towards social, economic and political change. Constructing a tangible sense of a modern state in urban Afghanistan, where modest services are available, has been easier than in the largely autonomous rural areas. Much of the political and social tension in Afghanistan revolves around this rural–urban divide, which pits conservatism against liberalism, the latter through association with the liberal communist past. The presumed profanity of urban life has resulted in a violent backlash and retribution being meted out on urban populations in recent years by the Taliban and other conservative forces.

Representing the state and local systems of governance presents the scriptwriters of *New Home, New Life* with difficult representational decisions We examine how creative and representational strategies were negotiated during the three different political periods. In doing so, we draw upon periods of ethnographic fieldwork in Afghanistan undertaken by Skuse (1996–2002), on qualitative and quantitative audience evaluation data derived from the BBC AEP (1993–2008) and on collaborative research between Gillespie and Skuse under the auspices of the current project: 'Tuning In: Diasporic Contact Zones at the BBC World Service'.

Representing the *Mujahideen* (1993–1996)

When the BBC AEP was founded in 1993 in the dusty back streets of University Town, Peshawar, Pakistan, the political landscape of Afghanistan reflected a patchwork of competing *Mujahideen* groups split largely along ethnic lines. For example, the Pashtun dominated *Hizbe Islami* (an Islamist group set up in Kabul in 1975 to combat communism in Afghanistan) competed directly with the Tajik *Jamiat-i Islami* (one of the oldest Islamic political parties and among the most powerful of *Mujahideen* groups) and the Hazara *Herkat-i Islami* (Islamic Movement of Afghanistan) a registered political party. The primary goal of each group was to defend its own ethnicised territory rather than to seek domination of an opponent (Maley, 1998). The fracturing of the country into discrete enclave states in which warlords held sway made cohesive politics and stable structures of governance untenable. A weak coalition of *Mujahideen* groups *did* manage to form a government in the immediate post-communist period (1992), though this alliance quickly gave way to a protracted and bloody civil war. This led to the destruction of Kabul and a further disintegration of state-wide civic institutions such as the education system, the police and the judiciary (Naby, 1986; Rais, 1994). The patchwork of *Mujahideen* affiliated warlords and commanders or the new *khans* (a term associated with traditional landlords) exerted their influence across Afghanistan during this period. This magnified the feudal politics of patronage and the conflicts which ensued provided dramatic material that could be easily woven into the narratives of *New Home, New Life*.

Faced with a society undergoing radical transformation and political disintegration, the dramatists of *New Home, New Life* sought to write stories that might help to strengthen existing traditional political and legal institutions, especially as the civil war intensified. Political and moral turbulence had ruptured contemporary Afghan society, tearing apart traditional legal/mediatory institutions such as village *jirgas* (councils) and age-based moral frameworks, such as the Pashtun tribal honorific code of *Pashtunwali* (Edwards, 1996; Roy, 1990).[1] *New Home, New Life's* melodramatic narratives attempt to address, albeit in oblique fashion, the political, legal and moral shifts created by war and social disintegration and guide the listening Afghan public about how to manage change and strengthen social bonds. Much of the 'positive change' promoted by the donors and dramatists of *New Home, New Life* involved the reinvigoration of tradition. Certain socio-cultural conventions, identified as being beneficially or benignly 'traditional', such as *jirgas* (village councils) and *khans* (landlords) are narratively marked as positive and socially strengthening. In contrast, other practices, such as giving women to enemy households to settle blood debts (see Chapter 13) are identified for stealthy, yet dramatic erosion. This strategy has contributed to the re-invention of tradition for contemporary political purposes (cf. Hobsbawm and Ranger, 1983).

During the *Mujahideen* period, *New Home, New Life* expended considerable melodramatic effort in representing traditional forms of mediation and governance. They had come under severe pressure as a result of the radical politicisation and militarisation of Afghanistan following the intervention of the Soviet Union in 1979. The influx of weapons and money from the United States, the United Kingdom, India, Saudi Arabia and elsewhere into Afghanistan that followed Soviet occupation quickly eroded traditional hierarchies. This led to a significant shift in power and status away from *spingheri* (white beards) and traditional landlords (*khans*) towards younger 'political *khans*' (typically military commanders) who had both guns and men at their disposal (Roy, 1990). This shift in social and political hierarchies meant that traditional governance and mediatory institutions, such as the village *jirgas*, lost their authority. As a result the settlement of local disputes and the allocation of natural resources (such as water and land) became highly problematic.

In Afghanistan, the title *khan* is conventionally used to mark out well-respected men in diverse fields of public service, in addition to its more common usage as a title for landowners or elders. In a detailed examination of tribe–state interactions, Anderson argues that the term 'conveys a notion of deploying others in one's own enterprise' and that it 'signals a man whose authority runs beyond his own household and beyond the general run of householders thereabouts' (J. Anderson, 1983: 133). The *khan* acts as the bridge between opposing social and political groups, and his mediating skills have long been exploited for economic, social and honorific gain. The *khan* mediates between *qawm* (tribe) and *gund* (faction), *atrap* (countryside) and *shahr* (city) and *hukumat* (place of government). The *khan* operates as a broker at the intersections of groups, locations and insitutions, building social relationships of varying closeness, from *malgarey* (companions), *nazir* (overseer), to the less intimate *hamsaya* (clients), reflecting relations based on business or indebtedness.

Historically, the social standing of the *khan* has been defined with regard to his social conduct. Piety, generosity and wisdom are considered as the most important honorific characteristics (Azoy, 1982). Traditional *khans* were akin to 'self-financed' public servants who, in benefiting the community, increased their own wealth, holdings and status in the process (J. Anderson, 1983). The traditional *khan* may be thought of as the village organiser of economic and social well-being. However, attacks on the perceived feudalism of the *khanate* system by communist reformers (1978–1989), radically altered the political, religious and moral landscape of Afghanistan. The gradual undermining of their role and status by far younger men ready to forge new 'out-group' political and military alliances in the face of the Soviet intervention (1979–1989) also profoundly altered the social, economic and moral connotations of the *khan* (Edwards, 1996; Roy, 1990; Rubin, 1995).

In the context of such a rapidly shifting political landscape, an initial goal of *New Home, New Life* was to problematise the excesses of the *Mujahideen* and represent a more morally infused representation of civil society in which key social roles and institutions such as *khans* (in their new military guise) and *jirgas* (councils) played a crucial part. The representation of new modern political realities combined with an older vision of a traditional society with *khans* and *jirgas* at its centre (cf. Lindholm, 1982). The redefinition of a familiar moral economy was of crucial importance to the production. Yet it was recognised early on that too close an association with one or other politico-religious groups was fraught with danger and could lead to accusations of political bias. A former BBC AEP Manager reflecting on how BBC notions of impartiality, normally associated with news, also pervaded the drama explained:

When we talk about Impartiality in *New Home, New Life* it's not just the impartiality they are talking about in Bush House [the BBC World Service's headquarters in London], it's more complicated. You have to be impartial as far as your accent is concerned. You have to be impartial where the language is concerned. You have religion, politics, culture, all sorts of different levels. That's very important. We could lose everything without impartiality.

(Shirazuddin Siddiqi, Interview, Peshawar, Pakistan, 1997)

Dramatists pursuing development goals have to become adept at balancing diverse local and translocal cultural codes and conventions if they are to be successful, but the additional impetus to strive towards BBC values of impartiality makes this task all the more complicated. *New Home, New Life* has to walk a tightrope between a fragmented social fabric, competing political discourses, conflicting political parties and militarised networks of patronage. Yet the producers strive to maintain a very clear policy of political impartiality via the representation of the generic *khan* and 'commander'. The complex political context paradoxically made it easier to portray political plurality and more difficult for audiences to identify with any one amongst the welter of competing groups vying for power. The representation of activities such as looting, robbery or generational conflict provided both a wide avenue of creative expression forscriptwriters and clear scope for the promotion of morally infused political themes. Nonetheless, producers recognised that *New Home, New Life* was far from 'realistic' in harking back to a time when *khans* performed a very different social, politico-moral and economic function.

New Home, New Life's representation of *Mujahideen* era politics resonated with the experience of many listeners who felt a profound sense of loss, bitterness and resentment over the social, material and moral disruption that they caused. The new political *khans* were regarded with contempt for ostentatiously flouting kinship norms, marital codes, social duties and property rights, all of which are synonymous with the Pashtun concept of *namus* (honour) and fundamental to Pashtun culture. Such transgressions substantively undermined moral and honorific sensibilities, leading many male listeners, in particular, to castigate some of the characters for doing the same:

... Fateh Khan [a representation of a negative militarised *khan*] should not behave like this as he is the chief of the village, so he should show better ways and not motivate people to bad activities [referring to land disputes]. Nowadays there are not so many *khans* and their time has passed. The new *khan* Commander Shakoor Khan is a better character and, hopefully, all of our countrymen will come to act like Shakoor then our country will not be destroyed like this. Some commanders don't care about the villagers. They act like *shaitans* [devils] killing people for small gains.

(Interview, Wardak Province, 1997)

In the absence of formal structures of governance in rural areas and extremely weak governance in urban areas, *New Home, New Life's* representational strategy was straightforward. The drama could be easily appropriated and understood by listeners precisely because it represented the Afghan political context in a rather vague manner, consisting in a diffused range of traditional and newly politicised *khans,* such as local military commanders. At the same time, it maintained some semblance of political impartiality by presenting a plurality of groups. However, it was clear to see that audiences were encouraged to identify the negative 'public' behaviour of the more 'militarised' characters and applaud the drama's positive portrayal of others, as they attempted to fulfil a more traditional and socially redistributive role.

The portrayal of the 'state' in *New Home, New Life* during the *Mujahideen* era focused on social disintegration, the localisation of political conflict and appeals to tradition and morality. Tribe–state interactions have always been beset with difficulty in Afghanistan, but the early 1990s was a period in which experiencing, let alone imagining, the state—in the sense ascribed by B. Anderson (1983) and Gupta (1995)—was particularly problematic. The lack of public services, the dearth of government offices and officials and their replacement by highly localised politico-military authorities necessitated a 'non-state' approach by the BBC AEP, albeit one that still sought to highlight and promote observance of basic human rights. The state has always been a weak and fairly fluid construct, especially in tribal Pashtun areas of the south and east of Afghanistan, and by the mid-1990s the political and military landscape of Afghanistan was undergoing a radical change. The BBC AEP found it much harder to represent change, not least because of their implications—namely, the radical conservatism of the Taliban and the emergence of a radically conservative religious state bureaucracy.

Representing and Refuting The Taliban (1997–2001)

The fragmentation of the country into warlordism and personal fiefdoms began to shift following 1994 as *Talibs* (students of religion) emerging from traditional *madrassahs* (religious schools) began to organise themselves against the *Mujahideen* groups.[2] Despite gains across the Pashtun south and southeast, where *Talibs* typically went into 'battle' with the Koran held high and where bloodless capitulation often followed, the producers felt that they were unable to reflect this new politico-religious reality despite their stated commit-ment to social realism. The BBC AEP soon realised that the conservative values of the Taliban were completely at odds with the donor-derived 'neo-liberal' objectives of *New Home, New Life*, as well as with thepersonal beliefs and convictions of the production team.

Qualitative data gleaned from ethnographic research carried out between 1996 and 2002 suggests that writers actively used the drama to keep alive liberal values—such as education for all, freedom of expression and, to a degree, freedom of choice—albeit choice framed by *Mujahideen* politics. Ironically, writers and producers used BBC editorial policy to block the influence of the Taliban, again citing the need for impartiality. Confronted with the conservative challenge of the Taliban movement, it remained far 'safer' and easier for *New Home, New Life* to portray politics as rooted in the recent tradition of new *khans*, tempered by traditional values and moralities (Edwards, 1996). But the emergence of the Taliban as a potent political force was not 'lost' on audiences. For example, one young male listener summed up a commonly held view: 'the role of the commander should be reduced to some extent because the days of commander [new *khans*] have passed and now we have the days of the Taliban' (Interview, Wardak Province, 1997).

The goal of the Taliban, aside from the conquest of rival groups, was the strict imposition of *Shari'at* law, which entailed a focus on the moral propriety expected of the general public (Butt, 1998; Davis, 1998; Marsden, 1998). The movement's politico-religious stance was clearly discernible in its own modest broadcasting efforts, with the following passage being representative of the religious rhetoric promoted on the only national broadcast competitor to the BBC WS, namely Voice of *Shari'at* Radio:

> The Taliban, who have emerged from the masses of the people, have started their struggle to deliver their compatriots from pain and hardship, to ensure complete peace and security across the country by collecting weapons, by doing away with feudal principalities [this being an attack on the enclaves controlled by rival political factions, rather than an attack on the feudalism of landlords, which was a feature of communist radio broadcasting] here and there in the country and by creating a powerful Islamic government in Afghanistan.
>
> (Voice of *Shari'at* Radio broadcast 5/11/96; cited in Marsden, 1998: 62)

Faced with a radically alternative polity to that previously portrayed, the ensuing representation of Afghan politics in this period became nostalgic. For a majority of listeners, the BBC AEP's rendering of politics was perceived as a fiction, one that was overtly anti-Taliban in its stance. This is evidenced by the pointed absence of clearly identifiable Taliban characters in the production during the period of the Taliban's ascendancy (1997–2001). The emergence of the Taliban as a populist political entity, especially in ethnically Pashtun regions, placed considerable strains upon the social relations of production. These strains were expressed through internal debates over wider BBC impartiality. The new Taliban-inspired realities, such as the collection of weapons and a widespread reduction of crime and culture of impunity, were easily reflected in the positive stances adopted by Commander Shakoor, the production's 'new *khan*'. Yet, the numerous squabbles, conflicts and intrigues between traditional and political *khans* continued in the drama, leading some listeners in Taliban-occupied Afghanistan to query why the movement should have ignored such criminal and clearly 'dishonourable' behaviour. In discussion with a group of *Talibs* in the town of Khost, Paktia Province, the realism of the production was challenged in an interesting, though not uncommon way, with listeners (the Taliban included) blurring fictional misdeeds with reality: 'Tell us where these *khans* are and we'll go and deal with them, no one has the right to hold weapons and collect taxes, [or] extract money with menaces, from the people' (Interview, Paktia Province, 1997).

Without a clear *Talib* presence in the drama at the village level, it fell to traditional, but morally negative characters such as Jabbar Khan, to oppose 'emancipatory' issues in 'the style' of the Taliban, as one of *New Home, New Life's* former managers, Shirazuddin Siddiqi, notes:

> ... we have a rigid guy [Jabbar Khan] who is opposing the idea of girls' education. His wife has a problem, but he doesn't like a male doctor touching her [as this is considered a breaking of *purdah*], he wants a female doctor, but at the same time Upper Village doesn't allow women to go to work, they don't allow their daughters to go to school to become doctors. And Jabbar Khan himself doesn't allow this. So tell me what's the option? What should Jabbar Khan do in this situation?
>
> (Interview, Peshawar, Pakistan 1997)

Resistance to the introduction of Taliban-like characters was typically couched in terms of the need for the BBC AEP to observe impartiality by not 'over-representing' any one political entity, hence the safety of maintaining a vague and politically fragmented representation of *Mujahideen* era politics. However, this representation was significantly at odds with political realities and became increasingly untenable as the influence of the Taliban grew to the extent that they controlled and loosely 'governed' the vast majority of Afghanistan.

With Taliban gains, in-house BBC debates over the inclusion or exclusion of a *Talib*-like character within the drama intensified. Ironically, the most powerful voice for the inclusion of a Taliban presence within *New Home, New Life* came from its first Project Manager, John Butt. He trained as an *alim* (scholar of Islam) and lived in Pashtun tribal and non-tribal areas in northern Pakistan for many years. His outlook was shaped by local religious orthodoxies and conservatism. However, rather than discouraging scriptwriters from addressing radical social themes, John Butt's creative talents and cultural knowledge enabled him to act as a cultural broker, a critical cosmopolitan, capable of translating and localising key themes. He was able to mediate between the conservative and the more progressive liberal-minded writers and editors, many of whom favoured a more rigid interpretation of the BBC's policy on political impartiality in an attempt to block the dramatic presence of the Taliban within the drama.

BBC editorial policy and notions of impartiality were upheld for sound and expedient reasons, but clearly BBC policy is also malleable, and enacted strategically in ways that serve less tangible and transparent interests connected, albeit indirectly and subtly, with the UK Foreign and Commonwealth Office's public diplomacy strategic priorities. Many of the drama's creative staff favoured a representation of civil society in which the Taliban and their brand of religious and cultural conservatism were absent—or perhaps more to the point an absent presence. How, they suggested, could they ever return to Kabul and accept that their daughters could not go to school, university or work for a living (a key policy of the Taliban being the restriction of women's activities in pursuit of strict adherence to *purdah*), when they could so easily have done so before under former communist, republican and monarchist regimes? Representing the Taliban in the drama was, for some, tantamount to acknowledging their presence, and by implication affording them a degree of legitimacy.

Though resistant to the presence of a *Talib* in the drama, most writers when interviewed preferred to keep their own political leanings opaque. Many had past close affiliations with the Afghan Communist State. And rather than expressing overt political opposition to the Taliban in the drama, many preferred to adopt a more moralistic stance in which the Taliban's perceived abuse of power could be questioned:

> ... it is the characteristic of an intellectual, because if you're not critical of ruling powers, who is going to correct that power? So I think that's our characteristic, but I don't think we're pro-*Taliban* or anti-*Taliban*. I don't deny that some might be against or some might be in favour, but I don't say *all* are against.
>
> (Shirazuddin Siddiqi, Interview, Peshawar, Pakistan 1997)

There were significant concerns in the production team over introducing a *Talib*-like character and the kind of moral example he might set. After much discussion, a compromise was struck. A highly conservative 'authority' figure was introduced, although his home was situated in the nearby urban district centre, near to but outside the drama's village boundaries. These decisions were influenced by the expatriate Project Manager, John Butt, who favoured a more accurate social representation of village life in response to emerging governance realities within Afghanistan. With the decision made, in-house debate over the Taliban-like character's portrayal began in earnest:

> The *Talib* has come but I'm trying to get rid of him. Initially, he came with a lot of good things like collecting weapons and bringing security and things like that. But we have to be realistic, so I added these two other ingredients there to complete the phenomenon. One of them was girls' education and one was women's employment. Now, since we don't know what will happen three months later, I am a bit sceptical about covering this phenomenon in the drama and I'm tempted to get rid of him. Because I don't really know what to do with this phenomenon, is it a good or a bad phenomenon? I don't know, I can't decide.
>
> (Shirazuddin Siddiqi, Interview, Peshawar, Pakistan 1997)

The production team had to deal with not only the problem of the three-month lead-time between the occurrence of 'real' or newsworthy events and their representation in the drama, but also with the profound political instability and uncertainty that the Afghan people were living through. Political and military regimes in Afghanistan have long been prone to quick collapse. The production team were wary of replicating or following real political events too closely. Rather, they sought to insinuate them into the dramatic fabric of the drama in more subtle ways. But there came a point when the non-inclusion of a *Talib*-like character actually distorted everyday realities. The production team had to perform a representational balancing act between the Taliban's positive actions, such as collecting weapons and increased security, and the undeniably retrogressive violence of prohibiting girls' education and women from working, banning music and television.

Responses to this balancing act are clearly reflected in the sentiments expressed by listeners, especially female listeners. Mothers were chiefly concerned over their children's lack of educational possibilities. But when audiences discussed acts of the violent punitiveness of the

Taliban aired in the drama, these actions met with approval and stirred fiery responses within certain sections of the audience. Here a young woman notes that:

> Mirak [a minor character in the production] says that the new chief of the district [the *Talib* character] cuts thieves' hands off. I think this is good work because two or three years back there were so many thieves that you couldn't sleep at night. We were always afraid they would come and loot our house. Now all these thieves and killings have stopped [because of the Taliban]. Now all of the people live in security, but stopping women working and girls going to school makes us anxious, but we always hear from the *Taliban* that when the situation becomes normal [though this never occurred] they will allow it, then we become happy and think of our small daughters and hope they will learn something in the future.
>
> (Interview, Wardak Province, 1997)

Rural female audiences, in interview situations, often referred to the Taliban as 'brothers' as a mark of affection and appreciation for the very real security dividend that they brought to many areas. However, such sentiments were also routinely tinged with female concerns voiced over education, especially by women who had moved from the cities to villages in order to escape the largely urban conflict of the civil war. But for those with no knowledge of city life, education represented a dream that was only vicariously experienced. The moral dilemmas explored in the serial about the role of women in the home, their marital rights and duties and their educational needs and aspirations, resonated very deeply with the concerns of rural and, even more so, with urban women listeners who had been more acutely affected by Taliban rule. The *Talib*-like character receded into obscurity as the dominant reality of the production's representation of politics slipped back to prioritising new *khans* who played an increasingly political role. Nevertheless, even the actions of the new political *khans* was refracted in subtle ways through the prism of Taliban rule and realities as well as in relation to the more traditional and benevolent *khan*. This see-saw adjustment to political and social change coincided with the departure of the drama's initial expatriate project manager, John Butt, who was replaced by an Afghan manager.

The lack of a clear Taliban presence in the drama under the new project manager continued to confuse the audiences as a middle-aged female listener reported:

... Sheroo [a henchman for a military *khan* in the drama] is a man *begherat* [without honour] and gets his livelihood from harming others. There are many forms of work in the world and he should do something else. It was enough for him that he was with Haibat Khan [another of the production's *khans*] and looted lots of places. But the people of the village have reclaimed these things. Once he helped to make a checkpost on the roadside and got lots of money [the collecting of 'taxes' by commanders and *khans* was common]. When Haibat Khan became poor he just went to work for Fateh Khan [another *khan*]. A few years back these things happened in our country. If one person had a job in Kabul, when he was coming to his village during the night a few armed people would go to his house by order of the village commander and take him and nobody would know about his whereabouts. After sometime they would have found the dead body in the mountains or far from the village and his family would have lived alone. Now, thank God, such commanders are no longer here because of the *Taliban*, because no one can own a rifle [the *Taliban* have collected many of the weapons in the areas they control]. Now everyone can move freely in the village.

(Interview, Ningrahar Province, 1997)

Many of the listener's comments concerning *New Home, New Life*'s portrayal of governance and politics during the ascendancy of the Taliban highlight the extent to which they exerted control over areas that previously had been ravaged by warlordism and human rights abuses. Although the Taliban controlled these areas with a violent conservatism, they were, at least initially from 1994, well received by Afghans who were tired of the exploitation and atrocities of the *Mujahideen*. The Taliban's brand of religious conservatism was very familiar to those living in rural areas. For urbanites, used to far greater freedoms, their rule was felt to be punitively harsh. Despite this, the Taliban's military conquest of up to 90 per cent of the country allowed Afghans, for the first time in many years, to think of the State of Afghanistan in more concrete and holistic terms. However, the lack of public services or limited choice in news and information media (in some parts, audiences tuned in to the

BBC Pashto Services to check what was happening locally), meant that identification with anything other than the disciplinary functions of the Taliban's state, as meted out through their religious police, remained weak. For many listeners, the very idea of a benevolent state, or even a state that citizens could access and use to pursue their interests and needs, remained an aspiration at best. It is perhaps unsurprising that the BBC AEP struggled over whether and how to represent the Taliban in *New Home, New Life*. Ironically, this in no way stopped it from maintaining its huge popularity amongst the audience, due in part to the radically limited intertextuality of media within Afghanistan during the 1990s. Thus, the choice by the BBC AEP to represent the Taliban obliquely through a hardening of traditional values and attitudes in some characters *did* work to a degree. This strategy provided a foil against which some of the more radically conservative injunctions of the Taliban, such as restricting girls from going to school and women from employment, could be problematised. The period of Taliban ascendancy was harsh, but in keeping with Afghan political history, it also proved to be relatively fleeting, forcing yet another representational conundrum on the *New Home, New Life* production.

Representing 'Liberal Democracy': The Period of Renewed International Influence (2002–Present)

During the months of October and November 2001, the US military completed an emphatic victory over the Taliban in direct response to the attacks of 11 September 2001 in New York that had been attributed to Osama Bin Laden, a long-time guest, financier and supporter of the conservative Islamic regime. In the initial period of conflict, occupation and uncertainty *New Home, New Life's* objectives took on new emphasis that resulted in the production being decoupled from routine audience evaluation and needs assessment processes (see Chapter 4), as recalled by a former BBC AEP manager:

> … the US-led war was a difficult period emotionally and operationally for everyone in the project. At the beginning there was a sense of shock and no one knew what to do. There were voices coming from London saying that *New Home, New Life* wasn't relevant and that information—in

other words news—was what was required. People in the BBC AEP were almost resigned to accept this view and agreed with stopping the broadcast [of the drama]. At one point the director of the project returned from Islamabad from a meeting were one of the DFID [UK Department for International Development] had summoned NGOs to persuade them to work closely with the military. The official was accompanied by British Army officers and asked colleagues [at the BBC AEP] to reflect on their own experience of the civil war. That meeting determined a new direction for the whole team and people brought their own personal experiences to the table, which resulted in a number of storylines for the drama and a huge number of programme ideas for AEP's educational features. This was one of the only occasions where storylines were not based on needs assessment but on the personal experiences of AEP's people.

(Personal Correspondence, 2008)

In an immediate sense the invasion and post-invasion periods of intense conflict allowed the production to revert to its favoured representational strategy, of vaguely identifying with a number of competing political groups, albeit enduring a more intense than normal period of military conflict. Here, *New Home, New Life* ostensibly connected to the experience of writers and producers who reflected on the intense conflicts of the Afghan–Soviet war (1979–1989) through which most of the writers had lived and worked. In this respect, a BBC AEP producer notes that 'we didn't reflect the US invasion as such. All we did was try and help people to behave as safely as possible under those circumstances'.

With the battle for military supremacy quickly over, the job of reconstruction and establishing a new democratic regime began in earnest. These two processes were reflected in *New Home, New Life's* ever-shifting narratives. Once again the fairly constant character set of the drama were heard to take on new roles, which were often connected to the re-emergence of some semblance of liberal democratic governance, as a young female listener notes regarding the new character role of the *Malik* (traditionally a local official that provides a link between government and village):

It [drama] explains to us what our *Malik*, elders, leaders and others do ... We were thinking that our *Maliks* are very good people, now we know the reality about some of them ... If a *Malik* is doing poppy trade, as a result he should go and hide with the animals which is so much shame for a well-respected person in society.

(Interview, Paktia Province, 1997)

A link between the three political moments identified in this chapter concerns the way the drama invokes tradition. In keeping with political practice in Afghanistan at moments of constitutional crisis, a grand assembly of tribes, elders, religious leaders and politicians—a *Loya Jirga* (Grand Assembly)—was called to redefine the political landscape of Afghanistan along liberal democratic lines. Subsequently, apart from informing Afghan citizens about their civic responsibilities and the electoral process, the drama quickly sought to reintroduce a more direct representation of government by allowing certain characters to take local government roles. New characters (such as the *Malik*) were also introduced. The representation of a stable government marked a radical new direction for the drama. The drama quickly shifted to identifying poor governance and good practice in political office. For example, the collusion of the *Malik* character with one of the *khan* (commander/landlord) characters in an opium deal was called into question and this allowed broader issues of corruption and bribery to be aired. Here, a middle-aged male listener notes that:

> The government is not weak. Most of the countries of the world helped it and many countries forces are busy helping the government physically and financially in terms of security. Now unfortunately our own government is a thief and their pockets never get full. How can we point out a thief to such a government? It is like pointing out one thief to another.

(BBC AEP, Focus Group Data, 2008)

Audience research offered suggestions about how government corruption might be addressed by introducing characters to 'sort other characters out': 'Police should be added to this drama, they should explain how police take bribes from the people. Once police and the people hear it on *New Home, New Life* from Radio BBC it will have a very positive effect on both' (BBC AEP, Focus Group Data, 2008).

Listeners were sceptical of the integrity of the Afghan police as revealed in comments, such as, 'a traffic policeman will hire his hat out to others for a day', so they can use the power it bestows to raise unscrupulous revenue. *New Home, New Life* has sought to introduce aspects of civic accountability and human rights. One such storyline concerns the aforementioned collusion of the *Malik* and *Khan* characters in opium production and sale in which a minor character that had been beaten is encouraged to seek recourse from the relevant local authorities:

Synopsis Scene 1 (outside):
Said Muhammad is washing his hands and face. Ghafar approaches and Said Muhammad notices Ghafar's bloody face and clothes. Ghafar says Adam Khan has injured his head. Said Muhammad asks the reason. Ghafar mentions the money which Adam Khan had given him for the exchange of opium. Said Muhammad becomes shocked and recalls Adam Khan promising to accept his own money. Ghafar says that Adam Khan is a person who doesn't keep his promise and has bad dealings. Said Muhammad asks him to sit and wash his face. Ghafar refuses and says he will go in this condition to the government in order to complain about Adam Khan.

(Episode 2098, broadcast on 25/08/2007)

Such a storyline makes it possible for audiences to conceive of complaining to a government that would respond to their concerns and interests. It reflects the political and civic changes that have occurred since 1994 when *New Home, New Life* was first broadcast. The rehabilitation of the government as an imaginable entity in the minds of the listeners is clearly reflected in both listeners' comments on the various portrayals of government authority, corruption and practice, as well as in reflections on the nature of the Afghan state more broadly. Importantly, the post-Taliban state was not resisted by writers but embraced. BBC policy on impartiality was not invoked to resist the advent of the new political realities dawning in Afghanistan, suggesting again that such policy is used within production in a far more calculating and strategic manner than one might think.

Conclusion

This chapter has shown how *New Home, New Life* makes a sense of state imaginable and tangible even if the model of the state that is promoted in the drama conforms to the conventions of western liberal democracies. The co-presence of services, public works and a plurality of media discourses concerning the state mean that not only can it be imagined, but also accessed (Gupta, 1995). Further, the rapid expansion of the media sector in Afghanistan, as a central plank of its push towards plurality, transparency and democracy in the post-Taliban period, has helped to broaden public dialogue about the role of the state in local and national life. Nonetheless, the penetration of the state into rural areas in Afghanistan still remains weak, and the resurgence of the Taliban in many southern Pashtun areas suggests that the current democratic government has some way to go before it can meaningfully extend itself across the whole of the country. However, our research with *New Home, New Life's* listeners has shown that, over time, they have come to see the state as responsible for delivering public services. Prior to 2002, few listeners ever mentioned the possibility that the state might play an active role in their lives. Vague aspirations that some form of more fair and systematic governance and citizen entitlements were imagined but not thought of as being within the realm of the possible.

It is clear that imagining and constructing a meaningful sense of state and civic responsibility remains fraught in Afghanistan and that the re-emergence of the Taliban is placing new pressures on *New Home, New Life's* communication strategy. Of course, dramas do not simply reflect reality in a direct and neutral way. Rather, social realism is constructed in the interplay between the observed realities of the audience as identified through audience research (see Chapter 4), the neo-liberal themes of donors and the liberal politics of media producers working in transnational teams. Finally, we should not lose sight of the fact that drama for development is as much about communicating hope as it is about communicating hardship. In this respect, portraying a positive and morally infused polity, be it traditional or democratic, provides listeners with competing and alternative narratives of development (Galavotti et al., 2001). Rigbey (1993)—a former producer of BBC Radio 4's *The Archers* and an initial consultant to *New Home, New Life*—suggests that drama can help forge a sense of belonging and connection for audiences, connections that they are keen to 'latch on' to. But depicting a sense of belonging to the Afghan state remains inherently problematic for *New Home, New Life* and very much a 'work in progress'.

Notes

1. *Pashtunwali* is a tribal honorific code that underpins Pashtun society. *Pashtunwali* 'is' culture and culture is not simply a given. It is regarded as something you are submerged within, it is something that you 'do' (Ahmed, 1980; Atayee, 1979; Barth, 1959; Lindholm, 1982). In this chapter, the term *Pashtu*, rather than *Pashtunwali*, is more commonly used. It connotes more than just a language but an arena of visible human agency that manifests itself in social norms about honour (*namus* or *gherat*) and modesty (*sharm*). Not offering the appropriate *melmastya* (welcome) to a visitor would render the host *begherat* or without honour. *Nanawatay* (refuge) represents another key concept within the tribal code of *Pashtunwali*, with the right of protection being granted to whoever requests it. Grima (1993) suggests that it is key to the building of patron–client relationships. The protection afforded to others raises the social standing of the patron who is often a wealthy *khan* (landlord). Often, such clients become the trusted house servants to a *khan*, his male kin and honoured guests. In another usage, *nanawatay* means pardon, in which an offence potentially punishable by death, such as murder, is offset against a payment that is made by the offender, commonly referred to as 'blood money'. *Badal*, another core cultural concept is most often equated with revenge, something that is taken, usually a debt incurred by a criminal. Exchanges such as 'taking' a blood debt for a life are regarded as *begherat* (without honour) since such exchanges can never balance. In a more conventional sense, *badal* simply means exchange and to 'do' *badal* is indicative of honorific exchange between those of equal social standing. Petty gifts are given and reciprocated, loans are made and returned and daughters exchanged in marriage, all under the honorific rubric of *badal*. All these core cultural concepts are represented and negotiated in *New Home, New Life*.

2. Maley (1998), unlike many other commentators discussing the rise of the Taliban movement, argues that they did not simply materialise on the battlefields of Afghanistan. Rather, they stem from a conservative religious tradition, the roots of which can be traced to the conservative Deobandi school of Sunni Muslim Islamic education and nearby politicised *madrassah*s across Afghanistan's southern border in Pakistan that continue to provide Islamic education. Within Afghanistan, local and loosely organised groups of *Talibs* have always existed. Maley points to the writings of Winston Churchill who as far back as 1898 commented on the 'wandering *Talib-ul-ilms*', as well as to more recent commentators who were seen to be fighting amongst *Mujahideen* forces in the mid-1980s during the height of the conflict. Taking the Province of Paktia and the area surrounding Khost town as an example, by 1991 the *Jamiat-e Tulaba* of Khost had formed, though this organisation is pre-dated by eight organisations that operated at a tribal level and represented groups of *Talibs* drawn from such Pashtun tribes as Mengal, Zadran and Ahmadzai. Though the ground force of the Taliban movement can be seen to have already been in place prior to its formal establishment, the impetus for the mass organisation of *Talib* groups appears to stem from modest beginnings. Davis (1998) notes that according to 'official' Taliban history the movement can be traced to a *madrassah* in Singesar village in Maiwand district, Kandahar Province.

By mid-1994 Mullah Mohammad Omar the organisation's founder, whose contemporary elevation to Afghanistan's Amir (Defender of the Faith) belies his humble beginnings at this simple village *madrassah*, had become 'incensed by the excesses of predatory *Mujahideen* bands on the provincial highways where arbitrary 'taxation', robbery and rape had become a depressing norm' (Davis, 1998: 43). This led to the taking-up of arms against these groups and the 'clearing-out' of 'criminals' along the main Kandahar–Herat highway. Following this, closer links between the *Mujahideen* Rabbani government in Kabul and members of the Pakistani Inter Services Intelligence (ISI) began to form, with organisational and military assistance being subsequently provided and financial aid stemming from Saudi Arabia (Davis, 1998). Maley rightly points to the continuities and fluidity in Afghan politics, a fluidity that has allowed members of *Mujahideen* groups, as well as reformed *Khalqi* (Pashtun) communists to enter the Taliban fold. He notes that the majority of the current Taliban leadership is predominantly drawn from ex-members of *Mujahideen* groups, most notably of Mohammad Nabi Mohammadi's *Harakat-e Inqelab-e Islami* party, a conservative religious party favoured by clerics who had little time for alternative Islamist parties with their socialist leanings and their tight party organisation.

References

Ahmed, A. (1980) *Pukhtun Economy and Society: Traditional Structure and Economic Development in a Tribal Society*. London: Routledge & Kegan Paul.

Anderson, B. (1983) *Imagined Communities: Reflections on the Origin and Spread of Nationalism*. London: Verso.

Anderson, J. (1983) 'Khan and Khel: Dialectics of Pakhtun Tribalism', in R. Tapper (ed.), *The Conflict of Tribe and State in Iran and Afghanistan*. London: Croom Helm.

Atayee, M. (1979) *A Dictionary of the Terminology of Pashtun's Tribal Customary Law and Usages*. Kabul: International Centre for Pashto Studies, Academy of Sciences of Afghanistan.

Azoy, W. (1982) *Buzkashi: Game and Power in Afghanistan*. Philadelphia: University of Pennsylvania Press.

Barth, F. (1959) *Political Leadership among Swat Pathans*. London: Athlone Press.

Butt, J. (1998) 'The *Taliban* Phenomenon', in E. Giradet and J. Walter (eds), *Essential Field Guides to Humanitarian and Conflict Zones: Afghanistan*. Geneva: International Centre for Humanitarian Reporting.

Davis, A. (1998) 'How the *Taliban* Became a Military Force', in W. Maley (ed.), *Fundamentalism Reborn? Afghanistan and the Taliban*. London: Hurst & Company.

Edwards, D. (1996) *Heroes of the Age: Moral Fault Lines on the Afghan Frontier*. Berkeley: University of California Press.

Galavotti, C., Pappas-DeLuca, K. and Lansky, A. (2001) 'Modelling and Reinforcement to Combat HIV: The MARCH Approach to Behavior Change', *American Journal of Public Health*, 91(10): 1602–1607.

Grima, B. (1993) *The Performance of Emotion among Paxtun Women: The Misfortunes which have Befallen me*. Karachi: Oxford University Press.

Gupta, A. (1995) 'Blurred Boundaries: The Discourse of Corruption, the Culture of Politics, and the Imagined State', *American Ethnologist*, 22(2): 375–402.

Herzfeld, M. (1992) *The Social Production of Indifference: Exploring the Symbolic Roots of Western Bureaucracy*. New York: Berg.

Hobsbawm, E. and Ranger, T. (1983) *The Invention of Tradition*. Cambridge: Cambridge University Press.

Lindholm, C. (1982) *Generosity and Jealousy: The Swat Pukhtun of Northern Afghanistan*. New York: Columbia University Press.

Maley, W. (1998) 'Introduction: Interpreting the *Taliban*', in W. Maley (ed.), *Fundamentalism Reborn? Afghanistan and the Taliban*. London: Hurst & Company.

Marsden, P. (1998) *The Taliban: War, Religion and the New Order in Afghanistan*. London: Zed Books.

Naby, E. (1986) 'The Changing Role of Islam as a Unifying Force in Afghanistan', in A. Banuazizi and M. Weiner (eds), *The State, Religion, and Ethnic Politics: Afghanistan, Iran, and Pakistan*. Syracuse: Syracuse University Press.

Rais, R. (1994) *War Without Winners: Afghanistan's Uncertain Transition After the Cold War*. Karachi: Oxford University Press.

Rigbey, L. (1993) *How to Write a Radio Soap Opera*. Unpublished Mimeo.

Roy, O. (1990) *Islam and Resistance in Afghanistan*. Cambridge: Cambridge University Press.

Rubin, B. (1995) *The Fragmentation of Afghanistan: State Formation and Collapse in the International System*. New Haven: Yale University Press.

Tapper, N. (1984) 'Causes and Consequences of the Abolition of Brideprice in Afghanistan', in N. Shahrani and R. Canfield (eds), *Revolutions & Rebellions in Afghanistan: Anthropological Perspectives*. Berkeley: Institute of International Studies, University of California.

Tapper, R. (1983) 'Introduction', in R. Tapper (ed.), *The Conflict of Tribe and State in Iran and Afghanistan*. London: Croom Helm.

8

DRAMATISING 'NEW NEPAL'

Andrew Skuse and Michael Wilmore

Introduction

Drama for development has long been understood as a 'world making' genre in the sense that its writers, editors and producers are actively engaged in challenging the socio-cultural contradictions, norms and mores that are perceived to act as 'brakes' on processes of social development, nation-building and modernisation (Allen, 1985; Das, 1995; Martín-Barbero, 1995; Rofel, 1995). The role of drama in problematising and promoting nationhood constitutes a particularly strong analytical prism within audience studies, with a focus on the emancipatory potential of drama being particularly prevalent (Abu-Lughod, 1995, 2004; Vink, 1988). Yet, promoting and representing aspects of modernity and nationhood is fraught with difficulty. Media environments are becoming increasingly complex and diverse and so the efficacy of 'nation-building narratives' become somewhat more diffused and dispersed. Further, audience engagement can never be assumed and responses to drama are inherently complex and contradictory. The style in which dramatic narratives are represented may work against the 'preferred meanings' that dramatists seek to embed within their productions. In seeking greater impact, many drama for development productions tend either to: (*a*) invest in complex evaluation regimes in order to better understand the informational needs and cultural dispositions of audiences so that a strong sense of social reality and subtlety in 'messages' can emerge; or (*b*) engage in radical innovation in creative styles and forms with a view to producing media that 'stands out from the crowd'. Both strategies involve 'working through' local cultural frames. This chapter examines the potential and challenges of radical creative innovation in drama for development.

The chapter focuses upon the BBC World Service Trust Nepal (BBC WST) *Katha Mitho Sarangiko* (*Sweet Tales of the Sarangi*)—a radio drama that adopts an innovative dramatic strategy to address some of the representational challenges associated with portraying shifts in contemporary nationhood in Nepal. *Katha Mitho Sarangiko* was broadcast on a national network of partner FM radio stations between 2008 and 2009, ran for 48 episodes and, like many other BBC WST radio dramas, was 15 minutes in duration. It continues to be broadcast/rebroadcast to this day. The drama sought to bridge a number of key political, ethnic and regional divisions in Nepal and consequently was set in the capital Kathmandu, the plains (*Terai*) town of Janakpur and the hills town of Pokhara. These three contexts are connected through the dramatic device of a wandering minstrel—the lead character Dilu, a *Sarangi* (bowed short-neck lute) player. The drama was part of a wider UNDP-funded peace-building mixed-media intervention (Nepal Conflict Transformation and Reconciliation Project) conducted by the BBC WST, focusing on peace-building and state reconstruction in the face of social and economic conflicts and changing political regimes. The drama, as evidenced by project documentation, addressed a range of 'key themes', including: (*a*) the culture of impunity and criminality (in the face of political fragmentation); (*b*) failure of local and national government to deliver change and civic services; (*c*) the bullying and disrespect perpetrated by political parties; (*d*) culture of protest; (*e*) ethnic and caste fragmentation into narrow interest groups; (*f*) frustration with the lack of change; (*g*) reliance on emigration; (*h*) unemployment of young men and (*i*) gender disparity (especially in the *Terai* [plains]).

Attempts to imagine Nepal as a modern and cohesive nation are beset by unhelpful dichotomies between modern and traditional and a static notion of nation and culture (see Burghart, 1984; Gellner et al., 1997; Whelpton, 2005). Liechty's recent examination of middle-class consumerism in contemporary Nepal reveals that:

> Nepal has long been a favoured site for Western projects of imagining 'tradition.' In almost all of these imaginings, Nepal and 'modern' end up on opposite ends of the conceptual spectrum. This contradiction presents Nepalis with a challenge—at once emotional, intellectual, and material—*to produce themselves* as members of, and inhabitants in, a world that is both modern *and* Nepali.

> (Liechty, 2003: xi)

Such imaginings of national community are frustrated by ethnic, linguistic and geographic (plains, hills and mountains) cleavages, as well as deep-seated inequalities relating to caste, poverty and disenfranchisement (Sharma, 2004). As Hutt (2003) observes, Nepal shares with Bhutan, and other multi-ethnic states of comparatively recent formation, the challenge of 'nationism' that is reflective of an ongoing search for a clear basis upon which a shared national identity can be built. Attempts to reassert Hindu monarchism as the rationale for shared national unity led to both political repression during the years of the *Panchayat* 'democracy' (1961–1989) and increasing unrest as the contradictions inherent in such a political strategy became evident. The *Panchayat* system rejected formal political parties in favour of locally elected pro-monarchists administrations, forcing many political groups to work clandestinely through such administrations. However, the power vacuum left by the collapse of royal rule in 1989 in Nepal and freeing of political organisation in 1990 has led to an increasingly fraught sense of ongoing political and ontological crisis over what constitutes Nepal as a nation. Consequently, the media in Nepal, and particularly the burgeoning radio sector, have thrived in response to audience demands for increased information, especially during the height of the Maoist insurgency and its immediate aftermath (Hutt, 2006; Onta, 2006; Whelpton, 2005; Wilmore, 2008). Further, increasing urbanisation, in part brought about by the flight of migrants fleeing violence in rural areas during the insurgency, as well as by rising living standards has increased the availability of media of all types.

In turn, this has led to new challenges in representing the Nepalese nation in which creative innovation, for example, playing with generic and narrative conventions plays a particularly important role in differentiating one broadcaster from another. As Benedict Anderson has pointed out: 'Communities are to be distinguished, not by their falsity/genuineness, but by the style in which they are imagined' (1983: 6).

Katha Mitho Sarangiko provides an excellent case study through which we can address some of the key questions facing the style in which the Nepalese nation is being imagined. What did creative innovation mean in the context of *Katha Mitho Sarangiko* and did it differentiate BBC WST drama productions from others? What creative strategies were employed by the dramatists? How did these strategies address the problem of representing Nepalese nationhood at a time of significant political change?

Katha Mitho Sarangiko's creative innovation can be located in the use improvisation and on-location recording, especially in the portrayal of the traditional practice of *miteri* (fictive kinship or 'blood-brotherhood'), and also in its approach to characterisation. These three creative strategies were designed to enable a sense of movement and connection between 'places' to be represented within the drama, and in the process, to convey the sense of an interconnected nation. In assessing these strategies, this chapter draws on qualitative data derived from focus group discussions conducted in the Kathmandu offices of the BBC WST with the production's Nepalese dramatists (Sushma Pandey, Deepak Rauniyar and Khagendra Lamichhane), Deputy Editor, Kedar Sharma and the British expatriate drama editor (Fiona Ledger).

'On-location': Innovations in Realism

On-location recording is the primary creative strategy used by dramatists to capture a sense of 'social realism' in *Katha Mitho Sarangiko* and forge a sense of dramatic connection between the capital Kathmandu with its urbane, intellectual and ethnically diverse population, Pokhara (a seat of Maoist influence) and the town of Janakpur (where *Madheshi's*, the plains population with historical and ethnic links to northern India are agitating for greater autonomy). Unlike its more conventional radio drama counterparts, the production is unscripted and based principally on a synopsis and guided improvisation. Its on-location recording utilises 'real' community members as actors—in addition to the small core of professionals the production employs—in the pursuit of more socially and culturally grounded drama output, itself a highly unusual and innovative strategy in the context of normally formulaic radio drama for development. The production's drama editor captures the nature of this improvisation:

> I think drama for development is heavily policed and controlled. [There is a] fear of not having a script! Nisha [an intern with BFM Biratnagar] was telling us that an NGO [she was familiar with] would sit in the studio and if one word was missing then it was 'stop the recording' ... [but] the message is in the aesthetics and if the creative side is done badly then there is no message! So you've got to write good drama number one, otherwise just forget it.

> (Fiona Ledger, Interview, Kathmandu, August 2008)

Here, the production logic seeks to escape formulaic and scripted dialogue in favour of 'good drama' based on social realist techniques that, it is hoped, can capture a more contemporary and 'realistic' portrayal of everyday life in which audiences can recognise their own lives. *Katha Mitho Sarangiko's* Nepalese dramatists suggested that by adopting an improvisational and context-driven approach, the production could help to 'mirror' real life with greater accuracy. In this sense, the use of on-location recording and improvisation reminiscent of the social realist traditions of British 'kitchen sink' drama of the 1960s as pioneered by directors and playwrights such as Ken Loach and John Osborne. British social realist TV drama in this vein uses improvisation to heighten social and political awareness and negotiate ways of tackling social problems (Heritage, 1998).

Social realist techniques often generate criticism among audiences more familiar with popular and formulaic dramatic conventions, but do culturally distinctive aesthetic sensibilities travel and make the translation of western social realist techniques difficult? Whether the use of improvisation and non-professional actors in *Katha Mitho Sarangiko* adds to the sense of social realism is uncertain. The BBC WST audience evaluation undertaken to date reveals a sense of appreciation and enjoyment by audiences, but also a sense of confusion over when and where the melodrama occurs. Such findings resonate with Burch's (2002) argument that culturally distinctive aesthetics are shared by regional audiences creating 'a kind of emerging South Asian [media] sensibility' and that these sensibilities may not mesh with Western tropes of realism, creative genres or technical norms. A similar point is made in Gillespie's (1995) ethnographic account of the confusion and distaste that mature-aged Asian viewers expressed regarding their viewing of Peter Brook's staged version of the *Mahabharata*, in contrast to their 'comfort' with the *Doordarshan*-made version of this sacred epic. When longstanding aesthetic sensibilities and conventions of realism are challenged or flouted, audiences may react with incomprehension or disdain.

Conventions of realism are culturally coded and relative which, we suggest, makes the translation of British social realism into other cultural contexts, particularly its associations with serious social messages, quite challenging. For example, for South Asian audiences the social 'seriousness' of a particular issue may be conveyed with greater dramatic force by visual iconography or by a combination of the tone of voice, the music, song and wider soundscapes that connect audiences to wider cosmological 'truths' than by more overtly didactic approaches to 'messaging' (Mankekar, 1999, 2002; Rajagopal, 2001). Likewise, the melodrama for which Bollywood cinema is especially famous, and which finds ready imitation in other media, might appear unsophisticated to audiences steeped in westernised realist traditions and regimes of representation. But Bollywood embodies 'a style that heightens dramatic contrasts and adds story emphases, pitching social change into the turbulence and uncertainty of individual experience' (Rajagopal, 2001: 97). Such covertly didactic strategies of contrast and emphasis that guide and lead audiences to certain understandings, may be particularly vital for audiences (especially those living in poverty with low levels of schooling and literacy) that rely in large part on popular oral, aural and visual traditions and cultural forms.

The use of innovative techniques in *Katha Mitho Sarangiko* broke the mould, but did social realist techniques, such as on location recording and the representation of three very different local dramatic contexts in one drama, 'translate' for audiences? The practice of on-location recording undeniably enables the production team to get 'up close and personal': to employ real people, places and the specific soundscapes that accompany them in a highly innovative way. The interplay of local sounds, voices, music and song plays a key role both in establishing the perceived 'realism' for writers and producers and is used in an attempt to both locate contexts and signpost scene shifts for the audience. The use of atmospheric and acoustic changes in sound, corresponding to the shifting of dramatic scenes and context, have been described as a key realist mechanism designed to appeal to what Rigbey (1993)—a former producer of BBC Radio 4's domestic production *The Archers*—calls 'basic ear psychology'. On-location recording shifts the impetus away from 'stock sounds', for example, of a certain context/thing, towards actual contexts and actual things (such as buses, teahouses, a door opening, etc.) and further explains production discourses concerning its own sense of 'supra-realism' and authenticity. For example, if the loose synopsis that the actors improvise from demands that a scene is set onboard a bus or in the ruins of a destroyed house, these locations can be sourced and a unique sound context captured. The realist impetus that on-location re-cording affords is also reflected in the performances of the actors which heightens the perceived sense of realism, as noted by the drama editor:

> For radio—we wanted them to use as much sound as they could. In fact, when you listen to the cut and mix we faded out about 4 seconds. To get the texture because this is a man, and that actor Suresh Chand, he's a professional actor but he was an internally displaced person and he lost his own property. So when he acted, that crying was very real because it came back to him. So the physicality of ownership, of coming back to your house and your land, and the way everything had been neglected, there were branches lying there, stones and sticks—so for radio there's a lot that can be communicated by sound—the locked door, the padlocked door.
>
> (Fiona Ledger, Interview, Kathmandu, August 2008)

The appeal of emotional and social realism in radio drama is very different to that of television or cinema, especially where representation of context is concerned. Hallam and Marshment (2000) describe visual media as immediate, 'actual' and 'iconic', while the anthropology of radio and sound highlights that an absence of visual imagery substantively contributes to both producers' and listeners' satisfaction with the media because far fewer constraints are placed upon the imagination (see Bull and Back, 2004). Though this suggests that radio might be more amenable than other media to imagining nationhood (among producers and audiences alike) than other media, on-location recording may serve to place checks on the ability of listeners to engage in such imaginative endeavours because the sounds captured during on-location may be too locally specific. This point is reflected in the comments of one of the dramatists who notes:

> You can hear the local language—areas are quite different. Different sounds from different parts of the country. Drinking tea in the *terai* [plains] and drinking tea in the mountains is quite different ... [we are using different sounds] to be accurate and authentic, but we've been criticised for it [by the audience] ... as people can't always connect these sounds to the place we record in.
>
> (Deepak Rauniyar, Interview, Kathmandu, August 2008)

The challenges of balancing dramatic depictions of the local and national, the particular and the general are considerable. Many listeners have little experience of life in the capital Kathmandu and even less of the regional towns of Pokhara and Janakpur. So while sonic realism creates a sense of local authenticity for some, it will inevitably be challenged by others. Might a more generic rendering of sound—vaguely capturing plains, hills, central or a mountain context—enable audiences to imagine and identify with particular locations as well as connect with national social and political issues? It is hard to say for sure but such creative decision-making is integral to making drama for development and gives us a glimpse into the challenges of translating cultural forms and conventions of realism.

Similar problems about balancing the local and the national emerge with regard to linguistic diversity, particularly in respect of the languages spoken in the *Terai* (plains). The desire to reflect language diversity appeals to the realist ambitions of the production, but the practicalities of broadcasting in a *lingua franca*, namely, Nepali and regional Nepali dialects takes priority over the representation of minority languages—as indeed it does in most drama serials across the world. However, some concessions are made to minority languages, as noted by the drama editor:

I don't think there was anything we recorded in the *Terai* that we didn't understand. Sometimes we had some of the characters—there was a young woman called Rinke who just lived in a house that we were recording because she was a bit of a charitable case because her husband had abandoned her, she was very shy and very pretty and we asked if she would like to have a small part in the drama—to come into the police station to report that her husband had been kidnapped in the drama. And she did that—because Dilu is friends with the police officer there was a kind of explaining [by Dilu] as we went along. If we said, 'right you've got to do it in Nepali' she couldn't have done it because you have to speak Nepali properly to be understandable. And so we let her [tell it in her own dialect]—and we let the emotions of it—it was a very short scene. She went off and with the money we paid her she went off and started a little snack business. We've used her again. We've used her twice. But somebody like that could never ever take part in a conventional drama.

(Fiona Ledger, Interview, Kathmandu, August 2008)

The improvisational approach to realist drama does allow for a more authentic and immediate feel to language diversity, and the kind of rapport struck up between local actors and the production team are clearly, at times, very consequential. But producers are quick to point out that the use of 'real-life' actors and 'real' locations, in other words cultural and contextual specificity, can only be pushed so far before it alienates the audience. This makes the tackling of broader agendas such as building a sense of national community and cohesion far harder to imagine. Close attention is paid to accents and customs in *Katha Mitho Sarangiko*, but language diversity also signals shifts in local context. Flashback devices are used to help the audience define when and where the drama is occurring. This is further strengthened through the use of additional 'directional' narration by the production's main character Dilu. Here, the drama editor notes:

… Dilu the storyteller narrator and main character has been clarifying links [between the three locations in the drama] and a lot of flashbacks are used. We had a lot of *Terai* wedding storylines and because in Pokhara the hill traditions are different in terms of dowry we had Dilu talk about his own traditions and how they are different and we flashback to a wedding where there is no dowry [so that comparison can be made] … [but] some people found flashbacks difficult and we've really thought about that and altered their pace ... to help people. More kind of recapping you know so you're really taking people by the hand and recognising difference, like with the wedding in the *Terai* and in Pokhara.

(Fiona Ledger, Interview, Kathmandu, August 2008)

The specificities of local culture and soundscapes produced by depictions of everyday rituals such as weddings that use flashback techniques may confuse audiences and so 'recapping' the key points is required to help audiences understand the subtleties of the production.

On-location recording clearly adds authentic sounds, characters, locations and ambience to the dramatic mix and augments the sonic, emotional and social realism of the drama. Like many other pro-social productions *Katha Mitho Sarangiko* is a fast-moving narrative propelled by the dramatists' creative instincts about what constitutes 'good drama'—and it is undoubtable that making good drama is the key goal. But good drama is a culturally relative aesthetic judgement which depends on levels of cultural capital and competences. Rigorous qualitative audience evaluation to assess audiences' informational needs and cultural dispositions may not always be possible due to budgetary constraints. On-location recording augments the sense of social realism but equating of the 'real' with the 'seriousness' of message does not necessarily deliver impact. Audiences listen with ears that are already accustomed to a preexisting Nepali mediascape in which the cosmic, the mythic and the fantastical may be equally important as the real (Mankekar, 1999, 2002; Rajagopal, 2001; Gillespie, 1995). It is interesting to note that initial ideas about connecting the production's three fictive locations via a chorus of Hindu Gods looking down from above were abandoned because such a strategy might have alienated non-Hindu audiences. But perhaps such a strategy might have had spiritual, sacred and cosmic resonances for a majority? As with the making of all cultural products, the outcomes of creative decision-making cannot be known in advance.

Prior familiarity with the Nepali mediascape and with the cultural consciousness and dispositions of audiences provide the most important resources at the disposal of dramatists. Creative innovation and the kind of playfulness with social realist techniques displayed in *Katha Mitho Sarangiko* are also necessary to pushing dramatic boundaries. But there is always the Brechtian dilemma that too much innovation risks alienating or confusing audiences if the drama fails to 'ring true' or conform to the expectations about what constitutes 'proper' drama (Mankekar, 1999, 2002; Rajagopal, 2001). Scripting and producing drama for development involves complex acts of cultural translation and transgression—playing with repetition and innovation, recognition and renewal and in doing so, it seeks to enact its own strategies of mediation to find a place in the imagination of the audience.

Fictive Kinship, Tradition and National Cohesion

The need to find a plausible way to bring together social actors within the drama who might otherwise exist in separate socio-cultural localities led the producers of *Katha Mitho Sarangiko* to employ the institution of *miteri*, described by Messerschmidt (1982: 5) as a 'form of fictive kinship'. This strategy, along with the primary device of using a wandering musician and storyteller as the main character, supported attempts on the part of producers to build links between the multiplicity of ethnic, caste and political affiliations in Nepal. In terms of the drama's role in building a sense of imagined national community, this dramatic device proved to be very useful because *miteri* is one of the few social institutions that have in the past been seen as capable of creating a sense of unity transcending cultural, caste and geographical boundaries. As a dramatic technique, it is not unfamiliar to Nepali audiences. Writers such as Munjushree Thapa in her acclaimed novel *The Tutor of History* (2001) used *miteri* to perform a similar function. Further, the practice is frequently represented in Nepali folk tales. Increasingly though, *miteri* is deployed as a symbol of a vanishing Nepal, emblematic of principles of unity and community that have been shattered by the violent events of past decades. So although its relevance to contemporary social life in Nepal is regarded as diminishing, analysis suggests that *miteri* is employed as a dramatic device to support and rationalise the 'national' wanderings of the central *gandharba* character, Dilu, as he travels to meet his *mit* (blood brother) friend Sukinder, the son of a Madhesi trader. These wanderings to different places (Kathmandu, Pokhara and Janakpur) serve to position the character as a living symbol, representative of an ongoing journey between past and future nations. *Miteri* not only provides a reason for

Dilu to pay frequent visits to places to which he would otherwise have no reason to travel, but it mediates a particular sentiment of nostalgic longing for previously lauded principles of national community that might resonate with the audience. Messerschmidt elaborates on the importance of the institution:

> Nepal's caste oriented society normally restricts kinship to the horizontal ties of consanguinity and affinity. The *miteri* allows the alternative of forming fictive kinship ties between members of otherwise endogamous groups and allows bonds of association to flourish vertically ... Such systems of relationship are often modelled on real kin ties and tend to link individuals, networks of individuals, and larger ... groups together for both affective and instrumental reasons. They are often found at the forefront of social change movements, serving in some instances to buffer individuals from change, and in other instances to enhance social mobility and ease adaptation to change.
>
> (1982: 5–6)

Popularly perceived as a form of 'blood brotherhood or sisterhood' the *mit* (male) and *mitini* (female) relationship is sealed via a formal initiation ceremony in which the 'blood brothers' or 'sisters' exchange gifts, agree to adopt the same formal obligations implied by biological kinship and thereafter feast. This point is reinforced by the Nepalese drama writers who all acknowledge that whilst *miteri* is now somewhat unfashionable in a formal sense, lots of people still hold such ceremonies informally, due to the perceived benefits of having what amounts to a duplicate non-kin family at one's disposal. As the drama editor notes, '... it's the one traditional institution that sanctions close relations with people from totally different castes and different areas—that's why it is rather extraordinary' (Fiona Ledger, Interview, Kathmandu, August 2008). The ability of the production to link characters of differing caste across regions is of fundamental importance given its development brief of problematising the fractious nature of Nepali politics at a moment of pivotal change, nationhood, governance and civil society, much of which reflects the contradictions and constraints of caste.

Ethnographic data highlight both affective (mutual affection) and instrumental (access to resources and social mobility for lower caste people or to neutralise the bad horoscope of an upper caste person) reasons for engaging in *miteri*. Typically the practice involves (ritualistically) creating bonds between people of a similar age who observe the key lifecycle events and rituals of their *mit* or *mitini*. In *Katha Mitho Sarangiko* a key element of *miteri* bonds relates to regional trade within Nepal and here Messerschmidt (1982) observes that hospitality is a key obligation associated with the practice, it being common for traders to organise *mit* (male blood brothers) along favoured trade routes to ensure access to food and accommodation. The use of *miteri* provided the audience with a familiar cultural institution and plausible reason to creatively link 'people' across both time and space. Although a clever device in this context it may be regarded as 'nostalgic' or at least an attempt to create a bridge between the past and present for as stated above, *miteri* was always at the forefront of social change.

Nostalgia, as Battaglia (1995) and Strathern (1995) argue, can be used actively and effectively as a creative ingredient in the reconstruction of 'ways of life' for the displaced. Here, linking to the past is critical to the search for stability during unstable times, and the use of the practice by producers can be perceived in a similar light. *Miteri* invokes a time when Nepal was more stable, more cohesive and subject to the rule of law. Though clever and creative, this strategy also runs some risks, because images of 'community' and 'stability' are inevitably written into both the past and tradition (cf. Williams, 1973). Consequently, those who are most often represented in these terms, primarily the majority of Nepalese living in villages, may find themselves politically marginalised, as the past and tradition connote significant aspects of disempowerment and marginalisation. Here, Pigg suggests:

> The category of the village follows the channels that connect Nepal to other places. It connects the cosmopolitan Nepalis who can recognize villagers to a worldwide discourse about the Third World and modernity. It translates the particularities of Nepal into the Esperanto of global social categories. Nepali villagers are seen to be more like any other Third World villagers than like Nepalese elites. By virtue of their participation in this language of categorization, cosmopolitan Nepalis stake out their place in a global society and legitimate their political authority over villagers who do not understand their villageness.
>
> (1992: 511–512)

The deployment of *miteri* therefore solves some practical problems for the drama producers, enabling the connection of characters that would otherwise remain socially remote from each other. Nevertheless, it also runs the risk of introducing alternative forms of social distancing, predicated on divisions between rural and urban localities into the programme. However, the producers' parallel strategy of 'realism', including improvisation and the incorporation of real people on-location, militates against the types of stereotyping observed by Pigg (1992) in everyday discourse and the Nepali media through the disruption of such expectations. Again, the producers tread a fine line between creative innovation aimed at challenging hegemonic socio-political expectations, and the repetition of conventional dramatic tropes directed at working within the parameters of what a highly diverse audience can 'digest' in terms of mediated discourse, the term representing a popular metaphor used to describe feelings about media content that audiences variously like or dislike (Wilmore, 2008).

Capital, Hills and Plains: Weaving the Nation through the Movement of Characters

One of the principal problems *Katha Mitho Sarangiko* faced in addressing national reconciliation and cohesion is reflected in the different cultural contexts that the production tries to weave together—capital, hills and plains. The drama, in pursuit of its contribution to the 'goal' of peace-building and reconciliation, sought to structure dramatic bridges between these very different geographical and ethnic contexts through the travels of the central character and wandering *sarangi* player Dilu, who fulfils a traditional *gandharba* (musician and storyteller) role within the drama. Whilst the practice of *miteri* outlined above provided some of the 'reason' for the character to move between the dramatic contexts of Kathmandu, Pokhara and Janakpur, BBC WST production notes also point to the dramatic scope of his role:

> ... striking up friendships and making connections between the different communities, exploring the tensions and the conflict—both social and political in Nepal. Dilu is both a key character and a narrator of events

in his own life and—in much the same way as a Greek chorus—the lives of others. A key friendship that emerges early on in the series is the relationship between Dilu and a *Madheshi* [Ramcharan Gupta] trader whose business has prospered through his friendship with a *Pahardi* trader [Bhim Bahadur]. Both men are subject to threats from *Terai* extremists. Through this storyline the tensions of the *Terai* are explored.

(BBC World Service Trust Nepal, Production Notes, n.d.)

The *gandharba* character was not the first choice of main character for the production. Rather a 'guru-type' role was the first suggestion by the writing team. This was discarded (along with the previously mentioned idea to link the regions represented in the production through Hindu Gods) because of a potentially negative identification with current political conflicts, for example, Hindu extremists. Many BBC WST dramas for development tend not to explicitly name political or religious groups in a given context, preferring instead to take a more vague approach to representing social and political events (BBC World Service, 1993; Skuse, 2002, 2005). Ironically, such restrictions may act as a check on innovation in social realist terms, especially when we consider the political complexity and animosity that has plagued Nepal in recent years.

The production uses the *sarangi* player, Dilu, as a connecting link. As a travelling musician, he had a clear and plausible reason to travel between the contexts of Kathmandu, Pokhara and Janakpur in pursuit of his profession. These travels, in the eyes of the drama writers and producers, serve to weave together the disparate ethnic, caste and political stances that characterise contemporary Nepal. In keeping with the realist credentials and aesthetics promoted by the production, the role of Dilu was filled by a 'real-life' *gandharba* (Prakash Gandharva), who is described by the writers as a 'naturally gifted' actor. His ability to actually play the *sarangi*—his major prop—is perceived by writers to add to the 'authenticity' of the production. The *gandharba* role, like that of the kin-practice of *miteri*, is also nostalgic and likewise appeals to a mythic past of social and political stability. The portrayal of national stability across the regions, as well as problematisation of recent instabilities, is a key goal of the production, with the definition of this character helping to throw light on a wide range of political and caste issues of relevance to the emerging 'new Nepal':

... there are some *gandharba* who have become very successful. We met some really good *gandharba* who were really professional. But there are some who kind of float around Kathmandu serving kind of toy *sarangis*—slightly degraded. Their status is ... I mean I think that of all the *dalits* [lower castes], they have a kind of sort of freedom that other *dalits* don't have. They can sort of come and go in a way. I think they're very interesting as a group. They have this kind of traditional role of spreading stories to communicate the news.

(Fiona Ledger, Interview, Kathmandu, August 2008)

The traditional role of wandering minstrels as storytellers and precursors to the tabloid press is common across many cultures, and it is clearly a useful device in this context. However, vagrancy arising from landlessness is particularly prevalent amongst Nepal's *dalit* population, and the result of extreme poverty and caste-based discrimination and therefore not freedom as such (Salter and Gurung, 1996: 39).

The *gandharba* character is not the only character in *Katha Mitho Sarangiko* to transcend space and perform a creative 'linking' function. The role of the police and the two traders that Dilu regularly encounters on his travels serve to link ethnic groups, different castes and discrete geographical regions together, and therein an implicit sense of nationhood. Frequently, the target for Maoist violence during the civil conflict (1998–2008), the police constitute a key force for its preservation, for corruption and also conflict. The rehabilitation of the police as a credible force that upholds human rights and justice was perceived by the production to be critical to its goal of strengthening 'the rule of law' and reducing the 'culture of impunity' still evident in many contexts.

The representation of *Terai* violence and the police response to it is a major dramatic theme of the production. In this context, extremist threats against the character Bhim, a *Pahadi* (hills-dweller) trader, and his friend Ramcharan, a *Madheshi* (plains-dweller) trader, lead the policeman character, Binayadhos, to dutifully investigate them. This elevates the police character above the ethnic and caste-based politics that pervade the region and positions him as a force for 'good'. The policeman is a family friend of the *gandharba* Dilu, and though originally from the *Terai* he worked for many years in Pokhara, Dilu's own town in the hills. The production uses supporting characters with 'experience' of the nation and national issues and weaves them into the fabric of the drama. The police provide a critical bridge between regions, ethnicities and castes through their movement. Such mobilities are designed to remove them from the potentially corrupting influences of local political, ethnic and kin connections, which may dilute their resolution to uphold the rule of law.

Conclusion

Though many dramas for development claim 'social realist' credentials, few have achieved such a clear sense of immediacy and social intimacy as *Katha Mitho Sarangiko*. Its deployment of radical creative innovation and on-location recording pushed the boundaries of the genre. The creative devices used to link the three contexts of the production highlight the opportunities as well as the constraints of balancing the use of traditional institutions as dramatic devices and adopting a playfulness with realist conventions. Working through the numerous cultural and political contradictions that threaten the national cohesion of Nepal while applying innovative aesthetic forms and conventions requires complex cultural negotiation and translation. Social realist dramas are often assumed to embed 'serious' messages about social change, but dramatists and producers have to develop narratives that have broad cultural appeal and seriousness may be conveyed very differently in different performance traditions. Conventions of social realism are historically and culturally relative and so achieving social, sonic and emotional realism via the realist technique of on-location recording may challenge, disappoint or even offend the aesthetic sensibilities of audiences trained in different traditions and used to different conventions of realism.

In *Katha Mitho Sarangiko*, an overtly didactic realism is eschewed in favour of illuminating social realities that speak to the hardships and uncertainties of contemporary life in Nepal:

> ... we didn't want to preach anything through our drama. We just wanted to present the real situations of our country. People should understand the circumstances clearly. If they do, we believe they are mature enough to take their own decisions.
>
> (Khagendra Lamichhane cited in Kathmandu Post, 12 January 2008)

Critically engaged audience evaluation is important to assessing the success of creative innovation and realist techniques, but experimentation is also the life blood of creating valuable dramas for development. The employment of 'pedagogic' devices such as flashbacks and narration that provide the audience with signposts about shifts in context were combined with the improvisational techniques—and this mix of old and new, innovative and traditional—characterises the creative strategy. The *Katha Mitho Sarangiko* production team were aware and responsive to the fact that some audiences found their use of novel techniques confusing. The use of creative linking strategies, including the use of traditional practices such as *miteri* and of mobile characters such as the *gandharba* and policeman character were used to 'weave' a sense of nation and problematise cultural and political contradictions.

Clearly, a great deal of cross-cultural 'coalescing' and creative innovation took place during the production of *Katha Mitho Sarangiko* production, but this was in the context of a rapidly changing Nepalese mediascape. The production, like so many other dramas for development, forged a realist path in pursuit of the 'seriousness' that the weighty themes of national cohesion and stabilisation seem to demand. The radical creativity of on-location recording, improvisation, the use of non-professional actors, the employment of traditional fictive-kinship practices, the use of nationally 'mobile' characters and close attention paid to the authenticity of sound and dialect all contribute to the augmented sense of realism. This chapter has reflected selective perceptions of the creative team about realism as technique, aesthetic and discourse and our analysis of those perceptions. What audiences made of the drama remains a story yet to be told in full, though it is clearly one that is worth telling.

References

Abu-Lughod, L. (1995) 'The Objects of Soap Opera: Egyptian Television and the Cultural Politics of Modernity', in D. Miller (ed.), *Worlds Apart: Modernity Through the Prism of the Local*. London: Routledge.

———. (2004) *Dramas of Nationhood: The Politics of Television in Egypt*. Chicago: University of Chicago Press.

Allen, R. (1985) *Speaking of Soap Operas*. Chapel Hill: The University of North Carolina Press.

Anderson, B. (1983) *Imagined Communities: Reflections on the Origin and Spread of Nationalism*. London: Verso.

Battaglia, D. (1995) 'On Practical Nostalgia: Self-prospecting among Urban Trobrianders', in D. Battaglia (ed.), *Rhetorics of Self-Making*. Berkeley: University of California Press.

BBC World Service. (1993) *BBC Producer's Guidelines*. London: BBC World Service.

BBC World Service Trust Nepal. (n.d.) *Production Notes*. Mimeo.

Bull, M. and Back, L. (2004) *Auditory Cultures Reader: Sensory Formations*. Oxford: Berg Publications.

Burch, E. (2002) 'Media Literacy, Cultural Proximity and TV Aesthetics: Why Indian Soap Operas Work in Nepal and the Hindu Diaspora', *Media, Culture and Society*, 24: 571–579.

Burghart, R. (1984) 'The Formation of the Concept of the Nation-state in Nepal', *Journal of Asian Studies*, 44(1): 101–125.

Das, V. (1995) 'On Soap Opera: What Kind of Anthropological Object is it'?, in D. Miller (ed.), *Worlds Apart: Modernity through the Prism of the Local*. London: Routledge.

Gellner, D., Pfaff-Czarnecka, J. and Whelpton, J. (1997) *Nationalism and Ethnicity in a Hindu Kingdom: The Politics of Culture in Contemporary Nepal*. Amsterdam: Harwood Academic Publishers.

Gillespie, M. (1995) *Television, Ethnicity and Cultural Change*. London: Routledge.

Hallam, J. and Marshment, M. (2000) *Realism and Popular Cinema*. Manchester: Manchester University Press.

Heritage, P. (1998) 'The Promise of Performance: True Love/Real Love', in R. Boon and J. Plastow (eds), *Theatre Matters: Performance and Culture on the World Stage*. Cambridge: Cambridge University Press.

Hutt, M. (2003) *Unbecoming Citizens: Culture, Nationhood, and the Flight of Refugees from Bhutan*. New Delhi: Oxford India Paperbacks.

———. (2006) 'Things That Should Not Be Said: Censorship and Self-censorship in the Nepali Press Media, 2001-02', *The Journal of Asian Studies*, 65(2): 361–392.

Kathmandu Post. (2008) 'Radio Drama Series through Dilu', *Kathmandu Post*, Kathmandu, 12 January.

Liechty, M. (2003) *Suitably Modern: Making Middle-class Culture in a New Consumer Society*. Princeton: Princeton University Press.

Mankekar, P. (1999) *Screening Culture, Viewing Politics: An Ethnography of Television, Womanhood, and Nation in Postcolonial India*. Durham: Duke University Press.

———. (2002) 'Epic Contests: Television and Religious Identity in India', in F. Ginsburg, L. Abu-Lughod and B. Larkin (eds), *Media Worlds: Anthropology on New Terrain*. Berkeley: University of California.

Margulies, I. (2002) 'Bodies Too Much', in I. Margulies (ed.), *Rites of Realism: Essays on Corporeal Cinema*. Durham: Duke University Press.

Martín-Barbero, J. (1995) 'Memory and Form in the Latin American Soap Opera', in R. Allen (ed.), *To Be Continued … Soap Operas around the World*. London: Routledge.

Messerschmidt, D. (1982) 'Miteri in Nepal: Fictive Kin Ties that Bind', *Kailash: Journal of Himalayan Studies*, 9: 5–43.

Onta, P. (2006) *Mass Media in Post-1990 Nepal*. Kathmandu: Martin Chautari.

Pigg, S. (1992) 'Inventing Social Categories through Place: Social Representations and Development in Nepal', *Comparative Studies in Society and History*, 34(3): 491–513.

Porton, R. (2002) 'Mike Leigh's Modernist Realism', in I. Margulies (ed.), *Rites of Realism: Essays on Corporeal Cinema*. Durham: Duke University Press.

Rajagopal, A. (2001) *Politics after Television: Hindu Nationalism and the Reshaping of the Public in India*. Cambridge: Cambridge University Press.

Rigbey, L. (1993) *How to Write a Radio Soap Opera*. Mimeo.

Rofel, L. (1995) 'The Melodrama of National Identity in Post-Tiananmen China', in R. Allen (ed.), *To Be Continued … Soap Operas around the World*. London: Routledge.

Salter, J. and Gurung, H. (1996) *Faces of Nepal*. Lalitpur: Himal Publications.

Sharma, P. (2004) *The State and Society in Nepal: Historical Foundations and Contemporary Trends*. Lalitpur: Himal Publications.

Skuse, A. (2002) 'Vagueness, Familiarity and Social Realism: Making Meaning of Radio Soap Opera', *Media, Culture and Society*, 24(3): 409–427.

———. (2005) 'Voices of Freedom: Afghan Politics in Radio Soap Opera', *Ethnography*, 6(2): 159–181.

Strathern, M. (1995) 'Nostalgia and the New Genetics', in D. Battaglia (ed.), *Rhetorics of Self-Making*. Berkeley: University of California Press.

Thapa, M. (2001) *The Tutor of History*. New Delhi: Penguin India.

Vink, N. (1988) *The Telenovela and Emancipation: A Study on TV and Social Change in Brazil*. Amsterdam: Royal Tropical Institute.

Whelpton, J. (2005) *A History of Nepal*. Cambridge: Cambridge University Press.

Williams, R. (1973) *The Country and the City*. London: Chatto and Windus.

Wilmore, M. (2008) *Developing Alternative Media Traditions in Nepal*. Lanham: Lexington Books.

9

A DYNAMIC ENCODING PROCESS

MAKING THE CAMBODIAN *'TASTE OF LIFE'* DRAMA

Lɪᴢᴢ Fʀᴏsᴛ Yᴏᴄᴜᴍ

Introduction

This chapter uses the BBC World Service Trust (BBC WST) Cambodian television drama, *Taste of Life*, as an entry point to examine shifting priorities among the key players involved in making a drama for development. It traces how various logics of practice (Bourdieu, 1990) influence how and when the development, drama, audience, media and managerial/editorial players exercise varying degrees of power at different stages in the drama-making process. It highlights the tensions between the competing concerns and logics of practice among the different players and fields involved in making an entertainment-education (E-E) drama that engages audiences while simultaneously achieving development-oriented outcomes focused on social change.

The production of a drama for development is a complex and multi-layered series of staged activities in which a range of dynamic interactions emerge between key players (donor, technical, managerial and creative). The production process occurs within larger professional and organisational processes. The processes have both complementary and contradictory aspects. These are implicitly and explicitly acknowledged to varying degrees by the various key players. Despite tensions that arise, the participation of the key players is predicated on the need to work together to achieve the common aim of making a drama to advance specific development objectives. This chapter presents and examines the various stages involved in making a drama for development. In doing so, it explores the roles of key players and how they negotiate their power and position to meet their professional and practical interests. Milestones in the drama-making process are identified in which the negotiated transfers of power can be identified as both instrumental and productive. Drama production is referred to and examined up to the point in the process that a script is approved for actual recording, as well as after it has been recorded and is presented to audiences. The technical processes of recording and editing the drama are not included (see Chapter 4 in this volume for more detail on production and editing processes) despite the important role they play in crafting the audio and visual outputs with which audiences engage. The insights presented in this chapter draw on six years of experience working with projects that produce dramas for development. The specific information about the Cambodian *Taste of Life* drama is supplemented with interview material from dramatists involved in other BBC WST drama productions.[1]

The *Taste of Life* Drama Project: Players and Logics of Practice

Taste of Life was a television drama serial produced under the auspices of a broader project funded by the UK Department for International Development (DFID) titled 'Strengthening Cambodia's Response to HIV/AIDS'. In Cambodia, an estimated 1.9 per cent of the population between 15 and 49 years of age are reported to have HIV, making it a significant national health issue (National Centre for HIV/AIDS, Dermatology and STD, 2005). However, at the project's inception, epidemiological evidence indicated a decline in HIV prevalence since 2000.

To broaden its health focus, the BBC WST undertook an assessment of other health issues affecting the population and identified infant and child (under 5 years old) mortality rates in Cambodia as among the highest in Southeast Asia. Accordingly, senior managers based in London renegotiated with DFID to extend the project's remit to cover maternal and child health in addition to HIV and AIDS.

Each of the players involved in making a drama for development has his/her own orientation. This orientation is shaped by their organisational and professional affiliations and their roles and responsibilities within the project, essentially, what Bourdieu (1990) calls their 'logics of practice'. Bourdieu's writing about social forms, symbols and practices speak to the non-formal, but deeply ingrained methods, processes, symbols and orientations that people adhere to and use to guide their interactions with others. These logics of practice emerge from one's *habitus* (commonly translated as 'field'), which can be understood as: 'sets of norms, values, and unwritten laws upon which the actions of all players in a field are based' (Eikhof and Haunschild, 2007: 526).

This sense of competing agendas and power struggles between the players involved in drama production is akin to Adorno's notion of *kraftfeld* or force-field (see Jay, 1993: 2) and is similar to Lewin's (1941) earlier concept of the term. Lewin (1941) points out that field theory 'emphasizes the importance of the fact that any event is the result of a multitude of factors' (1941: 293). He asserts that any description of a situation needs to 'include (1) the relative position of the parts of the field at the time; (2) the direction and the velocity of the changes going on at that time' (Lewin, 1941: 299). Lewin also points out that 'the boundary conditions of a field are essential characteristics of that field' (1941: 307). His subsequent 'force-field analysis' model describes a level of performance as being a state of equilibrium between driving, encouraging forces and restraining, discouraging forces. For the BBC WST, these fields are embodied and exert themselves both internally and externally. The analysis undertaken herein is driven by a desire to understand and make explicit all forces acting on a given issue or situation, in order to explain the equilibrium and how it may be changed.

Bouman (1999) identifies four distinct institutional models that can be applied to 'collaboration' in E-E projects and describes the different power relationships in each. Bouman also describes collaboration, such as the BBC WST's work in making dramas for development, as 'high-risk ventures' in which 'an asymmetry of power between two collaborating professional fields' is evident, namely, between 'television and health communication professionals' (2002: 241). She elaborates, noting:

> In E-E collaboration, many stakeholders struggle for control or access. This is a dynamic interactive process in which some of those who participate in the creation have more power in determining the content than others ... If some stakeholders who participate in the design process have more power and influence to determine the content of the programmes than others, the balance of power may become asymmetric.
>
> (Bouman, 1999: 132)

Tensions—Paradoxes of Creativity

This chapter draws on Hall's model of the 'circuit of culture' to illuminate the production cycle and key players involved in the dynamic process of meaning creation. The model stresses the sequence of communication moments, the cyclical nature of the sequence and the dynamic interrelatedness of the moments (1997: 1–11). Hall (1990) identifies five 'linked but distinctive moments' in the process of communication: production, circulation, distribution, consumption and reproduction. The 'object' of these practices is the meanings that are conveyed via a range of specific, recognisable symbols and signs. Hall notes that the production process requires 'material instruments—its means as well as its own set of social (production) relations—the organization and a combination of practices within media apparatuses' (1990: 508). During the production moment, 'production constructs the message' (Hall, 1990: 509).

Useful as Hall's model is for thinking through the wider institutional processes of production from a 'sociology of culture' perspective, it does not reflect the contingencies of specific projects in the field of drama for development. In this respect, the case study of film-making by DeFillippi and Arthur (1998) is helpful in highlighting key aspects of 'project-based' enterprises from strategic, management and career perspectives. The authors describe these aggregations as 'companies formed to pursue a specific project outcome' (DeFillippi and Arthur, 1998: 125). For those involved in project-based careers, their work typically involves the performance of highly skilled, 'complex, non-routine tasks that require ... collaboration of diversely skilled specialists' (DeFillippi and Arthur, 1998: 125). Moreover, their work, requiring crucial inputs into the final product, is often produced as fragments of a finished product that is in the process of construction and compilation throughout: 'Very few film project employees participate in all stages of production' (DeFillippi and Arthur, 1998: 131). In fact, the project staffing is characterised by a 'pattern of progressive dissolution' and departures of those involved in making a film concluding their involvement in the production long before the film's release.

DeFillippi and Arthur (1998) refer to two distinctive sets of participants in a film-making project: those with 'creative/artistic' roles and those with commercial or economic roles. Noting that independent film-making is financed by project-specific capital investments, those in commercial roles are under strong business obligation to the investors: 'The overall effect of these temporary capital investments is to constrain the level of autonomy for the project-based enterprise' (DeFillippi and Arthur, 1998: 130). Managers and other participants in creative and cultural industries have to address challenges posed by seemingly contradictory practices. Practices of managing creativity revolve around 'two key foci: (i) managing creative personnel and (ii) managing creative processes' (DeFillippi et al., 2007: 515). They note:

> Managing creative personnel poses challenges because of tensions that arise based on the dual goals of commerce and art, often associated with exploitation for efficiency and profitability contrasted with exploration in which returns are both uncertain and not limited to economic ends.
>
> (DeFillippi et al., 2007: 515).

In the case of making a drama for development, these management challenges are compounded by the necessity for the project to be accountable to multiple players who have differing priorities and concerns: the investor—the donor—for its development objectives as well as economic investment; to the multitude of international, national and local 'stakeholders' for whom the expected development practice is that projects will consult; as well as the media broadcasters who are key to actually delivering the drama to audiences.

The Players and What They Represent in Making *Taste of Life*

A number of key figures that were both internal and external to the BBC WST played a role in producing Cambodia's *Taste of Life*. They were from different types of organisations and institutions, different sectors of the economy and had different professional backgrounds. Broadly, the five fields they represented were: (*a*) development; (*b*) media; (*c*) drama (writers); (*d*) the audience and (*e*) management and editorial staff. These players had different functions and concerns, reflecting those of their organisations and their own professional expertise (see Table 9.1).

There are not only internal and external dynamics but also significant differences in priorities and power relations that have to be negotiated across fields and their logics of practice.

Table 9.1
***Taste of Life* Drama Production Constellation**

	Inhabitants of the field	
Key fields	*Internal to the BBC WST*	*External to the BBC WST*
Development	Project Director	Donor: DFID, Campaign Working Group members
Drama	Executive Producer, Dramatists	
Audience	Drama Researchers, Audience Researchers	Audience
Media	Project Director, Executive Producer,	Broadcast Partners (TVK, TV5) and their competitors (CTN), Media Regulatory Authorities
Management/ Editorial	Project Director, London Project and Senior Management	

Source: Author.

Securing the Drama Project, Establishing the Message Brief

> The institutional structures of broadcasting [...] are required to produce a programme. Production, here, constructs the message. In one sense, then, the circuit begins here.
>
> (Hall, 1990: 509)

The BBC WST's establishment of a contract with a donor can be regarded as the formal 'start' of a drama for development project, as well as the beginning of the initial production moment in the 'circuit' or 'loop' of communication. The development field dominates the commissioning stage of the drama project, by the donor stating its programmatic aims, funding priorities and budget limitations.

> ... via a proposal that we submitted to a funder, which would be in response to a call for proposals typically, or whether it's a direct approach from a funder to the BBC WST asking to run a project on their behalf [...] then from there, you would sit and agree what the overall aims and the highest level goals of the project are.
>
> (*Taste of Life* Project Manager, Interview, 2008)

From the outset of the production process the donor, as inhabitant of the development field, determines what the drama's focus and agenda will be, as well as the criteria by which its success will be measured. The dominance of development players at this stage of a drama project does not change even if there are multiple donors with competing priorities and agendas; however, donors with conflicting agendas can create a problem in obtaining clarity of focus and establishing which issues should take priority in the drama. The proposal and contract use words like 'objectives', 'intervention', 'target audiences', 'indicators of change', terminology with a development logic of practice. The process and its products are described in concrete, economic terms such as 'outputs, timeframes, personnel' that refer back to the monies being granted and their use.

The business development aspects of the project do not involve dramatists, and tend to occur before the appointment of many of the BBC WST's project staff, of which dramatists are key. With the exception of advice, in some cases, on drama budgeting, the commissioning is completed without input by creative staff.

You would suggest, for example, okay we have a budget of X million dollars, we're going to design five different outputs which we think we can afford and among them will be these short adverts, which will have purpose X […] and we will also create a drama, and the drama will also have purpose X plus purpose Y and purpose Z, because each of the outputs has a different purpose.

(Taste of Life Project Manager, Interview, 2008)

The production that had been started was prompted by reference to conditions and meanings that existed in Cambodia prior to the project being commissioned. They were generated from the Cambodian audience's prior 'reproduction moments', in the sense of representations drawing upon what was already known about the audience (Hall, 1997): In Cambodia, there existed conditions (the health status of the population) which the donor decided to address. In the *Taste of Life* instance, the donor agreed to a TV drama as part of the intervention: the stated aim of the drama was to address maternal and child health and HIV and AIDS. Once the overall aims of the drama are established and the contract secured, more detail about the information about these issues is needed.

Then within those issues, you have to start breaking them down: what are the causes of these problems, these diseases, or whatever it may be, and what can we do with a campaign-type activity, what could we do in terms of information.

(Taste of Life Project Manager, Interview, 2008)

The BBC WST's Management/Editorial response to this need is to construct a template borrowed from the Media world of advertising, known as a 'message brief' (see Table 9.2).

A range of tools and processes were used to generate this brief. In Cambodia, a Campaign Working Group, drawn from the Development field, was established to serve as technical advisors over the course of the entire project, and messaging workshops were conducted to engage and inform key 'stakeholders', as well as to obtain their technical guidance/expertise. The stage of work that sets the message brief, like the stage securing the project funding, is dominated by Development considerations, objectives and outcomes.

Table 9.2

Taste of Life HIV and AIDS Messaging Brief

HIV/AIDS Behaviour Change Objectives by Topic and Audience Segmentation

THEMES	Behaviour Change Objectives	General audience	*Sexually active men and women	Sexually active men	Sexually active women	Married couples or partners	Married men	Married women	Pregnant women
Sexual Health and Personal Vulnerability	1a) Talk about sex and sexual health			X	X	X			
	1b) Talk about personal risk		X		X				
	1c) Increase personal risk assessment		X					X	
Partners Reduction and Faithfulness	2a) Talk about the value of 1.1 test and be faithful		X		X				
	2b) Reduce number of partners and always use a condom		X						
Condoms	3a) Talk about using condoms		X		X			X	
	3e) Don't be embarrassed about buying and using condoms		X	X					
	3b) Use condoms every time you have sex			X					
	3c) Use condoms in sex outside main partnership						X		
	3d) Use condoms in main partnership						X	X	
Testing	4a) Talk about testing		X		X				
	4b) Get tested and know your status		X					X	X
	4c) Get tested before marriage (partners)					X			
Stigma	5a) Talk about discrimination against PLWHA	X							
	5b) Know that PLWHA have the same rights as you do	X							
	5c) Show support for PLWHA	X							

Target Audiences

Understanding the Social and Media Setting

Hall alludes to the importance of the 'story' to give meaning and that the 'decoding' which makes the meaning 'requires [the story] to be integrated into the social relations of the communications process as a whole of which it forms only part' (1990: 509). Once the drama project has been commissioned, with its programmatic aims, funding priorities and budget limitations stated and agreed, the early production activities focus on research and orientation to the drama's social and media context. This stage is dominated by considerations about audience and media.

Dramatists undertake a process of cultural immersion, to learn about settings, characters and situations for the drama's storytelling (see Chapter 6 in this volume). Audience researchers review existing research and conduct formative studies to find out more about things such as lifestyle, identity and the values of target audiences, particularly as they relate to the drama's aims and concepts. Formative and baseline evaluation studies focus on the programmatic aims and issues of the drama, typically assessing awareness, opinions, beliefs and practices related to the issues in the drama's message brief. This aspect of the production also refers back to 'reproduction moments' in the circuit of culture. Here, the focus is on increasing the management and drama staff's knowledge concerning existing audience conditions and meanings.

At this early moment in the production process, media markets, habits and preferences are also closely reviewed, either using existing data or via bespoke research studies. These data become the basis for strategic decisions about the drama platforms (radio, TV, Internet and mobile phone), broadcasters, time slots, the competition faced from other dramas and promotion of the drama. Media considerations—both commercial and regulatory—dominate the negotiations of the BBC WST's broadcast agreements, or 'memoranda of understanding', but underlying them are always concerns about audience.

> If you're trying to get your product seen by as many people as possible, which is usually what you want to do [...] I mean, it needs to be seen by the right people as well, so obviously if you're running maternal health programming, you'll want to be seen by women [...] so you have to consider their media habits.
>
> (*Taste of Life* Project Manager, Interview, 2008)

Creating the Characters and Stories to Deliver the Messages

In order to get started, the dramatists need to be informed about the drama's topic, audience, length and budget, which comprises the 'drama brief'. These are all matters that are decided in management negotiations with the project donor. Once the brief is presented to the dramatists, and the drama creation stage begins, concerns shift to be dominated by drama considerations.

> So arriving here [...] to do this television drama—actually that's what they said, a television drama, and when I had it explained to me that they were hoping to get 100 episodes out of the money we were given—so that would have been almost a soap [unlimited duration serial drama], had it been transmitted, say 2 times a week [...]. The important thing there was that the first thing that we had to do [...] was to say what format can we tell whatever story we're going to tell in? What story will the budget allow you to do?
>
> (*Taste of Life* Dramatist, Interview, 2008)

Dramatists go through a series of steps to formulate the drama. First, they decide the format or develop several format options. The format is the premise of the drama: its setting, tone and core characters. The purpose of the drama, as well as its duration and budget, are key considerations in developing the format.

> Everyone says let's have a new soap, and everyone thinks what format can it be? What precinct can it be? You've got to know where your characters are based [...]. Where are you going to set the drama?
>
> (*Taste of Life* Dramatist, Interview, 2008)

In the BBC WST's dramas for development, these format propositions are typically presented for review to the BBC WST management and key development 'players', most notably the donor. This review is a key milestone in the drama-making process. It involves recommendations and revisions until the format is approved. Revisions or changes to the format cannot be easily made later on in the drama-making process because once scripting or recording is underway, changes would involve substantial additional costs and lost time. However, this was the case in

Cambodia, where the project brief was extended from HIV and AIDS to also include maternal and child health issues: an entirely new format had to be established.

> Once the brief had changed from being a pure HIV drama to being 50% HIV and 50% mother and child health messages, the original format I'd come up with, which was a family based drama, sort of a Romeo and Juliet type set-up, […] we came up with the format of a hospital based drama, to allow young nurses, student nurses, who'd be having sex with each other.
>
> *(Taste of Life* Dramatist, Interview, 2008)

Once the format is agreed on, the dramatists start to populate it with characters. They imagine and describe the characters as though they were real people. They develop their personalities, styles, values, histories, ambitions and relationships. With the characters established, long-running story arcs and shorter-term storylines are designed. This point in the process is when key dramatic events, encounters, conflicts, alliances, dilemmas and resolutions are planned. These may occur in single, or more typically, across multiple episodes of the drama. These structural elements and decisions are all developed and decided by the players in the drama field. At key moments, the outputs of this dramatic crafting process—storylines, plot summaries and scripts—are presented for review. With *Taste of Life*, this review is conducted both by project management and selected development partners often convened as an advisory body.

During the production of a drama that does not have a development aim, it is typically the role of an Executive Producer, with a strong background in television or radio drama, to conduct these sorts of reviews. In drama for development, the project manager often serves this executive producer function. In some instances, the project manager has in fact had a background in drama as an executive producer. This was the case with one of the Project Managers interviewed for this study:

> … more usually [the Executive Producer] is the person who is the interface with the broadcaster really. So in other words, my job was to make sure the broadcasters were getting what they wanted and to make sure that the team was working effectively and properly and making programmes to a standard that we wanted. I suppose in overall charge.
>
> (BBC WST Project Manager, Interview, 2008)

In drama for development, when the person in that management role does not have a drama background, rather a media, journalism or development background, they need to learn about drama-making processes and logics. This is an extra layer of understanding that needed to be established within the BBC WST, in order for the project management to represent the drama and interact externally with the donors and broadcasters on behalf of the BBC WST.

Also with a drama for development, there is an added aspect to the creative work in deciding which characters can convey certain messages, and how they might do so. The 'educational' requirement in dramas for development, in terms of the development-oriented message brief, can be new to dramatists and even considered burdensome; at the least, they pose a tension and added challenge to creating a credible, entertaining and compelling story.

> We didn't want to break faith with the audience and lose credibility … you've just got to make a judgement there. If at every single opportunity, at the end of every scene, you had your heroine saying 'don't forget to use a condom', people are going to think it looks like […] a government announcement […] So you try to keep credibility as well as ticking the boxes and getting the messages [across].
>
> (*Taste of Life* Dramatist, Interview, 2008)

Checking the Drama Messaging

A key aspect of the accountability of a drama for development project to its funders is its ability to demonstrate that the development messages that were the raison d'être of the commission are being effectively delivered. While ostensibly dominated by development needs, the aesthetic qualities of the drama are considered and often firmly asserted, and tensions tend to arise during this review stage. The steps involving management reviews—of format, storyline outlines, production schedules and budget and so on—are familiar and routine to drama producers. However, for many dramatists working in drama for development, it can be unusual, unfamiliar and sometimes very uncomfortable to have scripts reviewed for their core development messages, instead of their storytelling or entertainment potential. However, at the same time the review is recognised as necessary to the 'drama for development' undertaking, with its focus on changing behaviour and identifying development constraints. Such reviews reflect a need for producers to demonstrate accountability to funders such as DFID.

> What's the point in making the most fantastically popular, successful programme if the messages you're giving out are the wrong ones?
>
> (*Taste of Life* Project Manager, Interview, 2008)

For many development players this review process is also new. While they may have been knowledgeable about the technical content of messaging, often they are not familiar with the way drama structures those messages. As a result, their feedback concerning *Taste of Life* was at times 'off the mark', focusing on characters or the storyline, rather than the technical content of the core development messages.

> Let's take a health campaign for example, they'll often come at it from a technical point of view, and they'd be very happy to see someone in a white coat telling someone how to take their diarrhoea treatment and they would regard that as an excellent programme on TV or radio [...] and of course, yes fine, the information is there, but nobody wants to watch that.
>
> (*Taste of Life* Project Manager, Interview, 2008)

This input needs to be balanced with the drama's needs to tell an interesting, credible story that will maintain the audience interest and attention.

> If you just sit there in the doctor's office and have a person in a white coat talking, the audience is going to drift away and then your entire project will be wasted, because without an audience, then what are you doing?
>
> (*Taste of Life* Project Manager, Interview, 2008)

In such instances the project manager plays an intermediary and interpreting role that seeks to explain how drama works and the importance of considering the audience:

> And I find myself explaining to the funders that: 'You might not be seeing the number of messages that you were hoping for here, but when the messages come on, people remember them, and we've built this story line with some very important points here which people will not forget.'
>
> (*Taste of Life* Project Manager, Interview, 2008)

Even getting clear and consistent advice about accurate technical content from the development players for the drama can be complicated for the management players and often involves negotiations within the development field. Here, a project manager reveals:

> Now in diarrhoea, you can follow the protocols of the WHO, which was one of the organisations on our advisory group, and we decided that we are following the WHO [World Health Organization] […] it is the highest-level health authority in the world. UNICEF didn't always agree 100% with them, but UNICEF was also on the advisory group so we took them into account as well, but then we bumped up against decisions from the government of Cambodia, which did not fall into line with WHO protocol […] so what do you do then, when you are a guest in a country and the government of that country is not agreeing with the WHO?

> (*Taste of Life* Project Manager, Interview, 2008)

Checking the Drama's Appeal and Story

Hall points to the importance of the production output to have a 'fit between codes' and to be recognisable to its audiences (readers) lest distortions or misunderstandings arise because of a 'lack of equivalence' or irreconcilable contradictions (1990: 515–517).

> It is in this set of decoded meanings which have an effect, influence, entertain, instruct or persuade, with very complex perceptual, cognitive, emotional, ideological or behavioural consequences.

> (Hall, 1990: 509)

According to Hall, the decoding process is not passive, nor is it is neutral. Hall refers to the receiver's use of three decoding positions vis-à-vis the ideological orientation of the sender, that is those involved in the encoding or production: dominant, negotiated or oppositional.

The most crucial aspect of a drama for development project's accountability to its funders is the ability to demonstrate that the drama is going to reach its intended audiences and that they will, at the very least, understand its messages and perhaps act on new information to their own benefit and the social good more generally. This stage focuses on a combination of audience, drama and development considerations, which necessarily require balancing:

> We were able later to check those storylines and find out that people did remember them; and check the messaging to find out that people did remember those messages. The funder of course always wants as many messages as you could possibly squeeze in, but as creative people we would know that would make for poor programming.

> (*Taste of Life* Project Manager, Interview, 2008)

Pre-testing is a widely accepted exercise in development communications to confirm that the outputs appeal to audiences and that the audiences interpret the messages as the producers intended. Pre-testing uses methods that are familiar to marketing/advertising media and typically focuses on issues of comprehension, credibility and production technical matters such as sound and image quality. It assists the encoding or embedding of donor messages into the drama serials. However, this does not guarantee that the audience decoding process will conform to donor or dramatist expectations. It is also difficult and more common to check shorter format outputs such as advertisements with more specific and direct messaging than it is to pre-test episodes of a drama serials.

For many of the BBC WST's audience researchers, pre-testing a drama was a specific and new undertaking that required extending their practice beyond knowledge of the development issue or confirming the clarity of short and direct messages. In order to do it well, both audience interactions with story and concerns about the drama structure and elements such as characters, situations and setting needed to be understood and examined. This is in addition to interpretation of any messages from the stories, relationships and events in the drama.

Testing the drama with audiences is for many dramatists a new and unfamiliar process that has to be incorporated into the drama production planning and can be seen to disrupt and interfere with creative processes. This adjustment to the plans is often a source of tension between the drama team, management and audience researchers. Eikhof and Haunschild refer to the 'importance of organisational routine that safeguards artistic logics' (2007: 523). In making drama for development, the routine not only has to be compatible with drama-making practices and schedules, but also audience research practices, as a project manager suggests:

> What we did was sat down with the research side and the creative side with me sort of sitting in the middle and we worked out a very clear timetable of how things would work [...] you just had to be absolutely methodical and absolutely adhere to deadlines and so on [...] which everyone in television is used to, but that was the key [...] [the audience researcher would say] 'Right, I need five days between when you give me the storyline and when I feed back to you, and feed back to the writers what the response of the audience was, which bits they liked, which bits they didn't like, which bits they got, which messages they didn't understand.' And then [the Executive Producer] would then talk to his team about how long they needed to do any changes in the script and so on, and so you just had to work back through it and stick absolutely to it [...]. That is the only way to do it, if you know from the start, that whatever it is that you're making has that extra dimension [the messaging] built in [...] because looking at 'normal' drama production, for want of a better word, that is not something you would normally do.

> (*Taste of Life* Project Manager, Interview, 2008)

Presenting the Drama to Audiences

The culmination of the drama-making is the actual broadcast of the drama. By this stage in the process, power rests with the media organisations actually broadcasting the drama and with the audiences, who may or may not watch or listen to the drama. Earlier audience research will have informed the broadcast agreements and the time slots for the drama broadcasts. However, concerns about media regulatory and audience public responses to the content still play a role in the final drama that is presented, especially in conservative contexts:

> Our writer wanted to build in a story about a gay man who was coming out and was therefore going to find out about his sexuality and HIV etc. Now, it's fair to say that HIV [-infection] levels [among] gay men are far higher than in the general population, so you could say it's a very

reasonable thing to do. The reason I vetoed it was because I was thinking of the big picture. The big picture was that we were a TV drama on prime time on the number one TV channel in the country, owned by the government, on behalf of the government, and to have put that storyline in there would have met such huge resistance from the people who were managing our project and the broadcasters who probably would have rejected it.

(*Taste of Life* Project Manager, Interview, 2008)

Managing Essential Concerns

In considering the key issues and sources of tensions in the stages of making a drama for development presented here, the essential concerns of the fields of the key players emerged as follows:

Drama = 'The Story'
Development = 'The Message', 'The Money'
Media = 'Census' (the audience size) and 'Censure' (standards, authorities)
Audience = 'Myself, My Life, My Society' or 'The Meaning'
Management = 'Facilitation' and 'Negotiation'

The more effective—that is, less controversial or resisted—management decisions tended to reflect the essential concerns of the dominant field at the stage in the drama-making process that a decision or resolution of tensions was required. Tensions were most acute when the players from a field that others did not consider to have priority tried to dominate the stage and assert themselves: those attempts to dominate were resisted and considered inappropriate by players from other fields.

Resolution of the tensions tended to be reached when the essential concerns that should dominate were recognised and could be agreed upon. These included: when storylines that did not match the development message brief were changed or removed; storylines and dialogue that would have been dull to audiences were changed; and scenes that could have been offensive to audiences or media authorities were removed. Bearing in mind that the players from different fields often had limited direct interactions with each other, the role of the project management was to represent the different players and their fields in order to negotiate these tensions. The management operated and navigated the drama-making project across the different fields, interpreting and negotiating their essential concerns.

Bouman talks of the importance of creating a 'joint frame of reference' in the form of a new television genre as a condition for success in E-E collaboration (1999: 201).

> Specific measures have to be taken to stimulate the fusion of one *habitus* with another and to build an E and E collaboration based on symmetry of power. What is required is a joint frame of reference which incorporates the habitus of both professional fields.
>
> (Bouman, 1999: 201)

The present examination of making drama for development concludes differently: It does not appear to be necessary for all the players to have a fully developed 'joint frame of reference' with their fields fused. Rather, the multi-disciplinary nature and wide range of highly specialised expertise required in the WST's projects making dramas for development, combined with the many economic, cultural and artistic pressures felt in such a high risk undertaking, suggest that it may be inadequate to establish a joint object of reference for their working relationships.

Bouman also stresses the importance of professionals in such an endeavour who are 'capable of dealing with the intrinsic tensions of combining entertainment and education and differences in work culture' (1999: 208). The findings here suggest the importance of strong, clear management structures and mechanisms to organise the staged activities in making development-oriented drama. A key function of the project management is to generate an organisational culture and relationships with key players that convey respect for their logics of practice and essential concerns. Internal management/editorial processes to ensure the integrity of the various logics of practice, included, but were not limited to: confirming and recognising that different essential concerns and logics of practice existed; developing a comparative, if not shared, lexicon or language to describe and explain the drama-making process and its stages; and planned, documented and marked activities, moments and events that generated a joint object of reference and demonstrated a sense of a joint undertaking.

The brokering role of the project management team was key to successful external relations between the BBC WST and other key players in the different fields. This was achieved by: engaging with and explaining to key development and media players about drama to acculturate them to the stages and dynamics of making a drama; at points when the fields did interface, establishing functional, task-oriented interactions; and interpreting and negotiating the different fields' perspectives. This often involved representing one domain's point of view or interests to the other, with the stated shared aim of keeping the drama-making process on course.

The approach to power (im)balances in *Taste for Life* has been to organise or to negotiate transfers of power from one asymmetry to another, rather than seeking symmetry in a new, fused *habitus*. While there is a joint *object* of reference—the drama—it did not necessarily shift the *habitus* or change the essential concerns of the five sets of key players and their fields. Rather these were brokered by the Project Manager as part of the management function, often done by representing the priorities and essential concerns of one field to another. This could be achieved because shifts of power are accepted (even expected) by dramatists at specific stages and moments in the drama-making process.

This exploration of making *Taste of Life*, combined with supplemental interview materials, suggests that to manage asymmetries of power, BBC WST project management established roles and agreements that identified key milestones, processes and points for input from other fields and players. These milestones and processes recognised and legitimised the expertise and essential concerns of the different players. Transfers of power, from one set of key players and their fields to another, occurred most functionally when they fit the drama-making routine. These included planned development input and consultation and audience testing and feedback. These were 'natural' milestones in the drama-making. Dramatists are receptive to these events when they occur at these points and are anticipated and planned. It was extremely disruptive to the creative stage, and inefficient to the overall process, when the testing and feedback was not conducted at these points. It is the role of the project management to negotiate these balances of power, to facilitate the transfers of power at different stages of the drama-making process and to safeguard not only the integrity of the drama's artistic logics and creative processes, but also of the logics and processes of development and audience research.

Conclusion: A Dynamic Translation Process

Making the *Taste of Life* drama, as well as the larger media project in which it was created, occurred within the parameters of the 'circuit of culture' as described by Hall (1990, 1997). The aim of the drama project and the craft applied to making the drama itself both focus on communication with preferred and intended meanings: it is a process of encoding meanings. Furthermore, those involved in the encoding and circulation of development messages, that is, the dramatists and broadcasters, do so with an acute awareness and consideration of how the audience and regulatory authorities will respond to and interpret it—the encoding is done with attention to decoding processes and how the negotiation of dominant and preferred readings takes place over the course of the serial drama. The commissioning and creation stages of drama-making are devoted to the craft of encoding, with pre-testing and feedback loops being provided by formative audience research focused on a close analysis of the decoding process. The players inhabiting the five fields involved in making a drama for development each have their own essential concerns and logics of practice: Drama—'the story'; Development—'the message' and 'the money'; the Media—'census' and 'censure'; Audience—the range of meanings' (about self and society) and the possible courses of action and response to new or renewed information embedded in the drama. These differing concerns and logics of practice dominate at different points in the drama-making process and it is the dynamics of this cross-cultural communication process that renders drama for development such a fascinating project of media and cultural translation for all players.

This case study has also flagged up the points of tension in the circuits of culture involved in drama for development. Indeed, those internal to the BBC WST with a management/editorial role navigate between the other four fields, and convey to all players respect for others' fields essential concerns and logics of practice. They play brokering, facilitating and regulatory roles: (*a*) the brokering role by representing the concerns and logics of practice of the fields from one to the other; (*b*) a facilitating role by generating organisational routines and structures for these exchanges to occur and for consensual transfers of power; and (*c*) an enforcement role when the asymmetries of power have not been resolved though those routines and structures. When there are tensions over imbalances of power, resolutions are achieved by deference to the essential concerns of the particular field that dominates at the particular point in the drama-making process. This reflection upon the dominance of different fields at different points in the production process, the tensions between the different players in the different fields, how the resolutions are achieved and how power is transferred support the assertion that making a drama for development is truly a dynamic encoding process.

Note

1. Secondary data included a review of project documents, correspondence, reports and presentations, and viewing sub-titled episodes of the drama. Primary data are eight semi-structured in-depth interviews conducted between March 2008 and August 2009. The first interviews were conducted face-to-face in Cambodia and London. Subsequent interviews were conducted via telephone. Most interviews were recorded; in some cases interview notes sufficed and key concepts and phrases were highlighted for later paraphrasing. When recordings were made, transcripts were used for analysis. The interviews were analysed with six codes: the four key players and their orientations—development, drama, media, audiences—and two other codes to designate milestones and negotiations.

References

Bouman, M. (1999) 'The Turtle and the Peacock: The Entertainment-Education Strategy on Television', PhD Dissertation, Wageningen Agricultural University.

———. (2002) 'Turtles and Peacocks: Collaboration in Entertainment-Education Television', *Communication Theory*, 12(2): 225–244.

Bourdieu, P. (1990) *The Logic of Practice*. Stanford: Stanford University Press.

DeFillippi, R. and Arthur, M. (1998) 'Paradox in Project-Based Enterprise: The Case of Film Making', *California Management Review*, 40(2): 125–139.

DeFillippi, R. Grabher, G. and Jones, C. (2007) 'Introduction to Paradoxes of Creativity: Managerial and Organisational Challenges in the Cultural Economy', *Journal of Organisational Behaviour*, 28: 511–521.

Eikhof, D. and Haunschild, A. (2007) 'For Art's Sake! Artistic and Economic Logics of Creative Production', *Journal of Organisational Behaviour*, 28: 523–538.

Hall, S. (1990) 'Encoding, Decoding', in Buring, S. (ed.) (1999), *The Cultural Studies Reader*. London: Routledge.

———. (1997) *Representation: Cultural Representations and Signifying Practices*. Milton Keynes: The Open University.

Jay, M. (1993) *Forcefields: Between Intellectual History and Cultural Critique*. London: Routledge.

Lewin, K. (1941) 'Defining the Field at a Given Time', Paper Presented at Psychology and Scientific Methods, Sixth International Congress for the Unity of Science, University of Chicago, Chicago.

National Centre for HIV/AIDS, Dermatology and STD. (2005) *Annual Report 2005: HIV/ AIDS and STI Prevention and Care Programme*, Ministry of Health, Phnom Penh.

10

JASOOS VIJAY

SELF-EFFICACY, COLLECTIVE ACTION AND SOCIAL NORMS IN THE CONTEXT OF AN HIV AND AIDS TELEVISION DRAMA

Lauren B. Frank, Sonal Tickoo Chaudhuri, Anurudra Bhanot and Sheila T. Murphy

Introduction

In India, as many as 3.1 million adults are HIV positive, which places critical emphasis on the urgent need to enhance prevention efforts and address the associated deep levels of stigma and discrimination that exist. The mass media and wider communication (peer, interpersonal and counselling) response to HIV in India has been significant, yet taboos associated with openly discussing issues associated with sex remain, reflecting the negative social and moral connotations of the disease. In the context of HIV in India enormous health communication challenges remain. Many of these challenges centre on the need for cultural sensitivity in communicating topics such as HIV, while simultaneously challenging current cultural norms. This chapter explores such issues via the example of the BBC

World Service Trust (BBC WST) *Jasoos Vijay (Detective Vijay)* through which viewers of this serial drama were exposed to issues that affect people living with HIV or AIDS.

Prior quantitative research has already demonstrated that viewing this drama had direct impacts on HIV-related knowledge, attitudes, and behaviour (Chatterjee et al., 2009). Consequently, following an introduction to the *Jasoos Vijay* production, this chapter presents a theoretical and thematic assessment of qualitative (letters, focus groups and interviews) and quantitative survey data, in order to identify key elements of the narrative that resonated with viewers. More specifically, we apply a number of relevant theoretical frameworks, principally emerging from the fields of health communication and social psychology, to explicate the shifts in viewers' HIV-related knowledge, attitudes and actions.

Various communication theories discuss the role of cultural context or social norms and their impact on behaviour. However, many such theories neglect the broader social and cultural contexts or 'fields' in which action occurs. They do not recognise that, 'complex cultural patterns of behavior are, in large part, transmitted and regulated at a social-systems level' (Bandura, 1969: 255). As Dutta-Bergman (2005) points out, the theories most commonly used to understand and measure the impact of health campaigns—such as the theory of reasoned action, the theory of planned behaviour and the more recent integrated model of behavioural prediction—acknowledge the role of social and cultural normativity and the collective nature of community, but remain largely individualistic in scope.

This individualistic orientation can be problematic for mass-mediated drama interventions produced for audiences in the so-called 'developing world'. This is particularly true within more 'collectivist' cultures, such as India, because the 'meanings associated with the behavior and the behavioral outcome might very well be located in the social networks, the collective fabric of the community' (Dutta-Bergman, 2005: 106). This point is supported by Sinha and Kumar, who note that:

> Indians possess both an 'independent' as well as an 'interdependent self' [...] The 'independent self' is associated with a desire to pursue individualistic goals whereas the 'interdependent self' is always concerned with fulfilling the expectations of others. The 'other' is highly evident in the consciousness of the 'interdependent self' and this leads

to a preoccupation with fulfilling the obligations of significant others [elders, husbands, caste groups, elites and so on].

(2004: 100)

In calling for a more culture and context-centred approach, Dutta-Bergman (2005) argues that the inclusion of subjective norms within these theoretical models does not make such models sufficiently social. Rather, the norms that these models tend to measure are those internalised and understood by the individual, rather than the collective. For development practitioners, this has both theoretical and methodological implications. In assessing some of these implications, this chapter draws upon qualitative and quantitative data to examine and challenge notions of collectivity, normativity and group dynamics and show how these concepts are mobilised, rightly or wrongly, in current theoretical models in health communication.

Jasoos Vijay: Background and Impact

In response to the growing number of HIV and AIDS cases in India, the BBC WST developed a broad programme of E-E interventions funded by the UK Department for International Development (DFID). *Jasoos Vijay* was specifically designed to impact viewers' HIV-related knowledge, attitudes and practices (commonly referred to as the KAP model of health communication). Working with the National AIDS Control Organization (NACO) and the national television broadcaster, Doordarshan, *Jasoos Vijay* was the centrepiece of the campaign to promote HIV and AIDS awareness. The BBC WST staff believed that an entertainment-based intervention would be most effective in achieving the objectives of the wider campaign which were: (*a*) increasing knowledge of how HIV is transmitted; (*b*) encouraging people to get tested and learn their HIV status; (*c*) challenging the culture of discrimination towards people who are HIV positive and (*d*) promoting support and treatment for those living with HIV or AIDS.

In conceptualising *Jasoos Vijay*, the BBC WST research team was particularly sensitive to the stylistic and genre preferences of the intended audience. In 2001, during the development of the drama, Nielsen's Television Audience Monitoring (TAM) data revealed that action or thriller genres were the second most popular type of content on general enter-tainment channels in India. Moreover, the creative team felt that the fast-paced action/thriller format and the constant stream of new cases for *Jasoos Vijay* to investigate and solve would allow them to easily weave key messages into the script without it appearing overly didactic. The series was shot with professional actors in various locations across India in order to forge a cultural and emotional connection to viewers from disparate parts of the country. Finally, *Jasoos Vijay* had all the ingredients of a *Bollywood*-style thriller—attractive heroes, evil villains, helicopters, car chases, suspense and, of course, lots of singing and dancing (see Dickey, 2007).

Jasoos Vijay was broadcast on the national television channel Doordarshan, the only freely available terrestrial channel in India, between 2002 and 2007. During that time, the BBC WST produced and broadcast 130 episodes of the drama. The key to the programme's longevity was its significant popularity. Television Audience Monitoring (TAM) data from Nielsen's audience panel showed that during its final phase, between October 2006 and September 2007, *Jasoos Vijay* reached a weekly audience of up to 15 million, and cumulatively it reached 70 million viewers over its last 52 episodes, making it one of the 10 most-watched programmes on Indian television.[1]

The drama's leading character was a male detective, Vijay, who was HIV positive. Vijay's HIV status was not revealed until the show had already become popular with the viewing public since the creative team did not want to risk rejection of the main character at the outset of broadcasting. Likewise, the way in which he became HIV positive was never disclosed. The fact that the central character was HIV positive allowed the programme to repeatedly address issues related to the care and treatment of those living with the virus, as well as the stigma and discrimination associated with HIV and AIDS. Here, Devika Bahl, the creative director for *Jasoos Vijay*, observes that:

> At the heart of the serial's success was our decision to portray the detective hero, Vijay, as HIV positive. Vijay's personal journey contributed greatly to dispelling myths and creating better awareness of HIV, its treatment and management [...] Vijay's first disclosure of his HIV status was to Gauri (his wife to be) after she professed her love for him. He maintained that an HIV positive person doesn't have to walk around with a sign

around their neck saying that he/she is positive but that if there is a risk of transmitting infection, then it is their responsibility to inform their partner and take precautions.

(Interview, 2009)

Jasoos Vijay was designed for mass audiences—cutting across caste, class and regions. For this reason, Detective Vijay was not given a surname, lest audiences perceive him to be upper or lower caste or from a particular locale or ethnicity. This purposeful ambiguity regarding Vijay's background was an attempt by producers to ensure that various audience segments would not feel alienated by a specific rendering of place, caste or ethnicity, allowing viewers more potential to project their own contexts and experiences onto the narrative. Though caste permeates all aspects of life in India, both the drama and its ensuing audience research efforts did not directly tackle the issue of caste. Instead, a deliberate strategy of being 'caste-vague' was employed, although it is possible that viewers may have made their own caste-related inferences with respect to Jasoos Vijay and his colleagues. Moreover, although Vijay and his team were shown to be from an urban background, they solved crime cases mostly in rural areas or villages, so as to further broaden the appeal of the programme and promote them to the status of 'visitors', freed from the specificities of context and therefore more able to intervene within that context in dramatic ways.

Jasoos Vijay managed to garner huge popularity in India. In evaluating the drama, the BBC WST conducted a quantitative baseline survey at the outset of the project that served as a benchmark of the public's HIV-related knowledge, attitudes and practices (KAP). After the campaign went off-air in 2007, an end-line survey was conducted using the same research methodology. This allowed for comparison of the baseline and end-line surveys, with potential respondents matched with respect to gender, age, education and location (specific town or village). The final baseline and end-line samples included 11,691 and 12,050 participants, respectively. Comparisons between the two surveys demonstrated that viewers did indeed change in terms of their HIV-related knowledge, attitudes and behaviours (Sood et al., 2006). More specifically, a higher percentage of those exposed to the *Jasoos Vijay* drama knew the different routes of HIV transmission and methods of preventing HIV transmission (for a more detailed analysis focusing on this quantitative data, see Chatterjee et al., 2009).

Although this quantitative research provides strong evidence that *Jasoos Vijay* was successful in achieving its stated goals, it does not answer the question of 'why' it was successful, or how the behaviour of audiences change. As Papa et al. point out, 'most past studies of entertainment education programs, with a few exceptions [...] have not provided an adequate theoretical explanation of how audience members' change as a result of being exposed to ... programs' (2000: 33). Indeed, understanding and utilising the theoretical elements that make a narrative impactful constitute a core challenge for future drama for development initiatives. Moreover, the success of E-E formats has often been judged (as outlined above) using multi-phase KAP surveys, which assess shifts in knowledge, attitudes and practices over time. The present chapter goes beyond this somewhat narrow quantitative focus to consider other outcomes and intervening factors that may be just as significant, such as social norms. Below we present a qualitative analysis of viewers' comments as expressed in letters, focus groups and one-on-one interviews, in an attempt to answer the question of why *Jasoos Vijay* was successful, while pointing out some constraints on success.

The letters included in our qualitative analysis were a subset of the letters and e-mails from the final year of the programme and included viewers from the Hindi-speaking states of Uttar Pradesh, Uttaranchal, Rajasthan, Punjab, Haryana, Madhya Pradesh, Chattisgarh, Bihar and Maharashtra. In addition, after the programme ended, 12 focus group discussions and 36 one-on-one interviews were conducted (between February and March 2007) with the audiences of *Jasoos Vijay*. After considering the logistics of inviting participants from a wide catchment area and with the intent of keeping travel to a minimum, 100 male viewers were invited and came from their home states to participate in 12 focus groups conducted in the nearby cities of New Delhi, Jaipur, Nagpur and Patna. To capture the opinions of those unable to attend the focus groups, the BBC WST audience research team travelled to a number of villages to conduct one-on-one interviews (all interviews were conducted by an interviewer of the same sex). A total of 36 interviews (18 with females and 18 with males) were conducted in rural areas in the aforementioned states. These data are supplemented by listener's letters received en masse throughout the duration of the production.

Thematic and Theoretical Analysis of *Jasoos Vijay*

Jasoos Vijay received more than 1,500 audience letters per month, and over 23,000 in its last year, providing further evidence of its popularity. The vast majority of these letters reflected positively upon the drama's impact, as a rural viewer of *Jasoos Vijay* mentioned: 'Earlier, family members used to get up and walk away whenever HIV or AIDS messages appeared on TV […] but not any more […] [after we started watching *Jasoos Vijay*] we all sit and watch and listen'. Moreover, many viewers reported impacts at the community level: '[…] inspired by your serial we have set up a group in our village which disseminates information on HIV, AIDS, STIs [sexually transmitted infections] among the villagers'. Such quotes typify the bulk of letter-based response from the audience, and together with BBC WST survey data, suggests that *Jasoos Vijay* had the potential to influence not only individual attitudes, but also cultural norms and beliefs held at a societal level (Chatterjee et al., 2009; Sood et al., 2006). In the following sections, we articulate the theoretical importance of this leap from individual attitudes and behaviours to collective norms and the implications for long-term sustainable behaviour change.

Social Cognitive Theory, Identification and Self-Efficacy

With its origins in social learning theory (Bandura, 1969, 1977b), Bandura's social cognitive theory (SCT) began with research that included media influences on aggression. Based on his experiments with children and adults, Bandura determined that people can learn vicariously by watching mass-mediated role models. Further, if an individual identifies with a role model, he or she is particularly likely to imitate that role model's behaviour (Bandura, 1969). Individuals are even more likely to perform a modelled behaviour if the role model is shown to be rewarded for the behaviour (Bandura, 1969). In the focus groups, participants frequently referred to Vijay's lifestyle and work ethic when discussing how people with HIV or AIDS should be treated: 'Jasoos Vijay is also suffering with this disease, and he is having and living a normal life' (male focus group participant, New Delhi). Similarly, another focus group participant observed that: 'even after getting HIV positive, Jasoos Vijay goes to villages and tells people about it' (male focus group participant, Uttar Pradesh). While fictional characters such as Vijay are often portrayed as free from the constraints of the socio-cultural context and the social mores and norms that define them, many audience members never-theless make a connection between the characters' on-screen conduct, how people living with HIV/AIDS (PLWHA) should live and how they should be treated by the wider community. Numerous letters received by the BBC WST reinforce this fundamental position.

But not all role models are equally effective. Prior research suggests that health information delivered through engaging storytelling, involving characters the viewer already 'knows' and cares about is more likely to be attended to and modelled in behaviour (Murphy et al., forthcoming; Singhal et al., 2004; Singhal and Rogers, 1999). For example, an analysis of listeners of the radio drama *Tinka Tinka Sukh* (*Little Steps to a Better Life*) in a village in rural India revealed that audience members who felt as if they had a para-social relationship with the characters were more likely to both discuss the issue of dowry and to take action in opposing it. Even within a single narrative, viewers appear to learn more from models—in this case, fictional television characters—that they identify with, like, feel as if they know, or perceive to be similar to themselves (Bandura, 2002).

The Vijay character was deliberately crafted to evoke such sentiments. However, it was not only Vijay's own behaviour that can be influential, but also the modelling of how others on the show react to him, as a man in Nagpur noted: 'The main character, *Jasoos Vijay*, is shown as HIV positive, but people are shown to treat him nicely in the drama' (Male focus group participant, Nagpur). Viewers also pointed to Gauri, Vijay's wife, as a positive role model for female viewers with respect to ways in which to interact with people who are HIV positive. For example, 'The one who performed the character of Gauri was also very good. Women have understood Gauri's message better' (male focus group participant, Uttar Pradesh). Similarly, 'Gauri's role was good, and its story was also good. I liked that Gauri as a lady could fight for AIDS' (male focus group participant, Maharashtra) or 'Gauri knew that Jasoos Vijay was HIV positive, and still she married him' (male focus group participant, Uttar Pradesh).

While much has been made of the role of central characters, it is crucial to keep in mind that supporting characters can likewise serve as significant role models. Indeed, Sabido (2004) highlights the use of supporting characters, particularly what he terms 'transitional characters', which begin as negative role models, but within the narrative, transition into positive role models. Sabido suggests such transitional characters can show audience members how to enact behaviour change through identification of first negative and then ultimately positive outcomes. However, within the *Jasoos Vijay* drama only a few main characters recurred throughout the series. Supporting characters only appeared in four-episode story arcs; thus, it is debatable whether viewers would have had sufficient time to clearly identify with such characters or for the story to show a believable transition from negative to positive role models. In turn, this suggests that the Bollywood-style of genre employed by the production may influence audiences in different ways, using different kinds of role models, than those typically employed in socially realist drama for development serials (see Chapter 8).

Nonetheless, for behaviour change to occur, individuals must not only know what to do, but must also believe that they are capable of performing that behaviour. Self-efficacy is the extent to which an individual feels able to perform a particular behaviour, which can be increased not only through personal experience and action, but also by the vicarious experience of observing others (Bandura, 1977a, 1982). An increase in self-efficacy resulting from engaging with the *Jasoos Vijay* drama was expressed in many viewers' comments. For example: 'I like the will power of *Jasoos Vijay* very much. The programme has taught me what we should do and at what time' (male letter writer, West Bengal). Similarly, and with regard to clear HIV-related messaging: 'So much change has come [as a result of watching the drama]. Now, when we go to doctors, we ask them to use a new syringe, when we go to the barbershop, we ask them to use a new blade' (male focus group participant, Patna). Other letter writers commented on the ambitions of spreading information about HIV and AIDS derived from *Jasoos Vijay* amongst their immediate peer groups. Such data reveal that viewers think not just of themselves when talking of efficacy beliefs, they also think of others, their peers and friends. In turn, this suggests that collective forms of efficacy may also derive from engagement with drama and effect change on a broader societal level.

Collective Efficacy

In its more recent form, social cognition theories seek to go beyond an analysis of the influences of drama serials on individual behaviour to include the broader social context (Bandura, 1998, 2001, 2004a, 2004b). Bandura (2001) suggests that personal, behavioural and environmental determinants all interact in producing thought and behaviour. Bandura also notes:

> The further evolution of the … [health communication] model treats personal changes as occurring within a network of social influences. It adds socially oriented interventions designed to provide social supports for personal change and to alter the practices of social systems that impair health and to foster those that enhance it.
>
> (1998: 633)

This position is supported by Law and Singhal (1999) who examined letters from listeners of the Indian radio drama *Tinka Tinka Sukh* and found considerable overlap between the concepts of self-efficacy and collective efficacy, as also suggested by Sinha and Kumar (2004) at the outset of this chapter. Likewise, the analysis of letters concerning *Jasoos Vijay* showed the importance of the related concepts of self and collective forms of efficacy and action. For example: 'Our villagers have become aware [of HIV and AIDS] mostly from your serial. My friends now use condoms to prevent themselves from [getting] AIDS. There are several slogans pasted on the walls of our village. We watch your serial to make ourselves aware of AIDS' (male letter writer, Rajasthan). Another letter writer draws a direct link between watching *Jasoos Vijay* and collective efficacy and action:

> It felt very good to watch your serial. It gives very useful information for illiterate rural people of India regarding HIV and AIDS and sexual diseases.

Inspired by your serial, we organized an association, an AIDS Eradication Society. We are providing AIDS information to the villagers.

(Male letter writer, Karnataka)

Interpersonal Discussion

Bandura theorised that media (and consequently campaigns that employ the media) can have 'dual paths of influence' (Bandura, 2001: 285). The first path is a direct pathway through which media influences behaviour change, and the second pathway is media that is effectively 'remediated' through people's interpersonal discussions (Bandura, 2001). Watching the drama helps people to talk to others about HIV and AIDS and watching often occurs in a group setting. Many of the focus group participants spontaneously mentioned co-viewing *Jasoos Vijay*. For example: 'All of the family watches the programme together, so we talk frankly about AIDS' (male focus group participant, Madhya Pradesh). While co-viewing is important, taboos on open discussion of sex-related issues still remain: 'We can't discuss. But *Jasoos Vijay* was so interesting that we could watch together at home' (Male focus group participant, Patna).

These quotes, and the many others like them, form a pattern. They suggest that although change is occurring, when it comes to discussions concerning sexuality and unsafe sex, many viewers (unsurprisingly and quite typically) are still constrained by socially held norms and taboos. These constraints remain so strong that many adolescents are not able to ask their parents questions relating to sexual matters (though discussion of sexual issues with peers would be more common). A recent study of Indian students reported (again, somewhat unsurprisingly) that most participants did not have open communication with their parents and other family members on sex-related matters (Selvan et al., 2005). By way of explanation, the study cited religious beliefs and the belief that sex is considered appropriate for discussion only after marriage and only with one's partner, as reasons for the poor communication between parents and adolescent children on sexual matters. In keeping with the work of Miller (1995) and Gillespie (1995), *Jasoos Vijay* appears to have provided a potentially safe impersonal outlet for engaging in discussions concerning sex and HIV. For example, 'all family members watch television together and tell our young how HIV spreads' (male focus group participant, Delhi) and 'we watch *Jasoos Vijay* together at home and now we openly discuss AIDS at home' (male focus group participant, Jaipur).

Social Norms

This safe environment may provide the potential for social norms about sex and HIV/AIDS to change. According to Bandura, norms work both through internal and external constraints on behaviour. Citing a health-related example, he notes that:

> Norms influence behavior anticipatorily by the social consequences they provide. Behavior that fulfills social norms gains positive social reactions. Behavior that violates social norms brings social censure. In addition, social norms convey behavioral standards. Adoption of standards creates a self-regulatory system that operates through self-sanctions. In this process, people regulate their behavior by self-evaluative reactions.
>
> (Bandura, 1998: 628)

Participants of both focus groups and interviews recognised clear social taboos surrounding matters relating to sex. These cultural norms become particularly relevant in understanding the hesitancy of Indians to talk about HIV and AIDS or condom use. All of the focus groups discussed the societal strictures against talking about sex-related issues. In the Madhya Pradesh focus group, the following conversation ensued: 'At first, "condom" was not thought to be the word of a gentleman; but after watching this programme, it has changed.' A fellow participant responded: 'When we go to purchase condoms at the medical store, the shopkeeper (chemist) does not look down upon you as a bad person' (male focus group participants, Madhya Pradesh). Participants readily identified *Jasoos Vijay* as crucial to their increased willingness to discuss condoms, condom use and HIV. For example: 'now we are more aware we can talk freely about HIV and AIDS. Earlier we were scared' (male focus group participant, Uttar Pradesh). This increased willingness to openly discuss HIV applies to men, as well as to women, with a female interviewee from Patna noting that 'whenever I go to the village, I tell them about it [AIDS]. Some people think that it is not correct to talk openly, but we ignore such thinking'.

Although viewers talk about their learning from *Jasoos Vijay* in a way that is reminiscent of a passive sender–receiver model, their choice to discuss HIV and AIDS and share their learning with others suggests an active and engaged audience. Not only did viewers report feeling able to discuss these previously taboo topics more openly, they also reported using *Jasoos Vijay* and associated storylines as a means to convince others to be more open as well:

> At first, the family members objected to my working for AIDS. They said it is not good. Then I explained to my father and asked him to watch *Jasoos Vijay*. Now he is convinced that it is a community awareness program.'
>
> (Male focus group participant, Maharashtra)

Gender

Unsurprisingly, gender was the most frequently cited barrier to discussion of behaviours relating to HIV/AIDS (for more on depictions of gender in *Jasoos Vijay*, see Chapter 5). In 10 of the 12 male focus groups conducted, participants spontaneously mentioned gender differences in social taboos relating to discussing sex. Male participants insisted that with few exceptions men and women could not discuss condoms or other sexual matters with each other. Rather, talk about sexual matters occurs for men and women within primarily separate and gendered social networks. A male focus group participant from Uttar Pradesh notes that 'married women talk among themselves—those who are educated. If they see a male, they stop talking'. Similarly, 'we cannot talk personally with women. We can go anywhere with an i-card [identity card for volunteers allowing them to talk about health matters] and discuss with women, but not personally' (male focus group participant, Nagpur). This suggests that discussion of sexuality and sexual practice is more accepted if it is conducted with a person performing some formal duty.

Data gathered by the BBC WST on this serial support this assertion. In four of the focus groups conducted, male participants suggested that nurses or midwives should be trained and encouraged to talk to women about HIV. For example, a male focus group participant revealed that 'I told the ANM [Auxiliary Nurse Midwife] to tell the women about it', while another suggested that 'my mother is an ASHA [Accredited Social Health Activist]. I told her to inform all pregnant women that they should go for an HIV test. If it [the test] is positive, take proper treatment, otherwise it can be dangerous for the child' (male focus group participant, Patna). Similarly, other men said that they had asked their mothers or wives to share information about HIV with other women within their community.

Even with medical professionals, women had mixed feelings about discussing sexual matters. When asked about their comfort in discussing urinary tract infections (UTI) with a doctor, one interviewee from Kotputli replied, 'yes, we can discuss it with a female doctor'. She emphasised that the only medical professionals with whom she would feel comfortable speaking were also women. Another woman similarly limited the amount of interaction she felt comfortable having with a doctor on sexual matters: 'Lots of women feel shy. I even ask my husband to write [her problem] on a slip of paper, and then I go to the doctor [and give it to him/her]' (female interviewee, Kotputli).

While our analysis revealed positive action on the part of many of the participants involved, a general reticence to discuss HIV and AIDS, particularly among/with women is still evident. In this respect, one woman commented that 'everybody stays in their own houses. Nobody talks about AIDS' (female interviewee, Jaipur). Interestingly, the most common discussion partner mentioned by women was their husbands: 'I don't feel shy talking to him [my husband] and we talk about condoms also' (female interviewee, Kotputli). Similarly, 'I have discussed this [HIV prevention] with my husband and he is convinced he should not have sex with other women' (female interviewee, Jaipur). This preference was also borne out in survey work, as female respondents were more likely to think it is alright to talk with their partners (96.0 per cent), than with friends or parents (87.6 per cent and 45 per cent, respectively). Chaudhuri (2007) further notes that women were more likely to face stigma as a result of being diagnosed with HIV than men; thus, their greater reluctance to speak may stem from a heightened fear of social and cultural ostracism.

Age and Generation

Age represented a second potential barrier that participants cited as affecting their willingness to talk about HIV. Social taboos in India limit the extent to which people should talk to children and young people, and many participants were shy or embarrassed to talk to their elders. A female interviewee from Maharashtra notes that 'whenever my brother asks about AIDS and condoms, my mother refuses to tell him [anything] as [she feels] he is too young to know about it'. However, highlighting the potential benefits of peer communication another interviewee from Madhya Pradesh reveals that 'I cannot talk about it [AIDS] with my neighbors and elders, but I can talk with people of my age group. For example, I discussed condom usage with my cousin who is getting married.'

The social strictures against speaking to children and elders about HIV and AIDS did not appear to be as strong as those relating to speaking to someone of the opposite sex. When asked whether he could speak to his elders, one man reported, 'not about condoms, but [we] are able to talk about injections and blood [donation/selling]' (Male focus group participant, Jaipur). This suggests that discussions about HIV and AIDS are not entirely taboo, provided they focus on the medical issues such as those associated with transmission, rather than sexual aspects of the disease.

Changing Attitudes

Discussion of HIV and AIDS was further facilitated by the interactive nature of the larger BBC WST campaign of which the *Jasoos Vijay* drama was the centrepiece. One man from Madhya Pradesh said, 'They [*Jasoos Vijay* anchors] also said that if you have any problem or want any information then write to us'. After having done so, he was able to use the information he received: 'We told them [our neighbours] that we are going to collect information regarding AIDS. They laughed. But when I gave this booklet to my friends and seniors, they read it'. The ability to distribute additional material has assisted people in sharing what they learned from the programme with others, which in turn increases the potential for self-efficacy.

Two of the key objectives for *Jasoos Vijay* focused on decreasing the ostracism of people living with HIV/AIDS (or PLWHA). In half of the focus groups, participants spontaneously mentioned that they had learned how to behave towards people who are HIV positive since watching the programme. When prompted, members of four of the remaining focus groups likewise noted the importance of not discriminating against, but instead caring for those with HIV. For example, 'in that programme [*Jasoos Vijay*], they tell about how we should behave with HIV positive people. We should sympathise with them' (male focus group participant, Maharashtra). Describing how his life had changed, another man said that we should 'give care and love to HIV patients' (male focus group participant, Uttar Pradesh). Survey data adds support to these findings. At baseline, 87 per cent of respondents agreed with the statement that 'PLWHA should be treated like a normal person', and 86 per cent of respondents agreed that 'PLWHA have the same rights as those who are not infected'. At follow-up, agreement with both of these statements had risen to 94 per cent.

As noted by the participants, these changing attitudes may have stemmed in part from an improved understanding of HIV and AIDS. Based on the knowledge gained from *Jasoos Vijay* about the routes of transmission of the disease, viewers reported feeling more comfortable interacting with people who are HIV positive:

> We got to know that if we shake hands, AIDS will not spread. At first, it was like: don't sit near him; don't eat with him. These fads have gone. We got information about [becoming] HIV positive. Now one hundred percent of our hesitation is gone.

> (Male focus group participant, Uttar Pradesh)

Reflecting a similar acquisition of knowledge concerning HIV transmission, another male focus group participant from Delhi reveals that:

> Our attitude has changed about people living with HIV/AIDS. It is not transmitted and spread by touching them or sharing their things. [There should be] no discrimination with them. Behave normally with them.

> (Male focus group participant, Delhi)

In these two quotations, the men show that their thoughts about how to interact with people who have HIV or AIDS have changed. However, their language reveals an us/them perspective that indicates a separation from people who live with HIV or AIDS. In contrast, a male letter writer from Rajasthan provides an example from his personal experience:

> We were not well aware of AIDS before this serial. My uncle is an AIDS patient and we avoided him. Now, our attitude towards him has changed and we decided not to misbehave with AIDS patients in the future. We hope that this serial will continue on Doordarshan.

Similarly, a female letter writer from Uttar Pradesh reveals that:

> My close friend's father has AIDS and he had given up hope to live. He had shut himself in a room and would not meet or talk to anyone. One day when I went to their house I persuaded him to meet me, had a cup of tea with him and spoke to him at length. I discussed with him about your programme and encouraged him to take a lesson from *Jasoos Vijay* who is HIV positive but is able to lead a normal life. Encouraged by this discussion he now wants to live.

These two participants discuss their experiences with people that they know who have HIV/AIDS. They do not differentiate themselves in the same manner, instead talking of 'we'.

In explaining why her opinion of HIV positive people did not change much after watching the programme, one interviewee identified a key variable that differentiates viewers, namely, level of education. Here, a female interviewee from Patna notes that 'illiterate people think that it [AIDS] is caused by touching. But I'm literate, so I already knew that it's a disease' (female interviewee, Patna). The survey data tended to confirm such observations. Agreement that people who are HIV positive should be treated normally and have equal rights was progressively higher with increasing levels of education, both at baseline and follow-up. Moreover, the change from baseline to follow-up was highest among people who were illiterate, with progressively smaller changes for those with a senior school certificate (SSC) and above. Because respondents with the highest level of education (graduate or higher) were more likely to know how HIV was transmitted and therefore support equal rights for HIV positive individuals at baseline, they did not have quite as large an increase, due to a 'ceiling effect'. None of the focus group respondents or interviewees refer to caste at any point nor was it directly probed by the moderators (possibly partially due to the deliberate downplaying of caste within the *Jasoos Vijay* programme), but mention of education or literacy level may be an indirect way of referring to caste differences.

Despite the general agreement among focus group participants, interviewees and survey respondents that PLWHA should not be stigmatised, many participants noted that people are not comfortable disclosing their HIV status. When asked whether he knew anyone who was HIV positive, a male focus group participant in Madhya Pradesh stated simply: 'People don't tell.' Similarly, another man pointed out the perceived need to be discrete: 'If anybody in the family gets affected by any disease, then we give him/her quiet [discrete] treatment' (male focus group participant, Madhya Pradesh). Yet other participants gave specific stories of people they knew. 'Our neighbor had contracted this disease and he hid it from everyone' (Male focus group participant, Uttar Pradesh). Even within families, HIV status can be a taboo topic: 'First my uncle got infected [with HIV] and then his wife, and then their small daughter, too. He died because of it [and] they feel bad if it is discussed in the family' (male focus group participant, Nagpur).

Thus, our analysis uncovered a discrepancy between viewers' stated understanding that the norm is that everyone should treat HIV positive individuals well and their unwillingness to inform others if they themselves were infected with the disease. The underlying cause of this discrepancy is unclear. It may be that focus group participants perceive their own attitudes to have changed more than the pervasive cultural norms. It is also possible that this discrepancy may reflect a tendency to provide politically correct or socially desirable responses with respect to individuals infected with HIV. Another possibility is that this discrepancy may reflect the difference between descriptive norms (beliefs about what people within the social context actually do) and injunctive norms (beliefs about what people should do) (Lapinski and Rimal, 2005). Although descriptive and injunctive norms may overlap when there is widespread acceptance of the behaviour in question, they are not theoretically constrained to do so. Additionally, even Vijay chose to limit disclosure of his status within the drama. There, too, the programme may have reflected a broader social norm concerning risk of ostracism, even as the show simultaneously attempted to reduce such stigma. The refusal among our sample of viewers to reveal their own HIV status suggests that despite the popularity of *Jasoos Vijay*, the cultural norms towards those with HIV and AIDS in India still have not shifted sufficiently.

Conclusion

Several factors were responsible for the success of the BBC WST's *Jasoos Vijay* drama. At the outset, an E-E approach was determined to be more promising than a didactic approach for achieving the specific behaviour change objectives of the wider campaign. The concept of a weekly action series that raised awareness of HIV and AIDS, as well as sensitivity towards people living with HIV and AIDS was then developed by experienced professionals, pre-tested and produced in a manner consistent with the high production values and standards of the broader BBC. *Jasoos Vijay's* colourful characters and stories succeeded in engaging a wide audience, as evidenced by Nielsen ratings and the thousands of letters and e-mails that arrived at the New Delhi offices of the BBC WST every month.

One of the major findings of the end-line quantitative research for BBC WST's HIV/AIDS Awareness Project was the mediating impact of self-efficacy and interpersonal discussions in changing viewer's KAP. Numerous psycho-social theories posit that self-efficacy mediates the relationship between attitudes and behaviours. Thus, more enlightened attitudes relating to HIV and AIDS may serve to make individuals more confident that they can successfully perform safer sex behaviours and this self-confidence, in turn, increases the likelihood that they actually do engage in safer sex practices. Similarly, exposure to the programme led to increased interpersonal communication, which, in turn, related to shifts in HIV-related behaviour, such as getting tested for HIV, using condoms and being faithful to one partner (Chatterjee et al., 2009). Both of these findings reinforce Bandura's assertion that in addition to direct effects, the media can also influence audiences indirectly along a 'socially mediated pathway' (Bandura, 2002: 141).

In addition to self-efficacy, collective efficacy and co-viewing appear to be important in understanding the context of dramas for development. Moreover, this analysis reinforces the notion that social norms play a pivotal role in behaviour change communication—potentially acting as either barriers or facilitators. These findings lend support to the growing chorus of voices calling for more ecological models of health (e.g., Dutta-Bergman, 2005). By situating dramas for development within the socio-cultural and social group contexts, they may be better able to achieve change at the individual, community and societal levels.

Importantly, the programme promoted a sense of efficacy among viewers with respect to HIV, making them feel that they could take action both at the individual and collective level. The series not only pierced cultural and social taboos by delivering messages related to sex, HIV and condoms on prime time television—but it also encouraged individual and community dialogue about these topics. Both the current analysis and a quantitative comparison of the baseline and end-line BBC WST surveys show conversation with family and friends about HIV to be a crucial factor in changing viewers' attitudes and knowledge of HIV and AIDS.

Clearly, drama producers must work with diverse communities to determine relevant cultural norms, and how those norms may vary across key segments of the target audience (by gender, age, religion, region, HIV status and so on). While prevailing norms should be acknowledged throughout the design process, it does not follow that all norms must go unchallenged. *Jasoos Vijay* highlights that sometimes changing existing norms is the primary goal of a campaign. However, researchers must tread carefully and thoughtfully before determining their campaign objectives and manner of implementation. For instance, many campaigns are designed to deliver specific behavioural objectives in the short term with little regard to potential long-term outcomes. Here, Wilkins and Mody (2001) rightly caution against taking such a myopic view. In producing drama for developing countries, producers are morally obligated to not only understand the nuances of the culture in which the campaign will take place, but also to anticipate the potential impact of the campaign both in the immediate and more distant future.

Note

1. Note that Nielsen's panel does not cover towns with populations of less than 100,000. Consequently, the actual reach may have been significantly higher than the figures reported by TAM data.

References

Bandura, A. (1969) 'Social Learning Theory of Identificatory Processes' in D.A. Goslin (ed.) *Handbook of Socialization Theory and Research*, pp.213–262. Chicago: RandMc-Nally.

———. (1977a) 'Self-efficacy: Toward a Unifying Theory of Behavior Change', *Psychological Review*, 84: 191–215.

———. (1977b) *Social Learning Theory*. Englewood Cliffs, NJ: Prentice-Hall.

———. (1982) 'Self-efficacy Mechanism in Human Agency', *American Psychologist*, 37(2): 122–147.

———. (1998) 'Health Promotion from the Perspective of Social Cognitive Theory', *Psychology and Health*, 13(4): 623–649.

———. (2001) 'Social Cognitive Theory of Mass Communication', *Media Psychology*, 3(3): 265–299.

———. (2002). 'Social Cognitive Theory of Mass Communication' in J. Bryant and D. Zillman (eds), *Media Effects: Advances in Theory and Research* (2nd ed.) (pp. 121–153). Mahwah, NJ: Lawrence Erlbaum Associates, Inc.

———. (2004a) 'Health Promotion by Social Cognitive Means', *Health Education and Behavior*, 31(2): 143–164.

———. (2004b) Social Cognitive Theory for Personal and Social Change by Enabling Media, in A. Singhal, M. Cody, E. M. Rogers and M. Sabido (eds), *Entertainment-Education and Social Change: History, Research, and Practice*, pp. 75–96. Mahwah, NJ: Lawrence Erlbaum Associates, Inc.

Chatterjee, J., Bhanot, A., Frank, L.B., Murphy, S.T. and Power, G. (2009) 'The Importance of Interpersonal Discussion and Self-efficacy in Knowledge, Attitude, and Practice Models', *International Journal of Communication*, 3: 607–637.

Chaudhuri, T. (2007) 'HIV Stigma in India: A Gendered Experience?', paper presented at the Annual Meeting of the American Sociological Association, New York, 11 August. Available online at http://www.allacademic.com/meta/p182903_index.html (accessed on 20 January 2011).

Dickey, S. (2007) *Cinema and the Urban Poor in South India*. Cambridge: Cambridge University Press.

Dutta-Bergman, M. J. (2005) 'Theory and Practice in Health Communication Campaigns: A Critical Interrogation', *Health Communication*, 18(2): 103–122.

Gillespie, M. (1995) *Television, Ethnicity and Cultural Change*. London: Routledge.

Lapinski, M.K. and Rimal, R.N. (2005) 'An Explication of Social Norms', *Communication Theory*, 15(2): 127–147.

Law, S. and Singhal, A. (1999) 'Efficacy in Letter-writing to an Entertainment-Education Radio Serial', *International Communication Gazette*, 61(5): 355–372.

Miller, D. (1995) 'The Consumption of Soap Opera: *The Young and the Restless and Mass Consumption in Trinidad*', in R. Allen (ed.), *to be continued … Soap Operas around the World*. London: Routledge.

Murphy, S.T., Frank, L.B., Moran, M. and Woodley, P. (forthcoming) 'Involved, Trans-
ported or Emotional? Exploring the Determinants of Change in Knowledge, Attitudes,
and Behavior, in Entertainment Education', *Journal of Communication*.

Papa, M.J., Singhal, A., Law, S., Pant, S., Sood, S., Rogers, E.M. and Shefner-Rogers,
C.L. (2000) 'Entertainment Education and Social Change: An Analysis of Parasocial
Interaction, Social Learning, Collective Efficacy, and Paradoxical Communication',
Journal of Communication, 50(4): 31–55.

Sabido, M. (2004) 'The Origins of Entertainment-Education', In A. Singhal, M. Cody,
E.M. Rogers and M. Sabido (eds), *Entertainment-Education and Social Change: History,
Research, and Practice*, pp. 61–74. Mahwah, NJ: Lawrence Erlbaum Associates.

Selvan, M.S., Ross, M.W. and Parker, P. (2005) 'Societal Norms and Open Communication about Sex-related Issues as Predictors of Safer Sex', *Indian Journal of
Community Medicine*, 30(4): 10–12.

Singhal, A. and Rogers, E.M. (1999) *Entertainment Education: A Communication Strategy for
Social Change*. Mahwah, NJ: Lawrence Erlbaum Associates.

Singhal, A., Cody, M., Rogers, E. and Sabido, M. (2004) *Entertainment-Education and Social
Change: History, Research, and Practice*. New York: Lawrence Erlbaum Associates, Inc.

Sinha, J. and Kumar, R. (2004) 'Methodology for Understanding Indian Culture',
The Copenhagen Journal of Asian Studies, 19: 89–104.

Sood, S., Shefner-Rogers, C.L. and Sengupta, M. (2006) 'The Impact of a Mass Media
Campaign on HIV/AIDS Knowledge and Behavior Change in North India: Results
from a Longitudinal Study', *Asian Journal of Communication*, 16(3): 231–250.

Wilkins, K.G. and Mody, B. (2001) 'Redeveloping Development Communication:
Developing Communication and Communicating Development', *Communication
Theory*, 11(4): 385–396.

11

'PASSPORT TO LOVE'

DRAMATISING FORCED MARRIAGE BETWEEN PAKISTAN AND THE PAKISTANI DIASPORA

Introduction

In 2006 the BBC World Service Trust (BBC WST) piloted an Urdu language radio drama entitled *Piyar ka Passport* (*Passport to Love*).[1] It was broadcast in both Pakistan and the United Kingdom in 2006 with a view to raising awareness and stimulating dialogue on human rights and gender issues—most notably on 'forced marriage'—amongst Pakistanis in these two countries intimately connected by history and migration. Forced marriage, in this chapter, refers to a marriage conducted without the valid consent of the people involved, and where pressure or abuse is used in order to achieve it.[2] The idea of addressing the issue of forced marriage emerged from the Public Diplomacy Section of the British High Commission in Islamabad, which at that time was helping British Pakistanis in Pakistan who had become the victims of forced marriage.

Simultaneously, the Forced Marriage Unit (FMU), a small unit of the United Kingdom (UK) Foreign and Commonwealth Office (FCO), was working in the UK to prevent the forced marriage of young boys and girls and to assist those that had been victims in their integration back into their existing families and/or into new social lives.

Research on the Pakistani diaspora (Anwar, 1979; Ballard, 1994; Werbner, 1990, 2002) suggests that migrants to the UK maintain strong links with families back in Pakistan and despite long periods of staying abroad, kinship occupies a significant place in their lives. Strength of family bonds is further maintained through transnational marriage arrangements, often and ideally between the children of siblings, for example, marriage between first cousins (Charsley, 2003, 2005; Shaw, 2000). In these cases, often, one of the marriage partners has to leave their country of residence after the ceremony. Frequent cases have been observed where girls (born or brought up in the UK) move to Pakistan to marry their cousins or male spouses come to the UK and attain UK nationality through marriage. Here, a member of staff from the BBC WST suggests: 'they [FCO] were rescuing girls with British passports and almost every instance of forced marriage that they came across was instigated for the sake of the passport.' Since such marriages were initiated by relatives based in both Pakistan and the UK, the FCO felt it crucial to address the issue with Pakistanis based in both countries. The FCO approached the BBC WST and invited them to create a radio drama that would engage and educate audiences by embedding narratives about forced marriage in the context of wider social issues identified as salient. Alongside this, the project also addressed other subjects of interest to the British High Commission in Islamabad, such as illegal immigration and drug smuggling, which were also of concern to the British Government. In response to the request from the FCO, the BBC WST designed a multi-media project, including a radio drama, live phone-in discussions and a website to encourage audiences in Pakistan and the UK Pakistani diaspora to reflect on and debate the issues raised by the drama. Drama, as the principal media vehicle, was seen as one of the few options capable of addressing the highly sensitive and complex subject of forced marriage, an issue not openly debated in Pakistani culture and media. Serial drama has a unique ability to enable audiences to get close to characters and the dilemmas that they face, and to use the dramatised conflicts to engage in vicarious discussions about their own personal experiences or of those close to them. Audiences can make moral evaluations, and the process can be didactic and effective in shifting attitudes and ideas.

The FCO turned to the BBC WST to implement the project for two main reasons. First, the BBC Urdu Service has huge popularity in both Pakistan and the UK and so the BBC brand is trusted and respected. Second, they perceived the BBC WST as having the necessary expertise in drama production within the region; most notably through previous Pashtu language dramas produced to support humanitarian efforts in the context of the Afghan civil war (see Chapters 4, 7 and 13).[3]

Once funding was secured from the FCO, the BBC WST commissioned formative research in which 12 focus group discussions were conducted in Pakistan in December 2005 (SB&B, 2006).[4] This research was conducted to provide insight into what audiences regarded as the most pressing social issues, their feelings about how such social issues might be or should be represented in radio drama and what elements a radio drama needs in order to achieve impact. Each focus group comprised 8 to 10 female and male participants, aged between 15 and 44 years, from both rural and urban areas. Participants were asked to discuss some of the most important problems facing people in Pakistan. Unemployment, lack of educational opportunities, corruption, poor governance, poverty and lack of infrastructure were problems explicitly highlighted by the participants. Marriage proved to be a cross-cutting theme and a number of forms of marriage in Pakistan were identified by the groups. The findings shed light on some of the core attitudes surrounding marriage more broadly, such as preference for marriage within families, the use of marriage to settle financial or family disputes or to consolidate ownership of family property (see Chapter 13 for a discussion of forced marriage in Afghanistan).

The BBC WST developed the drama storyline in response to the request from the FCO, a request subsequently informed by the findings from the focus groups. Six scriptwriters were employed to write the drama and actors were selected to bring the scripts to life. This team was selected in Pakistan with the help of the director of the BBC Urdu Service and his staff who were working in Pakistan and the UK (BBC WST member of staff). Later, the BBC Urdu Service also participated in producing the drama and moderating the phone-in and online discussions that took place during and after the programme. They cooperated with the scriptwriters, arranged live talking points (in which the public could call the writers and ask questions) and conducted an 'end of drama' workshop in Lahore, Pakistan.

The drama was the result of an intensive collaboration between experienced and new Pakistani writers under the editorial control of the drama's producer and director. The lengthy inception phase involving meetings and workshops in London, Islamabad and Lahore, allowed the purpose, approach and storyline to unfold in an iterative manner taking account of diverse perspectives.

Twelve 15-minute episodes were broadcast over two weeks (during 2006). The live radio phone-in programme on the BBC Urdu Service with additional phone in programmes on partner FM stations in Pakistan and live radio debate were held simultaneously in Lahore and London to facilitate a lively transnational debate. The websites of BBC Urdu and BBC World Service Trust featured content in Urdu and English, respectively, and provided background information on the project, details about the drama and characters and an online forum for discussion.[5] A multi-platform/media approach was deployed to encourage listeners to share their views and contribute to online debates regarding forced marriage and family life in Pakistan. The live link-up debate in Lahore and London, in particular, promoted a very animated discussion and confirmed that the drama had indeed, as intended, stirred up a considerable amount of public debate and interest in these sensitive subjects (BBC World Service Trust, 2006b).

Impact research conducted with radio audiences in Pakistan (BBC World Service Trust, 2006a) revealed that the drama was seen to reflect differences in the contemporary lives of Pakistanis living in Pakistan and abroad (notably the UK), and was able to engage audiences in its storylines. This was precisely what the project aimed to achieve from the point of view of funders. However, a majority of listeners—while recognising that the drama was both entertaining and original—felt that it focused too heavily on what were perceived to be negative aspects of life in Pakistani society, in particular, on the repression of women, corruption and fundamentalism, whilst ignoring more important and routine issues affecting Pakistani society, as identified in the formative focus group research.

In contrast to the aforementioned BBC WST audience study that assessed the impact of drama in raising awareness and stimulating dialogue on forced marriages in Pakistan (BBC World Service Trust, 2006a), this chapter examines the drama through a different lens, from the perspective of donors and dramatists. It aims to understand the connections and differences evident between media practitioners, human rights and development constituencies, donors and audiences, and analyses the processes by which British and Pakistani perspectives were negotiated. In particular, it examines processes of cross-cultural exchange and translation and highlights differences in perspectives on marriage practices between the various actors involved. The chapter argues that the drama provided a focused cross-cultural 'contact zone' that allowed for the examination of the relationship between these diverse actors; how they negotiate and perform everyday acts of cultural translation or cultural diplomacy for Pakistani audiences; how decisions are made and information contextualised to make it comprehensible for audiences and how assumptions about the intellectual level of the audience are taken into account. These issues are examined especially in relation to the problem of tackling 'forced' marriage—a term with many connotations and uses.

Data for this chapter was collected between June and September 2008. Four in-depth and open-ended interviews were conducted with staff from BBC WST, BBC Urdu Service diasporic staff and the FCO. Interviews were transcribed and translated into English where they were conducted in Urdu. Drama scripts, episodes, documents relating to discussion of the scripting process (i.e., formative discussions of the dramatists and researchers around the themes to be dramatised), BBC WST reports (2006a, 2006b) and the formative research study (SB&B, 2006) were also collected and analysed. Although like all research this chapter offers a partial account, it offers a glimpse of the kind of everyday translational and transnational media and cultural knowledge practices that have to be negotiated in drama for development.

The Drama: *Piyar ka Passport*

The drama presented 5–6 main storylines that ran across the 12 episodes produced. One of these stories ran throughout the drama, others were fed in during the episodes and a couple were left open ended to stimulate discussion amongst the general public. In all episodes, the drama team tried to maintain the dual objectives of creating an entertaining and engaging piece of drama using plausible characters, lively humour and dramatic conflict and suspense to hook its audience into the narrational process. It approached central issues, such as forced marriage, from as many perspectives as possible, in order to speak *to* and *for* diverse audiences (BBC World Service Trust, 2006a). Each episode had an overarching theme, such as illegal immigration, class conflict in Pakistan, division of land, rapid industrialisation, people smuggling, corruption and drug-related crime. However, most of the stories concerned women and focused on issues of marriage.

The drama presented the main story of two branches of a Pakistani family, one based in the UK and the other in Pakistan. The elder brother Ahmed (56 years old) moved to 'Steadford' (a fictional version of Bradford in the north of England) 35 years ago and started his own business. He lived happily with his wife Saleema (45 years old), son Javaid (25 years old) and two daughters, Safia (20 years old) and Sitara (15 years old) when he decides to retire and fulfil his desire to return to Pakistan. His wife endorses his decision as her daughters have reached a certain age; she glimpses the godlessness of the West in their attitudes and behaviour, and fears it will only get worse. Safia and Sitara are 'good girls'; they embody Pakistani values of modesty despite being brought up in a liberal western culture. However, living in Steadford has given them a sense of individuality, a capacity for critical thinking and questioning intelligence that Saleema finds hard to cope with. She and Ahmed think that the sooner they are married off, the more completely they will have discharged their parental duties to the girls. Their son Javaid does not want to go with them but acquiesces when his work with a charity in the aftermath of the 2005 earthquake in northern Pakistan brings him closer to his family's homeland.

Ahmed's younger brother Niaz (52 years old) lives back in Pakistan looking after the extended family, including his wife Sarwat (43 years old), two sons Anwaar (25 years old) and Shehzad (22 years old), daughter Zeenat (12 years old), his old mother (70 years old), his divorced cousin Zahooran (38 years old) and Zahooran's daughter Razia (21 years old). Niaz is close to bankruptcy. Ahmed has been sending him money ever since he moved to Steadford in the UK to buy land and build property for the day when he would eventually return. Niaz hasn't spent the money appropriately and, instead, spends it on his own failed businesses or the extended family. He keeps lying to Ahmed that a property has been bought in his name, with the help of his corrupt friend Patwari (the land registrar) who has a reputation of exploiting his position for personal gains.

When a family wedding in Pakistan reunites the two, the brothers decide to strengthen family ties by arranging a marriage between their respective children, Shahzad and Safia. However, this 'well intended' proposal quickly leads to conflict. Shahzad is a lazy boy with no ambition and continually gets in and out of trouble with organised criminals. He depends on this marriage to both repay his debts and to get a UK visa to enjoy the 'delights of England'. Safia, on the other hand is not willing, as she does not want to marry at all. Three months before they came to Pakistan, she was raped—a secret held between her and her mother Saleema. Saleema thought that Safia would be unmarriageable forever if the secret were to be disclosed and that her marriage with Shehzad would put the rape firmly in the past. However, when Safia discloses this secret out of her honesty, Shehzad's family refuses to accept her. 'Why should my son marry such a girl? Is there a shortage of girls that my son has to accept left-overs?' says Sarwat.

Tensions arise between the families not only because of the collapse of the proposal but also due to the fallout resulting from the inappropriate investment of Ahmed's remittances and the realisation that he has no property to return to in Pakistan. Ahmed, who is keen to see the fruits of his wealth, gradually realises that the house he thinks is his own is only rented. However, Niaz carefully lays a plot to fool his brother again; his corrupt friend Patwari offers to help him once more, but only on condition that he arranges his second marriage with Niaz's distant niece Razia. Upon hearing about the proposal, Razia is furious, for she is 21 years old and Patwari is 58 years old and also has a reputation for beating his first wife. However, Razia's mother Zahooran accepts the proposal as Patwari is a rich man and her daughter would at least not face the financial hardships that she herself had faced in life. When she sees no hope of escaping the marriage Razia elopes with her love, Abbas (28 years old), a hardworking intelligent man but from a lower caste—a factor that would have prevented him marrying Razia in any case. When the family discovers that Razia and Abbas are missing, they keep it a secret to protect the honour of the family. However, Ahmed's son Anwaar chooses to pursue the couple with a gun. He says, 'a girl of my family is not home where she belongs and that is enough for me. I will kill her and the man she is with.' However, Niaz reports to the police that Razia's disappearance is a case of abduction in an attempt to mitigate the situation. Razia is soon found and subsequently clarifies her marital status in court and the police case of abduction is dropped. Nonetheless, she arrives back to a barrage of slaps and swearing, but her grandmother and Javaid support her saying that Islam allows a marriage of choice.

Since the marriage between Patwari and Razia does not materialise, Patwari puts the entire blame of the property deception on Niaz and tension between the two families grows. Niaz feels that a marriage would heal the rift between the two brothers' so he proposes to arrange *wata sata* (an exchange marriage in which two families decide to marry two children each, for example, a son and a daughter of one family marry the son and daughter of the other family) between Shehzad and Sitara, as well as Javaid and Zeenat. Sitara refuses to marry Shehzad not only because she does not like him, but also because her willingness would have endorsed that her sister Safia is unmarriageable (due to her being raped), which would consign her to a life without 'identity'. Her refusal to marry makes her parents assume that she has a boyfriend in England, which fires their determination to wed her into safety, but despite being a good daughter she feels forced into disobedience by the situation. On the other hand, Javaid and Zeenat half-heartedly submit to their elders' decision thinking that their parents would decide what is best for them. Meanwhile, the police arrive and arrest Niaz on charges of fraud. Ahmed pays money to bring Niaz home. Shehzad is impressed by the generosity of his uncle and Niaz is grateful. The whole family becomes truly united when Shehzad gets up and announces that he is willing to marry Safia. However, Safia refuses gently and the drama finishes.

By focusing on the major themes of forced marriage, rape and migration, the drama took account of a number of culturally sensitive issues, for example, the marriage of young girls to older men, marriage to obtain visas, marriage for the sake of money or to retain wealth within the family, honour-related violence, class and caste discrimination, corruption and the position of victims of sexual abuse. It also showed some distinct values of Pakistani culture, such as the value of blood relations and how these relations do not fade with distance, power of forgiveness within families, importance of holding one's clan close, importance of the decisions of elders in weddings and Pakistani migrants' desire to return to their country despite having comfortable lives abroad. In doing so, the drama highlighted and encouraged the public to engage in debates on topics such as the maltreatment of victims of sexual abuse, forcing children into marriage and the need of women to stand up for their own rights.

Interaction between Funders and Dramatists

Turning from the drama's storylines to aspects of production, the FCO had, in principle, given complete creative freedom to the BBC WST in deciding what to broadcast and how, so long as the broad issues of forced marriage, illegal migration and drug smuggling were addressed and audiences were effectively and actively engaged. The FCO and the BBC WST sought a clear separation in their roles. According to the FCO, any involvement on their part in the creative process of script writing, mise-en-scène or performance was clearly beyond their remit. The BBC WST had the relevant expertise as well as an excellent reputation for the delivery of effective drama for development:

> … we didn't want to get involved in pulling the individual chord of scriptwriters, and telling them what we want them to do, so what we decided to do was, we had a kind of joint discussion to discuss the best way forward, and decided that we would commission the BBC World Service Trust to produce a drama for us that would cover the issues in a way that wasn't preaching to the people that 'you must do this or do that' but, more in a way, to engage them in a real life situation [which drama is deemed capable of stimulating].

> (FCO member of staff, Telephone Interview, 29 August 2008)

In the process of developing the drama, the BBC WST met with members of the FCO team tasked with responding to alleged cases of forced marriage. These discussions were helpful in providing the scriptwriters with material for the drama based on real cases that the FCO team had dealt with. The BBC WST also liaised with the British High Commission in Islamabad to share what was being covered in the scripts and how. Following the hiring of the drama team, the BBC WST held meetings with the writers about how to develop the drama. The most enduring tension throughout the project was the insistence on the part of the FCO to focus the drama on forced marriage specifically and the resistance of the writing team, who argued for the importance of locating the practice of forced marriage within a broader set of cultural and social relations. The final storyline is the result of a series of shifting production priorities from the original narrow remit to focus on forced marriage to a creative response to the broader interests of the audience to an embedding of the forced marriage storyline within a richer contextual narrative that addresses human rights, gender issues and cross-cultural relations.

> We [BBC World Service Trust directors and producers, and writers in Pakistan] talked about the issues surrounding it [the drama], talked about ways of approaching it and talked about other soaps in Pakistan and, you know, how large a family to represent, and how complicated a story to pursue, and sort of issues like that. I came back to London after that and it wasn't revealed until after the first meeting with the writers that actually a lot of the story of the soap was sort of pre-dictated by the funder [FCO] so quite a lot that we came up with the first meeting was then scrapped.
>
> (BBC World Service Trust member of staff,
> Interview, London, 21 August 2008)

In the view of the BBC WST, the FCO funders wished to present an extreme example of forced marriage based loosely on a case that they had dealt with in their work. In turn, they wanted the drama to have a very precise and immediate impact on attitudes to a very specific form of forced marriage. However, drama tends only to have high-level, immediate impact if it is supported by extensive and intensive outreach work, marketing and the scheduling of related debates about a particular issue. Further, *Piyar ka Passport* was always intended to be a pilot project designed to understand both the potential and the limitations of the drama format to address such a sensitive topic in Pakistan in the medium and long term. Nevertheless, the 'great expectations' (see Chapter 2) of the donor agency prevailed throughout the drama-making process and afterward.

> Drama is a very good way of meditating an issue but it is unlikely to change the world without a lot of accessory behaviour and I think, in fact, the project didn't quite have enough, we had very good debates, we had good phone-ins, but the marketing wasn't very strong on it. Really the British High Commission [in Islamabad] wanted to change the national consciousness for a few thousand pounds and immediately have less incidents of forced marriages. They would, ideally, have liked to have solved the problems but, you know, that wasn't going to happen and I think they were a little bit disappointed, but it was an unrealistic expectation to me.
>
> (BBC World Service Trust member of staff,
> Interview, London, 21 August 2008)

There were significant differences concerning how to broadcast other socially and culturally sensitive issues through drama. The BBC WST producers felt that not all issues could be covered through the drama in a way that the FCO wished, as it was deemed vital to take into account what is seen as 'appropriate' within Pakistani culture:

> The funders had very strong ideas about what should be in the soap [drama] and that was fine and it was their money, but some of the ideas they had were culturally not all that likely to make it through the process of discussion and writing. We had a scenario which the writers group in Pakistan were keen to pursue of a British girl who had been raped, been taken to Pakistan and married to her cousin and funders were very keen that the rape should be on air and I couldn't find anybody in Pakistan or in the Urdu Service to even consent to that as something to fit in to a drama ... none of the writers had a problem with rape being part of the story, they just didn't want it to put on the air, so we didn't put it on the air.
>
> (BBC World Service Trust member of staff,
> Interview, London, 21 August 2008)

While the Pakistani writers acknowledged that rape does occur in Pakistan and it is important to raise awareness of the issue, none of them thought it was culturally appropriate to openly and explicitly broadcast the act of rape. This view was linked to ideas of honour and shame in Pakistani culture. Issues pertaining to sex, rape or physical relationships tend not to be openly discussed or represented in the media, particularly in the rural settings that the donors wished to target.

Tension was also observed regarding 'who to reach'. The British High Commission in Islamabad wanted to reach audiences in Pakistan and the UK Pakistani diaspora as they saw the problem as a problem of transnational migrant communities. Ideologically, they were against forced marriage in any part of the world. They saw their role as 'rescuing' British girls with British passports and, according to the British High Commission, almost every case of forced marriage was motivated by a desire to obtain a British passport on the part of Pakistani families.

The BBC Urdu Service was also faced with the additional problem of having to appeal to male audiences who were mainly interested in listening to news on the radio. The genre of drama serials was seen as a 'feminine' genre, offering little appeal to men:

> ... there was already a small degree of tension on what the Urdu service wanted on their network and what the British High Commission wanted in the soap [drama] and it was a difficult relationship ... the funder had a very specific market in mind and the BBC World Service Trust took the project to the Urdu Service who weren't particularly reaching the market that the British High Commission had in mind and actually ... the BBC Urdu Service is a news service primarily and has a very male audience and *Piyar ka Passport* was quite a female story really and although the male characters in it were strong and intelligent ... the average listener to the Urdu Service wasn't interested in having that story to listen to before the news in the evening. So in that sense it was a bit of a mis-marriage between the Urdu Service and the soap, a forced marriage.

(BBC World Service Trust member of staff,
Interview, London, 21 August 2008)

However, this tension was resolved when the programme was aired on the BBC Asian Network, which had a much wider coverage than the BBC Urdu Service. The Asian Network replayed the drama in the UK, which was also a key target audience for the FCO. Despite funder–producer tension over the substance of the drama during the discussion process, and the difficulties over its appeal to male audiences, perhaps the most serious issue was its narrow portrayal of forced marriage in the face of a wide range of culturally and normatively sanctioned marriage arrangements.

Forced Marriage: A Wide Spectrum of Arrangements

In Pakistani society, marriage takes many different forms. For example: (*a*) arranged marriage initiated by parents and consented to by both partners; (*b*) love marriage initiated by the couple, but with the consent of parents; (*c*) court marriage without the parents' consent; (*d*) barter marriage (*wata sata*) where one marriage partner may be marrying out of choice, but the other is forced; (*e*) forced marriage—initiated by parents and resented by one or both partners; (*f*) marriage for money; (*g*) marriage to heal a family feud and (*h*) marriage to keep property within a clan, to settle debts and so on. In both rural and urban societies, people generally understand the distinction between these forms of marriage and recognise that such forms co-exist. However, arranged marriage is a widely accepted custom as it is generally believed that parents decide what they 'genuinely' think to be good for their children. The marriage partners may initially be reluctant to accept their decision, but in the long term, they realise that their parents made the right choice. Moreover, since parents take the main responsibility for marriage decisions, the marriage partners enjoy support from both sides of the family, which is often seen as helpful to sustaining the marriage over time. The reverse is the case in love marriage where the marriage partners have the entire responsibility of making the marriage decision, often against the wills of their respective families. Many of the live phone-in calls associated with the drama confirmed this explanation: 'they [parents] know what's right for their children and will never harm them'. For love marriage, the views were: 'the girl or boy may be temporarily blinded by love and would not be able to make the right choice' and 'love marriages are mostly a flop and have a lower success rate in any case'.

The detailed description above suggests that the idea of forced marriage is complex. Further, it was contested and debated among the stakeholders. As mentioned earlier, the initiative came from the FCO who, as 'donors', aimed to apply a 'rights-oriented' approach to the perceived/actual rise in the number of forced marriages of Pakistani women occurring in the UK and Pakistan. On the other hand, the BBC WST was thinking critically about what audiences felt about the issue and how it resonated with contemporary life. They also knew from their formative research that other issues were more important to audiences than forced marriage. Hence, the dilemma was—how to create a dramatic world that touches on issues close and distant to audiences while encouraging them to listen? Another critical question was—what is forced marriage? They considered it as one end of a long spectrum of arrangements, levels of involvement and decision-making. The challenge was how to unpack this issue and how to focus on more tricky issues of autonomy, the balancing of loyalties and implications of decisions about marriage and not just focusing on an extreme manifestation of the forced marriage:

> ... forced marriage is a degree of abstraction ... the issue ... is a very difficult one to tackle head on simply because ... the funders had come across instances of very brutal forced marriages where they were rescuing girls from extremely violent coercive instances but sort of on a sliding scale between forced marriage and arranged marriage there are huge areas that are grey where girls want to do what their fathers tell them to do and where parents genuinely believe that they know better than their daughters and with the best will in the world that they still force them into something.
>
> (BBC World Service Trust member of staff,
> Interview, London, 21 August 2008)

The BBC Urdu Service staff also recognised the significance of forced marriage as it affects Pakistani society, and that a variety of perceptions exist in people's minds that needed to be better understood. For example, what is normally seen as forced marriage in the West may be seen as 'arranged marriage' by most people in Pakistan:

> People don't think that there is anything like forced marriage of women, people think that they just arrange a marriage, they don't consider it as forced marriage ... I personally thought that it would be good to have a discussion on what exactly is forced marriage.
>
> (BBC Urdu Service member of staff,
> Interview, London, 28 August 2008)

Some of the drama writers clearly thought that 'arranged' marriages were not only culturally appropriate, but were, eventually, 'good' for women. The producer had to balance the perceptions of its writers with the demands of the funders while ensuring what was broadcast was also culturally appropriate. According to some writers, the best approach is to use open-ended narratives that enable audiences to debate and comment on the characters and their actions and decide for themselves where the boundaries between arranged and forced marriage should be drawn (see Appendix 2).

Donors', Dramatists' and Listeners' Views and the Drama Objectives

While all the scripts were translated into English, the FCO staff working on the project did not know the Urdu language and hence could not understand the nuances of the drama. Nonetheless, they attended the live link-up debates associated with the drama and were generally happy with its achievements. It was evident through the high level of participation of people in the debates that the broader objective of raising awareness in public was achieved:

> As far we are concerned we would say it was a success, I mean it is difficult to clarify what a success is, if the success is a reduction in forced marriages or is it an increase in the amount of people who come and talk to us about it? If you look at the website and the amount of responses that have been reported on the website and the people that listen to it and not just in Britain and Pakistan but across the world I think you see that it has covered a wide audience and a lot of people have been impacted by its discussion, so yes it was a success and any subject raised in the drama to raise awareness amongst people and engaging them in it is a good thing.

> (FCO member of staff, Telephone Interview, 29 August 2008)

The Trust also felt that the drama was innovative and broke new ground, particularly in terms of developing links between the UK and Pakistan. The idea of the associated media debates was particularly acknowledged: '… the other idea that we developed was the idea of discussion, you have a drama, you have strong narrative, some very strong ideas in terms of people and their stories and then having discussion programmes around it, is, was very positive, very good' (BBC World Service Trust member of staff, Interview, London, 22 July 2008).

Largely, because their target audiences are different, the BBC Urdu Service differed from the BBC WST and FCO regarding the openness of the listeners. For example, in contrast to some staff at the BBC WST and FCO who thought that Pakistan—not being an 'open' society—may not be receptive to open discussions on culturally sensitive issues such as molestation and forced marriage, the BBC Urdu Service felt that this was not the case. They suggested that such discussions are, in fact, very common in urban areas and amongst elite groups; however, they are not so accessible to people in rural areas. However, since the BBC World Service has a wide coverage in rural areas, such discussion 'did' reach these areas, engaging the general public in the process:

> It wasn't that we had introduced this idea for the first time in a unique way. There is very much a discussion and debate on these issues in Pakistani society but the difference was that such discussion is limited to elite classes in urban areas, but the Urdu Service's reach is in rural areas, villages, in areas where there are no TVs ... so if this drama and discussion introduced a debate in such areas, that was a big achievement and we were giving such people a new thought ... and to a large extent it was independent, and we as a team try to keep it as independent of the influences of the donors as possible.

> > (BBC Urdu Service member of staff,
> > Interview, London, 28 August 2008)

The Pakistani staff at the BBC Urdu Service also felt that the issues surrounding forced marriage were significant, needed to be addressed and that the drama 'did' address them. However, the last sentence of the above quotation suggests that the BBC Urdu service also recognised the need to resist the influence of the donors and to maintain creative and editorial control of the content, and to encourage the audience to come to an independent assessment about the dilemmas involved in marriage arrangements. The Urdu Service staff felt they were successful in achieving their goal of enabling listeners to express their views openly, even if they did not match with those desired by funders. A range of views was published on the related website and was open for comments.

In this sense, the online contact zones of the BBC WST became a place where competing views could be represented and contested, managed and moderated.

Spontaneous reactions to *Piyar ka Passport* tended to comprise of favourable responses from the listeners. The listeners genuinely appeared to have been positively influenced by the overall effort and supported their comments by appreciating the unique selection of topics relating to both Pakistani culture and environment; a realistic portrayal of family life; a good blend of romance, family conflicts and emotions; a comparison of immigrant and Pakistani lifestyles and effective use of characters and voices (SB&B, 2006): '*Piyar Ka Passport* succeeds in touching upon various relevant and inter-related topics ... while skimming over certain controversial issues' (excerpt from radio phone-in programme, BBC World Service Trust, 2006b). However, listeners also thought that the production should align its themes with religious dictum and never cross that line. Islam and the Quran, it was suggested, could be used effectively to discuss marriage and consent, but with caution as nothing should be misquoted or used out of context. It was thought that religion could also be used to help counter misconceptions. 'Islam allows a marriage of choice' was an argument used by Javaid and his grandmother to support Razia after she eloped. However, this could be taken further in the debates that followed the drama in which Islamic principles and guidelines regarding marriage could be brought to light, for example, Islam condemns forced marriage and gives liberty to both marriage partners to exercise their will. *Nikah* (matrimonial contract) is not complete without the verbal and written consent of the bride and groom in the presence of three witnesses from each side.

One listener took the view that the problems raised in the drama represented the past and that there has been a recent transition in the concept of marriage in contemporary Pakistani society:

> If this drama had been broadcast ten years ago it would have been relevant. But now, the situation in Pakistan has changed. That's why the plot and dialogue in the drama seem quite outdated. Don't you think that by keeping in mind the current situation the story could have been improved?
>
> (Excerpt from radio phone-in programme, BBC WST, 2006b)

Another listener suggested that '... after having listened to six episodes, I'm not impressed with the story. It's quite an exaggerated version of what actually happens in Pakistan' (Audience feedback to BBC Urdu Service, excerpt from BBC WST, 2006b).

On the whole, audiences appreciated the initiative and the way that the issues were presented through the drama. However, some people had reservations about the drama's content. They felt that it presented issues that were more a matter of concern for western societies and their governments, rather than for Pakistanis. Some felt that the production was unrealistic and to some extent shied away from some of the harder hitting issues. There was a view among some members of the audience that, although there were cases where spouses 'are' forced into marriage, the scale of such marriages may be far less than funders perceived it to be. The BBC Urdu Service also endorsed this view:

> ... the drama reflected many real issues but it did not present many issues that were crucial for people in Pakistan, for example, rape is something that is not so [common] ... they said it was western propaganda and western thoughts that the British government wished to impose through media, so there were some conflicting views ... they said that we have introduced western ideas about marriage and forced marriage in the society.
>
> (BBC Urdu Service member of staff,
> Interview, London, 28 August 2008)

This quote highlights the complexities and challenges, the inherent tensions and conflicts involved in the processes of cross-cultural communication and translation that are required to make good drama for development. Inevitably then, how such creative and political tensions are negotiated will shape the outcomes and impact of the drama. But as academics and practitioners, we have much to learn from these cultural encounters over dramatising development issues.

Conclusion

Literature on communication for development implies that mass media can play an important role in social change (Hemer and Tufte, 2005). Communication through media is seen as an important 'agent of surveillance' (Shaw and McCombs, 1974) and a tool of modernity, modern thinking and emancipation. In particular, entertainment-education programmes are perceived as instrumental in facilitating development (Jones and Lewis, 2006; Singhal and Rogers, 1999) by exposing audiences to new ideas, behaviours, practices and ways of thinking. However, Melkote and Steeves (2001) assert that audiences are not passive receivers of ideas; they critically engage and question the assumptions of broadcasters. Hence, communication for development cannot be seen as a delivery system in which messages for social change are often conveyed according to implicit or explicit assumptions and perceptions of external 'others'. Unlike the top-down model of modernisation—that initially influenced communication for development practice—the process should rather be seen as inseparable from culture and aim to facilitate intercultural communication and social change by understanding local contexts.

The analysis presented in this chapter brings into focus issues of translation, tradition and modernity as prevalent in an experiment 'genuinely' aimed at addressing and redressing what is perceived as rights violations, through communication. While cases do exist where girls are forced into marriage, at a wider level, there is the possibility that marriages seen as 'forced' by the West may be regarded as 'arranged' at the grassroots. Clearly, there is a continuum and a diversity to marriage arrangements that is often overlooked. Rarely are such marriages arranged simply to procure a passport alone. More importantly, they are arranged to balance loyalties, strengthen family bonds, settle feuds or debts and so on. The case presented here points to the potential representational challenges involved in translating concepts of human rights couched in universal terms at the specific local cultural level. Arranged/forced marriage implies traditionalism and conservatism. The project was clearly positioned by the FCO as a human rights project, but no doubt public diplomacy outcomes were hoped for even if they were not part of the primary purpose of the drama. Clearly, promoting more liberally infused versions of Islam is in the interests of western governments and central to their associated efforts of public diplomacy. It could be argued that the general thrust of the FCO's perspective on *Pyar Ka Passport* is close to wider UK government concerns about the export of Islamist influences (especially radicalising influences) from

Pakistan to the UK. Read in this light, the diasporic connection is also an issue of national security. Resisting extreme practices—such as forced marriage—is both a human rights and a public diplomacy issue. It is difficult to ignore this wider political context when analysing *Piyar Ka Passport*, though of course, policies, partnerships and principles translate into practice, often in unforeseen and unexpected ways.

This analysis also links us to Foucault's (1970, 1982, 1991) notion of structure and agency and more recent debates on the relationship between the two (Giddens and Pierson, 1998). Giddens regards structure and agency as reciprocal and interactive and emphasises 'mutuality' of the processes in which people shape systems and the systems shape their practice. The presentation of diverse perspectives in this chapter does not, of course, exhaust the full range of views that exist among all the various actors involved in the finding and making of this drama serial. But it does suggest that drama is being mobilised to raise awareness and catalyse change at a community level in contemporary media battles over ideas; however, people are enmeshed in cultural contexts that constrain the change. A linear approach, as criticised by Melkote and Steeves (2001) towards addressing the issues without much cultural sensitivity also characterises a lack of 'mutuality', itself reflecting a more recent critique on the theories of communication for development.

As the centrepiece of a multi-format pilot initiative, the *Piyar ka Passport* drama presented many forms of marriage as identified above (elopement—Razia and Abbas; *wata sata*—Shehzad and Sitara, as well as Javaid and Zeenat; marriage for money—Razia and Patwari; arranged/forced marriage—Safia and Shehzad). While presenting the issues associated with marriage, the drama unpacked a range of other issues concerning the diaspora, as well as the home-based Pakistanis. Studies conducted on the Pakistani diaspora in the UK (Anwar, 1979; Ballard, 1994; Donnan, 1997; Shaw, 2000) highlight the issues as echoed in the drama. Those specifically conducted on Pakistani marriages (Charsley, 2003; Das, 1973; Donnan, 1988; Fischer, 1991; Fischer and Lyon, 2000; Naveed-i-Rahat, 1990) discuss the issues of autonomy in kinship and marriage, loyalties with clan, masculinities of male marriage partners (Charsley, 2005), resistance of female partners, effects of marriage on the wider clan and so on. However, what comes out clearly from the studies, as well as the drama, is the need to recognise the gap between the perceptions of those aiming to address the issues of marriage and those practicing and experiencing marriage. The FCO's perception of forced marriage varied from that of the drama writers as well as the listeners. The extent of marriages really considered to be 'forced' was seen as less significant by the audience than by the FCO. Unfortunately, no quantitative evidence existed to locate the 'problem' of forced marriage or to substantiate the ratio of forced marriages to arranged marriages. First, given the complexity of the term, it is hard to locate cases into any discrete categories of 'forced', 'arranged' or any other. Second, as the analysis suggests, the phenomenon is subjective and culturally determined. Forced marriage 'does' exist as an issue in Pakistan and amongst the diaspora, and real examples 'are' found where girls are truly forced into marriage. In the case of *Piyar ka Passport*, I argue that the donor's assumptions concerning forced marriage seem ethnocentric. This case highlights the value of research that can inform how the processes of creative decision-making occurs in similar dramas and how broadcast services such as those provided by the BBC WST or BBC Urdu Service challenge donor agendas.

Notes

1. Information presented about the drama in this section is primarily based on interviews with member of staffs from the FCO, BBC WST and BBC Urdu staff. Specific references are cited in the text.
2. See FMU (2010).
3. Further, the BBC WST has a long-standing interest and engagement in mediating human rights and gender issues. It was involved in 'user-generated' media content projects focusing on women's lives in the Middle East, and was interested in taking up work in Pakistan. The proposal from the FCO offered the BBC WST an opportunity of both working in Pakistan as well as working on gender issues. The Trust refers 'user generated' to those projects which are developed in consultation with the audience. Audiences' opinion is sought on the issues that concern them and effort is made to produce dramas close to their real lives.
4. SB&B is a research company based in Pakistan. They were commissioned by the BBC WST to do the pre-drama research to indicate key issues faced by Pakistanis in the rural communities.
5. The multi-platform approach, particularly the Internet element, worked well for diaspora audiences in the UK and was effective in engaging them. The two websites provided background information on the cast and the characters, provided a daily

guide to the unfolding stories and featured articles which tackled themes such as rape, drug addiction, relative freedom of movement of poorer girls as opposed to middle-class girls, positive values among young Pakistanis (Ahmed's love and desire to serve Pakistan, Safia's courage to confess the truth, Zeenat and Javaid's respect to their elders' decision). A complete version of the public radio debate webcast on www.bbc. co.uk/urdu/ further encouraged comments and contributions from the public. The programme had a much wider coverage when broadcast on the BBC Asian Network, an unintended consequence that was not a part of the original brief. However, the online element was nearly meaningless for audiences in Pakistan, particularly those based in rural areas with no or very weak internet connections. Moreover, where Internet facilities are available, the issues of 'how to use the Internet' persist particularly among women audience. Therefore, most audiences in Pakistan could only make use of limited aspects of this multi-platform approach. This also prompts us to think that views obtained on the online forum only represented the views of urban youth who had access to and capacity of using Internet in Pakistan. People based in rural areas could have entirely different views on the issues addressed by the drama.

References

Anwar, M. (1979) *The Myth of Return*. London: Heinemann.

Ballard, R. (1994) *Desh Pardesh: The South Asian Presence in Britain*. London: Hurst.

BBC World Service Trust. (2006a) 'Piyar ka Passport: Using Radio Drama to Foster Dialogue about Social Issues in Pakistan', Series 01, No 2, October 2006.

———. (2006b) 'Final Report on the Pilot Radio Drama Project for Pakistan "Piyar ka Passport"', July 2006.

Charsley, K. (2003) 'Rishtas: Transnational Pakistani Marriages'. PhD Thesis, University of Edinburgh.

———. (2005) 'Unhappy Husbands: Masculinity and Migration in Transnational Pakistani Marriages', *Journal of Royal Anthropological Institute*, n.s., 11: 85–105.

Das, V. (1973) 'The Structure of Marriage Preferences: An Account from Pakistani Fiction', *Man*, n.s., 8: 30–45.

Donnan, H. (1988) *Marriage among Muslims: Preference and Choice in Northern Pakistan*. New Delhi: Hindustan Publishing Corporation.

———. (1997) 'Return Migration and Female-headed Households', in H. Donnan and F. Selier (eds), *Family and Gender in Pakistan: Domestic Organization in a Muslim Society*. New Delhi: Hindustan Publishing Corporation.

Fischer, M. (1991) 'Marriage and Power: Tradition and Transition in an Urban Punjabi Community', in H. Donnan and P. Werbner (eds), *Economy and Culture in Pakistan: Migrants and Cities in a Muslim Society*. Houndmills: Macmillan.

Fischer, M. and Lyon, W. (2000) 'Marriage Strategies in Lahore: Projections of a Model Marriage on Social Practice', in M. Bock and A. Rao (eds), *Culture, Creation and Procreation: Concepts of Kinship in South Asia*. Oxford: Berghahn Books.

Forced Marriage Unit (FMU). (2010) 'What is Forced Marriage'?, Foreign and Commonwealth Office, UK. Available online at http://www.fco.gov.uk/resources/en/pdf/2855621/what-is-forced-marriage (last accessed on 16 September 2009).

Foucault, M. (1970) *The Order of Things*. New York: Routledge.

———. (1982) 'The Subject and Power', *Critical Theory*, 8(4): 777–795.

———. (1991) *Discipline and Punish*. London: Penguin Books.

Giddens, A. and Pierson, C (1998) *Conversations with Anthony Giddens: Making Sense of Modernity*. Stanford, California: Stanford University Press.

Hemer, O. and Tufte, T. (2005) *Media and Glocal Change: Rethinking Communication for Development*. Buenos Aires: CLACSO.

Jones, S. and Lewis, P. (2006) *From the Margins to the Cutting Edge: Community Media and Empowerment*. Cresskill, NJ: Hampton Press.

Melkote, S. and Steeves, H. (2001) *Communication for Development in the Third World: Theory and Practice for Empowerment*. New Delhi: Sage Publications.

Naveed-i-Rahat. (1990) *Male Outmigration and Matri-weighted Households: A Case-Study of a Punjabi Village in Pakistan*. Delhi: Hindustan Publishing Corporation.

SB&B Marketing Research. (2006) *Research Report on Post-broadcast Evaluation of Radio Drama 'Piyar ka Passport'*. Prepared for BBC World Service Trust Lahore, Pakistan, 25 May 2006.

Shaw, A. (2000) *Kinship and Continuity: Pakistani Families in Britain*. Amsterdam: Harwood.

Shaw, D. and McCombs, M. (1974) *The Emergence of American Political Issues: The Agenda Setting Function of the Press*. St. Paul, MN: West.

Singhal, A. and Rogers, E. (1999) *Entertainment-Education: A Communication Strategy for Social Change*. Mahwah, NJ: Lawrence Erlbaum.

Werbner, P. (1990) *The Migration Process: Capitals, Gifts and Offerings among British Pakistanis*. Oxford: Berg.

———. (2002) *Imagined Diasporas among Manchester Muslims*. Oxford: James Currey.

12

URUNANA AUDIENCES AT HOME AND AWAY

TOGETHER 'HAND IN HAND'?

HELEN M. HINTJENS AND
FORTUNEE BAYISENGE*

Introduction

Urunana (*Hand in Hand*) is Rwanda's first radio soap opera. The production emerged during the late 1990s from a three-way transnational production

*Special thanks to Narcisse Kalisa for agreeing to be interviewed twice. Thanks to Chris Miller, Charlie and Anna, and other Health Unlimited staff for helping us observe the BBC meeting with UDC and HU in July 2009, and for granting us interviews. We are also grateful to them for looking through a draft of this chapter, and their suggestions for improvement. Comments also came from the editors and these were very useful in rewriting this chapter. Narcisse Kalisa also commented on the draft, for which we are grateful once more, and he provided us with English translations of a number of *Urunana* episodes. We did some translations of our own, initially into French. We would like to thank an anonymous Rwandan student for translating some key episodes for us, as well as our thanks to all those Rwandan women who took part in focus groups discussions both in Rwanda and in The Netherlands. Thanks also to Andrew Skuse and Marie Gillespie for their editing work on the chapter.

partnership between: The Great Lakes section of the BBC World Service; the Well Woman Media Project of the London-based NGO, Health Unlimited; and a group of dramatists and broadcasters working in Rwanda. Broadcast by the BBC World Service, the production was initially produced and edited by Health Unlimited. It is now produced by the Urunana Development Communication (UDC) (formerly at www.urunanadc.org/; see also European Commission, 2010), which estimated that the programme is regularly listened to by almost 70 per cent of Rwandans.[1] *Urunana* is explicitly adapted for the Rwandan context from the format of a long-running BBC Radio 4 drama, *The Archers*, which highlights the ups and downs of a rural village in England (see Bielby and Harrington, 2002; Jordan, 2007: 7; Soares, 2008). Since 2008, when *Urunana* won a prestigious media development award for encouraging audiences to discuss safe sex, family planning and other issues that are generally considered taboo in Rwanda, the programme has started to be of interest to researchers in gender, health and media outside of the field of E-E.[2] Our interest in this chapter is in exploring how drama is produced, and how it has helped to promote women's sexual health and mend relationships in post-genocide Rwanda.

Telling Stories: Mending Relationships

The 'pro-social' stories that *Urunana* tells are challenging and controversial, but they seldom generate critical feedback from audiences. Rather, its successes have been much vaunted. The drama challenges religious, clan, gender, ethnic and class divisions and enables listeners to 'tell themselves stories about themselves'. Through everyday discussions of the drama, the production team and funders of the drama hope that audiences arrive at a better understanding of their personal lives and find ways to tackle the social and health problems that they face. Serial dramas provide 'safe spaces' through which the private concerns of citizens can be made public and debated (Werbner, 1997: 238). Tilly has suggested that for stories to 'work' to repair social relationships (in this instance in the years following the 1994 genocide) and to promote health, including the sexual and reproductive health of women, they need to 'rely on [or at least claim] membership in a shared community of belief' (2006: 27). From such a perspective, drama can be understood to help 'create, confirm, repair and recast' lives, or more simply stated, 'stories do social work' (Tilly, 2006: 74). In addressing the 'social work' that the *Urunana* drama routinely performs, this chapter considers how the production is understood and acted upon by Rwandan listeners. In doing so, we examine the views, mainly of women listeners—but also of men—both at 'home' inside Rwanda and 'away', in Western Europe (notably, The Hague, Netherlands).

Urunana's original focus, when it started in 1998, was on improving women's well-being and sexual health. It now targets younger groups and men, alongside women, presenting carefully constructed 'messages' regarding sexual and reproductive health and preventative approaches to public health at them in entertaining ways. In fostering dialogue among Rwandans about health issues, *Urunana* storylines also speak to broader issues of national identity and development goals that have been profoundly reconfigured in the post-genocide (1994) period (Health Unlimited, 2009b; Greene et al., 2006; Ram, 2005). We argue that *Urunana* has, over time, contributed to the process of reimagining the nation and to a sense of shared collective fate (Pottier, 2002). The drama has stimulated the reconstruction of national imagination 'from below' by fostering newly imagined social connections among listeners (Ingelaere, 2007). However, just as the role of radio in generating genocidal violence may have been exaggerated, so too should we avoid exaggerating the ability of a radio drama alone to mend social relationships in a post-genocide society like Rwanda (Straus, 2007). As Zorbas puts it: 'reconciliation is a vague and messy process' (2004: 29). Nonetheless, the representation of dramatic situations that elicit discussion about reconciliation must be considered alongside *Urunana's* more pragmatic focus on sexual and reproductive health. First we explore how *Urunana* dramatised themes associated with health before proceeding to a discussion of its role in reconciliation.

Our Approach

During three two-hour focus group discussions in Rwanda and in The Hague, in The Netherlands, two *Urunana* episodes were selected for discussion with groups of regular and occasional women listeners. These were episodes 936 and 960, both of which concerned the marriage of a well-known character, Mugeni, to a local shop owner, Muhire. A central theme in both episodes is HIV testing and transmission. We used the discussions to gain a deeper insight into how listeners felt about questions of sexuality, class and ethnicity and how it 'felt to be a listener' when these issues were being discussed by the characters. Episodes 936 and 960 both focus on arrangements for the marriage of Mugeni to the older man, Muhire, in Nyarurembo (the fictional village in which *Urunana* is set). Muhire had tricked Mugeni into sleeping with him by offering her gifts, and she became HIV positive as a result. This was the underlying dramatic tension in the marriage that the serial explored. Accordingly, these episodes also examine sexual relationships and reproductive health, dealing with the ramifications of two HIV positive partners entering into a married relationship.

Episode 936 centres on the traditional wedding or 'giving-away' ceremony of Mugeni. Two of the most popular characters in *Urunana*, Bushombe and his wife Kankwanzi,[3] are getting ready to go to a wedding. Kankwanzi can only find one shoe. 'Kankwanzi, but what are you doing?' asks Bushombe: 'Don't you know you're going to make me miss getting a lift in Ngarambe's [the wealthy man's] vehicle?' 'But Bushombe, you don't want me to go without finding the other shoe, do you?' she replies, to which he laughs: 'If you're not careful, you'll go to the wedding without shoes and if you don't find that shoe in any case, just stay at home. I don't want you with me. I am not going to let you embarrass me!' (*Urunana*, Episode 936). A secondary character complains that requiring poor people to wear shoes is a form of 'oppression', but a farmer replies: 'That's not oppression … If we all do that [wear shoes] then we can have a good and healthy life.' This dramatises an issue of hygiene which is subject to government regulation, as we will explain later. Not surprisingly, when we played this episode, we found very divergent responses to such plotlines among audience interviewees in rural Rwanda and more educated listeners overseas, in The Hague. For example, one focus group participant in The Hague commented that *Urunana* can sometimes appear like: '… a channel of the government … It's a play well done … which helps the low [poor or uneducated] population to know or understand different programs of the government, such as TB prevention, hygiene, family planning programs' (Focus Group Discussion, The Hague, 3 December 2008). This listener implies that the drama is didactic, for example, in stressing that 'wearing shoes' is healthy. This is an issue for rural Rwandan audiences, at whom the serial was aimed. Rural focus group participants notably had less sense of 'distance' about the plot and purpose of *Urunana*. They tended to talk about how they identified with the different characters and the sexual and health issues they were facing.

Episode 960 then looks at the marriage of Mugeni. The first scene revolves around a sub-plot involving a father who is left to look after the household whilst his wife has gone away for a week of training. In the morning, the father asks the son to do all the housework while he attends a wedding, modelling how when gender roles are disrupted in the household, fathers may not take on new duties. After the wedding ceremony, the father ends up drinking beer with his friends and in the next scene, the son rushes in to tell him that his daughter is seriously ill. The men finally stop drinking and go off to see if they should take her to hospital. In the next scene, the audience will discover that the father and son are too late. As the daughter lies dying, the audience is compelled to contemplate how father and son might have acted differently and thus saved the girl's life.

The last scene in Episode 960 shows Mugeni refusing to have sex with her husband. She knows that Muhire has given her HIV and she doesn't want to risk pregnancy. She later becomes pregnant, but gives birth to an HIV-free child. This is seen as possible because Mugeni has been able to get access to antiretroviral therapy (ART). On their wedding night, Muhire denies he has HIV (and later refuses to go for a test). The scene ends with Muhire becoming angry with Mugeni when she refuses sex on their wedding night. Focus group participants were asked about how they felt about such everyday—yet highly intimate—problems being discussed in a way that challenged patriarchal attitudes. This triggered discussions in both the Rwandan and The Hague focus groups about the moral and social responsibilities of men and women with HIV and AIDS, and the harmful consequences of avoidance and denial. However, from this, can we conclude that *Urunana* has a positive effect on sexual behaviour? This might not be a realistic conclusion from so narrow a sample, but our intention is to add qualitative data and depth to empirical data, made available to us by the BBC WST through their monitoring of listeners, which will now briefly be explored.

Assessing *Urunana's* Impact on Health

Does *Urunana* encourage listeners, especially women and young people, to actively seek better health care? Mortality levels and infant mortality in Rwanda remain extremely high. However, *Urunana* (UDC) staff, the BBC World Service and Health Unlimited and partners in the Rwandan government—all maintain that *Urunana* positively influences its listeners. Rwanda remains a very dangerous place to give birth and bring up small children. Overall: '… the lifetime risk of maternal death … [is] 1 in 16 in Rwanda, one of the highest in the world,' which, in turn, highlights how 'conflict can wipe out decades of progress in development indicators, including health outcomes' (Chandrasekhar et al., 2010: 3, 4). There have been some remarkable successes, with HIV for example. Estimates of prevalence rates of 2.5 per cent for men and 3.5 per cent for women in 2005, compared with around 11 per cent around the end of the genocide, are quite impressive (Kayirangwa et al., 2006). Alleged 'evidence' of the benefits of *Urunana* on audience behaviour should be treated with caution, however. The causes of behavioural change may be much more difficult to trace than donors, dramatists and producers would like to admit. Identifying the drama as a key causal factor in behaviour change is difficult to support with evidence, especially since self-reporting data, gathered in such circumstances, may suffer from the Hawthorne effect—where subjects improve or modify an aspect of their behaviour in response to the researcher and research context.

Despite these concerns, it may also be that, for many Rwandan women, to start believing that their own health 'matters', as both a private and public issue, does represent a quiet, but real, sea-change, which may be at least partly drama-inspired. UDC Director Narcisse Kalisa suggests that, prior to watching *Urunana*, rural Rwandan women were not as able to point to cases in which patriarchal domination and behaviour were successfully confronted in the private sphere (interview, London, 20 July 2009). *Urunana* stories have provided such examples, albeit through fictional devices, and in so doing have helped to shift the boundaries of what is thought possible in relations between public and private sexual health issues. Radio drama alone cannot change social attitudes, but drama for development, if closely linked to wider strategies for realising human rights to health, for example, can do a great deal to help to sustain and broaden the impact of public and developmental policies.

Many of *Urunana's* storylines have revolved around the growing proportion of newborn babies of HIV-positive women that are born HIV-free. In 2004, only 25 per cent of babies born to HIV-positive mothers were HIV-free, but this rose to 55 per cent by 2006 (Countdown, 2008). There are many reasons for this, including links forged between government and NGO health programmes and the provision of antiretroviral therapy (ART) to pregnant mothers to reduce risks of mother to child transmission (MTCT). One listener, 'Maria', explains how she identifies closely with the character Mugeni. Like Mugeni, Maria is HIV positive and finds herself pregnant. Maria reveals to Health Unlimited staff that:

> I was depressed about my baby. Then I said to myself that I was Mugeni [the *Urunana* character] and that I must go to seek treatment. So I went to the hospital and now I have a HIV negative baby girl, who I call Mugeni.
>
> (Health Unlimited, 2009b: 1)

While audience statements cannot be read as unmediated 'truth', it is clear that *Urunana* does have an impact on listeners like Maria. The UDC Director, Narcisse Kalisa, also explains that *Urunana* has become a part of Rwandan listeners' everyday lives and part of their 'lived' reality; 'Lessons' drawn from storylines can be experienced as 'meaningful' through the process of personal identification with various characters. In a special *Urunana* episode for World AIDS Day 2008, for example, Mugeni was featured feeding her baby with boiled breast milk from a spoon to avoid HIV transmission (Health Unlimited, 2009b: 2). Such 'true to life' stories can encourage improved health-seeking behaviour in women like Maria by showing them that by getting advice and timely ART treatment, their baby can be born healthy and remain free of HIV. Our own research supports UDC findings that the ability of radio to transmit important health messages across to young people constitutes an important element in the fight against HIV.

There is some evidence that *Urunana* encourages rural Rwandan women to seek better health care and also improves their self-care capacities (Myers, 2002; Ram, 2005; Greene et al., 2006). Unsurprisingly, urban, well-educated women in the diaspora feel less keenly the need to take sexual and reproductive health 'lessons' from *Urunana*. They, too, acknowledge how health messages in the programme can, at times dramatically, transform the lives of some poor rural women, especially their position in family and community relationships. The monitoring evidence from 2003/4 supports this and suggests that audiences translate storylines into their own terms, discuss them with others and often seek advice, before finally taking any health decision (Ram, 2005). However, this process is difficult to measure objectively (BCO, 2008). How information is translated into discussion and understanding, and from there into actions, is a complex and slow process that would require extended ethnography or 'control' data that this study could not manage. *Urunana* storylines are more likely to 'work' because, as UDC Progress Reports confirm, audiences already have a say in how storylines are developed through formative audience research. This allows audiences' concerns and issues to be included when writers allow plotlines in the drama to develop. Heavy and sensitive issues are balanced with elements of light relief and humour in this serial drama, as in others. This is important since: 'Before facts can take root in the human heart, they have to penetrate all the elusive psychological layers that are at work in our interactions with one another' [before we are] ... able to act ... without severely disrupting family and community norms' (Myers, 2002: 4).

Storylines that resonate with existing cultural norms, even if also challenging such norms, are more likely to be well received. On the other hand, there will always be resistance to change, however entertainingly—or diplomatically—its benefits are conveyed. Characters do things that can cause offence, and portrayals of negative behaviours can have consequences for people who may wish to emulate such characters in their daily lives. Behaviour deemed positive within the storyline, or by listeners, could also reap reprisals if it challenges authority. One young woman listener, for example, was reported to have been punished by her parents, and thrown out of the family home after she decided that like Mugeni, she would seek contraceptive advice (Health Unlimited, 2009a).

The discussion of sexual behaviour across the generational divide is difficult for many families, wherever they happen to live. Soap operas can make it possible for taboo issues that are difficult to discuss openly, to be examined through fictional characters and storylines. In the following comment from a focus group participant in Rwanda, we see how one woman listener gradually overcame her resistance to *Urunana* themes:

> ... well, I remember at the beginning of *Urunana* stories being on BBC, my children used to like it and listen to it so much, and sometimes I was disgusted by that, and I would not let them listen to the radio, because I was not interested in it. One day I asked a kid called Diane [not her daughter] what she was getting from *Urunana*, because she was very interested, and she told me 'now I prefer abstinence'. I asked her why ... then she said: 'Don't you know that a man can trick you and get you either pregnant or give you diseases?' We started discussing sexual issues, and this would not have been the case before. From that time, I realised *Urunana* stories are very important for children's education, especially concerning reproductive health and HIV/AIDS. I no longer refuse to let my children listen, and instead I encourage them and advise them to practise *Urunana* stories. I am interested too; and I am no longer afraid to discuss sexual issues with my children.

(Focus Group 1, Rwanda, July 2008)

Through engaging with stock character types who personify certain social issues or problems, Rwandan audiences can create their own 'common unitary narratives' and construct 'new moral and aesthetic communities imaginatively' (Werbner, 1997: 247, 242). *Urunana's* popularity ensures that the talking and thinking spaces for this process to occur are available. Listeners in focus groups tend to emphasise shared practical problems, given that most stories are about health, sexual relationships and similar topics. What many listeners seem to have in common is the incentive to find ways to improve their lives, and this is one reason why they are likely to carry on 'tuning in'. Arguably then, the BBC World Service, Health Unlimited and UDC have achieved their mission of creating a partnership that has actively engaged in crafting and translating complex development concepts and issues into local frames in ways that are intelligible and palatable to rural Rwandan audiences. This, they have done admirably well. The literature on E-E for health seems to suggest that engaging audiences in the early stages of production, via formative research, and gaining their trust, can be vital to the success of 'health messaging' (E-E Info, 2008). It is clear *Urunana* can and does contribute to engendering sustainable transformations in health-seeking and illness-preventing behaviour in Rwanda in the long term—a key mission of both Health Unlimited and UDC. We must also pay attention, however, to gaps and silences that our research, especially with diasporic listeners, helped to reveal. Diasporic Rwandan listeners offered alternative perspectives on the role of radio for sexual health and even for promoting peace.

Safe Spaces and Strategic Silences

Narratives about national, ethnic and social 'identities' have been strictly 'under the radar' of *Urunana* from the start. These issues were not discussed openly. This seems to have been a conscious and deliberate strategy, which 'worked well' for most Rwandan listeners (Interview with key informant, The Hague, 5 December 2009). With much subtlety and nuance, therefore, the virtual town of Nyarurembo became in a sense a 'safe space' where Rwandans could meet, imaginatively and then actually via their everyday discussions of storylines and plots. A 'strategic silence' around ethnic political divisions opened up spaces for ordinary Rwandan listeners to discuss the sometimes banal, sometimes dramatic, choices the characters faced without dwelling on the social divisions of ethnicity and identity. Listeners share the jokes, and question what are appropriate gender and sexual relations. And both inside, but also outside Rwanda, this sharing can help 'repair' social relations through stories that produce a sense of 'narrative indeterminacy' that encourages further discussion among listeners about what might happen, or what should be done, or who might influence who (Allen, 1995: 17).

It might be argued that such strategic 'silences' should not be maintained if they prevent acknowledgement of trauma and thus delay subsequent healing and 'reconciliation' in Rwanda (Zorbas, 2004). The first major five-year evaluation of *Urunana* noted that:

It will be odd if Nyarurembo [the fictitious town where *Urunana* characters live] is almost the only community in Rwanda that has no *Gacaca* [community justice] process. This will be a very difficult issue for the writing team to deal with … But avoiding such issues will risk undermining the close existing relevance of *Urunana* to people's daily lives.

(Greene et al., 2006: 19)[4]

Yet we suggest that it is precisely *Urunana's* relative neglect of *Gacaca* and similar genocide-prevention and retributional initiatives, its relative silence on the legacies of genocide, that have made it so popular, and ensured it is listened to by more than two-thirds of Rwandans. This mass audience cuts across all the major social divisions of Rwanda, with the possible exception of class (as we suggest later). Its broad-based appeal has helped fulfil the programme's original purpose of conveying health messages in a meaningful way to a wide audience, so as to encourage positive social transformation. *Urunana* has also provided people with topics of conversation around sexual health issues that are engaging, but not so painful as to risk being overly divisive. The focus on gender relations, sexuality and reproductive health helped to 'depoliticise' the programme in some ways, whilst politicising other issues besides race or identity.

It has been suggested that the 1994 genocide destroyed: 'the myths, rituals and symbols that were part of Rwandan culture', and that drama can play a part in reinventing cultural norms in Rwanda (Kalisa, 2006: 519). *Urunana* and similar radio soaps may indeed be re-creating stories and helping Rwandans to shared new myths about Rwandans. To replace old, more divisive and oppressive myths, including racialised myths of origin, is essential for peace in Rwanda.

The wide popular appeal of *Urunana* in its early phases could be partly attributed to its steering away from political controversy, whilst embracing controversy in matters of sexual, reproductive and public health. In later episodes, an attempt has been made to acknowledge the politics of trauma and genocide, and the need for reconciliation.

Health, especially sexual and reproductive health, can be emotionally charged concerns. In Rwanda, however, even sexuality is not taboo in the way that ethnic identities have become (it is illegal to stir public debate on the issue). It is ironic that it may have become easier, and safer, to discuss sexual health and HIV and AIDS than people's ethnic or 'race' identities. *Urunana's* plotlines can evolve: '… without taking a perceptible stand or proffering solutions' to the main issues that concern the post-genocide government (Allen,1995: 22). Despite creating a safe and open space on-air, and via phone-ins and online debates, there was no reference to genocide. However, the programme was not merely ignoring the issue. As Narcisse Kalisa confirmed in an interview, the idea of theatre as an instrument of politicisation or agitprop does not fit in with *Urunana's* philosophy of gently broaching controversial sexual health issues, especially for poor rural women.

We suggest that in part, *Urunana's* 'cult' status does depend on the 'strategic silence' it maintains around the genocide and questions of 'race'. Sympathising with one another is easier when it comes to health and sexuality questions that everyone faces, at some time, than on issues of genocide, culpability or even peace and justice. Common human concerns like family relations, making a living and keeping healthy concern us all. Poor and marginalised rural Rwandans, piecing their lives back together day-by-day, bit-by-bit, could fit *Urunana* into their mental and emotional jigsaw puzzle without questioning the 'hill' and 'valley' life of post-genocide Rwanda.

Racism has been a major problem in Rwanda's recent history, as well as during colonialism and post-independence (Hintjens, 2001). Radio in the run-up to and during genocide helped to poison relations between Rwandans (Li, 2004; Straus, 2007). We should not forget that: '[e]ffective anti-racist struggles depend on the evolution of common, unitary narratives and the suppression of cultural differences between victims' (Werbner, 1997: 247). A detailed empirical study on the role of radio in Rwanda recently concluded that radio can and does influence behaviour, promoting communication in ways that can contribute to greater tolerance between groups, and even reconciliation (Paluck and Green, 2009: 3). It may be that *Urunana's* search for popularity meant that the opportunity to weave more hard-hitting political issues into the drama was missed. But then the programme would not have proven to be as popular as it has undoubtedly been (Soares, 2008). Arguably, during its first 10 years of broadcasting, the 'strategic silences' in *Urunana's* storylines and plots both helped ensure the programme's huge popularity inside Rwanda, which in turn is a key factor in arguments that point to its widespread acceptance and internalisation by rural Rwandan women and men.

On Partnership and Production

Urunana deals with practical, daily issues that preoccupy most people, wherever they live—sexuality, family ties, friendship, relations between women and men, making a living and trying to get along with one's neighbours—all without breaking laws concerning ths portrayal and promotion of ethnic identities! *Urunana's* rural audience at 'home' and Rwandan diasporic audiences 'away' seem to appreciate how sensitive issues are handled by writers and actors, with a 'light touch' and an eye for humour. This helps reduce the risk that by discussing sensitive sexual health issues the programme might cause offence or even provoke a backlash. *Urunana* has thus proven a useful and highly 'resonant' vehicle for both the Rwandan government and also NGO partners and the UK government, and even the EU funders who became involved after 2008. Successful radio dramas like *Urunana* fall firmly within the ambit of the public diplomacy objectives of the BBC, for example. Development and diplomacy can proceed 'hand in hand', so that sometimes the relationship with government can look almost seamless, for example, when we conducted the focus group in The Hague, our diasporic audience distanced themselves somewhat from the radio soap, regarding it as primarily a tool of governance, or:

> … a channel of the government where they spread out their goals. For example the Ministry of Health gets the population to know about how to prevent TB [tuberculosis] and forbidding them to share straws for the low [poor or uneducated] category of the population.

> (Focus Group, The Hague, 3 December 2008)

In Episode 936, for example, that was played to focus group partici-pants, Kankwanzi and her husband Bushombe take a personal container to Mugeni's wedding, so they don't have to drink from a communal straw (to avoid the potential for TB transmittal). This represents a storyline that seeks to get 'public health information' across to rural Rwandans. The storyline suggests that there is close cooperation between UDC writers and government health and justice policies and officials. Cooperation with official institutions is viewed in positive terms in most reports on *Urunana*, including in the five-year Evaluation Report (Greene et al., 2006).

Close collaboration with government, however, also makes it more likely that the specialised health services referred to in *Urunana* storylines (e.g., HIV testing facilities, family planning provisions and police procedures for reporting rape) will actually be provided by government, and may prove more accessible when people who have listened to the programme seek to access such services.

In Rwanda, as elsewhere, one view of radio is that it should '… be used as a tool of enquiry that enables listeners to play a real part in the production of programmes' (Ilboudo, 2000: 47). A similar observation is that: 'audience research and participation is essential … as much as possible, members of the audience should assist in the design of E-E' (E-E Info, 2008: 1). The first *Urunana* evaluation in 2000 noted that: 'The best dramas are written on the basis of solid and ongoing audience research [through focus groups] … and immersion in village life' (Myers, 2002: 5). Actors and writers actually spend some time every year fully 'immersed' in one of the several (12–14) villages in Rwanda where the production team works with local people on pre- and post-episode testing. In this way: '*Urunana* writers based in the city of Kigali go and stay in villages for at least a week in a year to get more of a feel of the life of their audience' (Kyagambiddwa and Uwamariya, 2004). Spending even one week a year in a village—when you are a city-dweller—marks a radical break with the usual assumptions about 'what is important'. Immersion strategies like these help inform the writers' construction of events in Nyarurembo (Kyagambiddwa and Uwamariya, 2004). If plots and characters are convincing for rural listeners, as seems to be the case, then perhaps this quality makes the same storylines and personalities somewhat strange and unfamiliar (because they are unknown) to many of the more educated diasporic and urban listeners of *Urunana*. We found some evidence of this in our focus group research, as will be discussed later.

Health Unlimited staff in Rwanda regard *Urunana* as a 'needs-based and audience-driven production', employing 'a participatory process of producing and writing' (Kyagambiddwa and Uwamariya, 2004). Audience groups help co-design future production, with the goal that themes and storylines become as 'reflective of true-to-life health and social priority issues' as possible (Kyagambiddwa and Uwamariya, 2004). Surveys, phone-ins and focus groups also provide opportunities for audience feedback. Storylines can be tested with audiences in this way:

'A few skits are acted out and a question and answer session follows to gauge if messages are understood. Attendants also ask questions about the past programmes, which is an opportunity for more feedback and suggestions' (Kyagambiddwa and Uwamariya, 2004). Regularly trying out scenes with listeners is a good way to test whether audiences really understand the health messages being included (Ram, 2005). The goal is 'self-help' and mutual solidarity among listeners, sometimes termed 'self-efficacy' (E-E Info, 2008). Here, a focus group participant explains the extent to which the production had an impact on her own life:

> Yes it happened to my neighbour and for us also. There is a time when she wanted, as a woman, to stop/suspend giving birth by taking contraceptives, her husband refused to go with her to ONAPO [an organisation in charge of family planning in Rwanda] because he wanted to have other children. So, because it is her life, she decided to go to hospital without his agreement.
>
> (Focus Group 1, Rwanda, July 2008)

The woman is presented as ignoring conventional 'good' wifely behaviour, and instead doing what she considers 'good' for her health. This participant explains that her neighbour also referred to a character in *Urunana* in order to 'justify' her decision to go to hospital without asking her husband. When something has been culturally sanctioned by a popular radio programme, it becomes thinkable, and, eventually, doable. An 'alien' idea, if it comes from *Urunana*, becomes a suggestion from a relatively trusted source of advice and information (the characters in the programme). Emotional identification and trust-building are absolutely critical to effective development communication initiatives like *Urunana*, especially for sexual health, HIV and AIDS, as well as family planning purposes (Hawkins et al., 2005).

Consultations by the writing team with medical experts and good connections with the Ministry of Health and local government have also been critical in avoiding disinformation about health treatments and in tackling the role of 'magical' beliefs about health and sickness. Networks among women listeners and in schools are important in disseminating the messages, helping to ensure that the information *Urunana* conveys is trusted by listeners. Studies have shown that especially for young people, discussions with peers are a critical source of information about sexual and reproductive health issues, including HIV and AIDS. Young people who were asked about this: '... indicated that they regularly listen to the BBC ... and Radio Rwanda which broadcast a programme known as *Urunana*' (Nyirabahire, 2007: 52). Similar 'Peer to Peer' research involving young men and women confirms the importance of having 'characters' to talk about so that intimate personal issues can be debated as public concerns.

As Bird notes in her work, mostly with Burundian refugees in Tanzania: '... it was important for the respondents that the information they received ... was from a trusted source' (2007: 182). Myers (2002) has commented that trusted dramas are typically those that are 'grounded' in the pressing local, social and cultural realities (if not political realities) that poor people face, and which seek to continually respond to the actual problems and development constraints experienced by the audience. Such grounding occurs through productions being 'written on the basis of solid and on-going audience research' (Myers, 2002: 5–6). She also stresses that identification through emotional attachments means that unless production standards and processes slip, the chances are that listeners will continue to: '... tune in regularly to follow the trials and tribulations of their favourite characters, and remain hooked' (Myers, 2002: 5). Such qualities are clearly reflected in the *Urunana* production.

Diasporic Distance

Radio production and consumption in a digital age disrupts any neat geographical association between the local and global (Fardon and Furniss, 2000: 2). *Urunana* sits at the confluence of a number of institutional and social relationships that defy such easy classifications. The programme is 'global' in a sense, since it combines a globalised 'soap opera' format and international resources with localised content and production. As a translocal and transcultural institution, the programme has received support from a number of institutions, including its home organisation, UDC, and also the BBC World Service, the EU, the UK-based NGO Health Unlimited, different Rwandan Government Ministries, and local authorities, women's groups, listener groups and medical experts.

Mobile communications technologies and digital media have also created new opportunities for Rwandans at home and abroad to maintain strong connections (if so desired). They can listen to and discuss the same programmes—including *Urunana*. Local to global cultural dynamics are constantly shifting and, as we have argued, the spaces around *Urunana* include Rwandans both at 'home' and 'away' from home.

The Rwandan diaspora originated even before the 1959 'Revolution' forced the flight of many Tutsi Rwandans to neighbouring countries for protection. The return of this diaspora was viewed as a threat to national stability long before the genocide, but perhaps today the Rwandan diaspora is no longer seen as 'a fifth column set on penetrating and conquering the nation from within' (Friedman, 1997: 85). Media producers generally, increasingly appreciate that 'their global audiences are more mobile than ever. The once clear lines separating ... domestic and foreign audiences' have become blurred as diasporic communities have rooted and uprooted themselves globally (Gillespie, 2009). It is a good idea to remind ourselves, however, that '... global diasporas are not identifiable communities in any clear-cut geographical or cultural sense', especially since after the 1994 genocide millions of formerly exiled or refugee Rwandans have come home, most to resettle in rural areas (Andersson, 2008).

Diasporas can be agents of diplomacy, capable of influencing publics and audiences 'back home' for development and strategic purposes. Although *Urunana* is specifically aimed at rural Rwandan audiences, it is also listened to by some in the Rwandan diaspora. Our research with listeners in The Hague as well as anecdotal evidence suggest that, increasingly, the diaspora is listening in and participating online in discussions and debates around reconstruction and social change in Rwanda generally. It has not been possible to ascertain rates of listening among Rwandan diasporas.

Within Rwanda itself, the need to reconstruct post-genocide rural communities has produced new forms of social and cultural hybridity in terms of gender relations, forms of identity and religious beliefs, as well as in class, upbringing, status and 'belonging'. What has arisen in rural Rwanda are some very complex cultural processes of 'Rwandanisation', involving a 'mishmash, borrowings, mixtures' of polyglot culture, including from neighbouring countries of exile: Uganda, Burundi and the DRC as well as further afield (Friedman, 1997: 81). Not surprisingly, perhaps, highly educated diasporic listeners nonetheless express a distinctive sense of distance from most *Urunana* listeners at 'home'. In most ways, both the reality the soap opera seeks to portray and those it seeks to influence are likely to be remote from the daily concerns of diasporic, and more educated, Rwandans. One of The Hague focus group participants described *Urunana* as:

> ... really helpful to the population of Rwanda especially those who do not have a chance to go to school and the poor, because this is something that we take for granted ... most of the time. We think that what we know is also known by others, but that is not true! Of course we are lucky somehow since we know these issues, but I think these programs help them [other Rwandans] so much.
>
> (Focus Group, The Hague, 3 December 2008)

Diasporic listeners are acutely aware of the differences between themselves and their rural Rwandan compatriots, and though *Urunana* does not really address the diasporic audience, they engage with it ambivalently, with a dose of nostalgia. Sometimes, though, there was some hard-hitting criticism, as with this focus group discussant, who said of *Urunana* in general: 'I can say that ... it is not made for me, it is made for others' (Focus Group, The Hague, 3 December 2008). The 'away' audience's sense of non-identification is also clear in the following statement:

> ... what I can add is that, when I listen to *Urunana* stories, and hear what they are talking about: chickens, manure, the story of the child putting the shoe on the fire, and so on, it makes me feel sad, I feel a complex ... I feel that we are very behind, I feel that I will not go back.
>
> (Focus Group, The Hague, 3 December 2008)

The main points of identification for these educated diasporic Rwandan women was through laughter at scenes involving Bushombe and Kankwanzi in dialogue. Diasporic listeners may thus interpret *Urunana* from a position of relative privilege, yet the social import of *Urunana's* dramatic narratives are not lost on them either. Speaking of a scene in Episode 936, where a woman is Master of Ceremonies at Mugeni's wedding, one diasporic woman notes:

So, those broadcasts are made in order to change people's mind, especially old people who still conserve the cultural principles and expressions, such as 'no female chicken can speak in the presence of a male one', among others. All these [conventional] expressions show that, if a woman leads a wedding ceremony, it is like something abnormal, and may bring malediction.

(Focus Group, The Hague, 3 December 2008)

The same participant also noted that in fact, women do act as 'M.C.s' for public events in Rwanda. Thus, as she put it:

... women had been masters of ceremonies, sometimes on National Liberation Day. We hear women leading ceremonies, asking someone to receive the President of the Republic [others reply: 'Yes'] ... From that, I can say that our country Rwanda is promoting gender [equity] ... there is nothing that we can't do, and this can be also a challenge ... So, when people listen to that story in *Urunana*, it may help them to think that, if a woman can be a Mayor of a District or a leader of a Sector and Village, why can't she lead a wedding ceremony? What is hard in that?

(Focus Group, The Hague, 3 December 2008)

A marked sense of gender solidarity among diasporic female listeners thus contrasted with what appeared to be a feeling expressed, in some cases, of 'moral distance' to *Urunana* characters and storylines. For example, in Episode 960, as previously discussed, where Mugeni refuses to have sex with her husband, a debate among the women listeners in the diasporic focus groups ensued about talking about taboo topics:

... his wife replies that she is not ready to do it [have sex]. It is said publicly, everybody and even children listened to it [in *Urunana*]. It is not allowed in our culture that you are not ready to have sex with your husband, you have to be ready every time [all laughing] ... When you can say 'No' to your husband, it is a powerful step. You have to be ready like a sexual/material object.

(Focus Group, The Hague, 3 December 2008)

Interviewees are impressed by Mugeni being able to refuse her husband what are deemed to be his 'conjugal rights'. Another participant continues: '... you are supposed to always say "Yes" ... you should say

"Yes", "Yes", "Yes!" So, *Urunana* stories try to show that, to have sex with your wife when she is not ready, it is considered as a rape' (Focus Group, The Hague, 3 December 2008).

Even for diasporic women listeners, who in some cases distanced themselves quite unequivocally from the target rural 'home' audience of *Urunana*, this scene provoked strong responses of identification. Rural and diasporic Rwandan women thus converge in their interest in challenging the presumed conjugal rights of husbands and in openly discussing sexual and personal issues through the medium of the drama serial.

Urunana is hugely popular among a majority of the rural Rwandan population and can be heard on the streets, in bars and taxis as well as in homes. It is a private and public phenomenon and the issues it raises are widely debated. Diasporic Rwandans listen to the programme in relative isolation. Some who don't consider themselves regular listeners appreciate it vicariously, for example, through their children, as one woman notes: 'Sometimes they ask us some questions about cultural subjects, which they are not aware of and they benefit from this. So I think it [*Urunana*] might even be a way for people to get to know their own culture' (Focus Group, The Hague, 3 December 2008).

Some diasporic Rwandans claimed that listening to *Urunana* made them feel 'at home' even though they were 'away', in spite of the lack of resonance of the storylines and characters with their own lives. They appreciated the humour and the inter-generational and cross-gender negotiation of cultural values by the characters (Interview with Key informant, 6 December 2009). Rwandans 'at home' watch primarily because questions of sexuality between husband and wife, gender relations and issues of HIV/AIDS testing or access to contraception are all issues that concern them. These issues cut across differences of class, education, identity and location; the humour in the programme also cuts across differences of personality and politics.

All the focus group participants, whether in Rwanda or The Hague, expressed the most positive feelings when talking about Bushombe and his wife Kankwanzi, who are characters designed to make audiences laugh. Their popularity is apparent across listener groups both inside and outside Rwanda. *Urunana* listeners can vote for their favourite character on the official UDC website, and Bushombe regularly comes up top. Kankwanzi, and Mariana, the nurse, regularly compete for second place (UDC, 2009). Wanting to feel in touch with 'home' plays a part in diasporic listening to *Urunana*, and it may help to reduce homesickness, as this woman in the focus group in The Hague observed:

> ... when we came here ... me for example, as I couldn't access or listen to any radio/broadcast from Rwanda, I was happy listening to *Urunana* stories, as it helps me to stay connected to Rwanda. I can't say that it helps me in other ways, no, it only helps me feel at home. When I hear cows, goats and other animals, it makes me remember my home as my children used to listen to it [*Urunana*] there, and it reduces my nostalgia.

(Focus Group, The Hague, 3 December 2008)

When we contacted Rwandans living or staying for studies in Europe, we found relatively few of them listened to *Urunana* regularly. Some had never heard of it, having been away from Rwanda for so long. Some did regularly listen to *Urunana* through the BBC Great Lakes website, however, especially when they retained an interest in rural affairs (Interview with Key Informant, The Hague, 5 December 2009). Transnational identifications seem to be evolving between diasporic audiences and characters in *Urunana*. To encourage highly skilled and highly educated Rwandans to return home (as well as those accused of crimes of genocide), the Rwandan government is starting to promote Rwandans' transnational identifications. Returning diasporic Rwandans may soon even be included in the *Urunana* storylines (Interview with Narcisse Kalisa, 20 July 2009). Many Rwandans overseas live in a kind of permanent 'limbo', both 'at home' in their new place of residence and 'away' from the place they continue to call home, most often Rwanda. Many remain unsettled for many years, yet are unwilling to return home permanently. For those living outside Rwanda for a long time, *Urunana* may no longer be the reminder of home, since 'the "home" they used to know and identified with has disappeared' (Al-Ali et al., 2001: 583).

For Rwandan diasporic audiences in Europe and North America that have not returned regularly to Rwanda since 1994, or since their time of exile, television, film and Internet have become more familiar media than radio. But for those who study abroad, or who intend to return to Rwanda soon, listening to *Urunana* can keep them in touch with home even though they are temporarily away. Rwandan culture becomes translocalised, subjected to cross-cutting influences from home and away, and 'performed as a process of negotiation within, about and across "ethnic communities", involving renegotiation as well as legitimation of the status quo' (Baumann, 1997: 221). Rwandans, who want to stay closely connected to the 'mother' country, will tend to perceive *Urunana* as having a 'social and psychological function in linking people in exile with those at home' (Bird, 2007: 184). But this function has not been as evident among the diasporic Rwandans with whom this research has been conducted, as had initially been expected.

A great sense of distance between listeners 'away' from Rwanda and those 'at home' is perhaps unavoidable, given the close affective identification between intended rural audiences at home and the main characters and storylines in *Urunana*. Distance from more educated, urban and diasporic communities, whether or not they are in exile, may result from *Urunana* being firmly grounded elsewhere. It may even be a measure of the programme's success, since UDC Manager, Narcisse Kalisa, when interviewed, was quite clear that *Urunana*'s target audience remains poor rural Rwandans, especially women and young people (Interview with Kalisa, 20 July 2009). The 'away' audience would thus be expected to express a greater sense of distance than those listening at 'home'.

Conclusion

Urunana has created some safe listening and talking spaces among Rwandans, whatever their status and location, but especially among the rural poor and women. Hearing and (re)telling *Urunana* stories has become a common way for Rwandan people to share something beyond the great pain and suffering of the recent past. In this way, listeners are able to communicate by ignoring the many differences among them, and temporarily putting those differences aside. As Charles Tilly has reminded us, stories like *Urunana* can do 'social work', by helping to repair broken social relations. In our view, as an exercise in storytelling, *Urunana* has contributed to stitching back together the torn social fabric of Rwandan society. This has been more an accidental outcome, perhaps, of the way the programme was set up and run, rather than its main goal. In very tangible ways, listeners cross boundaries of location, religion, clan, ethnicity and class, as characters produce a new set of rural idioms and re-imagine Rwanda. Inside Rwanda, *Urunana* is respected as a 'resonant' cultural form that contributes to people's health and also to wider social and cultural reconstruction, especially in rural areas. Through skilfully crafted health messages, the focus of the drama is taken off tragedy and towards comedy, and from conflict towards peace. The drama depicts Rwandans, and especially Rwandan women, seeking and finding their own ways of improving their own health and well-being, not only by relying on outside intervention—from government and other health-providers, but also by asserting themselves in their private lives. By telling '… themselves stories about themselves', *Urunana* listeners work out their shared identifications and common concerns as Rwandan citizens, telling stories that cut across the sharp differences emphasised, and created, in the past (Werbner, 1997: 238).

This singularly Rwandan achievement has been created through the establishment of robust transnational networks that started with creative synergies between Health Unlimited, a UK-based NGO and *Urunana's* writers and producers. These networks work through the cultural brokerage of the BBC World Service, which also acts as the main broadcaster of the soap opera in the Great Lakes region. This case study has been invaluable because it shows how, in post-genocide contexts, the capacity of stories to help repair social relationships is particularly significant (Tilly, 2006: 27). Sharing stories can mean sharing lives, hopes and dreams. Arguably, one of the most significant aspects of a soap opera like *Urunana* for Rwandans today, whether at 'home' or 'away', is to contribute to recreating an imagined community with common interests and a shared sense of belonging and fate (Anderson, 1983). But the re-imagined Rwandan nation has strong ties to the global Rwandan diaspora who also play a role in reimagining and reconstructing the Rwandan nation. National and transnational ties thus intersect in new and unpredictable ways to influence the way in which *Urunana* represents Rwandan realities, both at home and away.

Radio is believed to have a significant impact in Rwanda, including on health and attitudes to sexual rights, for example. For young people and women, the influence of radio rises and falls in relation to levels of formal education and literacy, and our focus group participants at home and in Rwanda confirm this expectation. The process of social reconstruction and of promoting health and well-being in Rwanda is ongoing, and depends not only on changes in attitudes but also in behaviour. Such behaviour change is notoriously difficult to achieve, even when *Urunana* producers, writers and actors seek to depict the Rwandan reconstruction process through 'a multi-dimensional looking glass', and in all its complexity. The plotlines have included Twa (pygmy) characters, Burundian refugees and exiles, people returned from their studies abroad and so on. In fictional Nyarurembo, Rwandans' health and well-being are given much more importance than their history or past divisions (since these are largely absent from the drama). The post-genocide divisions of Rwandans into 'communities of suffering' and 'communities of criminals' break down, giving way to much more complex forms of cross-generational, cross-class and cross-gender identification and imagining. It is this that leads us to suggest that *Urunana* started out as being about sexual and reproductive health, especially of women, and has ended up being more than this. It has ended up as a form of glocalised and 'audience-led', imagined nation-building and reconstruction in an increasingly transnational world.

Notes

1. In 2007, from the original three-way partnership of BBC World Service, Health Unlimited and *Urunana* writers, actors and producers the Rwandan media NGO, *Urunana* Development Communication (UDC) was formed and which, now manages all production and outreach work in Rwanda. The main source of funding is presently from EU sources. Both the BBC World Service and Health Unlimited remain active 'brokers' for UDC, however, helping with negotiations with potential donors.

2. This was one of several awards that the programme received in 2008, in spite of this; by 2010 *Urunana* is in financial difficulties, with funding not being renewed by the EU funders after March 2010. Sometimes it may be that success does not result in tangible rewards, especially where entertainment-education (E-E) in radio is concerned. For details of the award, and examples of Urunana's links with the BBC and the Archers' radio soap, see the report at http://oneworldmedia.org.uk/awards/previous_awards/2008/urunana/.

3. In most episodes of *Urunana*, two characters, Kankwanzi and her husband Bushombe, talk over the business of the day. Most listeners consider this couple the 'beating heart' of the programme. They are people who muddle through in spite of poverty, to improve their chances through both error and design. Being the principal joker and village gossip, Bushombe especially makes listeners laugh. He is not well educated, but

is proud and willing to learn. A role model for some male listeners, he is portrayed as a loving father and husband, who even returns to school with his daughter to learn to read and write.

4. *Gacaca* are neo-traditional 'hearings' which started in 2003–04 and ended up considering over a million cases (because of plea-bargaining which encouraged people to name others during hearings). These 'courts on the grass' were never used for major crimes like genocide, of course, and have been adapted and made national institutions for the specific purpose of trying genocide crimes (all but category 1 crimes, which are the most serious). Sentences could be pronounced for lesser crimes, but cases were passed back to national Rwandan courts for confirmation in more serious cases. *Gacaca* hearings are attended by the entire community, and usually take place on Sundays. Their contribution to overcoming polarisation, and bringing healing, is debated both inside and outside Rwanda. For some excellent film material on early *Gacaca* by Anne Aghion, a French Canadian film maker, see http://www.anneaghionfilms.com/.

References

Al-Ali, N., Black, R. and Koser, K. (2001) 'The Limits to "Transnationalism": Bosnian and Eritrean Refugees in Europe as Emerging Transnational Communities', *Ethnic and Racial Studies*, 24(4): 578–600.

Allen, R. (ed.) (1995) *To Be Continued…Soap Operas around the World.* Oxford-New York: Routledge.

Anderson, B. (1983) *Imagined Communities: Reflections on the Origin and Spread of Nationalism.* London: Verso.

Andersson, M. (2008) 'Mapping Digital Diasporas', *World Agenda*, BBC World Service Journal. Available online at http://www.bbc.co.uk/worldservice/specials/1641_wagus08/page5.shtml (accessed on 29 June 2009).

Baumann, G. (1997) 'Dominant and Demotic Discourses of Culture: Their Relevance to Multi-Ethnic Alliances', in P. Werbner and T. Modood (eds), *Debating Cultural Hybridity: Multicultural Identities and the Politics of Anti-racism*, pp. 209–225. London and New York: Zed Press.

BCO (Building Communication Opportunities) (2008) *BCO Impact Assessment Study: The Final Report.* London: BCO Alliance.

Bielby, D. and Harrington, C. (2002) 'Markets and Meanings: The Global Syndication of Television Programming', in D. Crane, N. Kawashima and K. Kawasaki (eds), *Global Culture: Media, Arts, Policy, and Globalization*, pp. 215–232. New York: Routledge.

Bird, L. (2007) 'Learning about Peace and War in the Great Lakes Region of Africa', *Research in Comparative and International Education*, 2(3): 176–190.

Chandrasekhar, S., Gebreselassie, T. and Jayaraman, A. (2010) 'Maternal Health Care Seeking Behavior in a Post-Conflict HIPC: The Case of Rwanda', *Population Research Policy Review*. Published online on 2 February at http://www.springerlink.com/content/a62k66u1m21p4476/fulltext.pdf (accessed on 15 August 2009).

Countdown (2008) 'Countdown to 2015 Maternal, Newborn and Child Survival, Rwanda'. Available online at http://www.countdown2015mnch.org/documents/countryprofiles/rwanda_20080314.pdf (accessed on 21 September 2009).

E-E Info (Entertainment-Education Information) (2008) 'Entertainment-Education for Better Health', *Info Reports*, 17. Washington: Bloomberg School of Public Health, Johns Hopkins University.

European Commission (2010) Video: Urunana (Development and Cooperation), http://ec.europa.eu/europeaid/where/acp/country-cooperation/rwanda/video_en.htm (accessed on 10 January 2011).

Fardon, R. and Furniss, G. (2000) 'African Broadcast Cultures', in R. Fardon and G. Furniss (eds), *African Broadcast Cultures: Radio in Transition*, pp. 1–20. Oxford-Harare-Cape Town-Westport CT: James Currey/Baobab/David Philip/Praeger.

Friedman, J. (1997) 'Global Crises, the Struggle for Cultural Identity and Intellectual Porkbarrelling: Cosmopolitans versus Locals, Ethics and Nationals in an Era of De-Hegemonisation', in P. Werbner and T. Modood (eds), *Debating Cultural Hybridity: Multicultural Identities and the Politics of Anti-racism*, pp. 70–89. London-New York: Zed Press.

Gillespie, M. (2009) '"Anytime, Anyplace, Anywhere": Digital Diasporas and the BBC World Service', *Journalism*, 10: 322–325.

Greene, C., Odido, H., Mbeki, C. and Kabagire, C. (2006) *Well Woman Media Project, Africa Great Lakes Region: 2000–2005 End Evaluation*. London: DFID-Big Lottery Fund.

Hawkins, Kirstan, Nsengiyuma, Gregorian and Williamson, Winkie. (2005) *Making the Transition from Good Girl to Good Wife: Young Women and Sex-workers' Narratives on Social Life, Sexuality and Risk: Byumba, Rwanda*. London: PEER. Available online at http://www.options.co.uk/images/stories/resources/peer/rwanda_2005_young_women_sex_workers.pdf (accessed on 10 January 2011).

Health Unlimited. (2009a) *Building the Capacity of Urunana Development Communication in Rwanda, Progress Report*. London: Unpublished Report from HU.

———. (2009b) *2008/09 Progress Report: Urunana: Expanding Radio Health Education to Rural Rwandans*. London: Unpublished Report from HU.

Hintjens, H. (2001) 'When Identity Becomes a Knife: Reflections on the 1994 Genocide in Rwanda', *Ethnicities*, 1(1): 25–55.

Ilboudo, J.-P. (2000) 'Prospects for Rural Radio in Africa: Strategies to Relate Audience Research to the Participatory Production of Radio Programmes', in R. Fardon and G. Furniss (eds), *African Broadcast Cultures: Radio in Transition*, pp. 42–71. Oxford-Harare-Cape Town-Westport CT: James Currey/Baobab/David Philip/Praeger.

Ingelaere, B. (2007) *Living the Transition: A Bottom-up Perspective on Rwanda's Political Transition*, discussion paper 2007/06, IOB, University of Antwerp, Antwerp. Available online at http://www.diversitylaw.be/objs/00172206.pdf (accessed on 21 September 2009).

Jordan, C. (2007) 'Who Shot JR's Ratings? The Rise and Fall of the 1980s Prime Time Soap Opera', *Television and News Media*, 8(1): 68–87.

Kalisa, M.-C. (2006) 'Theatre and the Rwandan Genocide', *Peace Review: A Journal of Social Justice*, 18(4): 515–521.

Kayirangwa, E., Hanson, J., Munyakazi, L. and Kabeja, A. (2006) 'Current Trends in Rwanda's HIV/AIDS Epidemic', *Sexually Transmitted Infections*, 8(1): 127–131.

Kyagambiddwa, S. and Uwamariya, I. (2004) '*Urunana*: Creative Communication for Development', Health Unlimited, September. Available online at http://www.comminit.com/en/node/69884 (accessed on 15 June 2009).

Li, Darryl (2004) 'Echoes of Violence: Considerations on Radio and Genocide in Rwanda,' *Journal of Genocide Research*, 6(1): 9–28.

Nyirabahire, S. (2007) *A study of Sources of Information on Sexual Education Available to Youth in Rwandan Rural Areas: The Case of Impala District*, Masters Dissertation, University of Witwatersrand, Department of Sociology. Available online at http://wiredspace.wits.ac.za/handle/10539/2181 (accessed on 15 June 2008).

Myers, M. (2002) *From Awareness to Action: Tackling HIV/AIDS through Radio and Television Drama*. London: University College.

Paluck, E. and Green, D. (2009) 'Deference, Dissent, and Dispute Resolution: An Experimental Intervention Using Mass Media to Change Norms and Behavior in Rwanda', *American Political Science Review*, 103: 622–644.

Pottier, J. (2002*) Re-imagining Rwanda: Conflict, Survival and Disinformation in the Late Twentieth Century*. Cambridge: Cambridge University Press.

Ram, R. (2005) Unpublished report. 'Preliminary Evaluation of the Urunana KAP Monitoring Data'. Statement of Major Findings (September 2002–July 2005) (Provided by HU).

Soares, C. (2008) 'Rwandans are Hooked on Africa's Ambridge', *The Independent*, London, 9 June.

Straus, S. (2007) 'What Is the Relationship between Hate Radio and Violence? Rethinking Rwanda's "Radio Machete"', *Politics and Society*, 35(4): 609–637.

Tilly, C. (2006) *Why? What Happens When People give Reasons and Why*. Princeton-Oxford: Princeton University Press.

Werbner, P. (1997) 'Essentialising Essentialism, Essentialising Silence: Ambivalence and Multiplicity in the Study of Racism and Ethnicity', in P. Werbner and T. Modood (eds), *Debating Cultural Hybridity: Multicultural Identities and the Politics of Anti-racism*, pp. 226–254. London, New York: Zed Press.

Zorbas, E. (2004) 'Reconciliation in Post-Genocide Rwanda', *African Journal of Legal Studies*, June: 29–52. Available online at http://www.africalawinstitute.org/ajls/vol1/no1/zorbas.pdf (accessed on 25 June 2009).

13

GOSSIPING FOR CHANGE

DRAMATISING 'BLOOD DEBT' IN AFGHANISTAN

Andrew Skuse and Marie Gillespie

Introduction

A key contention among drama for development practitioners is that their serials and soap operas stimulate gossip about social norms and that such everyday discussions about the rights and wrongs of characters' actions can, albeit progressively, lead to socio-cultural change (Singhal and Rogers, 2004). From this perspective, serial drama is seen as a moral, normative and instructive guide to the pitfalls of modern life; a way of tackling the consequences of poverty; and a pathway to development and change (cf. Martín-Barbero, 1995). Serial dramas stimulate gossip about key social problems, contradictions and development constraints in particular ways (see Appendix 2). They offer a 'safe space' and recrimination-free communication zone in which discussions of social and cultural norms, self-realisation and social change may occur (Galavotti et al., 2001).

Talking about development issues and recognising solutions is the main desired 'audience effect' of development-oriented drama. Practitioners see social and behavioural change or 'effects'—as coined in the literature on Entertainment-Education (E-E)[1]—as being driven by 'talk', and 'talk' is driven by the narrative 'cliff-hanging' structure of modern melodramas that stimulate audience thirst for more knowledge and further revelations prior to a final moment of melodramatic resolution.

The central significance attributed to soap talk or gossip by practitioners is consistent with academic research in this field which shows how the temporal and narrative structures of open-ended drama serials are particularly conducive to ongoing discussion of key social issues in local communication networks (Geraghty, 1991; Gillespie, 1995). The interweaving of multiple overlapping narratives of different durations within soap operas is quite different to the structures of drama series or one-off dramas. They engage their regular audiences emotionally, morally and socially in powerful ways. Drama for development serials on radio and TV are often very effective precisely because they mimic existing social communication practices such as gossiping (cf. Abrahams, 1970; Gillespie, 1995, 2005, 2006; Haviland, 1977). The halting narrative structure of drama and the regular gaps that producers impose on its flow are structurally similar to the manner in which snippets of information are circulated in similarly episodic form in everyday gossip and rumour.

This chapter offers a critical appreciation of the intermeshing of soap talk and real life gossip in local cultural contexts, and the role that these seemingly trivial discussions play in mediating audiences' responses to development dramas. It draws on insights from the author's media ethnographies of serial dramas in specific local contexts, and on more recent developments in media anthropology (Gillespie, 1995; Skuse, 1999; Ginsburg et al., 2002; Wilk and Askew, 2002). What people say about serial dramas in naturalistic settings is one of the most important sources of data available to researchers of understanding how audiences 'make meaning'.[2] Drawing on the work of Martín-Barbero (1995), Tufte (2003) proposes a focus on analysis of the discursive '[re]mediations' of audiences, and in doing so suggests that soap opera narratives have distinct 'social lives' and are highly mutable/[re]mediated (cf. Appadurai, 1986). Tufte's (2003) study of Brazilian *telenovelas* and earlier ethnographic work specifically on drama for development (Mandel, 2002; Skuse, 1999) production and consumption alerts us to the fact that: (*a*) audiences are complex and bring many differing mediations to the same media content; (*b*) audiences are embedded in and constrained by socio-cultural, political and economic fields that affect their ability to act on informative content or even interpret it (UNAIDS, 1999; CFSC, 2002) and (*c*) the 'meanings' derived from content tend to derive from collective dialogues and negotiation within these fields.

Understanding the relationship between serial drama, gossip and social change forces us to ask a number of probing questions. If drama opens up safe talking spaces for negotiating cultural norms and social change, what kind of spaces are they? Are these talking spaces subject to rules? To what extent are they framed by the strictures of cultural norms? Can they be empowering or liberating? To what extent do drama narratives mimic the subtle styles and registers of gossip practices in the local contexts in which they are broadcast? These questions are of fundamental import to claims about behaviour change and 'audience effects' made by drama for development practitioners.

The very notion of 'behaviour change', which draws on psychological theories, invokes an image of morally and/or politically defined practices aimed at manipulating individuals. This chapter eschews psychological models of individual behaviour change in favour of a more subtle, long-term, culturally grounded ethnographic approach capable of eliciting meaningful qualitative data on grounded social communication practices (cf. Tufte, 2002). We argue that an ethnographically inspired approach to drama for development can help overcome or avoid essentialist conceptions of culture and the weaknesses of psychological modelling behaviourist approaches which ignore the fact that cultural differences are just as likely to occur within local contexts as across contexts. Media ethnography is a rapidly growing field and its academic practitioners can offer 'thick descriptions' of local cultures upon which dramatists and development practitioners can build. But we also recognise that extensive and intensive fieldwork is not practical or affordable for practitioner-based research and therefore would support hybrid models of the sort proposed by Skuse et al. (2007) that involve anthropologists and practitioners in the kind of collaborations that we have aspired to in this volume.

We draw together and synthesise various threads of argument in other chapters (specifically chapters 4 and 7) in order to elaborate the analytical framework presented in this book. We hope to demonstrate this framework using the example of the popular and long-running (1994–present) social realist BBC Afghan Education Projects (BBC AEP) Pashtu and Dari (Afghan Persian) language production *New Home, New Life*.[3] In doing so, we draw upon long-term ethnographic fieldwork conducted by Skuse in northern Pakistan and Taliban-controlled Afghanistan between 1996 and 2002, notably in the city of Jalabad in Nangarhar Province.

The Social 'Effects' of Gossip

A key tenet of the psycho-social and cognitive behavioural theories that underpin much drama for development practice is that audiences are able to recognise and identify behaviours deemed 'beneficial' to their well-being and social development (Galavotti et al., 2001; Inagaki, 2007; Rogers, 1962; Singhal and Rogers, 2004). The contribution of everyday discussions of serial dramas to 'self-realisation' and 'self-efficacy' are central to such approaches. The 'effects' of the drama are seen as being located in this talk. The anthropology of complex social communication practices such as gossiping can shed light on the underlying reasons why this may be so. For example, Gillespie (1995) draws on the anthropology of gossip and rumour to explain how British Asian youth translate and appropriate the Australian TV soap opera *Neighbours* into local cultural terms. She argues that real life and soap gossip about social transgressions both test and affirm social norms. Gossip may be lurid, but it is primarily a force for social conformity.

Haviland (1977) in his ethnographic work on gossip argues that it involves various degrees of risk, is socially coercive, often factional, frequently performative and inevitably pleasurable (see also Bailey, 1983; Brison, 1992; Grima, 1986, 1993; Hunte, 1991; Mills, 1990, 1991; Paine, 1967; Sood et al., 2004).[4] Pocock demonstrates that gossiping acts 'upon people—and so constitute acts of power [...] by informing them and so modifying their perceptions or by defining them and so modifying the ways in which they are perceived by others' (1984: 28; cited in Brison, 1992: 3).

A close understanding of oral traditions and conversational practice may yield benefits to drama for development practitioners trying to 'persuade' audiences to change their behaviour. Cynically, we might understand such projects as developing more subtle forms of 'pro-social' coercion. After all, if drama opens up a safe space for gossip or talk about development issues, we must consider the possibility that this space is, in Foucauldian terms, a space of subjectification in which diffuse power 'works through' serials and subjects in noncoercive but effective ways to produce audiences as subjects (Gillespie, 2005).

The anthropological literature on gossip highlights both the safety as well as risk and recrimination factors that are associated with gossiping. The literature on drama for development and E–E tends to posit a wholly positive orientation to the practice in which gossip affords a discrete and safe semantic space in which key development constraints can be freely problematised and discussed without risk of recrimination (Galavotti et al., 2001). This contention is supported by Miller's (1995) ethnographic work on the appropriation of the mainstream US television soap opera *The Young and the Restless* in Trinidad, which shows us that the potential risks and negative repercussions of gossiping are reduced when the 'medium of exchange' is soap opera narratives. It is far easier, and more enjoyable, to contemplate the problems of infidelity when they concern your favourite soap opera character, rather than your own spouse or neighbour. For people with 'inside' knowledge of 'real' sexual indiscretions within the locality, melodrama allows them to discuss the issue and pass moral judgement free from direct social recrimination. Similarly, Gillespie's (1995) study of the consumption of the Australian daytime television drama *Neighbours* by Punjabi youth from Southall, London, shows that the serial provoked discussions of gender and sexual issues that otherwise would be difficult to raise. Both these examples of cross-cultural drama consumption highlight how audiences apply local frames to their interpretations of globally distributed soap operas. However, as Hannerz (1990) highlights, drama serials made primarily for domestic consumption are often more popular, are highly debated and tend to be more closely scrutinised (by local audiences and opinion leaders) than productions consumed on a transnational basis (cf. Buckingham, 1987; Das, 1995; Hobson, 1982). Because of this, domestic soap opera producers often find themselves having to carefully negotiate conservative forces concerned with the representation of themes such as politics, gender, sexuality, violence and so on (cf. Hannerz, 1990).

Drama for development practitioners tend to focus their gaze on the socio-cultural and behavioural 'effects' of melodramatic narratives, often in an uncritical way. There is often little appreciation of the influence of local cultural context, the effects of social conservatism or the importance of taking into account the subtle registers and rules associated with social communication practices, such as gossip. The available literature appears to ignore or sidelines these issues (Singhal et al., 2004). If serial drama triggers gossip and like gossip, it is episodic, how might drama for development producers mimic the subtle devices, styles and registers of local oral cultures? The answer to this question rests not only with dramatists who understand linguistic and cultural norms but also with wider investments in formative qualitative audience research to help in pre-testing the serial. Where this investment is weak, an appreciation of social communication practices is unlikely to be forthcoming. In the context of *New Home, New Life*, audience research (see Chapter 4) provides a powerful lens through which melodramatic narratives can be matched to actual communication processes and practices. The acute conservatism of the Afghan context militates against social change and so finding ways of dealing with conservatism effectively is a real challenge. This conservatism, expressed as a caution not to offend or dishonour, manifests itself in particular ways in social communication and this has been replicated in the production's narrative style. For example, in discussing the solicitation of marriage as represented in the Afghan context of *New Home, New Life*, Shirazuddin Siddiqi, currently Afghanistan Country Director for the Trust and formerly a BBC AEP Manager, reveals the fundamentally oblique structure of this and many other forms of verbal encounter within Afghanistan (cf. Mills, 1990, 1991):

> It's never direct. For example, we are friends and we know each other. I'll come to you and I'll say 'I've been thinking about how we can make our friendship and close relationship even closer. I don't know about you, but I think it's quite important for us'. Then you might say, 'I can't really comment, I can't really say anything on it'. Then I would feel that

I have consent from you and I must pursue the issue, so then I'd send a representative to your house. Because I could see that you're not opposing it […] In our culture if you don't oppose it you are actually confirming it.

(Interview, Peshawar, Pakistan, 1997)

In the Afghan context of the *New Home, New Life* production, severe social sanctions can accrue to those who gossip, and even more so to those who are gossiped about. This is understood by both producers and scriptwriters, who also risk conservative backlash if they openly push the boundaries of social and cultural norms too hard. Consequently, the drama employs narrative devices, such as 'obliqueness', when dealing with sensitive issues that would tend not to be openly discussed within Afghan society. In Afghanistan, it is far more common to imply that a social transgression has occurred than to openly accuse. It is also more commonly acceptable to suffer stoically rather than to complain. Again, this is understood both by producers and audiences. In societies that place a high price on the maintenance of honour and social discretion, an oblique approach to tackling taboos reduces the risk of rebuttal and offence. This suggests that the safe talking spaces that are opened by drama narratives and which potentially allow for the discussion of sensitive development issues and challenges must be carefully managed so as not to broach topics of too sensitive a nature and therein risk offence (cf. Gillespie, 1995; Miller, 1995). A good deal of responsibility and care is exercised in an Afghan's choice of 'words', be they audience member or radio drama writer, this being reflected in the cautious manner with which *New Home, New Life* challenges social and culture norms and mimics social communication contexts, practices, styles and registers.

Conflict and 'Bride' Exchange: A Storyline

In order to illuminate the issues outlined above, we now examine a specific storyline relating to one of *New Home, New Life's* key female characters, Shukria, the production's chief malicious gossip and villainess. The issue of women's rights and domestic conflict dominates the storyline. Such rights-based agendas are promoted by donors. For example, the status of Afghan women who are traded to settle blood debts (typically incurred through accidental death or murder), represents an ongoing concern for the international community (Tapper, 1991). Though Afghanistan has a diverse cultural and ethnic heritage, it has a number of social commonalties such as a strong patriarchal system in which women are typically subject to 'barter-type' exchanges in both marriage and conflict mediation (Tapper, 1991). The dramatic potential of such an issue is clear, yet *New Home, New Life's* relatively liberal-leaning scriptwriters were initially reticent about addressing it due to its associations with cultural conservatism; however, opportunities to critique such practices were also evident. Shirazuddin Siddiqi, currently Afghanistan Country Director for the BBC WST, reveals that:

> None of them [scriptwriters] were happy with it. But this is a tradition. They're all very liberal. Another thing, it's not a very good practice to sacrifice a woman and pay for one mistake with another mistake, because Majid [one of the drama's characters] did something wrong and then you do something wrong to correct it. They weren't happy, but this is a tradition that is still quite common. The reason we decided on this theme was to show in the long term that it isn't the best solution to such problems. Because, you see everyone will suffer because of this forced marriage. The practice is quite common, it has happened in my village! One of my cousins was given to someone. It was my grandparents' truck, it was going to their village and a boy [from a different family] climbed on the back of the truck and he got stuck on a hook that went into his stomach and he hung there until he died, because nobody had noticed him. The elders were brought together and formed a *jirga* [council] and they convinced the two parties to sit together. Once they did this they said 'we need this amount of money, we need that amount of land and a girl from your side'. My grandparents said they didn't have a suitable daughter, but finally they said that they have one daughter who is blind and who was just six months old. They said 'that's it, we agree'. They said they would wait for the girl to become 15 years old and then they would take her, but you have to give us your word. After 15 years the girl was given and she didn't go back to her father's house. It's a common practice all over Afghanistan. It came up in script development meeting and I mentioned that it had happened in my village. It had happened to some of the other writers too, so we felt it would make a good storyline.
>
> (Interview, Peshawar, Pakistan, 1997)

For many young women marriage and especially forced exchange represents a time of acute emotional upheaval. The security of the family home is literally traded for the unfamiliar and often hostile household of their husband and his relatives. Constituting the 'aggrieved party', new mothers-in-law, sisters-in-law and co-wives can be openly hostile to the new 'bartered bride' entering the home, though with age and the birth of children, their position typically becomes more respected and even powerful, as their husband ages and his influence recedes (Lindholm, 1982; Tapper, 1981). In replicating these cultural structures, the *New Home, New Life* production uses the character of Shukria as the fountainhead of what constitutes normative hostility.

The particular storyline in question ran for several months (between 19 October 1996 and 8 March 1997) and was highly popular with both male and female listeners. The storyline indicates a number of things: (*a*) the extent to which challenging messages are carefully embedded in dramatic action; (*b*) the extent to which the production treads a careful and at times normative cultural line; and (*c*) the manner in which the production mimics gossip contexts and practice within Afghanistan. With regard to the former issues, explicitly didactic statements tend to be avoided within *New Home, New Life's* dialogue and it is often left to the listeners to draw their own conclusions from the moral and domestic dilemmas with which they are presented. This is very much in keeping with the oblique nature of Afghan criticism, which constitutes a key quality of its oral culture (Mills, 1990, 1991).

The story thread begins when Khair Mohammad, a widely respected village elder, is accidentally shot dead by the character Majid during a village conflict over ownership of a number of valuable artefacts that have been recovered in the village as a result of an impromptu archaeological 'dig'. A traditional village council (*jirga*) is called to decide what punishment Majid should suffer and it is decided that he must give his unmarried adult sister Sabira to Sher Mohammad, the son of the dead man. This social institution is called *bad* (in Pashtu), which literally translates as 'bad' and refers to the original deed or 'debt', in this case the accidental shooting that occurred (Atayee, 1979). Though other female characters are sympathetic towards Sabira, her new sister-in-law and co-wife immediately instigate hostile relations when she enters her new home. Sher Mohammad's first wife, Tahira, is upset that her husband has taken a second wife, though he argues that it was only as a consequence of his own father's death and could not be avoided. However, Tahira is adamant that he was already interested in taking another wife because she has remained childless. Sher Mohammad consoles her and asks her to try and make Sabira feel welcome by helping her to make some new clothes.

The 'blood-debt' storyline resonated with familiar cultural concepts of particular relevance to ethnically Pashtun listeners. *Bad* derives from the term *badal*, a key institution of Pashtun tribal culture, and *badal* can literally be translated as 'revenge'. However, a more subtle translation of *badal* is that of 'exchange', which implies balanced reciprocal transactions made between families of 'equal' standing and honour. Standing in stark opposition to such balanced and honorific transactions is the concept of *bad*. Atayee (1979) notes that *bad* is simply the antonym of good and in Pashtun tribal law it tends to be equated with a crime such as murder, itself perceived as a deviation from 'good'. Each *bad* has its corresponding *narkh* (punishment) and *sharm* (payment or shame), the two being synonymous with each other.

Audience interpretations of this specific cultural institution are normatively gendered in nature, reflecting the relative values that men and women attach to the practice. Here, a middle-aged male listener suggests that:

> The case of killing in the drama should not be taken so simply as to be solved by giving a girl. Majid killed Khair Mohammad and the *jirga* decided that he should give his sister to Sher Mohammad, but according to our country's customs it is a very little load that they have given the killer. In our country, in addition to some money, two girls are required for a solution to such a killing. So, if another case of killing occurs [in the soap opera] then the killer should be given as heavy a load as possible so that it can become an example for others [not to kill].

> (Interview, Nangarhar Province, 1997)

Following the settlement of the blood debt the storyline becomes more overtly 'domestic', and it is here that 'female' interest was significantly sparked within the audience, with particular concern being voiced for the plight of the young woman exchanged to settle the debt.

The storyline proceeds with Sabira's new sister-in-law Shukria attempting to stir animosity between the two women. She does this by snatching the new clothes that Tahira is making for her new co-wife, leaving Sabira with no clean clothes to wear. Sher Mohammad sees that his new wife is wearing old clothes and asks what has happened to the cloth that he had brought for Tahira to stitch. He confronts Tahira, who tells him that Shukria had taken it and locked it away. Sher Mohammad tries to persuade his sister Shukria that Sabira should be treated properly within the family, but is accused of wanting their father's killer to run the household. However, he is adamant that she should return the cloth so that Sabira can have new clothes. The cloth is eventually retrieved from Shukria and Tahira sets about sewing Sabira a new set of clothes in a gesture that is symbolic of her acceptance of her co-wife. Later, Sabira visits the *goder* (stream) to collect water, a public excursion previously forbidden to her by Shukria (Boesen, 1983). Traditionally, the *goder* has constituted one of the few public places that women in *purdah* are able to visit to exchange information and interact with other women, or more riskily interact with non-kin men. At the *goder*, Sabira meets some friends, who ask her about her new life. Unhappily, she says that it is all right. After leaving, however, her friends discuss how she must be having a very difficult time even if she never complains about it. Being stoical in the face of hardship constitutes a key quality attributed by women to women (Grima, 1993). It illustrates the emdeddedness of patriarchal power structures and the difficulties of challenging them.

Later, another friend visits Sabira to ask about some sewing work being undertaken for her daughter's wedding. During the visit she questions Sabira on her quality of life. Sabira responds, in typically oblique fashion, by saying that she is 'sailing on a broken ship'. However, her friend tries to reassure her by noting that when she has given birth to a baby (preferably a male) she will gain more respect within the household since her co-wife Tahira has no children (cf. Lindholm, 1982). She asks her why Tahira can't have children and Sabira replies that she may be infertile. However, Sabira reveals that she is also yet to conceive and that this is causing her sadness because she is keen to improve her own position. Eventually, a thread within the storyline turns to whether Sher Mohammad is sterile since he now has two wives and neither of them can get pregnant. Ultimately, Sher Mohammad seeks treatment, though his sister Shukria remains a thorn in Sabira's side in what constitutes a highly normative cultural display of hostility. Lurking beneath the emotional gloss of melodrama, several clear themes are at work within the storyline. These are: (*a*) the social consequences of public conflict and using weapons irresponsibly; (*b*) the practice of 'giving' a woman to settle a blood debt; the poor treatment of these women in receiving families; and (*c*) the issue of female infertility and male sterility. These topics represent highly sensitive issues, especially that of male sterility, and they are handled with considerable care by writers. In Afghanistan, many men take second wives because they simply cannot accept that they may be sterile, which has implications for perceived masculinity, social standing and honour.

In fulfilling the arch-villainess role within *New Home, New Life*, Shukria provokes highly emotional responses among female listeners that range from concern over her mental health, commonly described as 'nervousness' or 'jealousy', to sheer and unadulterated 'hatred' for her hostility towards Sabira. Many female listeners draw upon their own domestic experience and normative cultural conventions when questioning the perceived 'negative' traits of Shukria, a character purposefully designed by the drama's writers to create social division and disquiet. A young female listener reveals the degree to which the portrayal of discord in domestic relations within Sher Mohammad's household causes listeners to engage in critical dialogue with the soap opera:

> There aren't good relations between *ban* [co-wife], but why has *New Home, New Life* made the *ban* friendly? Shukria is so bad that both *ban* are in trouble. But its wrong, if a sister causes trouble with the *ban* of her brother than he would tell her to leave his home and take her children to her father-in-law's house. Once a woman is married she doesn't have the right to stay with her children in her brother's house.
>
> (Interview, Nangarhar Province, 1997)

Shukria's failure to conform to key social mores is partly attributed to the inability of her immediate male kin to effectively police her behaviour effectively, this being commonly defined as 'angry' by many listeners (men and women alike). Some male listeners suggest a 'good beating' might help. Others agree that Sher Mohammad is a sympathetic character who knows and understands that his sister is mentally disturbed. Concern over the upbringing of her children and the example she is setting for them also occupies women listeners, with the notion that through her poor behaviour she dishonours both herself and her family. The conduct of Shukria is judged by the female audience to be wholly poor when compared with the 'innocence' of other female characters such as Bas Bibi, who is described as a kind and considerate woman. Though other female characters cause domestic tension, they are redeemed in the audiences eyes by the fact that they also routinely display positive moral and cultural traits. Here, a young male listener reveals that while: 'Other characters are sometimes rude. They're also kind sometimes. She's [Shukria] always backbiting [gossiping] and this is the worst habit of women. But she'll never triumph and all her backbiting will never come to any good' (Interview, Nangarhar Province, 1997).

While indicative of normative cultural constructions concerning who does and does not gossip, this listener clearly believes that all of Shukria's malicious endeavours can come to nothing. This illustrated this young male listener's stock of knowledge concerning the serials' prior dramatic narratives, and successive failures of Shukria to influence the outcome of various crises (for further discussion of the narrative role of key gossip characters see Gillespie, 1995; Modleski, 1982). The mobilisation of prior knowledge about characters and their actions enables audiences to discuss how, as an Afghan woman, Shukria could challenge patriarchal power. This has further implications for the character's agency. Buckingham (1987) notes that soap opera characters (such as Shukria) tend to hover on the boundaries of permissible behaviour, periodically being drawn in and out of the fictive community at the behest of the serial's melodramatic needs. Whilst the 'gossip character' is perceived as the fountainhead of poisoned domestic relations and spite, the use of gossip within the soap opera acts as a stimulus for both 'pleasurable' engagement with the drama and also gossip beyond its bounds. Though generally derisive of Shukria's behaviour, the fact that the audience so eagerly engage with her malevolence also suggests that there is clear 'pleasure' to be had in despising her character.

No doubt pleasurable, the production's dialogue also feeds off the way in which Afghan women exchange information and gossip. Meetings at the village stream or *goder* where various female characters are heard discussing Sabira's wretched life significantly replicate the actual social communication practices experienced by Afghan women (Hunte, 1991; Mills, 1990, 1991). For example, in one episode a group of female characters is heard discussing Sabira at the *goder* and intimate that they feel 'sorry for her' and that her stitching of clothes had caused a big quarrel within the household, due principally to Shukria's intervention. The scene's well-meaning content is taken up in audience gossip as direct attacks upon Shukria, who is understood to be furthering Sabira's suffering following the ignominy of her being exchanged to settle the initial blood debt (*bad*). In this respect, a young female informant complains:

> ... God damn Shukria! Nobody should do the things that she's doing in her brother's house. She behaves very badly with her sisters-in-law [Sabira and Tahira]. In our country during the past war many women were widowed, even four to six members of one family have been killed due to war, but their women haven't got so angry as Shukria. She's got a son and was married once [widowed], so she should stay in her father-in-law's house. Whatever the father-in-law's house is like, it's better than her father's house because when her children get bigger it will belong to them [...] Shukria should think about her own future and let Sabira and Tahira live happily.
>
> (Interview, Nangarhar Province, 1997)

The extent to which drama characters and the gossip they stimulate serve to define a moral community is perhaps the area that is of most importance and interest to this discussion. Women can become powerful and domineering matriarchs within the home by drawing their children, especially male children, into close personal relationships designed to marginalise their husbands whose authority is inevitably undermined with age, since marriages are typically between older men and younger women (Grima, 1993). Though the dominant woman is an affront to male sensibilities, such divisive characters are a prosaic feature of domestic life, this being evident in the number of listeners (both male and female) who draw comparison between Shukria and their own female kin.

The common retort to 'quarrelsome' female behaviour within the households of listeners was found to be often framed in terms of it being 'learnt from Shukria', indicating a connection between drama narratives and what is, for all intents and purposes, everyday behaviour. For Afghan women, their moral universe is conventionally defined by patriarchy, notions of honour (*ghairat*) and control (*purdah*) (Tapper, 1981, 1991). Unsurprisingly, women listeners tend to reflect on Shukria's behaviour 'ideal-typically', enforcing the normative behaviour that men expect of them. Normatively, a young female listener indicates the extent to which the suffering of women must be endured in the name of socio-cultural conventions such as 'exchange' to settle a blood debt:

> Shukria hasn't got the right attitude towards others, she's not affectionate or kind and is mean all the time. She seems to be very rebellious. I don't like her behaviour because women should be sympathetic and must have compassion to other people [especially other women] and particularly their family. All the time she puts the blame on Sabira, uses rude words and tells lies every day. People think that she has a stunted mind and has got into a mess with some neurotic problem. I think that Sabira can't find a way out of her difficulties and get away from Shukria, so she must bear her cruel words and say 'what can't be cured must be endured' because what is done [the blood debt] can't be undone and Sabira's life just seems to go from bad to worse.
>
> (Interview, Nangarhar Province, 1997)

'Outsider' characters such as Shukria are periodically drawn in to the fictive community through the eventual transformation of their character and the negative traits that they display (Buckingham, 1987). Just such a transformation occurred for Shukria, with other characters—and ultimately the audience—becoming increasingly sympathetic to her as it is revealed that she is suffering from post-traumatic stress disorder caused by the death of her husband and the ongoing conflict. Consequently, she becomes the focus of an altogether more sympathetic storyline concerning recovery from trauma. Drawing the character Shukria into the 'caring' fictive community of *New Home, New Life* serves to promote powerful melodrama, since the revelation of 'character change' inevitably comes as a considerable shock for the audience who have invested so much energy and derived so much pleasure from 'hating' her. However, such is the nature of radio drama that as one villainess is redeemed another inevitably emerges to take her place, filling the dramatic role of social miscreant, gossip and dual object of disdain and pleasure for the audience.

The transgressions of the character Shukria, though highly pleasurable, ultimately works towards the questioning of areas of more insidious normative behaviour, such as the treatment meted out to women exchanged to settle blood debts. In working through 'the local' in a detailed, yet moderately conservative way, the *New Home, New Life* production subtly informs social opinion concerning how such women should be treated. In the process, the theme of blood debt and exchange articulates with a set of broader gender-based concerns relating to the aspirations of young women and about what married life may hold in their husband's household (Tapper, 1981; 1991).

In problematising aspects of normative culture, *New Home, New Life* closely articulates with the manner in which reputation and morality are assessed in Afghan gossip practices. Certain of the production's themes, such as those pertaining to domestic violence, blood debt and the treatment of women, are subtly worked into the dramatic narrative through replicating both the context and structure of gossip practice. The extent to which the production actively structures audience readings and stimulates similar patterns of gossip comes to the fore in the manner in which the sympathy expressed by Sabira's friends is replicated in the sympathy expressed by the female audience. Though both female and male listeners are highly critical of the transgressions from cultural normativity that Shukria displays, many also take pleasure in the way the character stirs trouble and disrupts the lives of others (cf. Abu-Lughod, 1995). Concern over her constant presence in her brother's household and her interference therein suggests for listeners that she has overstepped the mark. However, there is perhaps only so far that *New Home, New Life* can go in 'pushing' the bounds of normative cultural conventions, such as the exchange of women to settle blood debts. Here, the production does not mount a particularly vigorous challenge to patriarchal authority, since it is recognised that this would alienate more of the audience than it could possibly win over, rather, it seeks to work within the strictures of normative culture, eking out small spaces for manoeuvre in which moderate aspects of change can be advanced from within the relative safety of gossip about radio drama.

Research on *New Home, New Life* supports the findings of other studies that drama offers a neutral space in which discussion of a 'sensitive nature' can occur (Miller, 1995; Gillespie, 1995). However, unlike the local/global examples cited by Miller and Gillespie in which the cultural context of production is different from that of consumption, the context of *New Home, New Life's* production is ostensibly national and more prone to conservatism and the negative, yet highly influential, opinion of politico-religious voices. In mimicking the patterns, styles and even the obliqueness of Afghan social communication, the production stays within the bounds of the permissible and therein maintains its audience. Within such contexts, staying within such bounds is critical to the long-term sustainability of drama and accordingly we can confirm in the Afghan context that the role of 'soap talk' is something that is not free from rules or strictures of cultural normativity. Indeed, drama for development and E-E practitioners tend to posit 'soap talk' as a kind of *tabula rasa* where anything and everything goes, as a space in which all things, no matter how sensitive, may be aired and potentially resolved. The analysis of data presented in this chapter suggests otherwise and reveals the considerable care that is brought to bear within production in the knowledge that normative culture in Afghanistan can, realistically, only be pushed so far.

Conclusion

This chapter has proposed an analytical framework with which to analyse and explain how and why serial dramas elicit 'soap talk', and how the talking spaces created enables negotiation of social and cultural norms, albeit in ways that do not push moral boundaries too far—at least in the short and medium term. Investment in formative audience research is vital to understanding and capturing the subtleties of local oral cultures and social communication practice and help to create a sense of cultural authenticity by mimicking social communication practices, such as gossiping. *New Home, New Life* has become part of the common cultural currency in Afghanistan. Daily conversations of the 'did you hear…' are exchanged in countless households, bazaars and teahouses by men and women. The producers and writers of the production understand what can and cannot be broached in drama and know how far to push cultural conventions. Drama works to define a moral order. Gossip can reinforce cultural norms and mores deemed by producers as worthy of upholding, while subtly challenging others that are perceived by donors, advisers and the writers themselves to be negative in nature. The connections between drama, gossip and the potential for social change or some form of normative reinforcement are significant. Here, the anthropological work of Haviland is particularly relevant:

> If we observe gossips in action we soon understand that one does not just *appeal* to norms or rules; rather, one applies them, manipulates them, and interprets them for particular purposes. Gossiping *requires* such manipulations of rules; its great attraction and potency stem from the opportunity it provides to bend the 'moral order' to a particular purpose. And where there are alternative strategies for success, alternative sets of values and ends; gossip allows people to sound out the opinions of their associates and to influence the values and assumptions of their neighbours.
>
> (1977: 11)

Whilst the risk and recrimination factors associated with gossip and gossiping may be severe in contexts such as Afghanistan, we have seen how gossip-inspiring fictional media narratives such as *New Home, New Life* also provide an opportunity for communities who may be constrained by normative culture to engage in critical discussion about social change, albeit in a highly conservative and constrained sense. The relevance of such gossip practices to processes of human and social development in culturally conservative contexts is clear and unequivocal. Consequently, as a genre of social critique gossip about serial drama may well be at the vanguard of contemporary social change.

Notes

1. Existing E-E literature supports this contention but fails to fully or adequately analyse the 'how', 'why', 'what' and 'if' of E-E's purported behavioural 'effects' and how specifically they relate to gossip practice and wider oral culture (Ong, 1982). Little by way of insight into the qualitative subtleties of oral culture and communication practices can be gleaned from this literature, suggesting that drama for development practitioners may gain useful insights from other academic traditions

into the appropriation of dramatic narratives, their use by the audience and broader community, their 'effects' or indeed where they fit relative to other discourses that circulate within society. In this regard, a more critical body of literature can be found in Media, Cultural Studies and Anthropology, where analytical emphasis has been placed on the complexity of audience engagement with mainstream soap opera, gossip practices included. This literature highlights: (*a*) audience pleasure in seeing normative categories, such as gender, subverted (Hobson, 1982; Modleski, 1982); (*b*) the feelings that drama structures in the sense of audiences empathising with characters (Ang, 1985); (*c*) drama as an abstract and safe medium of social exchange (Miller, 1995); (*d*) how audiences recognise something familiar within it in a socio-cultural sense and construct social reality through their media engagement (Skuse, 2002; Spence, 1995); and (*e*) how audiences use drama to help recognise the problems and issues present in their own lives through gossiping (Gillespie, 1995).

2. Tufte (2002) defines several points of entry to the qualitative study of drama for development (in this instance the Latin American variant *telenovelas*) that resonate with media theory: (*a*) '*telenovelas* articulate strong emotional engagement and increase audience involvement' (cf. Ang, 1985; Geraghty, 1991; Modleski, 1982); (*b*) '*telenovelas* increase dialogue and debate, and can break the silence around controversial or taboo issues' (Gillespie, 1995; Miller, 1995); and (*c*) '*telenovelas* socialize viewers [or listeners] to new lifestyles and articulate cultural citizenship' (Martín-Barbero, 1995; Rofel, 1995; Tufte, 2003; Vink, 1988).

3. In Afghanistan, radio has always represented the mainstay of national mass communication, with the relatively limited urban presence of television and film representing the next most significant mass media. In areas controlled (1994–2001) by the orthodox Islamic students' movement, the Taliban (religious students, 'seekers'), bans on the production, mediation and distribution of images of the human form, which were deemed profane in Islam, resulted in the strict exclusivity of the medium of radio, albeit censored of all popular music, drama and female voices at national level. Further, this resulted in a deepening of the appeal of international broadcasters who eschewed such conservative conventions. Whilst the post-Taliban (2002–present) media environment is radically different to that which preceded it, the intertextuality of media in rural Afghanistan remains constrained by poverty, lack of access to electricity, the high cost of batteries for radios and preferences for international short-wave broadcasting with publicly perceived 'credible' news services, such as the BBC World Service Pashto and Persian Services.

4. Handelman (1973) suggests two types of gossip encounter; one is safe from social recrimination and is open and consensual. The other is risky, unstable and tending towards opposition, incident and conflict. From this perspective, we can see that gossip practice is clearly subject to differing risk and recrimination factors. Where cultural and moral conservatism acts to magnify such risk factors, gossiping may become a dangerous social pursuit if not managed with extreme care.

References

Abrahams, R. (1970) 'A Performance-Centred Approach to Gossip', *Man*, n.s., 5: 290–301.

Abu-Lughod, L. (1995) 'The Objects of Soap Opera: Egyptian Television and the Cultural Politics of Modernity', in D. Miller (ed.), *Worlds Apart: Modernity through the Prism of the Local*. London: Routledge.

Ang, I. (1985) *Watching Dallas: Soap Opera and Melodramatic Imagination*. New York: Routledge.

Appadurai, A. (1986) 'Introduction: Commodities and the Politics of Value', in A. Appadurai (ed.), *The Social Life of Things*. Cambridge: Cambridge University Press.

Atayee, M. (1979) *A Dictionary of the Terminology of Pashtun's Tribal Customary Law and Usages*. Kabul: International Centre for Pashto Studies, Academy of Sciences of Afghanistan.

Bailey, F. (1983) *The Tactical Uses of Passion: An Essay on Power, Reason, and Reality*. Ithaca: Cornell University Press.

Boesen, I. (1983) 'Conflicts of Solidarity in Pakhtun Women's Lives', in B. Utas (ed.), *Women in Islamic Societies: Social Attitudes and Historical Perspective*. London: Curzon Press.

Brison, K. (1992) *Just Talk: Gossip, Meetings and Power in a Papua New Guinea Village*. Berkeley: University of California Press.

Buckingham, D. (1987) *Public Secrets: Eastenders and its Audience*. London: British Film Institute.

CFSC/Rockefeller Foundation. (2002) *Communication for Social Change: An Integrated Model for Measuring the Process and its Outcomes*. New York: Rockefeller Foundation.

Das, V. (1995) 'On Soap Opera: What Kind of Anthropological Object is it?', in D. Miller (ed.), *Worlds Apart: Modernity through the Prism of the Local*. London: Routledge.

Galavotti, C., Pappas-DeLuca, K. and Lansky, A. (2001) 'Modelling and Reinforcement to Combat HIV: The MARCH Approach to Behaviour Change', *American Journal of Public Health*, 91(10): 1602–1607.

Geraghty, C. (1991) *Women and Soap Opera: A Study of Prime Time Soaps*. Cambridge: Polity Press.

Gillespie, M. (1995) *Television, Ethnicity and Cultural Change*. London: Routledge.

———. (2005) 'Television Drama and Audience Ethnography', in M. Gillespie (ed.), *Media Audiences*. Maidenhead: The Open University Press.

———. (2006) 'Narrative Analysis', in M. Gillespie and J. Toynbee (eds), *Analysing Media Texts*. Maidenhead: The Open University Press.

Ginsburg, F., Larkin, B. and Abu-Lughod, L. (2002) *Media Worlds: Anthropology on New Terrain*. Berkeley: University of California Press.

Grima, B. (1986) 'Suffering as Aesthetic and Ethic among Pashtun Women', *Women's Studies International Forum*, 9(3): 235–242.

———. (1993) *The Performance of Emotion among Paxtun Women: The Misfortunes Which have Befallen Me*. Karachi: Oxford University Press.

Handelman, D. (1973) 'Gossip in Encounters: The Transmission of Information in a Bounded Social Setting', *Man*, 8(2): 210–227.

Hannerz, U. (1990) 'Cosmopolitans and Locals in World Culture', in M. Featherstone (ed.), *Global Culture: Nationalism, Globalisation and Modernity*. London: Sage Publications.

Haviland, J. (1977) *Gossip, Reputation and Knowledge in Zinacantan*. Chicago: The University of Chicago Press.

Hobson, D. (1982) *Crossroads: The Drama of a Soap Opera*. London: Methuen.

Hunte, P. (1991) *Social Communications among the Afghans*. Peshawar: UNICEF (Afghanistan).

Inagaki, N. (2007) *Communications for Development: Recent Trends in Empirical Research*. Washington DC: World Bank.

Lindholm, C. (1982) *Generosity and Jealousy: The Swat Pukhtun of Northern Afghanistan*. New York: Columbia University Press.

Mandel, R. (2002) 'A Marshall Plan of the Mind: The Political Economy of a Kazakh Soap Opera', in F. Ginsburg, B. Larkin and L. Abu-Lughod (eds), *Media Worlds*. Berkeley: University of California Press.

Martín-Barbero, J. (1995) 'Memory and Form in the Latin American Soap Opera', in R. Allen (ed.), *To Be Continued...Soap Operas around the World*. London: Routledge.

Miller, D. (1995) 'The Consumption of Soap Opera: *The Young and the Restless* and Mass Consumption in Trinidad', in R. Allen (ed.), *To Be Continued...Soap Operas around the World*. London: Routledge.

Mills, M. (1990) *Oral Tradition in Afghanistan*. Philadelphia: University of Pennsylvania Press.

———. (1991) *Rhetoric and Politics in Afghan Traditional Storytelling*. Philadelphia: University of Pennsylvania Press.

Modleski, T. (1982) *Loving with a Vengeance: Mass Produced Fantasies for Women*. New York: Routledge.

Ong, W. (1982) *Literacy and Orality: The Technologizing of the Word*. London: Routledge.

Paine, R. (1967) 'What is Gossip About? An Alternative Hypothesis', *Man*, n.s., 2: 278–285.

Pocock, J. (1984) 'Verbalizing a Political Act: Toward a Politics of Speech', in M. Shapiro (ed.), *Language and Politics*. Oxford: Blackwell.

Rofel, L. (1995) 'The Melodrama of National Identity in Post-Tiananmen China', in R. Allen (ed.), *To Be Continued...Soap Operas around the World*. London: Routledge.

Rogers, E. (1962) *Diffusion of Innovation*. New York: Free Press.

Singhal, A., Cody, M., Rogers, E. and Sabido, M. (2004) *Entertainment-Education and Social Change: History, Research, and Practice*. New York: Lawrence Erlbaum Associates, Inc.

Singhal, A. and Rogers. E. (2004) 'The Status of Entertainment-Education Worldwide', in A. Singhal, M. Cody, E. Rogers and M. Sabido (eds), *Entertainment-Education and Social Change: History, Research, and Practice*. New York: Lawrence Erlbaum Associates, Inc., Publishers.

Skuse, A. (1999) *Negotiated Outcomes: An Ethnography of the Production and Consumption of a BBC World Service Radio*. PhD thesis, University College London, London.

———. (2002) 'Radio, Politics and Trust in Afghanistan: A Social History of Broadcasting', *Gazette: The International Journal for Communication Studies*, 63(3): 267–279.

Skuse, A., Fildes, J., Tacchi, J., Martin, K. and Baulch, E. (2007) *Poverty and Digital Inclusion*. New Delhi: UNESCO.

Sood, S., Menard, T. and Witte, K. (2004) 'The Theory behind Entertainment-Education', in A. Singhal, M. Cody, E. Rogers and M. Sabido (eds), *Entertainment-Education and Social Change: History, Research, and Practice*. New York: Lawrence Erlbaum Associates, Inc., Publishers.

Spence, L. (1995) 'They Killed Off Marlena, but She's on Another Show Now': Fantasy, Reality, and Pleasure in Watching Daytime Soap Operas', in R. Allen (ed.), *To Be Continued...Soap Operas around the World*. London: Routledge.

Tapper, N. (1981) 'Direct Exchange and Brideprice: Alternative Forms in a Complex Marriage System', *Man*, n.s., 16: 387–407.

———. (1991) *Bartered Brides: Politics, Gender and Marriage in an Afghan Tribal Society*. Cambridge: Cambridge University Press.

Tufte, T. (2002) *Soap Operas and Sense-Making: Mediations and Audience Ethnography*. Mimeo.

———. (2003) *Living With the Rubbish Queen: Telenovelas, Culture and Modernity in Brazil*. Indiana: Indiana University Press.

UNAIDS. (1999) *Communications Framework for HIV/AIDS: A New Direction*. Geneva: UNAIDS.

Vink, N. (1988) *The Telenovela and Emancipation: A Study on TV and Social Change in Brazil*. Amsterdam: Royal Tropical Institute.

Wilk, R. and Askew, K. (eds) (2002) *The Anthropology of Media: A Reader*. Oxford: Blackwell.

APPENDIX 1

SERIAL DRAMAS PRODUCED BY THE BBC WORLD SERVICE TRUST 1999–2010

Drama funder	Duration	Broadcast information	Country and language	Objectives
1. *Khana-e-Nau, Zindagi-e-Nau* (in Dari) *Nawe Kor, Nawe Jwand* (in Pashto) (New Home, New Life)	1994–present	2,471 episodes to date Radio: BBC Persian and Pashto Service	Afghanistan Pashtu and Dari	To provide educational messaging on a broad range of health, governance, gender and sustainable livelihoods themes. Major subjects covered have included the role of women in society, nutrition and malnutrition, basic hygiene, drinking water, maternal and child health, the Afghan Constitution, reintegration and repatriation, mine awareness, poppy cultivation/substitution, livestock management and a wide variety of livelihoods and agriculture issues.
EC				
AKDNOSI				
DAI				
IFC				
Norwegian Ministry of Foreign Affairs				
SDC				
FCO				
DFID				
ECHO				
UNHCR				
UNICEF				

Appendix 1: (*Continued*)

Appendix 1: (*Continued*)

	Drama funder	Duration	Broadcast information	Country and language	Objectives
	UNFPA UNMACA CIDA Oxfam Tearfund ICRC WHO UNESCO UNOCHA (later UNMACA) UNIFEM UNODC (formerly UNDCP)				**Target audience:** Mainly rural, reflecting the overall demographic and ethnic composition of Afghanistan.
2.	Rruga Me Pisha (Pine Street) DFID EUCOECRS C.S. Mott Foundation Headley Trust IFES IOM UNHCR UNDP UNICEF	1999–2001	100+ episodes Radio: Radio Tirana, Albania's national radio station	Albania Albanian	To promote 'tolerance and understanding in Albania'. To raise awareness and stimulate debate on issues and dilemmas common to everyday life including blood feuds, trafficking, local elections, domestic violence, institutional corruption, land disputes, temporary settlement camps, ethnic discrimination, HIV and AIDS, prostitution and illegal weapons. **Target audience:** Young people, nationwide.

3. *Jasoos Vijay* (Detective Vijay) DFID	2002–06	153 episodes Television: Doordarshan	India Hindi—dubbed into seven other languages.	To increase knowledge of how HIV is transmitted. To encourage people to get tested for HIV. To challenge the culture of discrimination against people who are HIV positive. To promote support and treatment for those living with HIV. **Target audience:** General population, nationwide.
4. *Thabygone Yuva* (Eugenia Tree Village) FCO	2003–07	72 episodes Radio: BBC Burmese Service	Myanmar/Burma Burmese	To raise awareness about poverty-related health issues including HIV and AIDS. To provide information about and practical solutions for everyday healthcare problems impacting Myanmar/Burma's poor. To challenge stigma and discrimination against people living with HIV and AIDS. **Target audience:** Rural populations, lower socio-economic groups.

Appendix 1: (*Continued*)

Appendix 1: (*Continued*)

	Drama funder	*Duration*	*Broadcast information*	*Country and language*	*Objectives*
5.	*Story Story, Voices from the Market* DFID	2004 to present	14 series, each consisting of 12 episodes Radio: 55 partner stations including Federal, State and independent broadcasters, as well as on the BBC World Service	Nigeria English spoken with local parlance	To explore issues such as governance, rights and responsibilities, while mirroring the realities of the audiences in order to engage them. To tackle and encourage wide debate around issues that 'stifle development' and the achievement of the Millennium Development Goals in Nigeria. Each series has an overarching theme: for instance corruption, ethnic tension, health service delivery or living with HIV and AIDS. To draw attention to the empowerment of women, education and environmental sustainability in particular. **Target audience:** Adults, nationwide.
6.	*Rous Cheat Chivit* (Taste of Life) DFID	2004–06	100 episodes Television: TV5 and by the government broadcaster, TVK	Cambodia Khmer	To improve sexual health. Included the promotion of condom use, partner reduction and voluntary counselling and testing for HIV. To address stigma and discrimination faced by people living with HIV.

				To promote maternal and child health. Included the promotion of antenatal care services, breastfeeding, hand-washing and treatment-seeking for ARI and diarrhoea.
				Target audience: 18–34 year olds (for HIV and AIDS messages). Pregnant women and carers of children under the age of 5 (maternal and child health messages). Urban and rural.
7. *Our Town, Our Future* EU and MOTT Foundation	2004–06	24 episodes Radio: 29 radio stations across Bosnia-Herzegovina	Bosnia-Herzegovina Local languages	To raise awareness of the current weaknesses, as well as the best practices, of municipal authorities.
				To promote democratisation, good governance and the rule of law in Bosnia-Herzegovina.
				Target audience: Municipal workers, their families, local politicians and the wider community who use their services.

Appendix 1: (*Continued*)

Appendix 1: (*Continued*)

Drama funder	Duration	Broadcast information	Country and language	Objectives
8. *Piyar Ka Passport* (Passport to love) FCO	2005–06	12 episodes Radio: BBC Urdu Service, FM radio broadcasters in Pakistan and the UK's BBC Asian Network	Pakistan Urdu	To raise awareness and stimulate dialogue around gender issues, including women's rights, forced marriage, rape and sexual abuse. **Target audience:** Adult men and women in Pakistan and within the UK diaspora.
9. *Filega* (The Quest) Ethiopiaid	2006–07	18 episodes Radio: Amhara Mass Media Agency	Ethiopia Amharic	To stimulate debate about rural lives and livelihoods. To reflect the practical, material and social problems facing people in rural areas, including: deforestation and soil erosion, access to water, food security, poor sanitation and hygiene, crop management, governance issues, gender disparities and relations, sexual and reproductive health, early marriage. **Target audience:** Rural populations: Amhara region.

10. *Wetin Dey* (What's Up) DFID	2007–08	48 episodes Television: Federal Government owned Nigerian Television Authority's network of television stations as well as 40 state and independent stations	Nigeria English	To raise awareness of HIV and AIDS and reduce stigma across regional, ethnic and class divides in Nigeria. To increase knowledge and attitudes conducive to safer sexual practices. To build an 'enabling environment' for other HIV/AIDS programmes in Nigeria. **Target audience:** Young people between 15 and 24 with a focus on lower socio-economic backgrounds. Mainly urban.
11. *Kyanmarye ne Naungye* (Healthy Today, Stronger Tomorrow) The Vodaphone Foundation IrishAid	2008–09	Short drama segment within 135 magazine programmes Radio: BBC Burmese	Myanmar/Burma Burmese	To promote good health and support disease prevention efforts. To provide psycho-social support to those affected by Cyclone Nargis. **Target audience:** People affected by cyclone Nargis, especially in the Delta Region of Myanmar/Burma.

Appendix 1: (*Continued*)

Appendix 1: (*Continued*)

Drama funder	Duration	Broadcast information	Country and language	Objectives
12. *Katha Mitho Sarangiko* (Sweet Tales of the Sarangi) UNDP	2008–present	48 episodes Radio: BBC Nepali Service and more than 100 FM stations of the National network	Nepali	Part of a broader project on peace-building and state reconstruction in Nepal. To explore key themes including; (*a*) the culture of impunity and criminality (in the face of political fragmentation); (*b*) failure of local and national government to deliver change and civic services; (*c*) culture of bullying and disrespect; (*d*) culture of protest; (*e*) ethnic and caste fragmentation into narrow interest groups; (*f*) frustration with the lack of change; (*g*) reliance on emigration; (*h*) unemployment of young men; (*i*) gender disparity (especially in the Terai); and (*j*) social exclusion and attitudes towards different ethnic and caste-based groups. **Target audience:** Adults from different ethnic, social, cultural and religious backgrounds. Nationwide.

13. *Old City, New Dreams* FCO IFC Norwegian Ministry of Foreign Affairs Belgian Ministry of Foreign Affairs UNHCR Ministry of Foreign Affairs of the Kingdom of the Netherlands	2009–present	200 episodes to date Radio: BBC Persian and Pashto Service	Afghanistan Pashtu and Dari	To tackle urban-related problems such as unemployment, high cost of living, lack of infrastructure and inadequate service provision. To provide educational messaging on the health, governance and gender themes also covered by *New Home, New Life*. **Target audience:** Rural migrants living in the rapidly expanding urban areas of Afghanistan.
14. *Life Gulmohar Style* The David and Lucile Packard Foundation The MacArthur Foundation UNFPA	2009–10	156 episodes Radio: All India radio, local FM stations, BBC Hindi online	India Hindi	To promote gender equality and reduce gender discrimination. To advance the sexual and reproductive health and rights of young women. To foster an environment that will support reductions in maternal morbidity and mortality. **Target audience:** Middle-class women and men in urban areas.

Appendix 1: (*Continued*)

Appendix 1: (*Continued*)

Drama funder	Duration	Broadcast information	Country and language	Objectives
15. *Bishaash*	2010	24 episodes	Bangladesh	To generate interest in learning English.
DFID		Television: To be broadcast on popular cable and satellite television stations	Bengali	To promote supporting 'learning English' products and services.
				Target audience: Young people seeking to improve their English language skills.

Source: Author's own.

APPENDIX 2

MODELS OF NARRATIVE STRUCTURE

These diagrams show how the most basic pattern of narrative development—harmony, disruption and resolution—varies according to genre.

Fairy story/Single play
A fairy story has a fairly simple, circular narrative form that returns us to a state of renewed harmony.

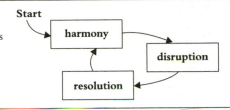

TV series/Situation comedy
Each episode of a situation comedy starts with a disrupted state and moves through a complication and a resolution but it always returns to a basic problematic—to an ongoing state of disruption.

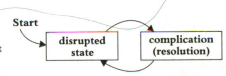

TV serial
The narratives of TV serials span weeks if not months. Each episode has its own particular disruption and resolution but the overall narrative has an overaching more general disruption and resolution which returns us to a state of harmony

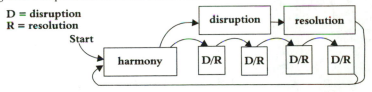

Long-running TV serial/Soap opera
The narratives of soap operas usually launch into an existing disrupted state. (It is arguable whether they begin at all, given that we appear to drop into characters' lives at a given moment.) The multiple, interweaving patterns of disruption and resolution are very uneven: some run parallel to each other while others are more quickly resolved. In any one episode several narrative strands develop at different rates. Some narrative strands may never get resolved - and that enhances the real-life quality of soaps.

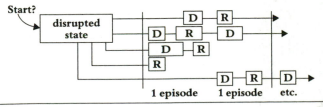

ABOUT THE EDITORS AND CONTRIBUTORS

Editors

Andrew Skuse is a senior lecturer in anthropology at University of Adelaide, South Australia and holds a PhD in social anthropology from University College London. His research addresses how the poor interact with information resources and how these resources affect areas such as livelihoods, health and social welfare. Skuse has researched widely on drama for development and is actively engaged in consultancy for various international development agencies. Prior to joining the University of Adelaide, Skuse worked as a Social Development Adviser for the UK Department for International Development (DFID), where he oversaw the specialist area of communications for development. His publications span both applied and academic fields, and he is currently active in undertaking research and consultancy in China, Philippines, Nepal and South Africa.

Marie Gillespie is Professor of Sociology at The Open University, and a Director of the Centre for Research on Socio-Cultural Change (http://www.cresc.ac.uk). Her research interests focus on issues of migration and media, diaspora and transnationalism in relation to questions of social and cultural change. Recent research projects include an exploration of the politics of security (http://www.mediatingsecurity.com), and a study of BBC World Service entitled *Tuning In: Diasporic Contact Zones at BBC World Service*, on which this book is based (http://www.open.ac.uk/socialsciences/ diasporas/). For a list of publications see http://www.open.ac.uk/socialsciences/staff/people-profile.php?staff_id=164735. Contact: m.gillespie@open.ac.uk.

Gerry Power holds a PhD (Communication Theory and Research) from the Annenberg School for Communication at the University of Southern California, USA. He is Managing Director of InterMedia UK, a global media and communications research and consultancy practice. From 2005 to 2010, as Director of Research and Learning at the BBC World Service Trust, he established an award-winning global network of researchers spanning 14 countries across Africa, Asia and the Middle East. He has taught at various universities including University of California Los Angeles, USA, Universidad de las Américas Puebla (Mexico), University of Texas at El Paso and the London School of Economics, UK. His work has appeared in the *International Journal of Communication*, *Communication Research*, *Human Communication Research*, *Journal of Communication Inquiry* and the *Journal of Health Communication*.

Contributors

Fortunee Bayisenge holds a master's degree in development (Women, Gender and Development) from the Institute of Social Studies, Den Hague, Netherlands. Bayisenge has conducted research on gender, empowerment and political representation in Rwanda, focusing on quota systems. Her work has a broad focus on women's issues, and she has previously worked within the local government in Rwanda focusing on gender, land and justice.

Anurudra Bhanot holds a master's degree in business management and has trained in advanced research analysis at the Indian Institute of Management, Ahmedabad (IIM-A), India. He is the Head of Research for South Asia with the Research and Learning Group (R&L) at the BBC World Service Trust in India. Over the last three years he has been responsible for directing and overseeing the implementation of formative, pre-testing, monitoring and summative research studies for the Trust's mass media projects in India, Bangladesh, Nepal, Afghanistan and Pakistan. Prior to joining the Trust, Bhanot headed research agencies in East Africa and Myanmar (Burma). His two-decade long career spans the advertising, pharmaceutical and dairy cooperative sectors in Asia and Africa.

Joyee S. Chatterjee is a PhD candidate at the University of Southern California's Annenberg School for Communication and Journalism, USA. Her research looks at the intersections of development communication and popular culture and its impact on gender norms in South Asia. She has a graduate degree in social work from the Tata Institute of Social Sciences and has a background in promoting Child Rights in India. Her recent projects have included research collaborations with the BBC World Service Trust in India on their campaigns promoting change in social norms among men related to HIV/AIDS prevention and condom use and campaign research for a radio drama to promote gender equity.

Sonal Tickoo Chaudhuri holds a master's degree in mathematics and business management. She is the Senior Research Officer with the Research and Learning Group (R&L) at the BBC World Service Trust in India. Over the last two years she has been involved in the design, implementation and dissemination of research work (formative, pre-testing, monitoring impact evaluation) for the Bill and Melinda Gates foundation-funded Condom Promotion project in India. In addition, she assists the Regional Head of Research with other research projects in the region as well as the business development team in mapping research scope for new projects in India.

Lauren B. Frank has a master's degree in health science from the Johns Hopkins Bloomberg School of Public Health, USA. She is currently a PhD student at the University of Southern California Annenberg School for Communication and Journalism, USA. Her research interests include health communication, mass media and organisational communication. She is particularly interested in means of disseminating public health messages.

Lizz Frost Yocum is a research manager at the BBC World Service Trust, currently managing research on a range of projects across East Asia and Africa—specifically Cambodia, China and Vietnam, Kenya, Somalia and Nigeria. Lizz formerly managed the epidemiology department for Médecins sans Frontières–Holland in Russia, monitoring and evaluating HIV and AIDS prevention work in Russia, Ukraine and Mongolia. She established the Médecins sans Frontières (MSF) field office in Uzbekistan, launching the nation's first DOTS tuberculosis control programme, and also acted as the epidemiologist during a meningitis epidemic in Ghana in 1997. Lizz has a master's degree in public health and a master's degree in social work from Boston University, USA, where she specialised in Epidemiology, International Health and Clinical Social Work Practice. She also holds a BA from Oberlin College, USA.

Helen M. Hintjens is a senior lecturer at the Institute of Social Studies, Den Hague, Netherlands. She holds a PhD in politics and an MA in political economy and international relations, both from the University of Aberdeen. She has researched extensively on Rwanda in the post-genocide period, examining issues relating to reconstruction, the politics of identity and conflict and the environment. Hintjens has also worked amongst the wider Great Lakes diaspora in relation to violent conflict and peace issues within the region. She has worked on media, but mainly specialises in human rights and social justice issues in relation to gender, identity and post-colonial relations.

Charlotte Lapsansky is a PhD candidate at University of Southern California's Annenberg School for Communication, USA. Her research focuses on evaluation strategies for development communications and communications for social change programmes. Prior to starting her PhD, she worked in India on media campaigns to address gender inequality and health. Gender and health, especially in the Indian context, continue to be thematic foci of her research. She has continued the exploration of masculinity, gender and health through collaborations with the BBC World Service Trust on the evaluation of a PSA campaign to promote male condom use as well as the campaign research for a radio drama to promote gender equity.

Emily LeRoux-Rutledge holds a master's degree in social and public communication from the London School of Economics, and a BA (Hons) in International Relations and English from the University of Toronto, Canada. She is part of the Research and Learning Group at the BBC World Service Trust, and has worked on a wide range of quantitative and qualitative research studies across Africa, the Middle East and Asia. Prior to joining the Trust, she worked at the secretariat of the Forum for African Women Educationalists in Kenya. She has conducted research on audience engagement in Nigeria, and on empowerment through mass media, specifically focusing on the BBC World Service Trust's Afghan Women's Hour project.

Carol Morgan holds a master's degree (Hons) in Literature and History from the University of Edinburgh, UK. She joined the BBC World Service Trust in April 2007 and spent two years working with the Research and Learning Group in London.

Carol is currently Country Director for the BBC World Service Trust in Sudan, where she runs media development projects and produces humanitarian and educational radio programming for community and government media networks. Her primary areas of focus are humanitarian media interventions and media for the promotion of sustainable livelihoods.

Sheila T. Murphy is an associate professor at Annenberg School for Communication at the University of Southern California, USA. Her research focuses on how people make decisions, and the factors that influence them including emotion, racial and gender stereotypes, cultural norms and cognitive issues such as how information is framed. Much of her recent work examines how people's attitudes and actions can be influenced through their favourite entertainment programmes. She has conducted numerous evaluations of entertainment education interventions as well as more traditional health campaigns for agencies including the National Institutes of Health, the Centres for Disease Control and Prevention and the BBC World Service Trust. She is also a principal investigator of the ongoing monthly Annenberg National Health Communication Survey.

Sadaf Rizvi is a Research Officer at the Institute of Education, University of London, UK. She has a PhD in social anthropology from University of Oxford, UK. Sadaf conducted her doctoral research on 'Muslim Schools in Britain' and explored the issues of integration and diasporic identities. She has been involved in the Economic and Social Research Council (United Kingdom) funded 'Shifting Securities: News Cultures before and beyond Iraq War 2003' and the AHRC funded 'Tuning In: Diasporic Contact Zones at BBC World Service' projects. She coordinated a BBC audience research project aimed at setting policies and recommendations for a new BBC Urdu website for Pakistanis in the United Kingdom and abroad. Her research interests are education and social cohesion, religion and media ethnography.

Caroline Sugg is a projects manager with the BBC World Service Trust. Since joining the organisation in 2003, she has developed and been involved with the implementation of numerous projects across Asia and Africa, including Drama for Development projects in Ethiopia, Nigeria, Cambodia, India and Nepal. Sugg has a particular interest and expertise in working with mass media to address public health issues. Prior to joining the BBC World Service Trust, she worked at Channel 4 Television and as a Strategy Consultant for an organisation specialising in providing advice to the media and telecommunications sectors. Sugg holds an MA in History from the University of Cambridge, UK.

Michael Wilmore is a senior lecturer in media at the University of Adelaide, Australia and Associate Dean (Postgraduate Coursework Programmes) for the Faculty of Humanities and Social Sciences. He holds a PhD and a master's degree in social anthropology from the University of London. Wilmore's research focuses on the uses of media by indigenous and other minority groups in post-colonial contexts, as well as on aspects of community media development, including cable television and radio, Internet and mobile media technologies. He has been studying the development of media in Nepal for over a decade and is currently examining the uses of FM radio by non-governmental organisations.

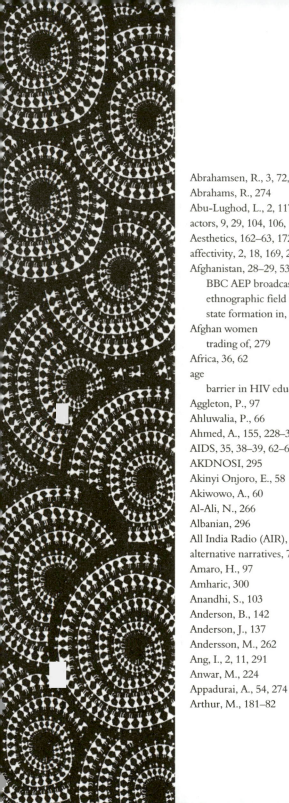

INDEX

Hobsbawm, E., 139
Hobson, D., 277, 291
Hodgetts, D., 47–48, 52, 61
Hornik, R., 8
humanitarian, 26, 46, 50, 72, 74, 136, 225
humanitarian information, 74
Human rights, 15, 25, 46, 142, 149, 153, 173, 223, 227, 232, 241–42
Hunte, P., 276, 286
Hutt, M., 160
Hygiene, 77, 249–50, 295, 300

ICRC, 296
IFC, 295, 303
IFES, 296
Ilboudo, J-P., 259
Improvisation, 161–62, 171, 175
Inagaki, N., 6, 8–10, 72–73, 276
India, 27–28, 44, 49, 68, 91–93, 100
Indian drama(s)
    strategies to reach men, 101–02
indigenous cosmologies, 61
Ingelaere, B., 248
innovative drama
    development storylines, for, 91–92
Institutional, 3–5, 24–25, 34, 44, 61, 119, 180–81, 184, 261, 296
International Center for Research on Women, 110
International radio broadcasting, 71
internet, 8, 187, 243–44, 266, 311
IOM, 296

Jamaica
    drama for development intervention in, 94
    Jasoos Vijay (Detective Vijay), 55, 92, 118, 297
    aim of, 102–06
    background and impact of, 203–07
    collective efficacy and, 210–11
    key objectives for, 216

thematic and theoretical analysis of, 207
Jay, M., 180
jihad, 74
Johns Hopkins Centre for Communications Programmes, 36
Jordan, C., 247

Kalisa, M-C., 256
Katha Mitho Sarangiko (Sweet Tales of the Sara), 161, 302
    addressing of themes, 159
    bridging of gap, 159
    deployment of *miteri* institution, 168–71
    didactic realism, 174
    display of creative innovation, 167
    on-location recording of, 161–68
    principal problems of, 171–74
    production team of, 175
    pro-social productions, 167
    use of innovative techniques in, 163–64
Katz, E., 1
Kayirangwa, E., 251
Khana-e-Nau, 295
Khmer, 298
Kimmel, M., 111
Kim, Y., 94
Kloos, P., 126
knowledge, 4, 6, 10–12, 18, 26, 38–39, 47–48
knowledge, attitude and practice (KAP), 49, 205
Kraftfeld notion, 180
Kumar, R., 202, 210
Kyagambiddwa, S., 259–60
Kyanmarye ne Naung ye, 301

Lapinski, M.K., 218
Latin America, 5, 100, 291
Law, S., 210
Leach, M., 9
Leaflets, 30